T0323784

IS THE TWO-STATE SOLUTION ALREADY DEAD?

Israel or Palestine?

IS THE TWO-STATE SOLUTION ALREADY DEAD?

A POLITICAL AND MILITARY HISTORY OF THE

PALESTINIAN-ISRAELI CONFLICT

HASAN AFIF EL-HASAN

Algora Publishing
New York

© 2010 by Algora Publishing.
All Rights Reserved
www.algora.com

No portion of this book (beyond what is permitted by
Sections 107 or 108 of the United States Copyright Act of 1976)
may be reproduced by any process, stored in a retrieval system,
or transmitted in any form, or by any means, without the
express written permission of the publisher.

Library of Congress Cataloging-in-Publication Data —

El-Hasan, Hasan Afif, 1932-
  Is the two-state solution already dead? / Hasan Afif El-Hasan.
    p. cm.
  Includes bibliographical references and index.
  ISBN 978-0-87586-792-2 (soft cover: alk. paper) — ISBN 978-0-87586-793-9 (hard
cover: alk. paper) — ISBN 978-0-87586-794-6 (ebook) 1. Arab-Israeli conflict—Peace. 2.
Palestine—Politics and government. 3. Israel—Politics and government. I. Title.
  DS119.7.E357 2010
  956.04—dc22
                              2010012020

Printed in the United States

To the Palestinian and Israeli generation of my grandchildren Laila, Hasan, Mariam,Yasmeena, Deena and Yara, to whom this study strives to pass the moral value of peace with justice

Acronyms, Abbreviations and Terms

AIPAC	American Israel Public Affairs Committee
ALA	Arab Liberation Army
ASU	Arab Socialist Union Party
BD	The Balfour Declaration
Nakba	Catastrophe, name given by the Palestinians to their defeat in 1948 war
DOP	Declaration of Principles
Emir	"Prince" in Arabic
FAO	Food and Agriculture Organization
Fallah	Palestinian farmer
Fatah	Harakat al-Tahreer al-Falastinia (Palestinian Liberation Movement)
GA	General Assembly
HA	Holy Army
Halacha	Jewish law
Hamas	Harakat al-Muqawama al-Islmiya (The Islamic Resistance Movement)
HRC	UN Human Rights Council
ICJ	International Court of Justice
IDF	Israel Defense Force
Intifada	Uprising
JNF	Jewish National Fund
MB	Muslim Brothers
Mufti	interpreter of Islamic law
OCHA	UN Office of the Coordination of Humanitarian Affairs
PA	Palestinian Authority
Pasha	Nobility title bestowed on accomplished individuals. It was originally used in the former Ottoman Empire.
PLO	Palestine Liberation Organization
PNC	Palestine National Council
PNGO	Palestinian NGOs' Network
Sharif	Nobility title of the descendents of the Prophet Muhammed.
UAR	United Arab Republic (Egypt and Syria)
UNGA	United Nations General Assembly
UNHCR	UN High Commissioner for Refugees
UNRWA	UN Refugees Relief and Works Agency
UNSCOP	UN Commission on Palestine
Wakf	Muslim endowment
Yishuv	The Jewish community in Palestine before the establishment of Israel
Zionism	Jewish national movement that promoted the establishment of Israel

Acknowledgement

Like all researchers and writers, I have relied on the advice and the professionalism of friends and colleagues. I have been unusually fortunate to have the support and encouragement of remarkably accomplished intellectuals. I am very grateful to Professor Wayne Martin of California State University, Dominguez Hills, for his ongoing good council and willingness to field my queries. I am especially grateful for his support and his interest in the subject of this book and the constructive analysis of Chapter 1. Thanks in particular to Professor Bronwyn Leebaw of the University of California Riverside for her enthusiastic support of the book project and for taking time from her busy schedule to review Chapter 4. And I owe a special debt to Professor Jon Hiskey of Vanderbilt University for his continuous encouragement to write on Middle East issues since my college years, and for his valuable comments on Chapter 11. I am particularly grateful to Algora Publishing for their untiring effort in editing the text of this book and for many valuable suggestions.

I should acknowledge the influence of having a family that talks politics and has a tradition of reviewing local and international issues any time they meet. My wife Haifa and our grown up children Afif, Muhammed, Hana and Firas engage me in serious and constructive discussions on the political thoughts that I put in writing in this book.

TABLE OF CONTENTS

INTRODUCTION

The "Palestinians" or "Palestinian Arabs" in this book are the people identifying themselves as Arabs who had been living in Palestine just before the establishment of Israel, as well as their descendants. The West Bank, Gaza Strip and East Jerusalem are referred to as "the occupied land." The Israelis call the indigenous Palestinians only "Arabs" to deny their linkage to Palestine and refer to the West Bank by its Biblical names "Judea and Samaria" to make the historical connection of the Jewish people with this land or the "disputed territory," to deny its status as occupied land. The Palestinian Central Bureau of Statistics (PCBS) estimates that there were more than nine million Palestinians scattered throughout the world as of 2006. More than one million were living in Israel proper, three and a half million lived in the West Bank and Gaza, two and a half million lived in Jordan and the rest were dispersed through the Arab world, Europe and North and South America. The American–Israel Demographic Group disputed these findings and concluded that the PCBS total numbers are inflated by one million three-hundred thousand.

I strongly argue against the concept of using ethnic origin to define nations today because every community within a geographic area is a mixture of races that came in contact through conquest, migration and intermarriages across time. This applies especially to the self-identified Arabs and Jews in Palestine. Arabs or Jews, or any race for that matter, throughout the world, cannot support their claim of being closely related genetically, by biology. Palestine was successively conquered by Canaanites, Philistinians, ancient Israelites, Egyptians, Persians, Greeks, Romans and Turks, by Muslims and by Christian crusaders. The groups that lived in Palestine fought, interacted and collaborated, but no group was obliterated in history. The Palestinians are the descendents of all the groups that inhabited the land since the ancient Canaanites and beyond. I therefore reject the myth of race and racial superiority including the ideology that fed the Fascism of the last century.

No population has struggled more than the Palestinians to hold onto their land or to return to the homes they were forced to leave — and achieved so little, if anything. Only the American Indian tribes and the indigenous peoples of New Zealand and Tasmania suffered similar injustice when they were systematically destroyed and ethnically cleansed to make room for British and European colonialists. The Palestinians used diplomacy, negotiations, protests, uprisings and wars but they have failed to save their lands and the refugees never returned to their homes. Even after the establishment of the State of Israel, the signing of peace treaties with Egypt and Jordan, and the recognition of Israel by the Palestine Liberation Organization (PLO), Israel still controls all of historic Palestine and the Palestinians, dispossessed and oppressed, are either living under brutal occupation in cantons surrounded by Jewish-only settlements and roads, check-points and the Israeli wall of separation, or they are living in refugee camps across the Middle East, and a sizable minority inside Israel is treated as second if not third class citizens.

This work condemns all violence for any reason and advocates for a just peace in Palestine based on human rights and international law, a peace which all parties to the century-old conflict and the people of the region need. To that end, the Palestinians should unite and do what is necessary to strengthen the "peace camp" in Israel; the Israelis should abandon the ideology of conquest and stop electing governments that may foreclose the possibility of peace with justice; and the international community (the US and Europe) should live up to the principles of justice that they claim their civilized societies hold dear.

Supporting the right of Israel to exist and prosper should not mean supporting it in subordinating Palestinians' claims to their historical rights and controlling their destiny. Many Israeli individuals and groups love their country and also support the Palestinians' right to have their independent state, but they are still in the minority. They question how their Jewish people can celebrate their ancient struggle against slavery and the anti-Semitism of today, claiming moral superiority, but at the same time accept oppressing another people, occupying and colonizing their land under false narratives. The Israeli novelist David Grossman spoke for many Israeli intellectuals and peace advocates when he wrote, "I could not understand how an entire nation like mine, an enlightened nation by all accounts, is able to train itself to live as a conqueror without making its own life wretched."[1]

This study will put the stories of the two parties to the Palestinian conflict, the Israelis and the Palestinians, side by side and leave it to the reader to conclude why a just peace that addresses the rights of the Palestinians serves the interests of the Israelis as well. To that end, I try to present a critical political discussion based on facts that Israel cannot be simply erased, and it will prosper and be more secure without being a colonial power. And despite their weakness, the Palestinians will refuse to continue living under oppression and in refugee camps. Chapter 1 summarizes what this study is all about. It is an effort to explain the historical and ideological background of the parties to the conflict. It covers briefly major historical events since the 19th century that led to the present sorry state. Only by understanding what has transpired in the past, the reader may grasp the Palestin-

---

1 Grossman, David, 1988

ian issue and why it is time the international community should act with more responsibility and a commitment to resolve the conflict according to international law and justice.

Chapter 2 is a brief review of the Arab nationalism since the 19th century. The link between Arab nationalism and the Palestinian issue today is more emotions and less substance, but under Arab nationalism, regular armies of the neighboring Arab states waged wars against Israel. Palestine was ruled by the Ottoman Turks as a part of Syria for four-hundred years before Britain and France defeated Turkey in World War I (WW I). Syria was the center of Arab nationalism when the Ottoman Empire was dismantled and Palestine was promised as a homeland for the Jews by the triumphant British. Syria was home of al-Baath Party and the Syrian Socialist National Party, organized nationalist parties that advocated the establishment of national state which included Palestine. The two political parties were strong opponents to the establishment of a homeland for the Jews in Palestine. President Nasser of Egypt championed the Palestinian cause as the self-proclaimed leader of the Pan-Arab nationalism. After the 1967 war, Arab nationalism has been replaced by local traditional and sectarian Islamic nationalism. But most Arabs today, even in the countries that made peace with Israel, continue to support the Palestinians and refuse to accept normalization with the Israelis before the Palestinian issue is resolved.

Chapter 3 is a brief history of the Palestinians since the dawn of the 20th century when Palestine was ruled by the Turks. It covers the pre-1948 period, the 1948 war, the PLO and Fatah history in Jordan and Lebanon and the rise of Hamas movement.

Chapter 4 is a review of Zionism and its early leaders and how it succeeded in the creation of modern Israel. The State of Israel has been the crowning achievement of the Zionist movement. Zionism has been the most successful international political movement in modern history. Its founder promised a homeland for the Jews in fifty years, and he was on target. The Jewish community in Palestine before the establishment of Israel is sometimes called the "*Yishuv*" in this study.

Chapter 5 is a narrative of the Hashemites' relations with Palestine since World War I. The histories of the Hashemites and Palestine are so intertwined that they can hardly be separated. Sherif Hussein Ben Ali, the patriarch of the Hashemite dynasty, lost his kingdom for refusing to accept the Balfour declaration, and when he was on his death bed, he asked to be buried in Jerusalem. King Abdullah the First of Jordan succeeded in keeping Jerusalem and the West Bank in Arab hands after the 1948 war. And until the 1967 war, the West Bank and Jerusalem were an integral part of the Hashemite Kingdom of Jordan. It was only in1988 that King Hussein Ibn Talal disclaimed his sovereignty over the occupied West Bank and recognized the PLO as the sole representative of the Palestinians.

Chapter 6 describes the relationship between Egypt and Palestine since 1914. Egypt fought four bloody wars against Israel, controlled the Gaza Strip from 1948 till 1967, and now it shares Gaza's life-line border. Jamal Abdel-Nasser championed the Palestinian cause under the banner of Arab Nationalism.

Chapter 7 reviews the development of Palestinian–Israeli relations after the 2003 Quartet "Roadmap for Peace" plan was announced. Representatives of the "Quartet," an ad hoc American-dominated committee made up of the US, the EU, Russia, and the UN, endorsed a 2003 US-proposed schedule of conditions and events dubbed the "Roadmap" for breaking the Palestinian–Israeli impasse and paving the way to a peace settlement based on a two-state solution.

Chapter 8 reviews the politics of the Palestinians after the Legislative Council Elections of 2006 and the Hamas victory. The victors in these elections were boycotted by the West, and Israel refused to cooperate with any government headed by Hamas. The Palestinian experiment in democracy was aborted by the very countries that rightly criticize Arab states for their lack of democracy.

Chapter 9 describes the 2006 Lebanese–Israeli war and its impact on Israeli politics. The Lebanese Shiite military group Hizbullah ambushed an Israeli military patrol in a cross-border raid; Israel responded by bombarding Lebanese roads, bridges, ports and airports, as well as other targets. Hizbullah's response was to fire hundreds of rockets on Israeli targets across the border, killing Israeli civilians including Israeli Arabs. Once it disengaged from Lebanon, the Israeli government was criticized for mismanaging the war, moved even more forcefully against the Palestinians, especially in the Gaza Strip which was governed by the Hamas faction and besieged by Israel.

Chapter 10 analyzes the so-called "peace process" including the 2002 Arab peace proposal and the 2007 US-sponsored Annapolis conference. The Palestinians have been clinging to the US "Roadmap" for peace and the Arab states have tried to revive the peace process, but Israel does not consider itself an occupier. Instead of withdrawing, Israel has built the separation wall and hundreds of new homes in major settlements in the West Bank.

Chapter 11, as the last chapter of the book, talks about the failure of Palestinian and Israeli negotiators to reach a final peace agreement. This study concludes that if there is any hope for establishing a sovereign Palestinian state, the Palestinians must end factionalism; the Israeli electorate political orientation must move away from the ideology of conquest; and the United States must transform its traditional Middle East policy of blind support to Israel into a genuine even-handed approach. The problem is that none of these players is ready to correct course. Chapter 11 thus reviews nonviolent options that the Palestinians may consider if the two-state solution is declared dead.

CHAPTER 1. THE ISSUE

The Zionists' dream of establishing the State of Israel in the middle of the Arab Middle East for Jews world wide has been fulfilled; and the "Jewish Question" has been resolved after the 1948 "War of Independence." A collective Israeli identity was created, the "Law of Return" was passed and absorption centers were established to incorporate into the Israeli society the new waves of Jewish immigrants who flooded the country, but the Arab Palestinian refugees were not permitted to return to their homes.

The declaration of independence includes a paragraph that calls for equality of all citizens irrespective of religion, race or sex. The commitment to the principle of equality was a condition for Israel to be accepted into the UN, but the official practice of the state strayed from the text. The Palestinians who remained in Israel were ruled by military ordinances until 1966, and when they finally were given the Israeli citizenship, they have been denied basic rights that the Jewish citizens enjoyed. The identity of the Israelis in their legal documents and ID cards is expressed in terms of their group religious affiliation as "Jewish," "Muslim," "Christian," "Bahai," "Durzi," etc., where all privileges are conferred by the state on the Jews by virtue of being Jews, thus making Israel an religio-ethnocracy rather than a liberal democracy. The Zionist movement major goal was achieved by creating a highly developed Jewish nation-state dominated by pioneering settler community, but the story did not end there. The recognition of legitimacy by the neighboring Arab states was not attained and the conflict continued. Then after three more wars in 1956, 1967 and 1973, Israel acquired control over the rest of historical Palestine which is densely populated by Palestinian Arabs and the new conquered territory was treated as a liberated Jewish "holy" land. Israel today is militarily secure, its economy is thriving, and it has been recognized by the largest and most populous Arab nation, Egypt. But Israel failed in bringing most of the world's Jews to Israel; its legitimacy has not been accepted by most countries of the region; there is discrimination in Israel against its Arab citizens and even against Jews who came from developing countries; there is internal tension between the religious and the secular communities and Israel remains dependent on massive US aid and diplomatic protection.

Although we understand what has happened in the last sixty or even hundred years and what is happening today, the problem with writing on the Palestinian question is the risk of being overtaken by developing events, mostly due to the unpredictable and unstable conditions created by internal Palestinian and Israeli politics and their agendas regarding the occupied land and the negotiations. Except for the power to mobilize its citizens for wars, Israel has been governed since 1977 by weak coalitions of fragmented parties of mostly big secular and small religious and extreme right wing parties that oppose compromises with the Palestinians. The religious parties in the government have bigger role than their sizes suggest; they have provided the needed Knesset majority support for fragile and ungovernable government coalitions. The ultra-Orthodox Jewish Shas Party with twelve Knesset seats, a partner in the 2007–08 Olmert Israeli coalition government and the Netanyahu 2009 government, can make or break the majority bloc of sixty-nine. Shas opposes any compromise on Jerusalem, an essential element of any future peace deal, thus making a peace agreement with the Palestinians less likely, even impossible. Extreme political parties became the major partners in the Israeli government coalition. Prime Minister Netanyahu is from the right wing Likud and the Foreign Minister in the 2009 government is from Yisrael Beiteinu Party (YBP) which received fifteen seats in the Knesset 2009 elections. YBP ran on a platform that calls for ethnic cleansing all Arab Israelis from Israel. Any right-wing party in the Israeli government coalition can withdraw its support and topple the government if it makes any concessions to the Palestinians that may be perceived a threat to the nationalist plans for "Greater Israel."

The Israeli State is still an active immigrant settler sociopolitical entity with no final boundaries or size or even a constitution, creating a sense of vulnerability among its citizens and endangering the stability of the region. Brutal military operations against the Palestinians and refusal of independent Palestinian state in the occupied lands are sold by the military establishment to the unsecure population as necessary security actions. A sizable segment of the Israelis view the Palestinians' demand for their civil rights as another form of the traditional anti-Semitism. And the Israeli public, religious and military education systems enforce this misconception by overemphasizing the Jewish link to the land, and purposely ignoring the history of the indigenous Palestinians. They were reduced to adversaries of the Jews and refer to them as "terrorists" or "gangs" seeking to foil the rights of the Jews to the "Land of Israel." The education system propagated the siege mentality and created generations of Israeli citizens who perceive the Palestinians including the Israeli–Arabs as transients in the "Land of Israel."

After the Zionists defeated the Arab armies in the 1948 war, they created the State of Israel and institutionalized a brand of vibrant parliamentary democracy for the Jewish citizens and they established freedom of the press tradition where it is easier to question Israeli policies and policy makers than in any country in the West. But Israel was created as an ethnocentric state for the world-wide Jewish people not for its citizens. Equality with the indigenous Palestinians on the same land was not considered an option by the Zionist ideology. Actions by the Israeli governments since the birth of Israel have been intended to rid Israel of its original Arab inhabitants. Israeli–Arabs can vote and run for elected public offices but they never enjoyed equality with the Jewish citizens, a basic requirement of liberal democracy. Israel enacted more than thirty statutes for the purpose of transferring private Arab lands to the state and the confiscated Arab lands have been sold or leased only to Jews. It created a legal system that protects the rights of women, homosexuals, and the disabled, but until 1966, the Israeli Arabs were ruled by military ordinances. Arabs are not trusted to serve in many professions and laws were passed to restrict their civil rights. The Israelis passed laws in accordance with Jewish history and complete disregard to the history of the Arab Palestinians who used to be the vast major-ity before the War of Independence. As of 1998, the Israeli courts have "dismissed all cases dealing with equal rights for the Arab citizens."[1] According to the news media, the Israeli Foreign Minister from 2006 to 2009, Tzipi Livni, who later assumed the leadership of Kadima Party and became the party's candidate for prime minister in the February 2009 elections, told school students on December 11, 2008 that Israeli Arabs must leave Israel and live in the future Palestinian state so that Israel may retain its Jewish character and democracy. What she suggested was that the only options for the more than one million indigenous Palestinians are either to live in Israel as second class citizens with no civil and political rights or to leave Israel. And in the territories that had been occupied in the 1967 war, Palestinian lands are illegally confiscated by the government, and Jewish settlers act outside the law, committing serious crimes against the Palestinians without incurring penal sanctions. John Dugard, the UN Special Rapporteur on the human rights situation in the occupied Palestinian territories (OPT), concluded in 2008 that, "Israel, since 1967, has been the belligerent Occupying Power in the OPT, and that its occupation of these territories has become a colonial enterprise which implements a system of Apartheid."

Avigdor Lieberman, the leader of Yisrael Beiteinu Party and the Foreign Minister in Netanyahu's 2008 government, stated, "When there is a contradiction between democrat-ic and Jewish values, the Jewish and Zionist values are more important." Israeli hard-lin-ers are following the political Zionist ideology of conquest to the letter, but since Judaism is defined by its ethics, they are breaching the Jewish Prophets' values of "justice, justice shall you pursue"[2] by denying the national-historical rights of the Palestinians over part of their own land. Israel accorded full rights only to its Jewish citizens and succeeded in concealing its racism and aggression against the Palestinians through its powerful defend-ers in the West. The establishment of Israel has interrupted the lives of the indigenous Palestinians, their lands were taken and their social and political rights have been violated. Historians like Benny Morris and Ilan Pappe detail the many ways in which the process of ethnically cleansing Palestinians and effacing the remains of their historical presence was achieved. The PLO, the internationally recognized representative of the Palestinians,

---

1 Adala Report of March 1998
2 Book of Deuteronomy

has formally and repeatedly accepted Israeli sovereignty over 78% of Palestine. It is willing to settle for the return of the 1967 occupied territories, but Israel has no intention of allowing the Palestinians have a sovereign state on one fifth of historical Palestine that was all theirs before 1948. Twenty-one Arab League states adopted the land-for-peace proposal that had been offered by Saudi Arabia in 2002 to solve the Arab–Israeli conflict once and for all. It called for withdrawal from all the territories occupied in the 1967 war, the establishment of an independent Palestinian state in the West Bank, Gaza Strip and East Jerusalem and resolving the refugees issue on the basis of the UN Resolution 194. In return, the Arab states would establish full normal relations with Israel. But the proposal was rejected by then Israeli PM Ariel Sharon and ignored by all successor governments, suggesting that Israel's governments prefer expansion over being integrated in the region. The Palestinians, dispossessed and oppressed, are either living under occupation and crippling siege paying high price for their resistance to occupation, or they are living in refugee camps across the Middle East, and a sizable minority are treated as second class citizens inside Israel, with no solution to their ordeal insight.

Many historians have written the narrative of the Palestinian–Israeli conflict within the context of the success in establishing the State of Israel in the Jews "historic homeland" that had been recognized by the international community in the 1947 UN vote. Others have considered it a history of injustice that has beset the entire Palestinian people through no fault of their own. Unfortunately, the Palestinians have lost control of their own history; and the history of their country has been mostly written by Westerners who made the connection between the Jews' suffering in Europe and the "morality" of dispossessing and expelling the Palestinians to resettle Jews.

The Palestinians' long journey to nowhere covers stages that were triggered by several major events over more than a century. These include the launching of the World Zionist Movement in 1897, the 1917 Balfour Declaration, the failure of the Palestinians 1936 rebellion and the abeyance of the Palestinians' national movement, the victory of Israel over Arab states in 1948 war, the 1967 occupation of the West Bank and Gaza and the 1993 Oslo agreements Palestinians' plunder. Other events occurred in between these major landmarks and impacted the Palestinian case. The 1979 Egyptian–Israeli peace agreement neutralized Egypt and transformed the Arab–Israeli conflict into a Palestinian–Israeli issue; the 1982 Israeli invasion of Lebanon sent the PLO into exile; the 1987 First *Intifada* (uprising) that created a new homegrown Palestinian leadership in the occupied lands; Iraq's invasion of Kuwait in 1990 ended the main financial support to the PLO; and the 1991 collapse of the Soviet Union left the US, the strategic ally of Israel, as the World's only superpower. These events weakened the PLO significantly and set the stage for the 1991 Madrid Conference and the 1993 Oslo agreements. Then after the September 11, 2001 terrorist's attack on targets in the United States, the US waged the war on terrorism and Israel launched its open-ended aggression against any form of Palestinian resistance to the occupation as a sideshow in the war against international terrorism.

The conflict, one of the world's oldest, has become an international issue involving big powers after World War I when the Ottoman Empire disintegrated. Palestine became a separate entity under the British control based on the secret British–French memorandum of understanding, known as the Sykes–Picot agreement of 1916 that divided the Arabian Peninsula and the eastern Mediterranean region between France and Britain. The area of Palestine was slated for international administration and subsequently declared a national home for the Jewish people, negating promises made by the British to Sherif Hussein Ibn Ali, of Arabia's Hejaz province, in the Hussein–McMahon correspondence. The 1916 Sykes–Picot agreement was denounced by Arab nationalists because it divided their lands between the two colonial powers and denied them the independence they had been promised, but the Arabs were too weak to do anything about it.

The British conquered Palestine in 1917 and issued in the same year the Balfour Declaration to create a Jewish homeland in Palestine. Chapter 4 describes in details how the Declaration came about. The League of Nations that was dominated by the victorious powers mandated Britain to administer Palestine with explicit commitment to create the right conditions for establishing a national home for the Jewish people against the will of its Arab population. Once the Palestinian Arabs learnt of the British plans for their country, they began organizing political protests, and later on they started active resistance that developed into the failed 1936–1939 revolt. When the British Mandate came to an end in 1948 and the UN General Assembly had passed resolution 181 to partition Palestine into two states in 1947, the State of Israel was born and recognized immediately by the US and key Western countries as well as the Soviet Union. Jews of the newly recognized Israeli State celebrated by dancing deliriously in the streets, but the Palestinians rejected the partitioning resolution even while they did not have a functioning national leadership or any state institutions. During the 1946 conference of the Arab leaders in Bludan, Syria, the self-appointed Palestinian leader Haj Amin al-Husseini rejected any form of Jewish national homeland and declared that the Palestinians' aim was to prevent it by force. The Jews, who had been preparing themselves since the early 1920s, were ready to run their state. During the Mandate, the pre-independence Jewish community (Yishuv) established the state institutions including well trained semi-military organization (Haganah) and their small settlements and kibbutzim were integrated into a national economy. The nascent Israeli State incorporated in its institutions the pre-state Yishuv organizations including the Haganah para-military, the bureaucracy, the political parties, the Histadrut labor union and the World Zionist organizations. But the Palestinians were never organized or united; they had not established government institutions and failed to impose general conscription; their poorly armed irregulars were operating without central direction or discipline, and the mutinies and desertions were common. The military of the nascent Israeli State succeeded in defeating both the unprepared Arab Palestinians and neighboring Arab states' military contingents that came to stop the implementation of the UN partition resolution. The Arab armies did not have the political will to fight; they were fighting more against each other than against the Israeli military.

When the guns fell silent in 1948, Israel controlled 78% of historic Palestine; 85% of the Arabs who were to be citizens of Israel had gone; their villages were demolished and their lands expropriated; the neighboring Arab countries signed truce agreements and most of the Palestinians ended up as refugees or under the protection of Jordan and Egypt. As for the Palestinians, it was humanly impossible for them to renounce their homeland, abrogate their own national rights and accept that another people had taken over their land, homes and farms. Sir Arthur Money, the head of the British Territory Administration in Palestine, wrote to Lord Curzon in April 1919: "The Palestinians in fact desire Palestine for themselves: and have no intention of allowing their country to be thrown open to hordes of Jews from Eastern and Central Europe."[1]

The Israelis on the left and right defend their military actions in the "War of Independence" that they were necessary to prevent the Palestinians and their Arab allies from committing genocide against civilian Jews and carrying out their declared aim of destroying their nascent state. They claim that the Palestinians and their Arab supporters who invaded the country initiated the war, the Jews were the weaker party and their victory was not expected by most observers. They ask why they had been castigated by some pro-Palestinian leftist historians for fighting back valiantly against the Arab invading armies and winning the war. According to Yaacov Lozowick, "The result of wars is normally a judgment on the cause of the combatants."[2] And as for the Palestinian refugees who were forced out of their homes, the Israelis argue that they had to force hostile Palestinian militias and their supporters out of the Jewish held territory to make it easy to defend. And since the Palestinians had rejected the UN recommendation to establish an Arab state in the part allocated to them, "the Israelis had no choice but to partition the country along more defensible lines." They add that the Arab countries had expelled all their Jewish residents including the 2,900-year-old Jewish community in Yemen and the Iraqi Jews who had been living there since Abraham 2,700 years ago. Even King Abdullah of Jordan expelled the few hundred Jewish residents of Jerusalem when his army conquered the Walled City in 1948, according to the Israelis. Since no Jews were left in the Arab countries, the Arabs effectively carried out an exchange of populations, according to Israel's defenders, and there would be no Jewish state today if there was no mass transfer (*nishul*) of Palestinians in 1948. The "Judaization" of Israel, which was the Zionists' main political goal, required the displacement of its Arab inhabitants. When asked about the Deir Yaseen massacre that was committed by the Jewish militias (hundreds of non-combatant Palestinians were murdered), Israelis say the massacre was a regrettable aberration and that the leadership of Israel sent a letter of unqualified apology to then King Abdullah of Jordan. They point out that massacres were also committed against Jews in the Arab countries, Algeria in 1934, Iraq in 1941, and Libya in 1945, and to this day, some Palestinians, Arabs and Muslims call for the destruction of Israel. The war, the massacres and the refugees in Palestine will be discussed in Chapters 3 and 4.

Israel was created on narrow ethno-religious grounds, replacing and dominating the Palestinians who lived there for centuries. With or without the tragedy of the Holocaust where millions of innocent Jews were slaughtered between 1933 and 1945 in Europe, the

1 Wasserstein, 1991, p.40.
2 Lozowick, Yaacov, 2003

West had already decided even before the 1917 Balfour Declaration to support and implement the Zionist project at the expense of the Palestinians. The Zionists have succeeded in securing the collaboration of the Western colonialists for their project since the dawn of the 20th century, long before the Holocaust, when Palestine and most of the Arab countries were part of the Ottoman Empire. But the sympathy with the Jews due to the Holocaust atrocities that was committed by the West has helped the Zionist enterprise after the establishment of Israel. It induced Western media and intellectuals to make connection between the collective memory of the Holocaust tragedy and the establishment of Israel. They tend to refrain from criticizing Israel and continue to generally ignore the repressive measures taken by its army and the settlers against the Palestinians after the 1967 war.

The Palestinians have been betrayed by the international community especially the West, the Arab governing elites and most certainly by their own leaders. Both, the Arabs under the leadership of the Hashemite and the Zionists allied themselves with the Western colonialists in World War I, but the Arabs were used by Britain only for defeating Turkey and exploiting the natural resources and strategic location of their lands. Western colonialists recognized the Zionists as carriers of Western civilization and Israel as the defender of their economical and political interests against what some Westerners call the inferior Oriental culture of terrorism and barbarism. To justify the morality of claiming a country that had been populated by its indigenous Arabs, Theodore Herzl, the father of Zionism used the same Europeans' justification for colonialism by elucidating that the indigenous Palestinians would benefit from the colonization of their land by the civilized European Jews. In search for legitimacy to the Zionist project, he argued that the Jewish-Palestinian issue was not a zero-sum situation. In his 1902 *Alteneuland*, Herzl wrote, "Those [the Palestinians] who had nothing, and who therefore could lose nothing, obviously gained. And they did indeed gain: employment opportunities, a livelihood, good conditions.... These hapless people have been made far more fortunate than they were before."

The British gave the Jews a homeland in Palestine and the British Mandate Authority created a dual society of Arab Palestinians and Jewish settlers where Jews occupied the senior positions in the Mandate administration and the Palestinians had to take the role of subordinates. While the Palestinians' method of protest was limited to petitions submitted to the administrators in Palestine whose job was to make the 1917 Balfour Declaration a reality, the Zionists had access to the policy makers at the highest level of government in London. The influence of the Zionists on the policies of the Western Powers never ceased even one hundred years after the inception of Zionism. If anything, it has increased especially since the demise of the Soviet Union and the rise of the US as the only super-power dominating the global agenda of economic and foreign policy and military operations. There has never been any significant support to the Palestinians among opinion or policy makers in the US, while the pro-Israel supporters include most of the policy makers from the two major parties in Washington, think tanks, intellectuals, journalists, business-people, authors and entertainers. The US support to Israel grew deeper over time and became rooted in the fabric of America's domestic and foreign policy.

The early Zionists won because, unlike their Arab opponents, they had dedicated leadership, superior organization, better planning and they had strong inside influence on the policies of the big Western powers. Palestinians have been at big disadvantage in the quality of leadership and in their relations with the West. The Palestinian conflict has been a global issue from the start involving big powers, and the Zionists have used their material and human resources to shape the policies of the Western governments and peoples in their favor. They extracted the Balfour declaration from Britain in 1917 and influenced the public opinion in the West to accept the idea of settling Palestine with Jews as a morally good solution to the "Jewish problem." The secular Westerners accepted Zionism as a secular national liberation movement while the religious Christians considered the creation of Israel a fulfillment of a Devine promise as the base for its historical legitimacy. Thus, the West disqualified the Palestinians' resistance to the Jewish settlers, who took their lands by force, as a legal struggle against colonialism. That denies the right to the occupied and victimized inherent right to resist occupation and seek national liberation.

After being defeated in war, Arabs everywhere have devoted too much time blaming Zionism and the West for the Palestinians' predicament and not enough analyzing the failures and incompetence of their own leadership and system of governments. The first generation of the Zionist leadership succeeded in uniting Jews, the secular European Ashkenazi, the traditional Sephardic, Yemeni Temani, and Ethiopian Falashas, the Orthodox, the Reformed, the Conservative, the Re-constructionists, the new Russian immigrants and Atheists. They came from multitudes of countries and continents, spoke different languages and grew up in diverse cultures. Each group holds on to its collective identity and political ideology, but the political Zionists devised a system where the military institution, the culture of insecurity and the common language became the glue that holds the Israeli Jews together. The three legends are the vehicles to penetrate the culture, the social and the political divergences of the different Jewish groups.

All Jewish men have to serve three years and the women two years in the Israeli Defense Force (IDF) then they go through annual military training after discharge. Every Israeli Jewish civilian is a life-long reserve soldier until the age of 45, ready for deployment at anytime he is called to serve. Civil militarism became a common denominator culture and a collective identity that united a large majority of the Jewish Israeli society. Besides the task of waging war, the Israeli military integrates the Jews and transforms every Jewish man and woman into an obedient soldier to the military generals and a Hebrew-speaking warrior. The feelings of insecurity that pervade Israeli society are rooted in the public, the religious and the military education systems that put too much emphasis on the history of the Jews suffering in Europe and their version of the struggle by the first generations of Jewish settlers in Palestine against the indigenous Arabs. This "education" has created a general feeling that the state is still threatened by the Palestinians and the neighboring Arab states, and most Israelis today believe reconciliation with the Arabs is hopeless. The Zionists succeeded in creating from the strange mix of the Jewish settlers a Hebrew-speaking nation, thus bringing a new life to a language that was spoken by few people outside the synagogue before the establishment of Israel.

In contrast to the early Zionist movement, the Arab tribal and clan system created local and regional Arab leaders driven by their own personal ambitions. Jewish leaders transformed Zionism into an institution that united a large mass of Jews worldwide in defense of Israel while traditional Arab elites reduced the concept of Arab nationalism to loyalties to feuding leaders. Arab and Palestinian leaders, with conflicting personal ambitions, could not effectively unite societies around a national cause, even when these societies were homogeneous and share land, history and culture. Sixty years after the first Arab–Israeli war, there is no movement toward democracy or human rights across the board in Arab states and the only major opposition forces are groups with Islamic religion agendas threatening the stability of their government's autocratic regimes.

With generous economic, military and material aid and access to know-how from the West, especially the US, Israel created the most powerful military in the Middle East and the most developed economy, efficient public and private sectors and a good system of accountability. It exports high-tech products to Europe and Asia, and since it had peace with Egypt and Jordan and established trade relations with many Arab and Muslim states, it has managed to penetrate the markets of the region. Israel's high-tech research and development puts it at the center of the information revolution. Deloitte and Touche 2008 survey showed that Israel ranked second only to the US in technical innovation in six key areas, telecom, microchips, software, biopharmaceuticals, medical devices and clean energy.

Like other Arab societies, the stateless Palestinian society has always been highly patriarchal and stratified where family and kinship ties determined the basis for political affiliation even when facing external forces. When the Zionist's project was launched in the last decade of the 19th century, the Palestinians primary allegiances had been to the family, clan and village and that was one of their weaknesses. Even when they knew how serious the Zionist threat was, the Palestinians could not shed their tribal culture of factionalism and blind loyalty to the big family (*hamoolah*) that made them easy to be drawn into their local leaders' personal feuds and rivalry that did not serve the national cause. That culture has produced corrupt and mediocre leaders. When the late PLO Chairman Yasser Arafat established the self-rule Palestinian Authority (PA) in 1993, he immediately created a typical corrupt Middle Eastern autocracy with all the powers granted to the Palestinians by Israel in his hands; loyalty dominated competency and his more than seven security agencies repressed dissent. His policies have undermined state building and economic and human development.

The Palestinians' leadership reinforced and perpetuated the semi-feudal structure of the Palestinians' society which followed the leadership of traditional prominent families' elites and failed to rise up to the historic moments of dealing with the Zionists' global power. It took years to create the State of Israel gradually and incrementally, and the Palestinians' *Nakba* (Catastrophe) did not happen over night or few months as many historians suggest. The *Nakba* started decades before the Israeli War of Independence or the ethnic cleansing of the Palestinians' towns and villages, when the rivalry between the Husseinis and the Nashashibi families rendered the Palestinians' struggle futile.

The national Palestinian social structure underwent full disintegration and an effective national leadership was missing many years before Israel was officially created. The Zionists planned and worked indulgently for half a century before establishing the State of Israel while the Palestinian leaders and their followers engaged in furious recriminations accusing each other for cooperating with the Jews and lack of patriotism. For more details on the pre-1948 Palestinians' infighting, see Chapter 3.

The uncompromising Palestinian leaders rejected the UN partitioning plan that gave them 45% of historic Palestine and they demanded control of all the country without having the resources to back-up their defiance or plans to defend their territory and their people if attacked. When the British terminated their role as the Mandate power and left the Arabs and Jews in confrontation in 1947, the Palestinians had no military to defend themselves and no institutions to run a state. The Jews constituted only about a third of Palestine's population, but their militia that had been developed into an effective national military organization was able to capture Arab neighborhoods, villages and towns, and contend with the regular military forces and volunteers of the surrounding Arab nations. The Palestinian leaders, who were absent when their people needed them most, had to surrender the defense of their country to the Arab states which throttled their nationalism to its infancy. But the Jewish military operated according to previously designed plans with the aim to insure control over the area designated by the UN for the Jewish state, occupy hundreds of strategically located Arab towns and villages and banish their inhabitants in the process. After the war, the landlocked West Bank that was slated by the 1947 UN Resolution to be the heartland of the Palestinians was annexed to Jordan in 1949 until the 1967 war when Israel conquered it as well as East Jerusalem and Gaza Strip.

Leaders of the neighboring Arab states proved their incompetence once more by going to war in 1967, claiming they had been provoked by Israel, without learning from their own history or anticipating the consequences of war. When the Israelis celebrated the sixtieth birthday of their state in May of 2008, they were in control of all historic Palestine; and the stateless Palestinians were divided and confused over whether to come into the US fold (which offers very little to their national cause other than conditional financial support) or to join the armed resistance to occupation — at the risk of being stamped as terrorists.

Five things led to the Palestinians' failure to establish their state in the 22% of historic Palestine that Israel occupied in the 1967 war. First and most important was the decisive defeat of the Arab armies in that war and the surrender of the West Bank, Jerusalem, the Gaza Strip, Egypt's Sinai Peninsula and the Syrian Golan Heights to the triumphant Israelis. Israel feels entitled to reap the spoils of the war it won and the Arab regimes collectively and the Palestinians are too weak to challenge it other than by waiting for the US to come up with solutions. The second reason is the Oslo agreements that allowed Israel to intensify its colonization of the West Bank and East Jerusalem. After Oslo, the Palestinian leadership have been negotiating from a position of extreme weakness as local administrators under occupation. The third is militarization, that is, the Second *Intifada* and attacks against the civilians in Israel proper that weakened the Israeli peace camp and played into the hands of the right-wing Israeli parties. Since the Second *Intifada*, the conflict became a vicious intractable blood feud that fed on itself and morality no longer mattered. The fourth obstacle is the rift between the Fatah and Hamas factions that led to violent clashes and the political separation between the Palestinians in the West Bank under Fatah and in Gaza under Hamas rule. The fifth is the Palestinians' misplaced faith in the international community under the US leadership that has subordinated its relations with Palestinians to its alliance with Israel. The powerful international governments have failed to protect the Palestinians' human rights and pressure Israel to end colonizing the occupied lands.

There have been only two successful Arab negotiations with Israel since 1948, Jordan under King Abdullah the First in 1949 and Egypt under Anwar Sadat in 1979. Ironically, neither of these leaders was given credit by Arab nationalists, especially the Palestinians, and both were assassinated for their willingness to negotiate with Israel.

King Abdullah was also criticized for his close relations with the British and he was blamed for surrendering Lydda and Ramle towns in 1948 and the "Iron Triangle" area in 1949 without a fight. And Sadat was accused of abandoning the Palestinians and his 1973 war allies, the Syrians, in favor of pursuing a separate peace with Israel. King Abdullah of Jordan negotiated with the Israelis in 1949 as an equal after his army won the battle for East Jerusalem, a big achievement by a small army that was no match to the Israeli military. He was the only Arab leader in 1948 who recognized the power of the Zionists and understood that the Arab–Israeli conflict was an international issue, and that any part of Palestinian lands that could be saved from the takeover by the Jews could be achieved only by help from a great power. His military could not have stopped the Israeli military from over-running the West Bank, so he used his close ties with Britain to influence the outcome of the 1948 war partially in his favor; he managed to keep the West Bank and Jerusalem under his control at the cost of tarnishing his reputation among his fellow Arabs, including the Palestinians. After capturing Jerusalem, his Arab Legion stayed passive all through the 1948 war. The pragmatic King succeeded in signing a truce with Israel, keeping the West Bank and Jerusalem in Arab hands, using his diplomatic and negotiating skills and his friendship with the British. Critics of King Abdullah may accuse him of many things, but they cannot deny the obvious; he saved one fifth of Palestine, including East Jerusalem, against all odds. The West Bank and Jerusalem were incorporated into his kingdom until the 1967 war when Israel captured them, annexed Jerusalem and colonized the West Bank. If King Abdullah had been alive in 1967, he would not have rushed to go to war with Israel, knowing there was too much at stake; it would put at risk the biggest achievement of his life. He would have signed a peace treaty with Israel if he had not been murdered in 1951, according to the Israeli journalist and one time deputy of Mossad, David Kimche. Israeli military generals tried to convince Prime Minister Ben-Gurion to conquer all Palestine in 1948–49, but the Prime Minister refused to follow their advice. He argued that "the international community [read Britain] would not allow Israel to conquer an excessive amount of territory and leave nothing for the Arabs."[1] Chapter 5 has more on King Abdullah.

Anwar Sadat negotiated with Israel a peace treaty in 1979 also as an equal after his armed forces stormed the Israeli Berleev line defenses in the 1973 war; and he declared the liberation of all Sinai, which is not a Palestinian land, as the end game of the negotiations. In his 1977 address to the Knesset, Sadat said, "None of us can, or accept to, cede one inch of it [Sinai], or accept the principle of debating or bargaining over it." Like King Abdullah of Jordan, Sadat realized that the conflict was an International issue and he could not recover any part of Sinai without help from the US. The signing of the Egyptian–Israeli peace treaty was based on the principle of land for peace and the complete withdrawal from Sinai was based on the international law regarding occupied territories. But without the US pressure, Israel would have continued to act in Sinai as it has always done in Palestine and the Golan Heights, defying the international law. Unfortunately for the Palestinians, the Egyptian territory was ceded in order to neutralize Egypt and safeguard Israel's control of the West Bank. Chapter 6 includes more details about Sadat and the recovery of Sinai.

The Palestinians missed an opportunity to establish their state when the leaders of the PLO signed the 1993 Declaration of Principles (DOP). The DOP established a five-year interim process of negotiations between a dominant occupier and the PA, a self-rule authority under occupation, without clearly specifying what the final outcome should be. It gave the Israelis time to create facts on the ground, tighten their grip on the territories and ironically sustain the illusion that the Palestinian Authority rules the Palestinians. The important issues were left unresolved: the borders, the nature of the Palestinian entity, the settlements, the Palestinian refugees and the status of Jerusalem. After countless summit meetings, promises and negotiations, more land was confiscated, settlements were built and expanded and a viable independent Palestinian state became more difficult to realize.

The Palestinians in the occupied lands won the sympathy of World public opinion and many Israelis in the 1988 First *Intifada* when they did not resort to acts of violence or use firearms in the uprising and the Israeli government failed to justify killing and injuring unarmed civilians. Many in the international community recognized the right of the Palestinians to be free, until the exiled PLO leadership in Tunisia stepped in; squandered the gains of the *Intifada* by signing the Oslo agreements that set the stage for the failure of the so-called "two-state solution"; and brought the Palestinians to the present predicament of getting only a limited autonomy on few parcels of the occupied lands separated by Jewish-only-settlements and Jewish-only-roads, rather than a sovereign state. Israel as the strong party in the conflict used the Oslo agreements, to which the Palestinian cause is held hostage, to bypass the international laws and the previous UN resolutions. The Israelis were very careful not to refer to the West Bank, Gaza and East Jerusalem as "occupied lands" in the Oslo agreements or in the negotiation sessions. They referred to it as the "disputed territory." The negotiations, between a dominant force that can dictate

---

1 Kimmerling, Baruch, 2001, p.41

terms and a powerless occupied state without serious and sustained involvement of the US as an impartial mediator was destined to fail. Israel used the negotiations as the excuse to disregard the UN resolutions and violate the international laws. The Oslo agreements are discussed with more details in Chapter 3.

The so-called "two-state solution" should be re-named the "Palestinian-state solution" because the state of Israel has been established since 1948 on 78% of historic Palestine. Israel today is a fact of life that cannot be denied even by the Palestinians who aspire to have their own state. During the closing months of his administration, President George W. Bush launched the Annapolis meeting to deal with the Palestinian–Israeli conflict with the announced goal of reaching statehood for the Palestinians in 2008. The significance of the meeting was that the Arab states which attended the meeting formally surrendered the Palestinian issue to the US government and became just witnesses and spectators. The PA leadership negotiated with the Israelis until the last day of President Bush administration without reaching a much-desired peace. The Israelis had maintained that Jerusalem must be excluded from such negotiations; they announced plans for more settlements expansion in the West Bank and East Jerusalem and they refused to have the refugees' issue on the agenda. Israel has been negotiating to translate its 1967 military triumph and the weakness of the Arab regimes into annexation and permanent occupation of the conquered land. They are playing the Palestinian conflict today with impunity under the 19th century colonial-power supremacy rules, not according to the 21st century "rule of law."

From the outset, the issues of the Palestinian–Israeli conflict started mostly with land and people but the ideological, religious and primordial cleavages entered into the conflict in force at a later point after the 1967 war and it was re-enforced after Oslo agreements. In 1948, the Israelis celebrated the establishment of their state and did not mourn for losing to the Jordanians the Western Wall and other sanctified sites in Jerusalem or the semi-mythological and semi-historical places in the West Bank. But when Israel conquered the new territory that is densely populated by Palestinians in the 1967 war, the Israelis developed many schemes to settle the land and oppress its indigenous population based on religious sentiments, history and security. Immediately after winning the 1967 war through what was frequently described by Israelis as "divine intervention," the victors viewed the Jordan River as Israel's eastern security boundary; a new frontier was opened for settlement; and the conflict was refocused on the Palestinians' struggle against the notion of Jewish historic rights and connection to the land of "Judea and Samaria." Israel annexed Arab East Jerusalem, including the Old City, and declared Jerusalem its "eternal united capital." Israel has a dual secular-religious identity but on the right to colonize the occupied lands, the boundaries between the two identities blur. Members of the religious organizations subscribe to the "Promised Land Concept," the secular Zionists adopt the "Greater Land of Israel" doctrine and the governments since 1967 hold that no one should question the right of Jews to settle in the newly occupied lands of "Judea and Samaria." The religious movements claim that the occupied lands are the "cradle of Jewish symbols" and biblical sites from the ancient periods of the First and Second Temples. And the secular Zionists see all Palestine as a frontier even if the local Palestinians individually and collectively claim title to every tract of land there. Minister of Defense Moshe Dayan, who was one of the least influenced by a religious vision, declared after winning the 1967 war, "We have returned to our holy places and we will never leave them." Chaim Bar-Lev, the Israeli armed forces commander, stated in April 1968, "During the coming years we shall continue settlement in all the territories." Eliezer Livneh, a theorist of the liberal Mapam Party, founded the "Movement for Greater Israel" in 1967. The leaders of the movement included a cross-section of mostly secular intellectuals from all sectors of the Israeli society and parties; they declared in their 1967 manifesto that "no Israeli government had the right to hand back land won in battle." They recommended building new Jewish-only cities (settlements) next to the Palestinian cities of Nablus, Hebron, Jericho and other population centers. Bar-Ilan University rector Harold Fisch, a member of the "Movement for Greater Israel," wrote, "There is only one nation to whom the land belongs in trust and by covenant, and that is the Jewish people."[1]

Gush Emunim, a chauvinist group that derived its inspiration from various divine promises, has been one of the most salient hawkish movements committed to establish settlements and change the map of Jewish presence in the West Bank. After the 1967 war, the group succeeded in shifting the emphasis of the Israeli political alliance between secular and ethnocentrism from the Zionist secular hegemony to the religious and primordial elements of the Jewish nationalism. Gush Emunim members believe they are the modern pioneers and the settlements on the so-called "ancestral homeland" are central in creating modern Judaism. The group early generations were young people receiving their education in state run religious schools and the National Religious Party youth organization B'nai Akiva, which blends religious fundamentalism with co-operative socialism. The group appeared on the political scene in 1974 when a small number of its activists accompanied by more than 2000 of their supporters established a camp in an old railroad station in an area densely populated by Arabs in the West Bank. The Israeli government transferred them to a nearby army base where eventually they were given permission to build their first settlement. From 1974 on, members of the group set up so-called "unauthorized settlements," then they managed to have the government concede, legalize each settlement, provide electricity and water and build infrastructures. Gush Emunim members built several new settlements in the heart of Palestinians-inhabited lands with red-shingled roofs and private gardens on hilltops of the territory and constructed Jews-only roads to the settlements on confiscated Palestinian private owned land. They named the settlements after sites in the Old Testament, like Shiloh and Beit El, or Jewish legends like Elazar, Elon Moreh and Neve Daniel. And the Israeli governments, especially after the withdrawal from Sinai, moved rapidly to help the settlers create more facts on the ground which would make it difficult to withdraw from parts of the occupied lands. Gush Emunim spokesmen were present in every Israeli government including Yitzhak Rabin's cabinet.[2] Israeli governments encouraged both religious and secular Israeli Jews

---

1 Sachar, Howard M. 2007
2 Sachar, Howard M., 2007

to live in the settlements by offering financial incentives, cheap mortgages and lower tax tariffs. A large percentage of the national budgets has been allocated for the development and maintenance of the Jewish-only settlements even at times of economic crisis. But the problem facing the Israelis in the occupied land is that the Palestinians have no plans to abandon their homeland and leave (as their countrymen and women did in 1948/49). Thus the issue of the "demographics" in Israeli society arose. To accept the incorporation of a rapidly growing Palestinian population within their territory would threaten what the Israeli leaders call the "demographic composition" of the "Jewish" state that the Israelis hope to preserve. The Israelis fear that the joinder of the three million Palestinians under occupation to the one million Israeli–Arabs would sooner or later transform the "Jewish state" into an Arab-majority country.

Israeli policy makers, groups and individuals developed many plans, mostly provocative, for the future of the Palestinian inhabitants. Since they could not expel all the Palestinians as they did in 1948/49, the Israeli governments adopted a policy of containing them in defined enclaves within "Greater Israel." But in East Jerusalem that had been annexed after 1967 war, Israel has been systematically revoking Jerusalem residency in Jerusalem. In 2009 alone, 4,577 Jerusalem ID cards were confiscated from Palestinian Jerusalemites forcing them and their families into exile or illegal residency in their homes. Palestinian Jerusalemites cannot obtain permission for their spouses coming from other places to live in the city. Israel places severe restrictions on issuing permits for Palestinian houses in East Jerusalem, forcing them to construct without permits. As a result, hundreds of Palestinian-owned homes have been demolished since 1967.

To make Israel look less of an occupier and to maintain a tight grip on the territory, the Israeli governments of 1999–2001 Ehud Barak and the 2006–2009 Ehud Olmert proposed limited autonomy under a Palestinian Authority in apartheid towns and villages in the West Bank and Gaza, giving the illusion that Israel no longer governs the Palestinians. Both governments emphatically rejected the refugees' right of return and insisted that Jerusalem must remain undivided under Israeli control. Besides defending the right of Jews to settle in the occupied lands, they believed security for Israel could be guaranteed only by controlling all the land west of the Jordan River and not by peace treaties. The 2009 government of Benjamin Netanyahu (including the leader of the hawkish Likud bloc and the hard-line nationalist Yisrael Beitienu Party chief Avigdor Lieberman) is not expected to offer anything more than limited autonomy and continuous domination of the Palestinians. Like the previous Israeli governments, Netanyahu's government would not accept the legitimate rights of the Palestinians to have a sovereign state of their own on part of their ancestral land in return for real peace. Netanyahu proposed negotiations for establishing a Palestinian state in Judea/Samaria and Gaza, but he attached certain conditions to this offer. He would not stop expanding the settlements; Jerusalem would stay united under Israeli control; there would be no military for the proposed state; the Palestinian refugees would relinquish their claim to a right of return; and the Palestinians must recognize Israel as a Jewish state. On January 21, 2010, Netanyahu said that, "Israel must have a presence in the West Bank to stop rockets from being imported even after a peace agreement is achieved." This "will require an Israeli presence on the eastern side of any future Palestinian entity."

The failure to achieve a two-state solution that satisfies the minimum national ambitions of the Palestinians is a foregone conclusion under the present conditions because Israel has been allowed to flout international laws with impunity. There will be no viable Palestinian state unless the occupation ends and the settlements are removed. Prime Minister Netanyahu pledged on August 8, 2009 he would never evict Jewish settlers from the West Bank or Jerusalem as Israel did in 2005 in Gaza, calling that a "mistake," although Gaza is still a besieged territory and its residents are denied any contact with the rest of the world. Should the present conditions change and a sovereign Palestinian state solution be reached, the 2005 eviction of 8,500 settlers from small Gaza settlements as part of Ariel Sharon unilateral disengagement was a precedent of the reversibility of settlement presence. But number of Gaza settlers was very small compared to the hundreds of thousands who may not agree to leave the West Bank and East Jerusalem voluntarily and refuse to live under the Palestinian rule. As of 2008, there were more than 450,000 settlers living in 144 Jews-only settlements and 200 outposts in the West Bank and East Jerusalem. The right-wing and religious parties that control the Israeli governments are strong advocates of establishing and expanding settlements in the West Bank and East Jerusalem as a self-acclaimed historical right for the Jewish people based on Biblical scriptures and the claim of "uninterrupted" continuity of the Jewish presence in Palestine. Some settlements are built in close proximity to the Palestinian population centers making the separation impossible. In the case of Hebron City, a small number of armed fanatic religious settlers, who are against coexistence with the Palestinians, control the center of an Arab city of more than one hundred thousand people. Chapter 3 includes more details about the Palestinian-Israeli agreement on Hebron.

The preponderance of Jewish settlers in the West Bank is not struggling to find a roof to put over their heads; they are religious fanatics with the ideology of "redeeming" the land and a deep hostility toward the Palestinians. Right-wing Israeli settlers espouse conflicting positions. They want separation from the Palestinians to maintain the Jewish character of the state, but they build settlements next to the Palestinian population centers and they have no interest in a peace based on equality and justice. The settlers have strong supporters in the Knesset and all successive governments since 1967. They have been viewed by their supporters as today's pioneering Zionists like the pre-state early Jewish immigrants who settled the land and established the kibbutzim. Two ministers in Prime Minister Netanyahu 2009 government, including the foreign minister, live in settlements built on Palestinian land. Netanyahu rejected President Obama's call for freezing the settlements' expansion and offered to give the Palestinians a mutant state with no sovereignty, but surprisingly Obama's spokesman described the offer as an "important step forward." The US has recently retreated from its original demand for freezing settlement expansion by linking the end of building settlements with the normalization process between Israel and the Arab states.

President Obama said his administration was committed to pursuing lasting peace and stability in the Middle East, but there is doubt as to whether he will be willing to pressure Israel to end the 40-year occupation which is a requirement for a durable peace. Rhetorical promises to help Arabs and Israelis negotiate their differences and reach peace were regularly made by American presidents from Richard Nixon to George W. Bush. President Obama stated in speeches to Arab and Muslim audience that the security of Israel is "paramount" but he had nothing to say about the security needs of the Palestinians. Security cannot be guaranteed for one side without the other. He praised the Arab peace initiative; but his focus was only on Arab states normalization with Israel and nothing about ending the occupation. George Mitchell, Obama's envoy to the Middle East came to the region to "listen rather than to dictate," but he refused to listen to any representative from Hamas movement, which won the 2006 legislative elections and has controlled the Gaza Strip since 2007. He listened only to the US allies in the Arab countries whose opinion has already been known. And George Mitchell did not visit Gaza, the site of the unspeakable massacres committed by Israel military in December 2008 that took the lives and maimed thousands; and reduced homes, schools, mosques, government civil administration and civil infrastructures to rubble. See Chapter 10 for more details on the 2008 war on Gaza.

The tone of President Obama's speeches and interviews differ substantially from those of his predecessor, but on the Palestinian issue, he works within the same parameters drawn by the Bush administration. President Obama has spent too much political capital on many local and international issues and he does not have enough capital left to spend challenging Israel's supporters in Congress and the press by reversing the traditional pro-Israel US Middle East policies to solve the Palestinian–Israeli conflict. While US Senators Joe Lieberman and John McCain were visiting Israel on January 9, 2010, they assured the Israelis that if Obama tried to pressure Israel to freeze settlements in any way, they would stop him. Lieberman said, "Any attempt to pressure Israel, to force Israel to the negotiating table, by denying Israel support will not pass Congress of the Unite States. In fact, Congress will act to stop any attempt to do that."[1] The continuous blind support to the Israeli right-wing governments and the collective punishment and the siege of the Palestinians in Gaza suggests business as usual in Washington.

Even if President Obama is serious about forcing Israel to conclude a just peace as some optimists expect, it does not mean the Israeli government will compromise its strategic territorial objectives to appease its major ally and defender. The history of the Zionist movement before and after the establishment of Israel suggests that, when it comes to the interests of Israel, alliances do not count unless they serve its goals. The success of the Zionist project was possible only because the British conquered Palestine in 1917 and issued the Balfour Declaration to create a Jewish homeland in Palestine. But the Zionist military organizations carried out violent campaign against the British in Palestine demanding no

---

1 *Jerusalem Post*, January 10, 2010

restrictions on the Jewish immigration, killing and injuring scores of British soldiers in the process. Chapter 4 has more details on the Jewish terrorist attacks on the British.

The Israeli leaders feel confident the US would continue its traditional support even if there are disagreements on announced policies. That explained why the Israeli Foreign Minister Avigdor Lieberman reaffirmed Israel's determination to continue its settlement program while sharing the platform with the US Secretary of State, Hillary Clinton who was calling for complete halt to settlement expansion. Only days after President Obama had called for a total freeze on settlement construction, the Israeli government authorized the construction of 300 new homes in so-called "illegal outposts" and roads for them in the West Bank. And in November 2009, Israel defied the US again by approving the building of 900 homes for Jews on West Bank land that had been annexed to Jerusalem municipality.

Israel announced plans to build 1,600 housing units in East Jerusalem in March 2010 while Vice President Joe Biden was in Israel to show the US support for Israel and launch proximity talks between Israel and the Palestine Authority. The announcement caused the US embarrassment, and for the first time since President George Bush Senior administration, Israel was criticized publically by the US Secretary of State and other senior US Administration officials for undermining American foreign policy goals in the region. The news media reported tension between Israel and its most important ally and benefactor, and some officials called it "the worst crisis in US–Israeli relations". Prime Minister Benjamin Netanyahu apologized for the timing of the announcement but not for its substance. The US has the power to topple Netanyahu's government, but previous US–Israeli disagreements have not led to freezing or slowing the settlements expansion programs. Yitzhak Shamir lost the election in 1992 after disagreements with President George Bush Senior on the subject of settlements. Yitzhak Rabin and Shimon Peres Labor led governments that succeeded Shamir's continued his settlement policy even after signing the Oslo agreements. American Israel Public Affairs Committee (AIPAC) got the signatures of "more than three-quarters of the US House of Representatives [327] on a letter [sent to the Secretary of State] calling for an end to public criticism of Israel and urging the US to reinforce its relationship with the Jewish state."[1] Sadly, the US was forced to capitulate to Israeli intransigence on the settlements expansion. Obama's failure to persuade Israel to freeze settlements construction, even for a few months, subverts his pledge to reach a comprehensive, just peace in the region, which would require evacuating settlements.

If there is any hope for establishing a sovereign Palestinian state, there will have to be a basic course correction in the positions of the main key players in this conflict. Palestinians should end factionalism and pursue non-violent method of struggle; the Israeli electorate political orientation should move away from the ideology of conquest and accept the Palestinians right to self determination in a sovereign state of their own; and the

---

1 Guardian.co.uk, March 30, 2010.

US traditional Middle East foreign policy of blind support to Israel should end and start a real even-handed policy. The problem is that none of the parties is ready to correct course.

Once the two-state solution based on Palestinian–Israeli negotiations is declared dead, the Palestinians have the power to reject living under the status quo. They have many options to consider, but regardless of the option they choose, the Palestinian leaders need to patch up their differences, end the rift between their factions and unite the people behind a non-violent resistance strategy. Palestinian elites must rehabilitate their credibility among their people. As a starter, they should tear up the Israel-issued VIP identity cards that became a symbol of the virtual wall that Israel created to divide the Palestinians into two unequal classes in the national struggle — the people who suffer daily and sacrifice under occupation and the other Palestinians, a class of VIP elites plagued by endemic corruption who reap illegal personal benefits from the international aid that flows under the status quo. If the Palestinians fail to purge their own ranks and unite behind one strategy, they will have nobody to blame but themselves for being locked into a Bantustan that is not commensurate with the sacrifices that the Palestinians made over a century of struggle.

If the Palestinians fail to attain their sovereign state on even 22% of their historic homeland through direct negotiations, they have to choose other options and not accept the status quo. Under the present international conditions and the balance of power in favor of Israel, no option is guaranteed to give them the state they aspire to have. These are some nonviolent options that the Palestinians may choose to consider:

• Focusing on establishing a bi-national or a "one-liberal-democratic-state" in all historical Palestine that grants equal rights to all its citizens. This concept was promoted by the early cultural Zionists who opposed the establishment of a Jewish state.

• Accepting a state with provisional or temporary borders. This option has been suggested by some Israeli leaders and was rejected by Mahmoud Abbas in his speech to the Fatah Party conference in 2009.

• Declaring unilaterally a Palestinian state on all the occupied lands and asking for recognition from the international community.

• Disbanding the PA negotiating team and surrendering the negotiations to the pro-West Arab states. This casts doubts on the legitimacy of the PA leadership among their people since the only reason for the PA's existence has been to negotiate.

• Organizing a nonviolent campaign demanding the enforcement of the Fourth Geneva Convention and the previous UN resolutions in the occupied lands. The Palestinians have the right to use all means to resist occupation, but an effective option to garner the international support and strengthen the Israeli "peace" factions is to mount a concerted campaign of peaceful protest, civil disobedience and boycotting Israeli products. Chapter 11 provides analysis of these options.

The case of the Palestinians for justice is easy to explain. The Fourth Geneva Convention prohibits an occupying power from making the control of occupied lands permanent.

The Palestinians have a right of self-determination and to reject life under occupation or apartheid conditions in a non-sovereign Bantustan state. And Israel's need for "security," or the historical claim to the land based on "Old Testament prophecy" cannot justify violating international laws.

CHAPTER 2. ARAB NATIONALISM

The so-called "Arab world" includes countries stretching from the Atlantic Ocean in the west along the southern shores of the Mediterranean to the borders of Persia in the east, and the Arabian Peninsula. The majority of citizens in the Arab world are self-identified Arabs; they have adopted Arab traditions for generations and their formal mother tongue is the Arabic language, even if there are variations in how it is spoken in different countries and different regions. The Arab world came under Ottoman rule when the Turkish Sultan Saleem I conquered Egypt, Iraq and Syria in 1515–1517 from the Mamaleek, and Sultan Suleiman the Magnificent extended its domination in the 1530s to include North Africa's coast, Yemen, and Aden. These lands had been ruled by the Turkish sultans from Constantinople for four hundred years. The sultan was the center of the imperial power; the empire was divided into provinces (*vilayet*); and the authority to manage the provinces was entrusted to appointed officials. In the 19th century, Turkey was referred to as "the sick man of Europe" and many of its Arab provinces were taken over by the Europeans. Muhammed Ali imposed the virtual secession of Egypt and Ibn Saud of Najd extended his Wahhabi rule over a large territory of the Arabian Peninsula. Many overlords in the Levant (Eastern Mediterranean area) established their own principalities under adopted religious sectarian names like the Alawite or Druze or Maronites. And when the 1860 civil war broke out between the Druze and Maronites in Lebanon, where thousands were killed, the French Army occupied Beirut and forced the Turkish government to grant Lebanon self rule under an appointed Maronite chief. France took Algeria in 1830 and Tunisia in 1881, and Libya was lost to Italy in 1911.

Muhammed Ali, the titular military governor of Egypt since 1805, succeeded in defeating the Wahhabi tribes in Arabia in 1811 and conquering Sudan in 1823. He was trying to carve out parts of the Ottoman Empire for himself and establishing an Arab-speaking kingdom under his rule. When the Ottoman Sultan rejected his claim to Syria, Muhammed

Ali dispatched an army under the command of his son, Ibrahim Pasha, to take it by force in 1831. The overwhelming majority of Syrian notables and religious leaders welcomed Ibrahim.[1] The only serious resistance the Egyptian armies faced was in the Palestinian city of Acre, where Governor Ahmed Al-Jazzar put up a fight and Ibrahim had to destroy the city before it would surrender. The Egyptian armies marched into the rest of the Syrian cities, Damascus, Homs, Hama, and Aleppo, unopposed. By 1833, Ibrahim was formally recognized as the governor of Syria on behalf of his father.

The Syrian Arabs, Muslims and Christians welcomed the Egyptian ruler and perceived him as a liberator from the hated Turks. The Muslims aspired to live in a Muslim empire with an Arab caliphate that would give them more influence than they had had under the Turks. Arab Christians on the other hand believed that Ibrahim would treat them fairly because his father had been known for his tolerance and fair treatment of the Christians in Egypt. Only the Palestinian Arabs were divided regarding support for Ibrahim. Some of them supported his expansionist ambitions because the Turks had burdened them with taxes and failed to provide them with any social services or adequate security. Other Palestinians had reason to fear him because of their first-hand knowledge of his father's policies in Egypt, due to Palestine's proximity to Egypt. Many Egyptian dissidents had sought refuge in Palestine to avoid high taxes and the draft or to escape retribution for standing in the way of Muhammed Ali's rise to power.

The Western powers did not sit idly by while the Egyptians expanded their influence by dismantling the Ottoman Empire. Fear of Ibrahim's ambition and the further decline in Turkey's ability to defend its heartland led European states to intervene militarily. The navies and armies of Britain, Prussia, Russia, and Austria forced Ibrahim to withdraw his troops from Syria and end the occupation of Syria in 1840.

The British reaction to Egypt's military success against Turkey suggests, first, that the British had an interest in Syria due to its strategic location, and second, the British perceived an Arab kingdom under the ambitious Muhammed Ali to be more of a threat to their interest in the road to India than the Turkish occupation. Third, Britain would not tolerate Arab nationalists coming to power in Syria or other strategic areas unless they were controlled by Britain (or too weak to challenge its interests). With the Egyptian withdrawal from Syria, the plan for an Arab kingdom failed, but the short-lived adventure succeeded in laying the foundation of the Arab awakening.

ARAB NATIONALISM UNDER THE IBRAHIM ADMINISTRATION

Ibrahim's administration introduced significant reforms to the system of taxation, public education, justice, and security in Syria, but the legacy of his rule between 1831 and 1840 was the rehabilitation of Arabic as the language of instructions in public education and the improvement of the positions of the Christian and Jewish minorities. Ibrahim abolished the protection taxes imposed on non-Muslim minorities by the Ottomans. He appointed Christians and Jews to local councils, put an end to the Ottoman government

---

1 Donna Divine, 1994.

restrictions on building or repairing churches and synagogues, permitted missionary activities, and allowed the establishment of European consulates in Damascus, Beirut, and Jerusalem. Ibrahim's deference to the Christian and Jewish communities in Syria was motivated by fear of the European opposition to his military campaign rather than a commitment to religious equality.[1] When the Egyptians had to withdraw from Syria and surrender it back to Turkey, the Turks could not easily scrap the system of administration reforms that had been implemented by the Egyptians. The reforms included government supported primary education for boys, the policy of tolerating the activists of all religions, and the acceptance of the European consuls' presence in the main cities of Syria. As a result, the Jesuits and the American Protestant missions arrived in 1834 and the competition between them for influence on society through their educational institutions led to the revival of the Arabic language. The American mission moved a printing machine, capable of printing Arabic books, from Malta to Beirut.

At the time of Ibrahim's arrival in Syria there were no Arabic printing machines, Arabic newspapers were unknown, bookstores were nonexistent, and the spoken Arabic had degenerated into many debased and distorted dialects and idioms.[2] There were only elementary schools run by the mosques or the churches and the schools were dedicated to teaching the religion of the community. In the short period of Ibrahim's rule, a public education system was established with primary schools throughout Syria and high schools in the large cities. Arabic text books and Arabic translations of the Bible were printed and distributed all over Syria and many schools were established by the missionaries in Jerusalem, Beirut, and Damascus. The educational system and the tolerance of the Christian missionaries that Ibrahim started survived his departure and set the foundations of the Arab national consciousness.

ARAB NATIONALISM UNDER THE TURKS AFTER IBRAHIM'S RULE

The education system was used by a new breed of intellectual reformers as a vehicle to promote the doctrine of unity based on formal Arabic language heritage rather than sectarianism and a narrow national identity. Prominent men of letters such as Butrus Bustani, Nasif Yaziji, and Adib Is-haq were pioneers in propagating secular Arab nationalism based on knowledge and enlightenment. Bustani, an Arab Presbyterian, wrote books on Arabic literature, composed papers, taught in American missionary schools, translated the Bible, and compiled an Arabic language dictionary. He published an Arabic encyclopedia based on Arabic sources and European translations. He founded the first weekly political newspaper in Beirut in 1860, promoting knowledge as the means to bridge sectarian differences. He established his famous educational institution in 1863, the "National School," for boys of all religions and backgrounds; and he recruited the distinguished scholar and Arab nationalist Nasif Yaziji to teach Arabic language in the school.

---

1 Donna Robinson Divine, 1994.
2 George Antonius, 1979.

Bustani and Nasif Yaziji were members of the "Society of Arts and Science Society," established in 1847, which advocated the pursuit of knowledge even beyond the Arabic culture. This suggests that their concept of Arab nationalism was not hostile toward the Western culture. Some of the society members were foreign nationals residing in Syria, but the majority was Christian Syrians. Nasif Yaziji promoted the idea of reviving the Arab ancient civilization and urged the Arabs to free themselves from the Turks' domination.[1] Another society, the "Syrian Scientific Society," was established in 1857 mostly by Arab notables and heads of prominent families of all creeds living in Syria and some living in Egypt and Turkey. Among its members were the sons of Butrus Bustani and Nasif Yaziji. Unlike the "Society of Arts and Science Society," which was dominated by Christian members and had relations with missionaries, the majority of the "Syrian Scientific Society" was Muslim of different sects, and there was no missionary influence. The historian George Antonius argues that Arab nationalism as a movement to unite the country against the Turkish rule was secretly conceived by some members of the "Syrian Scientific Society" and promoted among students throughout the country by word of mouth.[2]

The Syrian Protestant College, which opened in Beirut in 1866, was the first high educational institution that trained Arab students in education, science, literature and medicine, and it has been credited with graduating many Arab nationalist pioneers. By 1873, the Jesuits had already opened schools in Beirut, Ghazir, Zahla, Damascus, and Aleppo. They established the University of St. Joseph in Beirut in 1875 and expanded their printing and publishing facilities. The American Presbyterians established a college, which has become the American University of Beirut. Many early Arab-Syrian intellectuals opposing colonial rule and promoting Arab nationalism were educated Christians who associated Arab nationalism with the Arab-speaking communities. George Antonius, the son of Christian Arab parents, argued in his book, *Arab Awakening*, that Arab nationalism in some parts of the Ottoman Empire had been sustained by the common language. Although Arab identity was indebted to Islam because Arabic is the language of the Koran, neither the religion of Islam nor certain ethnicities have ever been conditions for Arab nationalism. The Arab nation, according to Antonius, includes all Arabic-speaking people residing geographically in all north Africa, Sudan, the Arabian Peninsula and the region east of the Mediterranean.

The Arab national movement was launched by Arab literary elites in Syria who were educated in French or American missionary schools in Beirut and Damascus in the second half of the 19th century. Many of the early secular Arab nationalists were Christians, because they were the first to achieve the social status of the bourgeoisie, due to their easy access to education in the missionary schools.[3] Another factor for the strong Arab nationalism among the Christians was their feeling of alienation as non-Muslims living under the Muslim Turkish rule. Strong Arab nationalism emerged in the beginning of the 20th century to protect Arab political and economic interests when the "Young Turks" took power in Constantinople.

1 Ernest Dawn, 1973
2 George Antonius, 1979.
3 Sharabi, 1972.

Members of the secret association, Committee of Union and Progress (CUP) that had been established by the Young Turks staged a military *coup d'état* against Sultan Abdul-Hamid in 1908. The CUP was dominated by military officers of Turkish background, but other races from within the Ottoman Empire were represented in its membership including Jews and Arabs. Its objective was to end Abdul-Hamid's authoritarian rule and reform the government by resuscitating the 1876 constitution which established freedom of belief and equality of all citizens before the law. Arab nationalists, both Muslims and Christians, rejoiced and an Arab society of *"al-Ikha' al-Arabi al-Uthmani"* (Arab–Turkish Brotherhood) was founded for the main purpose of protecting the democracy that had been accorded by the new constitution. They aspired to promote the national interests of the Arab region on an equal footing with the Turks. Their agenda included teaching the Arab population in their own language and fostering Arabic culture. As a goodwill gesture toward the Arabs, the Young Turks released Sharif Hussein Ibn Ali from his forced residency in Istanbul and appointed him to be the Grand Sharif of Mecca. Unfortunately, the honeymoon was too short. It was only a few months before the good will and the alliance between the Arabs and Turks suffered a serious setback.

The rift started over the outcome of the 1908 parliament elections. Unhappy with the results, Arab nationalists accused the CUP of using unfair practices in favor of the Turks at the expense of the Arabs. The Turks were estimated to be only 34% while the Arabs constitute 48% of the total population of the Ottoman Empire in 1908, but out of 245 elected representatives in the Chamber of Deputies, the Turks won 150 seats, or 60%, and the Arabs had only 60 representatives, or 24%.[1] The elections were followed by government decrees banning societies that had been established by non-Turkish races and enacting laws that discriminated against non-Turks.

All this suggested there was a Turkish nationalist movement in the making. The government adopted a policy of more centralization for greater efficiency, which would take away the freedom of the Arabs and other minorities who preferred decentralization that allowed them to pursue their political and cultural development.

Arab nationalism increased rapidly as a reaction to the imposition of more laws that required using only the Turkish language in the administration, the courts, and the schools.[2] The new laws were perceived as deliberate attempts to subordinate the Arab population to the Turks. Organized Arab nationalism was strong in Syria and Mesopotamia (Iraq) in reaction to the new Ottoman policies that emphasized the Turkish rather than the Islamic identity of the empire. Some activists demanded Arab independence and others asked for political autonomy.

The Turks' policies provoked protests in Beirut in 1910 demanding that besides the Turkish language, Arabic should be allowed, especially in the courts, and that Arabic-speaking teachers should be appointed to teach Arabic in state preparatory schools. This came at a time when the Ottoman government was accused of condoning Zionist purchas-

---

1 George Antonius, 1979.
2 A.L. Tibawi, 1969.

es of Palestinian Arab lands from absentee owners. There was a strong Jewish presence in the government of the Young Turks.

Arab nationalism was strengthened in opposition to the Jewish national movement (Zionism). The tension between the two movements was aggravated by the realities in Palestine. According to the historian Yehoshua Porath, years before the First Zionist Congress was convened, frustrated Arab notables from Jerusalem submitted petitions to the Ottoman government demanding the end of Jewish immigration and land purchase. They charged that "the Jews were taking away all the land from the Muslims." Syrian nationalists saw the Zionist penetration of Palestine as an Arab national problem, and by 1911, Arab leaders in and out of the Turkish government launched attacks on the government for abandoning the Palestinian peasants who had been expelled from their homes and lands by East European Zionist settlers. There was an angry confrontation in the Chamber of deputies in 1912 when Arab members complained against the sale of Palestine's arable plain of Marj-ibn-Aamer (Vale of Jezreel) to a Jewish agency. Arab deputies Shukri al-A'sali from Damascus, Ruhi al-Khalidi and Sa'id al-Husseini from Jerusalem, and Rida al-Sulh from Beirut attacked the government for its anti-Arab bias and demanded limits on Jewish immigration to Palestine. In August 1913, the Arabic language newspaper *Palestine* called on wealthy Arab nationalists to buy government lands in Palestine before the Jews could purchase it.

Arab nationalism in Syria in the late 19th century coincided with the emergence of Egyptian reformers such as Refaa'h Tahtawi, Jamal Eddeen Al-Afghani, and Muhammed Abdo. They argued that the Arabs could rise to the challenge of the modern world only if they reformed and reinvigorated Islam. Muhammed Ali who ruled Egypt from 1805 to 1848 started the process of modernizing Egypt. Students were sent to Europe to study and by the 1830s, many of them had come back to teach and translate to Arabic modern secular political ideas. The Egyptian reformers tried to bridge the gap between Islam and modernity by promoting the secular state within more tolerant Islamic environment.[1] The writings of Al-Afghani and Abdo were an attempt to encourage the Egyptians to make the transition from a traditional society to a capitalist society without losing the Islamic culture.

The loss of the Arab country, Libya to Italy in 1911-12 was viewed by Arab nationalists as a sign of Turkey's weakness and many began to plan for an alternative to the Ottoman rule. Secret nationalist societies were developed by members of prominent Syrian families and ranks of Arab officers in the Turkish army. Arab officers, mostly from Baghdad and Mosul, formed the underground *"al-Ahd Society"* (the Compact Society) demanding reforms that would include recognition of Arab political rights and Arab culture. They aspired to work for achieving independence or at least greater autonomy for Syria within the empire. The feeling of being Arab was strong among officers who had been denied promotions because of their non-Turk nationality. During World War I, some Arab offi-

---

1 Bassam Tibi, 1982.

cers abandoned their Turkish military units and joined the British army and Emir Faisal's[1] army in the fight against the Turks. Although Emir Faisal was a close ally with the British colonialists, his accession to the throne in Syria, then in Iraq, was perceived by Arab officers as symbolic of an Arab nationalist struggle.

One of these officers was Nouri as-Said, who fought under Emir Faisal in the Arab revolt and led the troops that took Damascus when the Turkish army had to retreat in 1918. He served several times as a pro-British prime minister in Iraq during the British Mandate and under the monarchy. Nouri as-Said promoted and signed the 1930 Anglo–Iraqi treaty that was a prelude to Iraq gaining full independence although the treaty gave Britain many military and economic privileges. The treaty was bitterly resented by the Arab nationalists, poisoned Iraq's politics for decades and it was the main reason for uprisings. The pro-Britain Iraqi elites including Nouri-as-Said and members of the royal family and its supporters were massacred by the masses during the 1958 military coup led by Abdul-Karim Kassim.

Arab nationalism after World War I east of the Mediterranean was a natural reaction to the foreign rule and the desire to gain independence. The nationalists opposed the Mandates imposed by Britain in the south and France in the north. Greater Syria was divided by Britain and France into four statelets: Lebanon, Syria, Palestine and Trans-Jordan. The nationalists supported the Arab monarchy in Iraq under King Faisal despite his close relations with the British and the fact that the entity he ruled was a satellite state.

The significance of the post-World War I period was the establishment of political parties that called for unification. The Syrian Social National Party (SSNP) was established in Beirut in 1932 by Antun Sa'adeh. Sa'adeh advocated the establishment of a secular union that includes Syria, Lebanon, the historical Palestine, Sinai Peninsula, Cyprus, Jordan, Iraq, Kuwait and parts of southern Turkey. Geography was the main factor in Sa'adeh's conception of a nation. He believed it was the natural social unity in support of the rights and duties of the people sharing the geography define the characteristics of a nation rather than language or religion. Sa'adeh was opposed to the Balfour Declaration and he allegedly threatened the life of the British Secretary of State for Foreign Affairs, Arthur Balfour, while visiting Syria. Sa'adeh was accused of treason by the pro-France Lebanese authority, tried, and executed in 1949. The SSNP was heavily involved in the local politics of Lebanon and Syria including coup d'état attempts in Lebanon. Its military wing fought against the right-wing Phalangists in the 1958 Lebanese civil war and fought against the Israeli invaders of Lebanon in 1982. And in Syria, the SSNP was a popular party when democracy was restored in the early 1950s. But the party lost support and was barred by the Syrian government in 1955 when its members were accused of violent acts against leaders of the Baath Party. The SSNP was against Nasser's Arab socialism and the 1958 Egyptian–Syrian union. After it allied itself with the leftist parties in the Lebanese civil war against the Phalangists, the SSNP policy was approved by the Syrian regime, and it was legalized in 2005.

---

1 Emir means "Prince" in Arabic. Faisal was the future king of Iraq.

The "Arab Socialist Baath Party" (ASBP), a Pan-Arab secular nationalist party, was founded in 1940 by Michel Aflaq (Christian) and Salah Bitar (Muslim) in Damascus, Syria after the defeat of France in World War II. The party's name literally means renaissance; it calls for uniting all the Arab countries into one Arab socialist nation and freeing the Arab world from the Western colonialism. Its constitution which contained a commitment to unite the Arab world as its main goal was approved by its first congress in 1947. And in 1953, the party was merged with the Arab Socialist Party. The Arab nation as identified by the ASBP inhabits the area that stretches from the Taurus Mountains in the north to the Sahara in the South and the Arab Ocean from the East to Atlantic Ocean in the west.

Not all ethnic groups living among those defined by the ASBP as Arabs consider themselves Arabs. They define themselves as Kurds, Turkmen, Jews, Armenians and North African Berbers. The ASBP became the driving force for Arab unity in the 1950s; it established local organizations in many Arab countries including Syria, Jordan, Lebanon, Iraq, Yemen and Libya. The party was put to the test when Syria and Iraq were ruled by two branches of the Baath Party in 1963 and instead of unity, they brought division — even while they both professed the same unitary discourse. Syria even supported non-Arab Iran in its war against Iraq.

The "Muslim Brothers" (MB) was founded in Egypt by an educator, Hasan al-Banna, in 1928 to promote the traditional Islamic Sharia laws, and in few years the MB became a major political force in the Middle East. They considered Palestine to be one of the battlefields in the war against colonialism. When the Palestinians revolted in the 1930s, the MB supported them and initiated a fund-raising campaign on behalf of the Palestinians, and in 1948 thousands of MB members volunteered to fight in Palestine. They fought with enthusiasm as part of the Egyptian expedition force but their lack of military training rendered them ineffective as soldiers.

The ideology of the first modern radical Islamist thinker in the Arab world was preached by Sayyed Qutb, a member in the Egyptian MB organization. His philosophy that calls for armed revolution to establish an Islamic government in Egypt was conceived while he was exposed to the culture of Western enlightened liberalism. He felt revulsion against what he saw as decadence during visits to the United States in 1948–1950. Qutb followers did not see much difference between the Egyptian atheist regime and any "Western infidels". The MB has been banned in Egypt, but its members still run for election in the parliament as individuals. They have managed to have some of their members elected in every parliament since the 1970s and they became the major opposition group in Egypt. The MBs joined the Nasserites in bitterly opposing the 1977 Sadat peace initiative and the 1978 Camp David framework that led to Egypt's recovery of Sinai while abandoning the Palestinians and leaving Syria's Golan Heights under Israeli occupation. The MB branch in Jordan, known as the "Islamic Action Front," has been a strong supporter of the regime since it was allowed by King Hussein Ibn Talal to operate in 1948. Even when Jordan banned political parties, the "Islamic Action Front" was exempted.

THE ARAB LEAGUE

In March of 1943, the Egyptian Prime Minister Mustafa Nahhas proposed the creation of a league for the Arab sovereign states. Delegations from Egypt, Syria, Iraq, Lebanon and Trans-Jordan passed what they called "Alexandria Protocol" providing the basis for the creation of the "Arab League" in October 1944; Saudi Arabia joined the protocol in January 1945; and the League pact was signed in Cairo on March 22, 1945.The Arab League was established according to the wishes of Great Britain as a prerequisite for the admission of the Arab states to the United Nations. The announced goal of the League was to "draw closer the relations between member states and co-ordinate collaboration among them to safeguard their independence and sovereignty and to consider in a general way the affairs and interests of the Arab countries." Egypt used the League to pursue its ambitions of leading the Arab states and dominating the region by disguising its desire for hegemony as a solidarity scheme. The establishment of the Arab League created fierce competition between the ASBP party that called for wide Arab nationalism and the SSNP party that championed limited regional nationalism.

The most far reaching decision made by the Arab League was the 1948 military campaign against Israel where troops of Egypt, Syria, Trans-Jordan and Iraq invaded Palestine in an attempt to nullify the UN partition resolution and the establishment of the state of Israel. The Arab armies were defeated and humiliated by the newly created Israeli army. The Jews called this war "The War of Independence" and in Palestinian historiography it is called al-Nakba (the Catastrophe).

While Israel was strengthening its democratic institutions for its Jewish citizens after the War of Independence, very little attention was allowed for sustaining or developing democratic civil institutions in Arab countries that were defeated in the 1948 war. The defeat of the Arab armies in 1948 was the starting point of many cultural and political changes. Military coups, assassinations, and militarization and an all-out emphasis on establishing Arab nationalism overtook most societies in the Arab world at the expense of social, democratic and economic development, and Islamic religious extremism emerged as a force to be reckoned with.

The emergence of Jamal Abdel-Nasser in 1952 as the leader of Egypt started a new era in Arab secular nationalism. The charismatic Nasser, a veteran of the 1948 war, championed the Palestinian cause and Pan-Arab leadership. Nasser was admired by the Arab masses for his political, economic and social policies especially after the 1956 war, the nationalization of the Suez Canal and the recovery of Sinai (although it was US President Dwight Eisenhower and Soviet Prime Minister Nikolai Bulganin who forced Israel to withdraw from Sinai). Due to Egypt's large population, its highly educated middle class, and the fact that in the 1950s it had the only public universities, developed entertainment industry, and powerful media in the non-Jewish Middle East (the media reaching a large audience beyond its borders), Egypt was in a strong position to speak directly to the people of the Arab countries. Many Arab professionals who became the elite classes in their own countries received their training in Egypt, and Egyptian teachers, medical doctors and engineers volunteered to serve in other Arab countries.

Until the emergence of the military rule under Nasser, Egypt had been the only Arab country with long-established political parties under the monarchy, including al-Wafd, a secular party, one of the first in post-colonialism, and the Muslim Brothers Islamist party. Al-Wafd Party in Egypt and the National Congress Party in India were the first modern secular parties in the British ex-colonies to call for democracy, but unlike those in India, Egyptian military leaders put an end to the fledgling democracy in the 1952 military coup that brought Nasser to power. Nasser created a sense of pride among the Arab people, but at the same time he destroyed the democratic experiment in Egypt, and sadly other Arab leaders followed his example.

Colonel Hosni al-Za'im overthrew the democratically-elected government in Syria in 1949. And in the same year, another coup was staged in Syria by Colonel Sami al-Hinnawi then Colonel Adeeb Shishakli deposed al-Hinnawi. Shishakli abolished political parties, and when he was overthrown in a 1954 coup, power was concentrated in the military, the democratic institutions were weakened and the political parties were dominated by big landowners and city prominent notables. Civilian President Shukri al-Quatly of Syria had difficulty ruling his country after years of instability.

Fearing more coups, al-Quatly offered to have a merger between Syria and Egypt. Abdel-Nasser of Egypt accepted the offer and the two countries became the United Arab Republic in February 1958. Three years and eight months later, Syria seceded, following a military coup. The first Arab union was destined to fail because the Egyptians, who were dispatched to manage Syria, were military personnel with contempt for democratic principles and no real knowledge of the Syrian political culture. During the short-lived union, the Syrians were excluded from decision making and Syria became an Egypt-controlled province.

Then the decisive Arabs defeat in the 1967 war cast doubts on the legitimacy of Arab state governments, brought the end of Nasser's Pan-Arab dream, and saw the emergence of local traditional and sectarian Islamic nationalism. Israel conquered the West Bank, Gaza, the Egyptian Sinai, the Syrian Golan Heights and the Lebanese Sheba Farms. Less charismatic and less interested in Arab nationalism, the military figures Anwar Sadat then Hosni Mubarak followed Nasser's death in 1970. Sadat's and Mubarak's concern was to recover Sinai, King Hussein Ibn Talal of Jordan renounced his claim to sovereignty over the West Bank and Jerusalem, and Palestinian nationalism and militant organizations emerged. Chapter 6 has further discussion on Egypt and Chapter 5 goes into more detail on Jordan-Palestine relations.

With the passing of Nasser, Arab nationalism was replaced by local patriotism, and the Pan-Arab Baath Party (established in the 1940s, based on the goal of creating one united secular Arab nation) became a relic of the past. Before the Arab world had the time to recover from the serious political and intellectual trauma of the 1967 military defeat, the Arabs had to deal with new dramatic surprises that had great impact on Arab nationalism. In 1990, Iraq under Saddam Hussein invaded Kuwait and occupied the small state, a neighboring Arab country and a member of the Arab League. The occupation of Kuwait opened the door for the US to intervene militarily in 1991, with Egypt and Syria participating. The war extended the ongoing US military presence in the Gulf region, shattered the myth of the Pan-Arab regimes' solidarity, and meant the end of the Arab League as an organization to "safeguard the independence and sovereignty of its members."

Arab states entered the 21st century burdened by a failed Pan-Arab experiment and an undemocratic culture that undermines the conditions that an increasingly educated population with exposure to the rest of the world is coming to expect for its own: relatively free multi-party institutions, an independent judiciary, free speech and open media.

In the name of military security, emergency laws were enacted and military courts were established to deal with dissenters and critics. Militant Islamic organizations that had been trained and armed by the US in the war against the Soviet Union in Afghanistan founded an alliance named al-Qaeda under the leadership of Osama Bin Laden, a member of a rich Saudi family. Al-Qaeda called for ending the US military presence in Saudi Arabia and establishing a new Islamic caliphate to unite Arab and other Muslim countries. And like many political movements in the Arab world, Al-Qaeda accused Arab leaders of abandoning the Palestinians in their struggle to recover their land. Al-Qaeda militants established training camps in Afghanistan and it was accused of attacking Western targets in different countries, most notably on September 11, 2001. US President George W. Bush took the opportunity to declare "war on terror" and on this argument invaded Afghanistan.

The Taliban government was easily toppled, al-Qaeda camps were destroyed and their top leaders went underground and moved to the Afghan–Pakistan border. Then on March 20, 2003, the US military (supported by UK troops and small contingents from many other countries, but not any Arab or Muslim countries) invaded Iraq, an Arab state and one of the founders of the Arab League. The invading armies overthrew the Iraqi government, captured its president, Saddam Hussein (a former US asset), and allowed his pro-Iran political enemies to hang him in December 2006. A series of rationales have been offered for the invasion of Iraq that later proved to be false. They started with allegations that Iraq was developing weapons of mass destruction, in violation of a 1991 agreement, and actively supporting al-Qaeda. These assertions have been disproven.

After the US invasion and the collapse of the Baath regime, Arab nationalism in Iraq gave way to sectarian and ethnic civil war among Sunni, Shia'a and Kurd Iraqis that took the lives of many Iraqis and destroyed the social structure of the nation. Estimates vary regarding the number of Iraqis who died or were injured, left their country or were ethnically cleansed, that is, assassinated, but the figures are in the millions.

There was a transformation of the priorities in the Arab states when the last inch of Palestine was surrendered to Israel in the 1967 war and the Egypt–Israel and Jordan–Israel peace treaties were signed. Arab states washed their hands of Palestine and claimed the issue is not an Arab responsibility anymore. The abandoned Palestinians under occupation or in the refugee camps have to fend for themselves. And America's unconditional support of Israel and disregard for the Palestinians is no longer an important factor in the Arab states foreign policy.

In the January 2006 Palestinian Parliamentary elections, Hamas won 76 of the 132 seats in the chamber, making it the first time in the Middle East the Islamists could claim the right to head a government — although it was under Israeli occupation, but Israel, the US and the EU did not respect the results of the elections. Arab states have yielded to the Israeli–US-led campaign to refuse to establish normal relations with a Hamas-led PA government. And when Hamas took over Gaza by force, Arab regimes enforced the siege on the Palestinians in Gaza that was imposed by Israel and the US, while Gazans were dying as a result of the sanctions and the collective punishment.

By the first decade of the 21st century, Arab League membership increased to 22 states but the numbers are misleading. The idea of unity under Arab secular nationalism that gained popularity in the first half of the 20th century is being forgotten, and no one dares to defend it anymore today.

CHAPTER 3. PALESTINE SINCE THE 19TH CENTURY

Palestine is the territory from the eastern Mediterranean shore to the Jordan River. The name, ethnologically, means "the land of the Philistines." According to historians, the Philistine tribes settled in the land of Canaan around 1250 BC. They established five king-doms: Gaza, Ashkelon, Ashdod, Gath, and Ekron.

Palestine was known by the first Jewish settlers as "Eretz Israel." The Jewish commu-nity in Palestine before the establishment of Israel is sometimes called the "*Yishuv*" in this study. The word "*Yishuv*" means "settlement" in Hebrew, but it was used in Jewish litera-ture and history books as a shortcut for "Jewish settlers in Palestine" from the 1880s until 1948. Some Palestinian Jews claimed to be the descendants of a Jewish community that had lived there uninterruptedly since the days of the last ancient Jewish Commonwealth. Physically, the descendants of the Palestinian Jews have small bones and dark skin, and speak Hebrew and Arabic according to the historian Howard Sachar.[1] Some of them lived in the small village of Pekin, located in north Palestine, practicing agriculture and breed-ing silkworms. Howard Sachar refers to them as "little Arabized Jews" and "authentic" Hebrews who embodied "the physical connection with Palestine."

The claim to Palestine by religious Jewish groups was based on the right of conquest by the Jews in a campaign that took place more than 3,000 years ago. But the same land had been successively conquered by Egypt, Persia, Greece, Rome, the early Muslims and the Turks since then. Using the logic of the religious Jews, Christians would need to go back and build a Byzantine state in Palestine since Christianity arose 2,000 years ago, well after Judaism but before Islam. The Palestinians of today, Muslims and Christians, claim to trace their descent to all the peoples who have lived on this land from the time of the

---

1 Sachar, Howard, 2007, p.18

Canaanites. There are Arab Palestinian families called Cana'an and some people in Palestine have been using the name Cana'an for their children.

The main Jewish argument against the Palestinian Arabs' claim to their country is summed up in the phrase, "We were here from time immemorial." In this view the Arab Palestinians are newcomers. The Palestinians counter by claiming that their Canaanite ancestors settled the land in 1250 BC, long before the Jewish tribes led by Joshua invaded the interior of the land of Canaan and murdered most of its inhabitants (according to the Bible). During the closing decades of the 19th century, the notion of a Palestine entity was as yet non-existent. Palestine was ruled by the Ottoman Turks as a part of Syria from 1516 until 1919, when Britain and France defeated Turkey in World War I. On the eve of the war, Palestine was unanimously referred to as Southern Syria, part of Damascus province. Palestine was divided into three administrative districts, Sanjak of Acre, Sanjak of Nablus, and *Mutasarrifiyya* of Jerusalem. The Turks divided Palestine into governorates, with the administrative center changing from Beirut to Damascus over the years. By the middle of the 19th century, the administration district (*Mutasarrifiyya*) of Jerusalem was established. The self-identification and personal status of its inhabitants was mostly religious. Farmers populated the villages, and merchants, craftsmen, the landlords and money lenders lived in towns. The notables were the town's religious leaders, rich landlords or high ranking government employees.

By the middle of the 19th century, the population of Palestine was 84% Muslim Arabs, 10% Christian Arabs, 1% Druze Arabs (an offshoot of Shi'at Islam), and about 5% Jewish.[1] The 1858 Ottoman land reforms in the southern portion of Syria (that came later to be known as Palestine) was an attempt by the government to enhance its ability to mobilize people and increase tax revenues. The reforms led to other unintended social and political consequences that impacted the lives of the Arab population forever as well as the destiny of Palestine. Land was awarded to people esteemed for their services to the empire. Land ownership was allowed to be registered to the town notables, and the traditional clans, and created a new relationship among the population by expanding the power of the Arab notables beyond the small towns where their families lived.[2] The notables took possession of large estates in the most fertile parts of the country and used these assets as the new foundation of a dominating socioeconomic elite class that would lead the Arab Palestinians through the middle of the next century. A small segment of these wealthy Arabs lived in the main cities, held government positions and formed the ruling class.

The Arab Palestinian farmers were struggling to feed their families and meet their debts and tax obligations. Education for their children, even elementary, was a luxury they could not afford. Until 1833, when *Ibrahim Pasha* ruled Palestine as part of Syria, government-supported education institutions were not available in Palestine. There were only elementary schools run by the mosques or the churches and the schools were dedicated to teaching the religion of the community. Only the children of influential families

---

1 Don Peretz 1996.
2 Kemal Karpat 1968

could afford to acquire high education in Turkey or Europe and later on in Egypt. By 1871, there were only third and fourth grade public elementary schools in Palestine with enrolment limited to 341 pupils in Jerusalem, 255 pupils in Hebron, 235 in Gaza, 120 in Ramle, 190 in Jaffa, and 70 in Lydda.[1] In 1891 the first Palestinian secondary school was established in Jerusalem by the Turkish government, and by the end of the century, middle schools were set in the towns of Nablus and Acre. Schools and colleges teaching liberal European curriculums were established by Christian missionaries in Syria and Lebanon. The political and economic powers of the traditional prominent Arab families allowed them to have better education and travel abroad; they thought of themselves as the guardians of the national interests. Arab students in Istanbul's higher education institutions engaged in political activities and after graduation, they were given important positions in the government.

Before the surge of ethnic nationalism in Palestine, self-identification of the individual was religion. The clergy and the communal religious traditions controlled the social status and the rights of the individual at all stages of life including birth, marriage, divorce, death and inheritance.

The second half of the 19th century marked the birth of both Zionism and Arab nationalism, the two ideologies that have been at the center of the conflict in the Middle East. Arab nationalism was inspired by the demand of the Arab elites in Syria province to be free from the Ottoman Empire and to protect Arab culture from Turkish-ethnic Ottomanization. Pan-Islamists and the Christian Syrian and Lebanese intellectuals who were promoting secular Arab nationalism shared the opposition to Turkish domination. Pan-Islamists such as Abdul-Rahman al-Kawakibi argued that the Arabs rather than the corrupt Turks should lead the Muslim nation, and secular Christian Arabs insisted that the adversity of the Arabs had been a result of Turkish negligence. Even before Palestine was conceived as a separate entity, Arab nationalists such as Naguib Azoury predicted the inevitability of conflict between Arabs and Jews.[2]

For most of the early 19th century Palestinian Jews belonged to the Old *Yishov* community that had settled there to practice their religion rather than for political reasons. During the 400 years of the Ottoman rule, there was a steady emigration of Jews and expansion of Jewish communities in Palestine, mainly in the cities of Jerusalem, Safed, and Tibrias. Most of the emigrants were descendents of the survivors of the Spanish and Portuguese Inquisition. They were referred to collectively as the "Sephardim," or "the Spanish," in Hebrew. In the early 19th century, there was an attempt by the Jewish leaders in Tibrias to increase their community by attracting more settlers, but they failed due to local Arab opposition against land sales to Jews. A similar effort was mounted in Hebron where the site of the Hebrew patriarchs was located, but by 1890 the number of Jews in Hebron was less than 1,500, mostly living in the vicinity of Talmudic schools. Jerusalem, however, attracted more new settlers in the 19th century. As late as the 1840s, most Palestinian Sep-

---

1   Divine 1994, p.120.
2   George Antonius, 1979.

hardic Jews communicated with each other in Ladino, an old Spanish dialect.[1] The elected Sephardic Chief Rabbi, *Rishon l'Zion*, was officially recognized by the Turkish authorities as the representative of the Jewish community and the arbitrator of their disputes.[2] The Chief Rabbi controlled fees levied from Jewish communal functions such as the sale of some kosher food products and a monopoly on burial services.

In the first half of the 19th century, Czar Nicholas I used coercive methods to convert his Jewish subjects into Russian Orthodox Christians, but his strategies failed and Jews became united by their fear. Thousands of Jews unhappy with these policies escaped from Russia but only a small fraction of them chose Palestine as their destination. Even so, the steady influx of Ashkenazim Yiddish and German-speaking Jews from Europe and Russia into Palestine in the second half of the 19th century created demographic change within the Jewish community. The Ashkenazim became the majority.

Both the Palestinian Sephardim and the Ashkenazim follow the Orthodox Jewish religion but each group has its own rabbis. They differ in their traditional attire and pronounce their prayers in Hebrew with different accents. Economically, the Sephardim were engaged in trade and skilled crafts but the majority of the Ashkenazim depended on subsidies from families in Europe or charitable funds provided by the European communities' *Kollel* organizations.[3] The choice of Palestine as the destination of most Russian Jewish immigrants in the 1840s was motivated by religious conviction rather than the need for economic or physical security. Palestine was too poor to provide business opportunities equivalent to those in Russia. The majority of the Ashkenazim Jews devoted their time to praying and studying Jewish theology. Despite restrictions on Jewish immigration to Palestine by the Turkish government, many settlers made their way into the country. European Jewish philanthropists such as the industrialist/banking family of the Rothschilds provided financial backing to buy land and establish settlements in Palestine.

There was always tension between Arab peasants and the new Jewish settlers, even with the arrival of the *"First Aliyah"* Jewish immigrants of the late 1880s, who were not ideologists and in most cases were willing to employ Arab laborers under Jewish managers in the settlement farms. The second wave of Jewish immigrants, the *"Second Aliyah,"* who fled Russia after the pogroms of 1903 and 1905, were mostly militant Zionists with radical nationalist ideas. They were backed by the Zionist institutions and they used Marxist rationalization for their strong attachment to the land and labor. Yosef Brenner, a literary figure and a *"Second Aliyah"* immigrant wrote, "Only when we will have learned the secret of labor and committed to memory the hymn of those settled on their own soil shall we have deserved the title Man."[4] Their ideology reflected on their attitude toward the Palestinians, especially the farmers and the farm laborers. They were determined to defend

---

1 Arnold Blumberg, 1885.
2 Rishon l'Zion: Hebrew for "First in Zion."
3 Kollel: private organizations provide financial support to married men who devote their time to Jewish religious studies. The share of the fund appropriate to the Jews registered with a Kollel is called Halukah.
4 Howard Sachar, 1996, p. 75

disputed land that they acquired against the claims of aggrieved Arab farmers, and they considered replacing the Arab labor with Jewish workers as a national obligation.

PALESTINE UNDER THE MANDATE

Britain and France, victors of World War I, redrew the map of the Arab lands and declared their public support for the Zionists' aspiration by granting the Jews a homeland in Palestine. The Hashemites, who claimed to speak for all the Arabs, including the Palestinians, were close allies with the British during and after the war. Their army of Arab Bedouin irregulars fought side by side with the British against the Turks. The historical events before, during and after the war suggest that one purpose of Britain and France in World War I was to control the Arab land East of the Mediterranean for its strategic location and oil reserves. The war stripped the Turks of their Middle East Arab provinces, and Turkey under Mustafa Kamal recognized the Arab territories as a lost cause. The region was divided into small satellite states dependent on great powers for their defense, and the Arabs have never been in control of their destiny since then. There was nothing the Palestinians could do when Britain created the Palestine Mandate and gave itself the right to grant a homeland to the Jewish people in Palestine in the Balfour Declaration, as though Palestinian Arab inhabitants did not exist. The Declaration was viewed as an outcome of the convergence between the interests of international Zionism and British colonial ambitions. Once their country was under the British control, the Palestinians had to struggle — not only against the British colonialism and the resourceful and powerful international Zionism; they also had to contend with the Arab states' incompetent and sometimes collaborator leadership.

The country that was granted a Mandate was supposed to shepherd the natives toward the goal of governing themselves and eventually achieving complete independence. It was a form of trusteeship colonialism with a promise to develop a future nation-state. But the Mandate in Palestine was unique because of the conflicting obligations to the natives and the international Jewish population the British had assumed. The antagonism that Britain created between Arab Palestinians and Jews prevented the Mandate authority from developing foundations for effective self-governing institutions. The years of the Mandate were marked by many crises brought on by conflicts between the Palestinian natives and the Jewish settlers. Palestinian Arabs, Muslims and Christians alike, had resented the Zionists' activities in their country even before the creation of the Mandate. Local notables were enraged when the 1918 Zionist Commission, headed by Chaim Weizmann, asked to make Hebrew an official language alongside Arabic. Jews then constituted only 7% of the population and owned 1% of the land, but the British occupying military granted Weizmann his request.

When the League of Nations mandated Palestine to be governed by Britain, the majority of Palestine inhabitants supported the option of a union with Syria. They wanted the inclusion of their country in Syria under Emir Faisal's rule, but the Palestinians and the Syrians had lost control of their destiny. Strong Palestinian nationalism emerged after the fall of Faisal in 1920 and the realization that the Zionist aspirations constituted a threat to the Palestinians. If there was no Zionism, Palestine would have continued to be a part of Syria and the Palestinians would have become Syrians.

The Palestinians were mostly small farmers, and because of their attachment to the land, they were worried by the Jewish organizations purchasing land from absentee Arab landlords and indebted local farmers (*fellaheen*). Many Arab Palestinian farmers were already being dispossessed by local sheikhs, town-dwelling merchants and money lenders, absentee land owners, and government tax-collectors. Very little of the season's crop was left after distribution among all these, and as a result new debt had to be incurred to pay off the old, and more land was taken over by the creditors. This resulted in a mounting concentration of land in the hands of a small number of Arab landowners who mostly resided in the Arab capitals of Beirut and Damascus.

Zionist organizations that supported Jewish immigration took advantage of the existing commercial environment and easy access to land in Palestine. They purchased vast tracts of land, mostly from absentee landlords, and expanded Jewish settlements. Many of these land owners had ended up as citizens of Lebanon or Syria when the new international borders were drawn by the British and the French during the partition of the Ottoman Empire. Urban-based Arab Palestinians and Lebanese merchants, usurers (or financiers, to use today's term), and bankers acquired large tracts of land through financial activities, and some of them sold land to Jewish agencies. The non-Palestinian *Sursuq*, the *Aryans* and *Twaynis* families of Beirut, acquired ownership of 20 villages in northern Palestine, including the fertile *Marj Ibn Aamer* (Vale of Jezreel), through loans from international banks, and sold the land to Jewish groups before 1914.[1] More than 100,000 acres of farmland was sold to Jewish organizations during the Ottoman rule. Palestinian and non-Palestinian absentee landlords sold 94% and local landlords and small farmers sold 6% of that land.[2]

The Palestinians were at a big disadvantage in their competition with Jewish settlers, especially during the British Mandate. Their local economies were in decline while the well-financed and organized Jewish sector had capital and know-how. The Palestinians never had anything similar to the Jewish Agency that was financed by contributions from Jews all over the world or the exclusively Jewish trade union, the Histadrut, which was aiding and promoting Jewish immigration and labor. The Jewish Agency acquired 350,000 acres by 1936.[3] By the mid-1940s, Jews had acquired around 10% of the cultivated land, including half of the land used for the famous Palestinian citrus groves. Arab land sales had been a source of tension among the Arabs. As Jewish land buying stepped up, pressure on the peasants mounted. They had to move from the purchased land and seek employment in the cities or live on a shrinking share of the cultivated land.

---

1 Laurence Oliphant 1881, p.329.
2 Khalidi 1997, p.112.
3 Chaim Weizmann statement before the Palestine Royal Commission on November 25, 1936.

The Palestinian villagers and town dwellers had to place themselves under the protection of the wealthy families who had obtained their prominence through their bureaucratic services in the government, through the acquisition of land directly from the peasants, or through land concessions and patronage by the Turkish government. Many scholars attribute the political failure of the Palestinians in their struggle against the Zionists partially to the structure of their society, which relies heavily on political loyalty to a few prominent families.[1] Family and tribal loyalty created excessive internal conflicts and insurmountable obstacles to cohesive political development, and made it easy for the British to divide and conquer. As a matter of history, the Turks, the British, the Jordanians, the Egyptians and even the Israelis used members of the traditional prominent families as instruments of control.

The Palestinian conflict has been a struggle between the Zionists' ideology of conquest and the Palestinians' instinct for survival. Palestinian nationalism came into being as a defensive identity in response to the Jewish penetration of Palestine. It has been intensified by the failure of Arab leaders to protect the Palestinians who had been expelled from their homes and lands. Local populations, especially the tenant-farmers and agricultural laborers of the fertile lands, resented the establishment of Jewish colonies. The managers of the purchased land evicted the Arab tenants and replaced them with Jews.

As early as the second half of the 19th century, Arab Palestinians had resorted to violence against Jewish settlers on lands they used to cultivate. Arab peasants from the village of Yahudiyya attacked Petah Tiqva, a settlement that was established on land sold by absentee landlords in 1886.[2] They killed a settler and wounded many others. Similar attacks were carried out against the settlers of Rehovat and Hadera in the early 1890s.

The Zionist national movement and the Balfour Declaration shaped the concept and aspirations of the Palestinian nationalism which has endured decades but with no significant success of establishing an independent state. The Palestinian popular national movement emerged as a response to Balfour Declaration, the San Ramo Peace Conference resolution, the defeat of Faisal in Syria and the growing Jewish presence. It was obvious from the start of the British rule in Palestine that its policy favored the Jewish community at the expense of the Arabs. Hebrew was declared as an official language, and representatives of different organizations in the Zionist movement arrived in Palestine. These and the appointment of Sir Herbert Samuel as the high commissioner were signs of Britain's determination to establish a Jewish-dominated state in Palestine. Samuel, an Anglo-Jewish Zionist, had played an important role in introducing Weitzman to the British policy makers. He was firmly against the Palestinians' effort to dilute the British support of the Jewish national home. The Palestinians were frightened at the prospect of becoming a minority in their own country when Herbert Samuel summarized in a speech the main objective of the Zionist movement: "[to create] a purely self-governing Commonwealth under the auspices of an established Jewish majority."[3]

---

1 Yehoshua Porath 1974; Salim Tamari 1982.
2 Neville Mandel, 1976.
3 Bernard Wasserstein, 1991, p.76

On September 1, 1922, Sir Herbert Samuel proclaimed the "Palestine Order in Council" which defined the mandatory government obligation in Palestine. Besides providing for independent judiciary to protect the rights of the natives and the foreigners, the freedom of worship and liberty of conscience, it obliged the government to secure a Jewish National Home in Palestine. Even before the British occupation, when there were few Jewish settlers in Palestine, the Arab indigenous population perceived the politically committed and economically ambitious "Lovers of Zion" as a threat. The peasants and the economically humble and illiterate segment of society had been the first to feel the danger of the colonists. They were the first to come in contact with the settlers in their daily life when they were evicted from the land that was acquired by the Jewish Agency.

The collapse of the Faisal regime in Syria in July 1920 led to the relocation of the Palestinian activists' headquarters from Damascus to Jerusalem and the development of strong Palestinian nationalism. No help was expected from Faisal or from Syrian Arabs. Recognizing the failure of the Great Syria concept, the Palestinian notables decided, at the "Third Arab Congress" that was convened in 1920–21 in Haifa, to develop a strategy based on autonomy for the Palestinians. Musa Kazim al-Husseini, a previous mayor of Jerusalem, stated that "Southern Syria does not exist any more; we have to defend Palestine."[1]

The Palestinians formed associations to organize communications with the British occupation authority. The first Palestinian national organization was the Muslim–Christian Association, established in various towns. It sponsored a convention in Haifa that was called the "Palestinian Arab Congress and elected an Arab Executive" (AE) to organize a deputation to London in 1921. The Palestinian Arabs wanted the AE to be recognized by the British authorities as a balance against the Jewish Agency, but the High Commissioner, Herbert Samuel, refused to accept it as representative of the Palestinians because its members opposed the British Mandate and the Balfour Declaration.

The Mandate administration decided to arrange for the election of twelve members in a legislative council representing the three communities, Muslims, Christians and Jews. The majority of the Arabs, both Muslims and Christians, boycotted the primary elections, thus forcing Samuel to cancel the voting and the legislative council all together and establish instead an advisory committee with members to be appointed by the commissioner. The appointed Palestinians refused to participate in other than a democratically-elected self-government that would have favored the Arabs as a majority. Herbert Samuel asked the Palestinian Arabs to establish their own agency to cooperate with the Mandate government on matters that concerned their community as a counterpart to the Jewish Agency. Musa Kazim al-Husseini rejected the establishment of such an agency because it implied the recognition of the Jewish Agency activities. Al-Husseini was the mayor of Jerusalem, the president of many Arab Palestinian Congresses and the head of the Arab delegation to England to protest the Balfour Declaration. In response to the Arab rejection to cooperate with the Mandate authority, Samuel decided that the legislative and executive functions would be reserved to the High Commissioner person.

---

1 Yehoshua Porath, 1974, p. 107.

The Palestinians' struggle for national recognition in the wake of the British occupation has been articulated in peaceful protests interrupted by bursts of bloody violence. The central political issue during the Mandate period was whether the Jews would have unrestricted rights to immigrate and buy land in Palestine. The main Palestinian demands that had been the same throughout the Mandate period were spelled out by the Third Arab Congress and presented to the Colonial Secretary, Winston Churchill, in London by a Palestinian delegation in 1921.[1] The demands included recognition of Palestine as a distinct political entity for the people living there; the formation of a national government with an elected parliament; revoking the policy of creating a national homeland for the Jews in Palestine that entails the suspension of Jewish immigration which was detrimental to the Palestinian people; and restraining the grabbing of the lands by the Zionist organizations. Until the mid 1920s, the Palestinians tried peaceful means to persuade the British to change their pro-Zionists policies and adopt one based on the democratic principles of the consent of the governed. They sent petitions and delegations to the decision makers of the British Government in Palestine and London but they felt being always ignored. Petitions and memoranda were submitted to the League of Nations in Geneva but the Mandate Commission, that was controlled by the big powers and influenced by the Zionists, never responded to the Palestinians pleas. There was a well staffed Zionist office in Geneva to provide the Mandate Commission with information on Palestine in any language necessary. The Palestinians and the other Arabs had no such offices to present their views. According to the Palestinian historian Salman Abu Sitta, "when the Palestinian delegation arrived in London in 1922 to protest against the injustice of the Balfour Declaration, not one member [of the delegation] was fluent in English."

In 1929, a quarrel erupted between Palestinian Arabs and Jews on the rights of the Jews to bring religious furniture for praying at the al-Burak (Wailing Wall) in Jerusalem. The incident was followed by large riots and bloodshed in other cities including Hebron where 133 Jews and 116 Arab Palestinians were killed. The British Prime Minister, Ramsey McDonald, asked Lord Passfield (Sidney Webb) to investigate the incident and provide a solution. Passfield proposed revising the British policy in Palestine by limiting Jewish immigration and the creation of a legislative council with a majority of Muslim members. Ramsey McDonald rejected Passfield's recommendations to restrict Jewish land purchases and immigration. The Prime Minister decision to reject recommendations by his own appointee was included in a letter he sent to Chaim Weizmann in 1931. The cumulative effect of the British commitment to implement the Balfour Declaration and the League of Nations bias in favor of the Jews drove the Palestinians to resort to violence. Young Arab militants realized that the establishment of a Jewish homeland in Palestine was the preamble of the Mandate and therefore the Palestinians had to rid the country entirely from the British rule. They viewed Britain and the Zionists as allies in a conspiracy devised to deprive them from their national inheritance. They were enraged when the British au-

---

1   CO 733/14, Petition submitted by Muslim-Christian Delegation to the Colonial Secretary on August 12, 1921.

thorities provided rifles to the residents of Jewish settlements for defense against Arab rioters in the 1930s.[1]

Frustrated Palestinian peasants and small farmers turned to violence and armed struggle; they were disorganized and poorly led, but willing to kill and be killed. They never had the institutions and the leadership needed to succeed against the British and the powerful international Zionism. They had suffered series of defeats and their chances of having fully independent state of their own have receded. Even Vladimir Jabotinsky, the founder of the first right wing Revisionist branch of Zionism suggested in 1923 that there were Palestinian Arabs in Palestine and they loved their country. In his effort to justify the creation of a paramilitary Jewish self defense organization to defend the Jewish interests against the Palestinian nationalists, Jabotinsky wrote that "Palestine will remain for the Palestinians not a borderland, but their birthplace, the center and basis of their own national existence."[2]

During the British Mandate period, the Palestinian leadership failed to unite and never formulated a plan to meet the political and economic challenges of the Zionists activities in their country while the Zionists managed to increase the Jewish population to 28% of the total Palestinian population through European Jews immigration.

PRE-1948 PALESTINIAN POLITICAL PARTIES

Although the Palestinians considered themselves part of the Arab world, they espoused a Palestinian nationalism since their problems with the Zionists were not addressed by the other Arabs (who had their own local problems and had been too weak to help, anyway). East of the Mediterranean, Arabs were isolated within borders drawn by the European colonialists under leadership closely allied with the British, a perceived enemy of the Palestinians.

The late 1920s and early 1930s witnessed rapid political mobilization and activism among all sectors of the Arab Palestinian society. National parties were established, with pan-Islamic or Pan-Arab sentiments, but their effectiveness was compromised because none of the parties was a political party in the Western sense. They were groupings attached to individual families. The large constituency was controlled by competing families, rather than any unifying national movement.

The influential Jerusalem families of al-Husseinis and Nashashibis that had achieved prominence during the Ottoman era, in the 19th and early 20th centuries, maintained their leadership role under the British Mandate. There were thirteen mayors for Jerusalem from the al-Husseini family between 1864 and 1920. Musa Kazim al-Husseini started his career in the Ottoman bureaucracy, and then he became the mayor of Jerusalem until 1920, when the British ousted him for his stand against British policies, and replaced him with Raghib Nashashibi. Until his death in 1934, Musa al-Husseini was also the president of the Arab Executive that was established to represent the Palestinians as the counterpart of the

1 Baruch Kimmerling and Joel Migdal, 1993, p.99.
2 Mordechai Bar-On, 1996, p.12.

46

Jewish Agency. He headed four different Arab delegations to London under British rule. To underline the secular feature of Palestinian Arab nationalism, Christians and Muslims had been accorded proportional representation in the various delegations and in the Arab Executive, despite the Islamic background of the top leadership and majority of the Palestinian people.

Haj Amin al-Husseini, a close relative of Musa al-Husseini was the leading nationalist figure in Palestine during the Mandate. He was born in Jerusalem in 1893, received his higher education at the renowned al-Azhar University in Egypt, served in the Ottoman Army as an officer during World War I and returned to Jerusalem immediately after the war. Haj Amin was appointed to the position of "Grand Mufti of Jerusalem" (interpreter of Islamic law) by the British in 1922. His brother and three generations of his family before him had held the post of the "Hanafi mufti" of Jerusalem under the Turkish rule.

Later on, Haj Amin assumed the more influential presidency of the "Supreme Muslim Council," an institution established by the British to direct the religious affairs of the Muslim community as a counterpart to the Rabbinical Council of the Jews. In his official capacities, he had authority over all Islamic courts, educational institutions, and the extensive *Wakf* (Muslim endowment) properties. He used his authority as the guardian of the holy sites of Islam in Palestine to influence the emerging Palestinian nationalist movement.

His political power was enhanced more when his cousin, Jamal al-Husseini, founded the Palestine Arab Party in 1932. Haj Amin was able to mobilize the loyalty of most of the Muslim population. The Husseinis and their Palestine Arab Party were pan-Islamist and Pan-Arab. Haj Amin was recognized by the Islamic countries for his 1931 campaign to make the Islamic sites in Jerusalem, al-Masjid al-Aqsa and its surroundings, a center of Islamic culture. He formed the Arab Higher Committee in 1936 as the successor organization of the Arab Executive, although the British would not recognize either organization because of their opposition to the principles of the Mandate, including the Balfour Declaration.

Haj Amin continued to be the dominant political figure and the most outspoken critic of the Mandate policies during and after 1936. The British accused him of inciting the uprising of 1936, dismissed him from his position as the president of the Supreme Muslim Council, and forced him to exile in Lebanon then in Iraq. During the early years of World War II, he was in Nazi Germany soliciting its government's support for the Palestinians' cause. Even in exile, Haj Amin tried to consolidate his power and undermine his political opponents in Palestine. Many prominent members and local supporters of the Nashashibi National Defense Party were murdered or terrorized into leaving Palestine. The victims included mayors, members of municipal councils, village leaders (*Mukhtar*) and educators. Thousands of fugitives who had to leave Palestine to save their lives crowded into Cairo and Beirut. Fakhri Nashashibi, the leader of the Nashashibi faction, was shot dead in the streets of Baghdad after Aref Abdul-Razzak, a henchman of Haj Amin, issued a death warrant against him, calling him a traitor.

Not to be upstaged by the Husseinis, the Nashashibi family established the National Defense Party after the defeat of Raghib Nashashibi in the municipal elections of 1934.

Some business people, disgruntled Arab mayors, and middle class people who resented the Husseinis' power and patronage were among the supporters of the Nashashibis. The Nashashibis and their National Defense Party were more local in their orientation, took a moderate stand toward the British and the Zionists, and established good relations with Emir Abdullah of Trans-Jordan.

The two leading families had political power bases in their client town quarters and villages, and the lasting split caused by their rivalry was among the factors which contributed to the failure of the 1936 rebellion and the stalling of the national movement. It was this family rivalry that rendered the Palestinians' struggle against the British and the Zionist project ineffective and prevented them from creating national institutions in anticipation of their future state when the British Mandate would be terminated.

The first Palestinian national political party that was not dominated by the prominent families of Jerusalem was the *Istiklal* (Independence) Party. It was founded outside the influence of the traditional Jerusalem notables by young Muslim and Christian Palestinian activists and professionals from the National Congress of Arab Youth in Nablus and Jaffa a decade after the disappointing performance of the Hashemites in Syria and Trans-Jordan. They leveled sharp criticism at the Jerusalem-based national leadership and accused them of collaboration with the British authorities. The founders of the *Istiklal* Party proclaimed that the established Palestinian leadership had failed to defend the interests of the people, and they declared that the British imperialists, not the Jews, should be the main target of protest because they were responsible for creating the Zionist menace. Its leadership encouraged the Palestinians to defy the British authorities by staging incidents of civil disobedience and by boycotting their institutions. They called for an Indian Congress Party-style boycott of the British. The boycott idea held no appeal for the notables because most of them, including Haj Amin, were on the British payroll at that time. During some demonstrations against the Mandate authority, the *Istiklal* Party members assigned guards to protect Jews and their property.[1] Unlike the other political parties, the *Istiklal* refused to meet with the British high commissioner in 1935 and present him with its demands, and even declined to review his proposal for establishing a legislative council which was perceived as a concession by the British to the Palestinians. The legislative council plan, that would have given the Arabs more power proportional to their majority status, was later rejected by the British Parliament as a result of pressure from Zionist activists in Britain.[2]

In its 1933 meeting in Jaffa, the Arab Executive called for non-cooperation with all government institutions and high-profile British visitors. With no elected legislators to protect their interests or recognized organizations to air their grievances, the Palestinians had to resort to civil disobedience and violence to get the attention of the British authorities. With the outbreak of World War II in 1939, the exhausted Palestinian Arabs called a halt to the fighting and the revolt came to an end.

---

1 Baruch Kimmerling and Joel Migdal, 1993, p. 100.
2 George Antonius, 1979, p.388.

THE PALESTINIANS' EARLY ARMED STRUGGLE

When the threat of the Zionist movement increased due to the rapid Jewish immigration in the 1920s and early 1930s, the Palestinians responded with strikes and riots against Jewish neighborhoods. The two communities were separated by their incompatible political aspirations and clashes broke out in 1920 and 1921. Following rumors of Jewish plans to control religious sites in Jerusalem, riots erupted in the mixed neighborhoods in Jerusalem and Hebron. And as mentioned above, the 1929 incident concerning prayers near the Jerusalem holy site of al-Burak "the Wailing Wall" sparked violence and killing on both sides. In the early 1930s, Palestinian nationalism among peasants and poor city dwellers (who were not bound by loyalty to elite clans) was based on Islamic ideology. Some of the nationalists were followers of Sheikh Izz-al-Din al-Qassam, a mosque preacher and a fundamentalist Muslim who treated Zionism as nothing but a Western enterprise. He called for a holy war against the British and the Yishuv. In his sermons, he sought to inspire his supporters to rise up against the British and the Yishuv Zionists, but he argued that the Palestinians should be good Muslims first in order to defeat their enemies. He was a cofounder of Haifa's Young Men's Muslim Association and he formed a clandestine group of a few hundred followers who pledged to sacrifice their lives for Palestine. His followers were mostly uneducated, uprooted landless peasants from northern Arab villages, driven off the land that they had farmed for generations by the Jewish land purchases, and Arab laborers who were unemployed due to the exclusion policy of the Jewish National Fund.[1] They supplied their own guns and received military training secretly at night. Members of the al-Qassam group were accused of occasional raids against Jewish settlements and involvement in the 1931 Nabi Musa riots. Al-Qassam and an armed group of his followers set their headquarters in caves of the wooded hills of Ya'bad village, planning how to attack Jewish and British targets. Before it had time to act in any major operations, the al-Qassam armed revolt was suppressed, its leader and four of his companions were killed, and the rest of his men were captured in combat by a mixed team of British and Arab police recruits in 1935.

From a military point of view, al-Qassam rebellion was brief and futile, but the Palestinian nationalists saw its fallen leader who died gun in hand, the hero they needed to inspire resistance to the British and Zionists plans. In death, al-Qassam has been immortalized as a legend of the Palestinian nationalism. His action was the first organized armed uprising since the beginning of the Mandate. Reaction to his death suggests that he was more in tune with popular Palestinian sentiments than the majority of the traditional leadership. A large number of mourners marched behind his coffin for seven miles from the City of Haifa to his village, Yajour, shouting slogans against the British and the Zionists. While the Palestinians saw al-Qassam's actions as a glorious patriotic struggle, the British labeled him and his group as a band of thieves and murderers. Ben-Gurion understood al-Qassam revolt as the beginning of a serious phase of the Palestinian national movement. He compared the impact of his death on the Palestinian nationalism to the death of the

---

1 S. Abdullah Schleifer, 1993

Zionist pioneer and revisionist leader Joseph Trumpledor in the 1920 clash with Palestinians in Tel Hai.[1]

Al-Qassam's death was a national event that unleashed the general strike and the 1936–39 Arab revolt. Three generations later, the Islamic militants of the 2,000 uprising named their military wing and even their home made missiles after al-Qassam. His anti-British militant views that had been shared by other nationalists conflicted with some of the traditional Palestinian leaders who sought accommodation and cooperation with the British. Palestinian nationalism intensified with the increase of Jewish immigration from Germany after Hitler's rise to power in 1933, and by 1935 there were local strikes and armed violence, then the uprising against the British in 1936–39. The Palestinians could not tolerate Jewish immigration and the procurement of large tracts of their land any more. In the first sixteen years of the British Mandate, Jewish immigrants flooded into Palestine, increasing their population from 61,000 or 2% to 385,400 or 28.2% of the total population. The coastal city of Tel-Aviv that was established in 1909 became an exclusively Jewish city and in Jaffa Jews exceeded 30% of the population.

The general strike against the British was followed by a spontaneous bloody uprising that developed into the full-scale rebellion, triggered by the killing of two Arabs living in a hut near the Jewish settlement of Peta Tikvah on April 15, 1936. On April 19, there were rumors that two more Arabs had been killed by Jews in Tel Aviv. The Palestinians' reaction was mass rioting in Jaffa and a grass-root nation-wide strike initiated and coordinated by locally based national activists in Nablus and Jaffa. The violent reaction and the strike revealed the frustration with the British policies and the failure of the national leadership to counter the Zionist threat. After being criticized for their apathy, traditional leaders joined the militants by establishing the Arab Higher Committee (AHC) as a national organization with Haj Amin al-Husseini as its president to coordinate the resistance. Before aligning himself with the rebellion against the British, Haj Amin served the Mandate authority in his capacity as the "mufti"; and the British subsidized him when the "*wakf*" income declined after 1929.

Virtually all Arab businesses closed during the strike with the exception of government employees, the basic agricultural work in the villages and the produce distribution centers. Government employees did not join the strike for fear of being replaced by Jews, but they had to contribute part of their salaries to the strike fund. Some violence started when the government disregarded the strike demands and announced new less restrictive immigration law. To end the strike, the Palestinians demanded negotiations on forming a national government and suspension of Jewish immigration during the negotiations, but the British refused both conditions. The British offer was to have a Royal Commission to investigate and come up with recommendations but the strike had to end first. The Palestinians ended the 6-month strike when they realized that a deadlock persisted and the Jewish community had benefited economically from the strike.

---

1 Avi Shapiro, 1992, p.302.

The strike was followed by a bloody 3-year revolt that exposed the failure of the Palestinian traditional leadership to overcome their personal and tribal feuds and face the real challenge. The 6-month strike was as violent as the post-strike phase of the uprising, except that the Palestinians had been more unified during the strike. The Palestinians ended the strike on the advice of the rulers of the Arab states and at the request of the Arab Higher Committee. The violence had already caused the death of thirty-seven British, sixty-nine Jews and close to one thousand Palestinians.[1] The only concession the British made was to form another commission, but on the same day the members of the commission left for Palestine, the Mandate administration announced a new policy allowing more Jewish immigration. To the disappointment of the Palestinians, all the affronts that had led them to strike continued unabated.

THE EARL PEEL COMMISSION

The British government appointed Earl Peel, former secretary of state for India, as a head of a royal commission in November 1936 to investigate Arab grievances and make recommendations for the future of the Mandate. Initially, the AHC decided to boycott the commission unless Britain agreed to stop Jewish immigration. Under pressure from non-Palestinian Arabs, Haj Amin reluctantly agreed to testify in front of the commission, but the Jewish leaders, including Weizmann and Ben-Gurion, prevailed. After five months, the commission concluded that under the Mandate, the Arabs and Jews had failed to overcome their differences, and given their irreconcilable positions, the partition of the country into two separate states was necessary. The possibility of creating a state for the Jews was discussed openly for the first time.

Peel's report proposed dividing Palestine into three regions, a Jewish self-governed entity on 5,000 square kilometers comprising the north and the coastal plains, an Arab self-governed entity on most of the remaining 16,000 square kilometers, and a permanently mandated British enclave in the Jerusalem–Bethlehem area, with a corridor linking Jerusalem to the Mediterranean through Jaffa, Nazareth and the Sea of Galilee. The report also recommended that the Arab area to be united with Trans-Jordan and a ceiling set on Jewish immigration of 12,000 per year for a period of five years. A corollary to Peel's report recommended the exchange of 225,000 Arabs with 1,250 Jews to insure a Jewish majority in the prospective Jewish state, with fair compensation to the involved population.

The Zionist movement was divided on the Peel Plan but the majority of its leaders including Chaim Weizmann, David Ben-Gurion and Moshe Shertok accepted the plan for its offer of a Jewish state. They believed that Peel's Report gave legitimacy to the Zionist claim and marked the beginning of the birth of a Jewish state — with or without an agreement with the Arabs. Many Jewish leaders endorsed the Peel Commission's recommendations, especially the transfer proposal that would safeguard the Jewishness of the Zionist state. Ben-Gurion, as the head of a Zionist movement that wished to create a liberal democracy in a future Jewish state, strongly embraced the idea of transferring Palestinian

---

1 David Hirst, 2003, p. 209.

Arabs. He wrote in his diary on July 12, 1937, "The compulsory transfer of Arabs from the valleys of the proposed Jewish state could give us something which we never had."

The Zionist leadership accepted the partition only as the first step to establishing a Jewish state over all of Palestine. Ben-Gurion stated in an interview with the historian Yaacov Shimoni, "[We should] erect a Jewish state at once, even if it is not on the whole land. The rest will come in the course of time. It must come."[1] Those who opposed the Peel Report argued that the proposed Jewish state was too small to absorb all the future Jewish immigrants. They expected to have millions of refugees from Europe. The Zionists had been collectively working on establishing a Jewish state and any disagreements had to do only with the tactics. The 20th Zionist Congress was convened in Zurich a month after the Peel Report was issued in 1937. It supported partition but withheld announcing that approval until the Jewish Agency explored the plan and negotiated with the British government the conditions for implementation.[2] Ben-Gurion was elected chairman of the Jewish Agency with one goal on his agenda, to establish a Jewish State.

With the approach of the Second World War and the British desire to secure the support of the Arabs and Muslims against the Axis powers, the Peel Commission Plan was dropped.

The British government accepted the recommendations while the Arab Higher Committee rejected them out of hand and insisted on full independence in all of Palestine, with a ban on further Jewish immigration. They opposed any plan that would give the Jews any part of the country they viewed theirs, and they feared that a Jewish state would be only the first step toward taking over the entire country. Peel was criticized for giving the Jews the best agricultural land and a large Arab population, and the prospect of annexing the Arab sector to Trans-Jordan was a most unacceptable outcome for Haj Amin, Syria and Iraq. The Arab Higher Committee asked Arab and Muslim governments to reject the Peel Plan, which they did, except for Trans-Jordan and Saudi Arabia. Iraq and Syria warned Emir Abdullah not to collaborate with the British and the Zionists by accepting the Peel recommendations, and after hesitation, Abdullah joined the Arabs by publicly repudiating the Report in the Pan-Arab conference at Bludan, Syria. Iraq was concerned about the economic impact of partitioning on its Kirkuk crude oil sales, as the oil was carried by pipeline to Haifa's harbor, and the Syrians were against the partition for fear that annexing the Arab sector in Palestine to Trans-Jordan would be a step to establishing a "Greater Syria" under Emir Abdullah's rule.

The Arab population of the Galilee region understood that the Peel Report recommended giving their part of the country to the Jews. They were alarmed by the prospect of being dispossessed of their lands and deported to the desert. Lewis Andrews, the British District Commissioner for Galilee, was assassinated in September 1937 by an Arab when he emerged from a church in Nazareth. Due to pressure from the Zionists and the British press to hold the AHC responsible for killing Andrews, and other violent actions, the

---

1 Avi Shlaim, 2000, p. 21.
2 Haward Sachar, 1996, p. 207.

British dissolved the Committee, deported its members to the Seychelles Islands, and Haj Amin escaped to Lebanon.

The Palestinians perceived the British decision to proscribe the Committee as an insult to their community even if many of them had no respect for its traditional leadership. After the actions against Haj Amin, his supporters intensified the rebellion and the violence continued to escalate. By 1938, the rebels had overwhelmed the Mandate security forces, especially in the interior.[1] They disarmed policemen, collected taxes, raided banks and stores, established their own courts, executed Arabs who opposed the revolt, and intimidated the local leaders into cooperation. The Palestinian revolt that followed the strike was started by people from the lowest socio-economic segment, which had suffered the most from British policies and the Zionist invasion. The rebels were mostly peasants from the villages and workers from poor city neighborhoods. There was no coordination with the Palestinian leadership at the beginning of the revolt, but once it started, the traditional leadership under Haj Amin al-Husseini stepped in to maintain its own supremacy.[2]

The revolt succeeded in its early stages in harassing the British. But once Haj Amin stepped in and brought it under his control, the revolt became identified with him personally, even while he was in exile, and that led to internal division among the competing leading families and the factionalism of Palestinian society. The Nashashibi clan and their supporters opposed the revolt at the risk of being accused by the Husseini faction of aligning themselves with the British against the national aspirations of the Palestinians. The Palestinians were polarized. The lives of those who disagreed with Haj Amin were threatened by the rebels. An attempt on the life of Fakhri Nashashibi, allegedly by Husseini supporters, led the Nashashibis to openly back Emir Abdullah of Trans-Jordan, whose aim was to get a foothold in Palestine.[3] Given the alliance between the resourceful Yishuv and the powerful British Mandate authority against the rebels, the up-rising of the fragmented Palestinian society was destined to failure. In 1938, Britain decided to use its military superiority to "re-conquer Palestine" and restore order.[4] A state of emergency was declared, military courts were established to enforce its regulations, and an army of 20,000 troops was unleashed against the rebels. The British military used heavy-handed methods including ambushes, night curfews and blowing up houses to force the rebels to move out of the towns and eventually crush the rebellion.

After 1936, the Mandate authorities started adding thousands of new Jewish recruits to its police force, trained by the military, and by 1939 their numbers exceeded 14,000. Besides that, the British dropped their demands that the Jewish paramilitary organization, the Haganah, surrender their illegal weapons. When the revolt was crushed, there were significant human and economic losses among the Palestinians and no concessions from the British. The last two rebel leaders, Izzat Darwazi and Yusuf Abu Durra, crossed the borders into Syria and Trans-Jordan. The French administration in Syria arrested Dar-

---

1 *London Times*, September 6, 1938.
2 David Hirst, 2003, p. 204.
3 Yehoshu Porath, 1974, p. 242.
4 David Hirst, 2003, p.214.

wazi; and the Trans-Jordanians arrested Abu Durra and handed him back to the British authorities in Palestine, where he was tried and executed in 1940.

The Palestinian economy was devastated and more than 5,000 killed in battles or executed by the British, 14,000 wounded, 5,679 detained, many leaders were exiled, and the Arab Higher Committee was proscribed.[1] It was estimated that 10% of the adult Palestinian population were killed, wounded or exiled and the hope for independence was dashed. In the meantime, the Jewish economy thrived, its military capability improved, and Jewish immigrants continued to arrive in large numbers. While the British disarmed the Arab Palestinians, they allowed the Jews to arm themselves and the Haganah began manufacturing their own arms.

The *Yishuv* used the Palestinian strike as a pretext to replace the port of Arab-controlled Jaffa, where no single Jew used to work, with a modern port in Tel Aviv. Only Jewish workers were engaged to load and unload ships. When the phase of reliance on the protection of the Mandate was drawing to a close, the *Yishuv* had already developed a formidable quasi-military force that would fight the War of Independence, while the Palestinian military had collapsed, their political leaders were fighting each other in exile, and their society was fragmented.

MACDONALD'S WHITE PAPER

Despite the Palestinians' opposition, the pace of Jewish immigration continued to accelerate as anti-Semitism spread in Europe under Nazism in the 1930s. The Jewish population in Palestine approached half a million by 1939 and the British were pressured to do something to alleviate Palestinian fears. Secretary of State Malcolm MacDonald issued a White Paper on May 17, 1939, to settle the Arab–Jewish conflict by creating a unitary state. It called for gradually transferring the responsibility of governing to the people of Palestine, with a goal of creating a single independent Palestinian state for Jews and Arabs within ten years. It proposed sharp limits on Jewish immigration by allowing only 10,000 Jewish immigrants per year for five years plus a total of 25,000 refugees. After the five years, no more immigration would be permitted without Arab Palestinians acquiescence. Both Haj Amin and the *Yishuv* rejected the White Paper, each for their own reasons. The White Paper recommendation of establishing a single state should have satisfied the main Arab demand in their struggle, but the Arab Higher Committee objected to the length of the transitional period and other conditions to be met before establishing the promised independent state. The AHC rejected the stipulation that the establishment of the independent state required cooperation between Arabs and Jews which would give the *Yishuv* the power to demand parity in running the government. It has been suggested that the exiled Haj Amin refused the White Paper so that he would not lose his domination over the national movement to his bitter rivals, the Nashashibi clan and Emir Abdullah who supported the White Paper recommendations and were ready to fill the leadership vacuum.[2]

---

1   Walid Khalidi, 1971, p. 847.
2   Issa Khalaf, 1991, P.64-75.

The Nashashibis welcomed the White Paper recommendations and offered to cooperate with the British to implement them.

The Zionists perceived the White Paper as a British surrender to the Arabs and a sudden reversal of their support for a Jewish state. It would relegate the Jews to a minority in a Palestinian state and would limit immigration at a time when Europe was increasingly anti-Semitic. For the *Yishuv*, the Mandate had already served its purpose by 1939 and it was no longer helping the Zionist project. It was time for the Jewish community to affirm its self-reliance. The Jews of Palestine demonstrated throughout the country denouncing the White Paper, and some riots broke out. The *Yishuv* response was violent; they challenged the Mandate by waging their own rebellion against the White Paper, using the guns and the ammunition which the Mandate had given them to fight the Arab rebels. The studios of the Palestinian national radio station were bombed immediately after the news was broadcast; the government department of immigration in Tel Aviv was stormed and set on fire.[1] The Irgun Z'vai Le'umi organization bombed some government buildings and communication facilities. Jews demonstrated, Arabs in the cities were harassed, and British policemen were attacked in Jerusalem. The *Yishuv* encouraged clandestine illegal Jewish immigration and transformed the armed guards of the Jewish communities into the *Haganah* paramilitary force acting as a national military organization to defend the Jewish interests against the Arabs and the British. This became the nucleus of the future Israeli army that fought in the War of Independence.

With the outbreak of World War II, the *Yishuv* had to put their disagreement with the British aside and join them in the war against the Nazis and Fascists. By 1943, the British policy makers had second thoughts about the proposed single-state solution. They scrapped the White Paper and returned to the concept of partitioning. John Bagot Glubb suggested that fear of a Jewish rebellion in Palestine was the main reason for the British rethink on the White Paper. Glubb believed that, "If the Jews start a rebellion [against the British], it [would] be much more efficiently organized than the Arab Revolt [of 1936]" and more difficult to suppress.[2]

PALESTINE IN 1947–1948

Britain finally decided to end its Mandate and turn the issue of Palestine over to the United Nations General Assembly (UNGA). The UNGA passed Resolution 181 (II) on November 29, 1947 to partition Palestine into two states, a Jewish and an Arab, and international regime for Jerusalem area. Chapter 4 discusses the subject in more details.

David Ben-Gurion accepted the Resolution on behalf of the Jews; the Palestinians and the Arab states rejected it arguing that the future of Palestine should be decided by its rightful owners and that the General Assembly had exceeded its legal authority. The partition resolution was never implemented. Civil war between disorganized Arab irregulars

---

1 David Hirst, 2003, p.220.
2 Glubb, "A Further Note on Peace Terms in the Middle East," May 25, 1943: St. Antony's College Middle East Center Archive (Oxford), Glubb papers.

and the well-prepared Jewish military erupted with the early, gradual British withdrawal from major cities.

Jewish forces took over the area assigned to the Jews by the UN resolution and strategic parts of the Arab-allotted territory as well, plus areas earmarked for international control. In the process of capturing the Tel Aviv–Jerusalem road, the Jewish militia *Irgun Herut Leumi* (IZL) and *Lohamei Herut Yisrael* (LHI) attacked the village of *Deir Yaseen* in April 1948 and killed, mutilated and raped hundreds of its Arab residents, including women, children and the elderly. Palestinian villagers and town dwellers were alarmed as news of the massacre was reported by the news media. Fearful of becoming the next victims of Jewish atrocities, residents of neighboring and distant towns and villages started fleeing en masse. Israeli historians now acknowledge that Jewish forces committed more than 30 large scale massacres of civilians between November 1947 and May 1949 that helped precipitate the exodus of the Palestinian refugees.

The AHC, under the leadership of Haj Amin, who was residing in Cairo and Beirut during the 1948 war, established no institutions to link the Palestinian population in different regions to each other nor did he succeed in unifying the leadership of the prominent families which had dominated Palestinian politics since the 19th century. Haj Amin himself was a party in the traditional family feuds and disputes over the Palestinian leadership. As a result, following the termination of the Mandate, the leading Palestinian citizens did not coordinate or plan for defending their communities, there was no regular recruitment or mobilization, and no arrangements were made for weapon acquisition and logistics planning for defense like those achieved by the *Yishuv*. The fighting Palestinians were scattered, disorganized groups of poorly-armed, inexperienced young men tied to their local leaders — who had always been at odds with each other.

The AHC succeeded in recruiting a small group of volunteer irregulars, known as the Holy Army (al-Jihad al-Mukaddas), led by Hasan Salami and Abdul-Qader al-Husseini, the son of the late Musa Kazim al-Husseini and a close relative of Haj Amin.[1] The Holy Army was no match for the larger and well-organized Jewish military. Salami directed operations in the coastal area and Abdul-Qader commanded the fighters in Jerusalem and Hebron mountains. Abdul-Qader's unit controlled the main road between Tel Aviv and Jerusalem for a while, using small arms and displaying heroism, before the Haganah went on the offensive. Abdul-Qader al-Husseini, the most charismatic Palestinian military leader, was killed in the battle for al-Kastal in April 1948.

The Arab League formed its own 4,000-men volunteer force, the Arab Liberation Army (ALA), under a controversial military commander, Fawzi al-Qa'uqji, a Syrian Arab nationalist and a soldier of fortune. Al-Qa'uqji was more of a political figure than a military leader. He was appointed by pro-Abdullah Arab politicians as a counterweight to Haj Amin supporters. Haj Amin accused him of being an agent for the British and Emir Abdullah of Trans-Jordan. The Israeli Haganah Intelligence reported in February 1948 an agreement between al-Qa'uqji and Abdullah to the effect that the area which the ALA occupied,

---

1 Rosemary Sayigh, 1979, p. 77.

namely the Ramallah–Nablus–Tulkarm Triangle, would be annexed to Trans-Jordan.[1] The selection of al-Qa'uqji to lead the ALA, despite the objection of Haj Amin, relegated the Palestinian nationalists to insignificant players rather than partners in the 1948 war. Al-Qa'uqji excluded Palestinian volunteers from his army because, according to one of his officers, "they [the Palestinians] simply get in the way." Instead of cooperation, there were rivalries and frictions between al-Husseini Palestinian fighters and the ALA.

Al-Qa'uqji's betrayal of his Palestinian comrades-in-arms was demonstrated by his refusal to support Abdul-Qader al-Husseini in the battle for al-Kastal and Hasan Salami in the Ramle battles. More alarming was the tacit understanding that was reached between al-Qa'uqji and the Haganah intelligence officer, Josh Palmon, for the ALA to refrain from supporting the Palestinian fighters if the Jewish military decided to go on the offensive on the Jerusalem front.[2] The meeting between the two supposed adversaries took place in al-Qa'uqji's headquarters in Nur-Shams town on April 1, 1948. Al-Qa'uqji kept his promise to Palmon when the Haganah launched its offensive against the Palestinian Holy Army to open the Tel Aviv-Jerusalem road on April 4, 1948. The ALA military contingent did not help the Hasan Salami or Abdul-Qader al-Husseini fighters to defend the strategic road. When al-Husseini's irregulars ran out of ammunition, Al-Qa'uqji refused to help.

Ironically, after the collapse of the Holy Army, the ALA was the next to suffer humiliating defeats in the battles for the control of Tirat Zvi and Mishmar-Haemek, small settlements, by the Haganah defenders. Al-Qa'uaqji's actions suggest that he had no intention to fight or any confidence in the military that he was leading. He complained about the quality and the lack of preparedness of his ALA army. He wrote in his 1948 memoirs that "[his] officers and men lack military competence...Some of the men could not even load a rifle properly. [Also] among the officers there were some elements so corrupt that I did not know how the Inspector-General could have agreed to their being attached to the units."[3] The Jewish fighters made big territorial gains before the end of the Mandate. They took over towns and villages and "cleansed" them of Arab residents. Conquered areas included West Jerusalem, Haifa, Jaffa, Tiberias, Safed and Acre.

By the end of the British Mandate, the accumulation of many factors contributed to the failure of the Palestinians to hold onto the land they claimed or even the land apportioned to them by UN General Assembly resolution 181. First and most important, the Palestinians had never recovered from their defeat in the 1936–39 revolt. Their leaders were not even living in Palestine. They never created institutions for a future state, whereas the Jewish community had been laying the foundations of their state by establishing democratic institutions and a military force. As early as 1922, while the Palestinian leaders were feuding with each other, the *Yishuv* had their own elected political assembly, community councils, religious and social organizations. The Zionists' known ambitions made it more pressing for the Palestinians to work together on strategies, coordinate resources, and

---

1 Benny Morris, 2002, p.181.
2 Avi Shlaim, 2001, p.85.
3 *Journal of Palestine Studies I* (1972), p.48.

confront the impending danger. Instead, they relied on a political system based on traditional clan links and tribal loyalties.[1]

Second, the Palestinians rejected the UN resolution and launched an armed struggle — without the means to fight a war and without the political clout to challenge the Zionists within the international community that had created Israel. It was understandable that the Palestinians had not accepted the imposed decision to give their land to foreign settlers, but it was beyond their power to support their moral claim by war. In hindsight, since the Palestinian elites must have known their own vulnerability and the strength of the *Yishuv*, especially after the collapse of the 1936–1939 revolt, they should have known better. They could have bowed to the inevitable and accepted the UN resolution as a starting point, but they did not. Given the weak Arab conditions at that time, the 1947 UN resolutions offered the most viable basis for resolving the Palestinian question.

Third, the Palestinians did not take into account the influence of the Zionist organizations and their non-Jewish supporters on the decision makers and the public opinion in Europe and America. Prominent Zionists had access to Britain's cabinet members and members of Parliament at any time, while Arab delegations to London had only sporadic meetings with these officials and no means to influence public opinion.[2]

Fourth, the Palestinians overestimated the power of the Arab military and underestimated the Jewish military power and determination. The 500,000 Jews in Palestine were able to provide more fighting men and women than all the invading Arab armies combined. Their military planning and their determination to fight for their lives and for the cause that they believed in provided them with additional strength and superiority. Many of their fighters had military experience, having fought the Arab rebels in 1936–39 and later on the Nazis (with the British and the United States armies) in World War II. The highly-motivated veterans of the Haganah supported, by the armed members of the Irgun, Stern, and LEHI paramilitary organizations, were more than a match for the inexperienced Arab armies. Sir John Bagot Glubb, the British commander of the Trans-Jordan army wrote: "I knew the extent of the Jewish preparations. I know that the Arabs had no plan and there was no co-operation between them."[3] This simple observation suggests that Arab leaders must have been aware of their military shortcomings but they held back the truth from the Palestinian people. Arab governments raised the expectations of the Palestinians rather than restraining them.

Fifth, Palestinians trusting member states of the Arab League to make crucial decisions for them weakened their case in world opinion; it led to perceiving the conflict as an invasion of the newly-born Israeli state with less than half million Jews by the armies of six states of forty million Arabs. Israeli leaders and sympathetic writers portrayed Israel as a weak, besieged Jewish David attacked by a hostile Arab Goliath. This gave the Israelis the excuse to use their superior military power to occupy more Arab lands, remove by

---

1 Salim Tamari, 1982, p.179.
2 Ann Mosely Lesch, 1972.
3 Sir John Bagot Glubb, 1957, p. 101

force the remaining inhabitants of the areas they conquered, and take over their land as "absentee property."

The 1947–1948 period witnessed the watershed events that led to the birth of Israel and the flight and expulsion of much of the Arab population.[1]

POST-MANDATE PALESTINE

On May 14, 1948, one day before the British departure, Israel declared its independence and Israel was born with all its state institutions functioning. It already had well-organized and adequately-equipped regular and irregular forces in place to defend their state and expand its borders, dedicated leadership to manage the territory, and international network to provide armaments and political support. The Yishuv celebrated and Arab Palestinians declared a general strike.

The conflict was internationalized when more than 20,000 troops from Egypt, Syria, Lebanon, Iraq, and Trans-Jordan crossed the borders to assist the Palestinians in a war that has been called by Israel the "War of Independence." The leaders of the Arab states were high on rhetoric and low on military preparation and political competence.[2] The intervention in Palestine by the regular armies of five Arab states was decided in the April 29, 1948, Arab summit in Amman. They agreed to invade on May 15 but there was no coordination among the various Arab armies. King Abdullah was chosen as the commander in chief of the Arab military campaign, but he admitted that he "had not known anything about the Arab armies."[3] The real problem was the conflicting interests of the Arab states and the distrust of each other's intentions in Palestine.

Each state was assigned its own zone in Palestine and had its own independent command. Except for Trans-Jordan, Arab states committed only expeditionary forces and kept the bulk of their military at home. Egypt dispatched 10,000 men, Syria 3,000, Lebanon 1,000, Iraq 3,000, and Trans-Jordan provided 4,500 soldiers.[4] Full scale fighting erupted at many fronts, but militarily they were ill-prepared, battle-shy, and the lines of supply for the Iraqi and the Egyptian contingents were hopelessly extended. The Syrian and Iraqi military did not even have military maps for the terrain they were supposed to secure, and they had to rely on school book maps and civilian guides instead. The Iraqi line of communication exceeded 600 miles of mostly desert and the supplies for the Egyptian army had to be transported more than 200 miles across Sinai.

Count Folke Bernadotte, a member of the Swedish royal family, was appointed by the United Nations as a mediator to create a peaceful situation between Jews and Arabs in Palestine when the British Mandate expired and Israel was proclaimed a state. He succeeded in mediating the first truce between the two sides of the conflict on June 11. The negotiated truce banned the introduction of additional weapons and restricted the immi-

---

1 Michael Cohen, 1989, P.90
2 Pappe 2004.
3 Howard Sachar, 1996, p. 317.
4 Sir John Bagot Glubb, 1957, p.94.

gration of military armament to Palestine during the truce, but both sides did not observe such restriction.

Before the truce took effect, the Arab armies had limited military gain in establishing footholds in the Israeli designated territory. The Egyptian forces acquired positions deep in the Negev Desert leaving behind many fortified Jewish settlements. The Arab Legion took over the Old City of Jerusalem which had no strategic significance and it had been designated by the UNGA Resolution as part of the International sector of Palestine. Israel decided to commit its military resources in the area to defend West Jerusalem and several settlements in the Judean Hills after losing Old Jerusalem to the Legion. The Syrians barely crossed the borders in the Israeli territory. The Iraqis, the ALA and the Lebanese stayed within the Arab designated territory in the north.

The truce gave Israel time to break the arms embargo, bring large quantities of armaments and recruit thousands of volunteers from within and abroad, raising its military manpower from 35,000 to 65,000. Bernadotte proposed on June 27 a new comprehensive settlement plan that involved both Palestine and Trans-Jordan. He recommended annexing the Arab area of Palestine to Trans-Jordan, the Jewish and the Arab states to be joined in federal union, Jewish immigration to be controlled by the United Nations after two years and allowing the return of the Arab refugees to their own homes. The proposals were rejected by the Palestinians for dividing the country and Haj Amin al-Husseini followers were against annexing the Arab sector to Trans-Jordan. The Israelis rejected them because they were confident that they would have the upper hand and conquer more land should the hostilities resumed. Besides, the Zionists' goal had been to have a state of their own.

When the Egyptians violated the truce on July 8, they were unaware that the Israeli Defense Forces (IDF) had been rearmed, reorganized and ready to launch their counterattack on all fronts. In the next ten days, the IDF was on the offensive, capturing the ALA headquarters in Nazareth, the towns of Lydda and Ramle and most of their surroundings west of Jerusalem and Hebron from the Arab Legion and strategic parts of the territory controlled by the Egyptians.

The IDF launched a major offensive (Operation Dani) against the Arab Legion in the central front, but the Legion decided not to fight. Trans-Jordan did not commit troops to defend Lydda which had been under their control. It fell to the IDF on July 12 without a fight, and then civilian leaders of neighboring Ramle surrendered their town when they realized that Trans-Jordan military would not defend it despite appeals for help by its mayor and the town notables to King Abdullah. The Palestinians perceived the surrender of Lydda and Ramle without a fight, each with a population of 20,000, as a betrayal by Jordan.

Before the end of the Mandate, a political decision was made by King Abdullah and Glubb that Lydda and Ramle would not be defended because they were considered as Haj

Amin strongholds.[1] Immediately after conquering Lydda and Ramle, Ben-Gurion authorized the troops to forcibly expel their inhabitants from their homes toward the east to join the West Jerusalem Arabs who were driven from their homes at the same time.[2] The IDF carried out the orders and emptied the towns of their residents even using its own trucks to transport them to the east. The second truce was declared on July 19 and the guns fell silent for three months before the hostilities were resumed.

During the second truce, the Israelis bought large quantities of military hardware from Czechoslovakia and increased the number of their troops by more than 20,000 new recruits. When the IDF terminated the truce by attacking the Egyptians to break the siege of the Negev settlements, the Israelis had overwhelming superiority over the Arab armies combined including the Jordanian, the Iraqi and the Syrian military who were not involved in the fighting anyway. The Egyptian military lacked the manpower and ammunition to stop the IDF offensive that started on October 15. Seven days later, the IDF conquered Beersheba, Majdal and other Arab villages in the Negev area, forcing most of the Egyptian army to retreat from its positions in the Negev and Hebron-Bethlehem area to western Negev and Gaza Strip.

A sizable Egyptian force, estimated at four thousand men, was encircled in the Faluja area and remained surrounded until Egypt and Israel concluded the armistice agreement in February 1949. Jamal Abdel-Nasser, the future leader of the 1952 military coup that ended the monarchy in Egypt, was among the officers in the Faluja besieged pocket. During the whole military operation against the Egyptians and while the IDF was consolidating its gains, the rest of the Arab armies were watching from the sidelines.

Inter-Arab rivalry between the Jordanians and the Egyptians developed into open competition to dominate the territories when both sides established military presence in the same area during the first month of the invasion.[3] Hebron and Bethlehem had been the scene of confrontation between the two sides for the control of the area when a small detachment from the Egyptian army arrived from the south in June of 1948. The Arab Legion had control of the two towns since April after disarming the pro-Mufti Palestinian fighters. Each of Egypt and Jordan appointed a military governor and tried to establish a police force and its own municipal management. Jordan won the contest by providing salaries to its supporters while the Egyptians proposed collecting taxes from the local population.

When the Egyptians had to withdraw from Hebron-Bethlehem, Jordan rushed military units to replace the Egyptians in the two towns. In the middle of the battles for Nagev when the Egyptian army sustained heavy losses and faced possible defeat at the hands of the Israelis, the Jordanian army stood idle and Abdullah even prevented the Iraqis from providing assistance to the embattled Egyptians.[4] King Abdullah was so much against the idea of "All Palestine" government in the Arab sector that he would rather have its sponsors, the Egyptians, lose to Israel than win and establish such a government. The success

---

1 Benny Morris, 2002, p.173, 276.
2 Benny Morris, 1999, p.240.
3 Avi Shlaim, 1988, p. 328.
4 Yoav Gelber, 2004, p. 70.

of the Israeli offensive in the Nagev brought about the end of the Egyptian control over strategic areas, the irrelevance of "All Palestine" government and ironically left Israel in a strong position to negotiate with Abdullah.

While engaging the Egyptians in the south, the IDF expanded its operations by conquering the remaining Palestinian enclave under the ALA control in the north. Within the last three days of October, the IDF crushed the ALA completely, crossed the international borders with Lebanon and occupied many villages in South Lebanon up to the Litani River. The IDF exploited its success on the battle field and the weakness of the Arabs by marching unopposed from the just conquered Beersheba town to the Dead Sea.

In December 1948, Ben-Gurion government decided to launch the second military offensive against the Egyptians to drive them out of all Palestine except Gaza Strip and force them to accept an armistice.[1] The Israelis believed that once the Egyptians signed an armistice agreement, the rest of the Arab states would follow suit. The IDF tightened the siege on the Egyptian military units in Faluja. In Operation "Horev," Israel dispatched a mechanized column toward the Egyptian town of Al-Arish with the objective of isolating the bulk of the Egyptian military in Gaza Strip. In its thrust westward, the IDF crossed the international borders with Egypt provoking a strong protest by Britain which had a defense treaty with Egypt. By January 6, 1949, the IDF cut al-Arish-Rafah road, thus disrupting the main supply line to the Egyptian force in the Gaza Strip. Few days later, there was a serious confrontation with the British on January 7, 1949, when a formation of Israeli airplanes intercepted and shot down five British reconnaissance planes over Sinai. On December 29, 1948, the United Nation Security Council called for a permanent armistice between Israel and the belligerent Arab states, Egypt, Lebanon, Syria and Trans-Jordan. The Egyptians officially agreed to negotiate not directly face-to-face with the Israeli representatives, but through a mediator from the United Nations. Egypt was the first to conclude an armistice agreement.

An unwritten political agreement had been brokered by the British between King Abdullah of Trans-Jordan and the Jewish Agency before the invasion. Abdullah promised not to cross the borders of the newly recognized Israel and the Jews undertook not to interfere with the Trans-Jordanian army invasion of the Arab sector of Palestine. The Arab Legion stayed within the area allotted to the Palestinians by the UN partitioning resolution, and the only territory that its military units contested was the old city of Jerusalem, which had been designated an international zone within the Arab state by the United Nations. But the Arab Legion surrendered the cities of Lydda, Ramle and Latrun that the UN had earmarked for Arab sovereignty. And later on, King Abdullah surrendered the so-called the "Iron Triangle" area in the northwest of Palestine through the 1949 negotiated armistice agreement.

Many post World War II Jewish settlers had been veterans of the war against Germany. They constituted the core of the Israeli self-sufficient military forces that fought in the War of Independence. They defeated the inexperienced Arab armies and the disorganized

---

1   Ben-Gurion, 1982, entry on December 19, 1948, p.886.

Palestinians in 1947–49. The Israelis were highly motivated, well organized, and they were fighting for a cause they believed in under dedicated leadership. By the end of 1948, Israel had taken 2,000 square miles beyond the partition borders and even crossed into Egypt's Sinai Peninsula. While the State of Israel controlled 8,300 square miles, Egypt was able to save the southern coastal Gaza Strip (140 square miles), or about 1% of Mandate Palestine. The pre-war Gaza Strip population of 80,000 was joined by more than 179,000 refugees after the war; and the Egyptians became the custodians of this territory. Egypt limited its role to that of a caretaker in Gaza, preserving the Strip (not preparing i) to take its place in a future Palestinian state). The governor general wrote to the Defense Minister in 1960 that the Egyptian administration in Gaza was "to build a democratic social society and create cooperation among Palestinians to liberate the rest of their country."

Under Egypt, Gaza Strip was never formally annexed to Egypt and the Egyptian rulers never fostered alternative nationality to its citizens like what the Jordanians did to the West Bank residents. The Egyptians advocated a temporary political status for the Strip that could be reversed only if all Palestine is liberated. Palestinian refugees in Gaza constitute 70% of its total population and Nasser made no effort during his entire tenure to improve their economic conditions. They had no job opportunities in Gaza and they could not work in Egypt proper due to Egypt's discriminatory laws. Gaza refugees lived in limbo under Egyptian military rule in severely overcrowded camps as beggars depending on the UN handouts. Because refugees were the large majority of Gaza Strip's population, Egypt shared administrative responsibility of the Strip with the UN Relief and Work Agency (UNRWA). UNRWA provided the refugees with food rations, education and some employment. Nasser failed to extend his social and economic revolution to help the most vulnerable Arab constituency, the Palestinians.

Trans-Jordan managed to save the eastern mountainous part of Palestine (2,270 square miles) or 20% of Mandate Palestine, which was later called the West Bank. Once the Arabs lost the war and it was too late to undo the Balfour Declaration and its effects, it was the right decision to annex what was salvaged from Palestine to Trans-Jordan. Besides losing territory allocated to the Palestinians in the war, there was the exodus of hundreds of thousands of Palestinian refugees from their conquered cities and villages to the West Bank, Trans-Jordan, Lebanon and Syria.

The evidence clearly suggests that while the Arab leaders were giving rhetorical backing to the Palestinian cause, they acted only to serve their own interests. The main objective of King Abdullah of Trans-Jordan, the commander-in-chief of the Arab forces in the 1948 War, was to annex those sectors allocated to the Arabs in the partition resolution.[1] He was reportedly involved in secret negotiations with Israel and had the blessing of Great Britain to divide Palestine between his kingdom and the Jewish state. Secret negotiations or no, King Abdullah was the only Arab leader to claim success in the 1948 war. It is unfair to fault Abdullah for using diplomacy and negotiations to keep the West Bank and Jerusalem in Arab hands. Trans-Jordan had no natural resources and its population

---

1 Peretz 1996 p. 40; Shalaim 1988.

was half that of Syria and no more than 8% of Egypt's population. The King knew the imbalance of power that favored the Jewish establishments in Palestine and internationally, and he recognized the political and military limits of the Arab states, especially his kingdom. Two years after the 1948 war, the West Bank and Jerusalem were annexed and the Emirate of Trans-Jordan became the Hashemite Kingdom of Jordan. Gathering support from those who mistrusted this maneuver, King Farouk of Egypt tried to use the 1948 war to strengthen his leadership role in the rest of the Arab world.

The 1948 War has been remembered in the collective national memory of the Palestinian Arabs as *al-Nakba* and it has been proudly depicted by the Israelis as a "War of Independence" that was won against all odds. The Arabs' defeat in this war cast doubts on the legitimacy of their civilian governments and set the stage for military rule in Egypt, Syria and Iraq.

In the aftermath of the 1948 War and after the signing of the permanent armistice agreements between Israel and the belligerent Arab states, the Arabs were divided among themselves. The West Bank residents were given Jordanian citizenship; Gaza Strip was administered by an Egyptian appointed military governor; and the Palestinians who went to other Arab countries were granted the status of refugees. To counter Jordan's claim to the West Bank, the Palestinian AHC under the leadership of Haj Amin al-Hussein and the sponsorship of Egypt set up the "All-Palestine" government in Gaza with Ahmad Hilmi as its prime minister in September 1948. "All-Palestine" was only a government on paper because it had no jurisdiction over any part of the area under Jordan control and not even over the Gaza Strip, where its prime-minister resided. The symbolic "All-Palestine Government" was dissolved by the Arab League in 1952; Arab governments became the official guardians of the Palestinian cause; and active Palestinian nationalism receded significantly until the emergence of the PLO and Fatah.

Personal animosity among the leaders of the Arab governments was reflected on the policies toward the Palestinians. They never agreed on a plan or a strategy on the Palestinian issue. Egypt, Iraq, Jordan and the AHC continued to have different plans regarding the Palestinian entity biased by their leaders' personal ambitions and hatred to each other. The severity of the split was especially obvious in the late 1950s and early 1960s, when Nasser of Egypt and Abdul-Karim Kassim of Iraq had been competing on the leadership of Arab nationalism. Both Nasser and Kassim argued that Jordan's annexation of the West Bank had been illegal. Kassim, however, considered Egypt as guilty as Jordan for occupying Gaza Strip. Kassim afforded to be more hawkish than Nasser in his rhetoric against Israel because unlike Egypt, Iraq was too far from Israel and it never signed an armistice agreement with Israel. He believed that the Palestinians should use armed struggle to recover their land, following the example of the Algerian war of independence against the French. To prove that he could improve on anything Nasser could do, Kassim proposed establishing a Palestinian Republic to be supported by the Arab states. Its sovereignty would be over the West Bank and Gaza Strip and later on over the land liberated from Israel. Kassim referred to the West Bank, Gaza Strip and Israel as "the territories that were usurped by three thieves: one of them hostile to Arab nationalism, Zionism, and the other two from within the Arab camp: Egypt and Jordan."[1] Kassim promised Iraq's support to a Palestinian Republic with financial aid and military needs.

Egypt proposed establishing a Palestinian entity (al-Kiyan al-Filastini) that would represent the Palestinians as a people rather than refugees at a meeting of the Arab League Council in 1964. The Egyptian plan included the election of an assembly by the Palestinians in the Gaza Strip, Jordan and Lebanon, which in turn would elect an executive branch to represent the Palestinians in the international arena. The Palestinian National Council (PNC) met in Jerusalem in 1964 and established the PLO, which gained legitimacy among the Palestinians — especially after the defeat of the Arab armies by Israel in the 1967 War.

THE PALESTINIAN ISSUE AFTER THE 1967 WAR

The war lasted only six days but it has changed the politics and geography of the region for ever. It left Israel in control of all historical Palestine, Egypt's Sinai Peninsula, Syria's Golan Heights, Lebanon's Shebaa Farms and small areas of Jordanian territory. Chapter 4 reviews with more details about the war.

Most important, the war put an end to the Pan-Arab project of Nasser and set the stage for Sadat's peace initiative with Israel, and the rise of the Palestinian nationalism.

The defeat in the 1967 war, and the 1970 civil war in Jordan that resulted in the demise of the pro-Jordanian elites in the West Bank, created an environment of nationalism among the Palestinian bourgeoisie living outside Palestine. Driven by their nationalist fervor, they supported Arafat's liberal Fatah faction of the PLO. By 1974, they succeeded in enlisting Arab league recognition of the PLO as the only representative of the Palestinians. The Rabat Conference of Arab nations decided to give the PLO recognition as their "sole legitimate representative." And in November of the same year, Arab and Islamic governments managed to extend an invitation for Arafat to address the UNGA on behalf of the Palestinian people. Representatives of some countries, including Israel and the US, walked out during the speech. Shortly after that appearance, demonstrations by PLO supporters in the occupied lands erupted, followed by strikes and civil disobedience in large and small towns, and Israel retaliated with curfews and deportations.

Then the Israeli government authorized West Bank municipal elections in 1976, where men and women were allowed to cast votes. The activists who ran for election were concerned about Palestinian national identity rather than municipal issues. The competition was between two groups, the pro-Jordan coalition and the PLO supporters. The young Palestinian voters delivered a decisive victory for the PLO and repudiated the pro-Jordanian candidates. King Hussein Ibn Talal of Jordan could have ignored the municipal elections as a referendum on his rule over the West Bank — if he had been able to reach an acceptable solution with Israel on the occupied lands.

---

1 Moshe Shemesh, 1988, p. 12.

When the Israeli leaders shunned his effort to arrive at a solution, King Hussein Ibn Talal decided in 1988 to disclaim his sovereignty over the occupied West Bank and Jerusalem, and he recognized the PLO as the sole representative of the Palestinians. Egypt had already signed a peace agreement with Israel in 1979, thus ending the confrontation between Israel and the most populous Arab country.

Then, in 1990, in the context of confusing diplomatic signals from the United States, Iraq invaded Kuwait. The US led a multinational coalition military campaign to liberate it and restore its sovereign government in only four days of fighting. The Kuwaiti war was followed by the collapse of the Soviet Union, the end of the Cold War, and the emergence of the USA as the world's sole superpower.

In the fall of 1991, the US-led Arab–Israeli peace process was inaugurated in Madrid and supported by the PNC. Yasser Arafat signed the Declaration of Principle, known as Oslo I, in September 1993, and in the same year, Jordan signed a peace treaty with Israel. Egypt was the only country that recovered all its occupied land, namely the Sinai Peninsula. But the Palestinians, Syrians and the Lebanese were left alone, struggling to recover their lands.

THE PLO

The Palestinians had been always under foreign rule, or under the guardianship of authoritarian Arab governments that had not achieved liberation for their own countries. This allowed the Israelis to claim, in the words of Golda Meir, that, "It is not as though there was a Palestinian people in Palestine, considering itself as a Palestinian people, and we came and threw them out and took their country away from them." The Palestinian people as such "did not exist"[1]

Even the Balfour Declaration and the League of Nations Mandate that authorized Britain to govern Palestine referred to the Palestinians only as "the non-Jewish communities." The failure of the regular Arab armies to protect the Palestinians in so many encounters with Israel led the Palestinians to lose faith in the Arab governments' ability to liberate any of their land.

The Palestinians, indeed, had no unified leadership until the coming of the Palestine Liberation Organization (PLO) that was created by the Arab states after their 1948 defeat, and the militant Fatah, established by expatriate Palestinians as an alternative to the guardianship of the Arab governments.

Fatah and the PLO had no choice but to be fostered and protected by Arab regimes and become another Arab state establishment because they were created outside Palestine lands. Fatah and the PLO were liberation movements, but they had to conform to the host country politics and abide by their laws. When Fatah and the PLO merged their organizations, the leadership proved to be no different from the other Arab leaders.

Different leaders of Fatah recite different narratives showing how their organization started, each giving himself an important role, which suggests that it was the creation

1 *Sunday Times*, June 15, 1969, as quoted in David Hirst, 1977, p.264.

of a team of activists who had been working in Kuwait. According to Yasser Arafat, he started Fatah in 1959 by publishing an underground magazine in Tripoli, Lebanon, that called on the Palestinians around the world to stand up and fight for the liberation of their homeland.[1] Most of Fatah leaders, however, were working in Kuwait as contractors and civil service employees, and some had known each other as students in Egypt. When the organization was underground, it was controlled by the Kuwaiti-based group.

Besides Arafat, known leaders included Khalid al-Wazeer, Mahmoud Miswaddy, Munir Ajour, Yousof Ameerah, Ahmad Assadi and Adel Abdul-Kareem. Some of these with roots in the Muslim Brothers movement withdrew from Fatah because of their suspicion that Arafat, who was trying to dominate the organization, was an agent of the Egyptian secret service.

Willing Palestinians were recruited and organized in few underground cells throughout the Middle East and Europe. The survivors of the original 15 central committee members of Fatah that was formed in 1963 continued to be powerful members within the organization, but Fatah had been dominated by Arafat who made all the decisions until his death in 2004.[2]

Fatah had no political ideology, but it was committed to fighting a guerrilla war against Israel, similar to the Algerian war of independence. Its strategy was to stage limited raids across the borders to provoke Israel into attacking Arab countries and start a war. The Syrian army trained and equipped its fighters and it was the raids of Fatah into Israel from the Syrian–Israeli border that started the tension which eventually led to the 1967 War.

A campaign of violent attacks on Israeli targets at the border was carried out by Fatah irregulars. Its first military operation against Israel took place in 1965 when an armed band placed a bomb in an Israeli water project. The leader was killed by a Jordanian soldier while crossing the border into a Jordanian-controlled area after the raid.

By 1964 and while Fatah was expanding, a new Palestinian organization was formed by the Arab League. At Nasser's invitation, an Arab League summit meeting was held in Cairo in January 1964 to discuss the problem of Israel's plan to divert water from the Sea of Galilee to the Negev desert. The summit endorsed Nasser's proposal to create an official organization with both political and military wings to represent the Palestinians and share in liberating their homeland. To ensure King Hussein's consent, Nasser as the main sponsor of this project accepted Hussein's condition that the proposed organization should not be a front for a Palestinian entity.

Later on in the same year, a group of leading Palestinians from throughout the Middle East and Europe convened a conference in the Arab sector of Jerusalem. The conference established the PLO under the chairmanship of Ahmad Shuqayri, a former lawyer from the Palestinian city of Acre. Shuqayri was imposed on the Palestinians by Egypt to appease King Hussein because of his relatively good standing with Jordan.[3] The conference created

1   Janet and John Wallach, 1990, p.106.
2   Janet and John Wallach, 1990, p.108.
3   Moshe Shemesh, 1988, p.40.

the PNC and drafted two documents, "al-Mithaq al-Watani al-Filastini" and "al-Mithaq al-Qawmi al-Filastini." These documents functioned as the constitution of the PLO and a declaration of independence, known as the "National Covenant." They defined Palestinian political goals and Palestinian rights as envisioned by a new generation of Palestinian nationalists. The covenant stated that after liberating all of historic Palestine, it would be part of a united Arab nation.

Soon after that, the Palestine Liberation Army (PLA) was established as the military arm of the PLO. In choosing representatives of the 319 members of the PNC, Shuqayri appointed 216 members from Jordanian-Palestinians. Over 100 of the PNC members came from the ranks of the Jordanian Government officials, thus the interests of Jordan would not be compromised. The 422 delegates who attended the conference endorsed the PLO constitution and the Palestine National charter that called for the destruction of the Zionist state through armed struggle. And to alleviate the fear of Jordan, the PLO covenant stated that the PLO would not assert any territorial sovereignty over any land of Palestine currently under the control of the Arab states. Only after liberating their homeland, the Palestinians would exercise self-determination. Shortly thereafter the Palestinian Liberation Army (PLA) was established by Egypt.

To insure his control over the organization, President Nasser allowed the PLA to have their military bases under Egyptian oversight in Sinai and Gaza Strip and supplied them with light arms. Egypt's tight control over the PLA was accredited for the absence of serious violent incidents across Gaza-Israel armistice lines between the creation of the PLO in 1964 and the 1967 war. The Egyptian administration in Gaza used hard measures to restrict the freedom of the press and all forms of political expression in the Strip to prevent the frustrated refugees from incursions into Israel. Nasser did not want the Palestinians to carry on raids in Israel, wreck the 1957 armistice agreement, and draw Egypt into another war with Israel. He thought war with Israel was unavoidable, but he did not want others to decide its timing. Unlike Fatah which was established by Palestinian nationalists, the PLO was created and completely controlled by the Arab states establishments. Fatah, which was competing with the PLO over the loyalty of the Palestinians prior to the 1967 war, had been given more freedom to operate against Israel by the Syrians.

The idea of creating an organization to speak for the Palestinians was originally suggested by the US Undersecretary of State George Ball to Nasser, according to Hani al-Hasan, a Fatah central committee member. He recalled that "Shuqayri told [him] that Nasser and the Arabs in cooperation with George Ball helped to create this organization."[1] The farfetched allegation of US support to the creation of the PLO suggests that al-Hasan was spreading an obvious smear campaign against the PLO on behalf of Fatah to disqualify it from representing the Palestinians. Linking the creation of the PLO to the US policy makers damages the credibility of its establishment among the Palestinians who perceive the US too close ally of Israel. Fatah announced its opposition to the PLO from the beginning accusing it of being just an arm of the Arab governments rather than an independent

---

1   Janet Wallach and John Wallach, 1990, p. 110.

organization. Few years after the interests of the two organizations clashed, Fatah would join the PLO and eventually Arafat managed to replace Yahya Hammodi the new chairman of the organization. Arafat dominated the PLO since then through the control over the financial contributions of the Arab governments to the Palestinians. Arafat personally had been in control of the PLO finances which included direct financial aid from oil rich states and 5% of the salaries of tens of thousands of Palestinian workers in the Gulf area. Arafat control of the purse put him at a special advantage above all other Palestinian leaders.

The PLO leaders, however, wasted their energies challenging the governments of their Arab hosts in Jordan and Lebanon and taking sides in intra-Arab conflicts that had nothing to do with Palestine. They posed more threat to their hosts than to Israel, thus losing the needed support and sympathy of most non-Palestinian Jordanian public, the Lebanese and the Gulf population. Their irresponsible behavior reinforced tribalism and sectarianism in the host countries at the expense of the Palestinian cause. By losing the support of the people in the region and severing the traditional Jordanian-Palestinian ties, the PLO became the Palestinians worst enemy.

THE PLO IN JORDAN AND IN LEBANON

When the PLO failed to establish a presence in the occupied West Bank after 1967, and as Israel refined its methods of sealing the border, Jordan which had a large population of Palestinians in its midst could not refuse it a refuge. King Hussein allowed Arafat's Fatah men and members of other PLO umbrella organization to move in the Jordan River valley only with a warning that they would not carry out commando attacks against Israel. Despite the warnings, the Palestinians shelled the kibbutzim and mined border roads inside Israel. In a 1968 incident, a bus load of Israeli children on a school outing hit a mine in the road and two children were killed. The Israeli response was a tank and infantry attack on Fatah military base across the border with Jordan near the town of "Karamah." The Palestinian fighters supported by the Jordanian army artillery put up a stiff resistance in a bloody battle. The Israeli attackers retreated leaving behind four tanks and four armored vehicles. Israel lost 29 soldiers dead, the Palestinians suffered 97 killed and the Jordanians lost 129 dead. The Jordanian military participation made the crucial difference in the outcome of the "Karamah battle."

The number of casualties in Karamah suggests that the Jordanians had been the major participants in the fight, but this battle was perceived in the Arab press as a victory by the Palestinians over Israel, and Arafat took the credit. In many interviews through the years since 1968, Arafat and other members of the PLO continued to talk about the victory in the battle of Karamah. Even in the 2009 Fatah Bethlehem convention, Mahmoud Abbas mentioned the battle of Karamah in his rhetorical speech. Arafat used his verbal skills to spread the word about Karamah and boost the reputation of Fatah. Thousands of young Palestinian recruits flocked to the camps of Fatah and other revolutionary groups that had been banned in Jordan including Marxists, Maoists, socialists, Communists and Ba'athists. Guerrilla raids and Katusha rockets attacks against Israel continued until the

Israelis started responding with heavy military reprisals depriving the Palestinians of their sanctuaries in the Jordan River valley and forcing them to move their bases inland mostly in refugee camps. The Israeli retaliation destroyed the farms along the Jordan River and disrupted the economy of Jordan which had been dependent on agriculture. In the meantime, the Jordanian army had to stay in the front line while thousands of Palestinian irregulars roamed the capital and other towns.

Soon after moving their headquarters to the Jordanian cities, the PLO leaders and fighters disregarded their status as guests of a sovereign state and that they should act as such. They took the advantage of their popularity after the Karamah encounter by creating an outlaw state within a state. Rifle-toting Palestinian militias ignored the Jordanian laws and moved through its towns wearing uniform, manned roadblocks, and allegedly committed murders and extortion. Some guerrilla leaders spoke of transforming north Jordan into an autonomous area controlled by the PLO. Others challenged the government by demanding the removal of some government ministers for their views on the PLO conduct. They led Palestinian refugees in demonstrations and forced King Hussein to rescind his order to enforce an ordinance that forbade people from carrying weapons in the capital. Armed Palestinian guerillas raided hotels in Amman and held foreign guests as hostages when members of armed Palestinians were apprehended for violating the law. The PLO actually posed a greater threat to Jordan than to Israel. By 1970, clashes between the well armed Palestinian guerrilla and the splintered Jordanian army became common place and its society was disintegrated into two tribes, one supported the Palestinian guerrilla and the other supported the King.

When the Popular Front for the Liberation of Palestine, a member organization in the PLO, managed on September 6, 1970, to land and blow up three hijacked airliners in Jordan, King Hussein decided to use his army to reclaim control of his country by force once and for all. On September 17, he launched his forces against the PLO stronghold in the refugee camps and villages. During the ensuing nine days, 3,000 Palestinian fighters and many thousands of civilian refugees were killed, and the Palestinians memorialized it as the "Black September Massacre." This battle had international implications when Syria backed by the Soviet Union intervened in what looked like a bid to help the Palestinians against the government of Jordan. At the height of the crisis, King Hussein sent an urgent appeal for help from Washington when a Syrian armored column crossed the border. Israel, backed by the US, put its air force on alert, mobilized troops at the border with Jordan and declared its intention to prevent the Syrian advance in Jordan. With heavy artillery and air bombardment and without the need for Israel to intervene, the Jordanian military succeeded in driving the Syrians out of Jordan after inflicting heavy losses on their retreating tanks. The Jordanians moved to consolidate their gains against the PLO, launched an attack against their last encampments in the north killing hundreds and capturing thousands of fighters and many of their leaders. After their decisive defeat, the PLO lost access to the large Palestinian population in Jordan. A PLO unit allegedly assassinated Wasfi Tal, who had been the Jordanian prime minister and defense minister during the Black September massacre, while attending a conference in Egypt. Wasfi Tal was the second Jordanian prime minister assassinated while in office. The first was Prime Minister Hazza' Majali who was killed in 1960 by a bomb planted in his Amman office. Both Tal and Majali belonged to prominent Jordanian families known for their strong loyalty to the Hashemite dynasty. The lasting damage done by the PLO behavior in Jordan was one of the regrettable alienation of the non-Palestinian public in their support of the Palestinians. Jordanian society has suffered deep division and mistrust between its Palestinian and the East Jordanian communities. Jordan's 1970 decision not to tolerate any attempt to attack Israel from its side of the Jordan River was perceived by some Palestinians as a betrayal to their cause. But the circumstances suggest Jordan had to re-establish its sovereignty over its territory and borders with Israel.

Following their bloody eviction from Jordan, the PLO reestablished itself in Lebanon which had more than 235,000 Palestinian refugees, and Arafat set up his headquarters in West Beirut. Based on an agreement brokered by Nasser in 1969 to give the PLO control over the refugees in Lebanon, Arafat acted as a head of a mini-state within a state in the refugee camps. He used the $400 million in annual contributions from Saudi Arabia and other Gulf States, to develop institutions in the refugee camps that included labor welfare, some clothing and household goods factories, courts, armed security forces, hospitals and clinics. The PLO had news agency, radio station, and bank and telex services in Beirut. In short, the PLO established a quasi-government over the archipelago of the refugee shantytowns. Many of the refugees became PLO guerrilla recruits moving freely in towns in violation of Lebanon's sovereignty. Lebanon with its mixed Christian–Sunni–Shia–Druze sectarian and ethnic division was helpless to impose restrictions on the PLO guerrilla activity in the country and the excursions through its open borders with Israel. Then the PLO participated in the Lebanese bloody civil war supporting the Muslim faction against the Christians, thus alienating a large segment of the Lebanese population against the Palestinians and prolonging the civil war which claimed the lives of tens of thousands from 1975 to 1990. With the support of the PLO, Muslim Sunni, Shiite and Druze battled the Christians for controlling the country. The Syrians intervened on behalf of the Christians and the country was mutilated.

Israel invaded Lebanon in June of 1982 in response to members of Abu Nidal faction of the PLO attempt to assassin Shlomo Argov, the Israeli Ambassador to Britain. After a week of fighting, West Beirut was besieged by the Israelis and the PLO fighters were rendered helpless. An agreement was negotiated with the help of the United States where the 14,000 Palestinian fighters and their leaders were disarmed and withdrawn to Syria then exiled to Tunis. After removing the PLO from Lebanon, Israel withdrew from Beirut and kept under its control a security belt two miles deep in Lebanon across its border. The delicate Lebanese political system was de-stabilized and its independence was compromised when the PLO moved to Lebanon. Lebanese Christian hatred for the PLO was so deep that Christian villagers in the south tolerated and even supported the Israeli presence in their lands. A Christian militia army financed, armed and trained by Israel was created to support the Israelis in the security zone of South Lebanon. Palestinian refugees in Lebanon have become even more unwelcome group today. They had to endure massacres of Sabra,

Shatila, Tel al-Za'atar and Dbayyeh at the hands of bitter Lebanese allied with Israel in 1982. The Lebanese Phalangist para-military, supported by the Israeli troops, massacred almost 2,000 Palestinian refugee civilians during the 1982 Israeli invasion of Lebanon. The February 8, 1983, Israeli **Kahan Commission** determined that the massacre was carried out by the Phalangist unit, acting on its own but the last page of the official Israeli report held Ariel Sharon "personally responsible" for the massacre.

Despite the generous Kuwaiti contributions to the PLO, Arafat refused to join the anti-Iraqi coalition of the Arab states and denounce the Iraqi invasion of Kuwait in 1990. He traveled to Baghdad to embrace Saddam Hussein after the invasion perhaps hoping that Saddam might help in liberating Palestine. His stance was construed by the coalition and the people in the Gulf as approval of Iraq's naked aggression against Kuwait and Saudi Arabia, thus eroding much of the goodwill the Palestinian community in the Gulf States had accumulated through the years. Until 1990, the Gulf States had been providing generous financial contributions in support of the PLO military, social and administration programs. Kuwait collected 5% of its Palestinian employees' income as a "liberation tax" that was given annually to Palestine National Fund which had been controlled by the PLO. After Kuwait was liberated from the Iraqi invaders, the financial contributions to the PLO were cut off. The PLO faced a great deal of hostility from the governments and the general population of the Gulf region, and most expatriate Palestinian workers lost their jobs and had to leave to Jordan.

HAMAS

The Islamic Resistance Movement or "Harakat al-Muqawama al-Islmiya" in Arabic referred to as "Hamas" drew its ideology from the Egyptian-based Muslim Brothers movement (MB). Palestinian branches of the MB were established in Jerusalem and other Palestinian towns during the British Mandate. By 1947 there were more than thirty MB branches with few registered members. Ahmed Yasin, a charismatic Islamic preacher and a leader in the Palestinian wing of the MB organization, transformed Hamas from a religious group into a militant social and political nationalist organization in 1987 at the beginning of the First Intifada. Hamas become the political alternative to the PLO during the First Intifada. Israel tolerated the emergence of Hamas in Gaza in the late 1960s as a spiritual alternative to Fatah and the PLO. Israel authorized Hamas to build mosques, schools, clinics and infirmaries. Just like America that supported Bin Laden and Al-Qaeda in Afghanistan in the war against the Soviet Union, the Israelis tolerated but did not support the establishment of Hamas which later on became irredeemably hostile to Israel, demanding all Palestine for the Palestinians.[1] Yasin became Hamas' spiritual leader until he was killed by an Israeli guided bomb in 2004, and his successor and cofounder of Hamas, Abdul-Aziz al-Rantissi was killed four weeks later.

According to Hamas's narrative, its evolution entailed more than one stage. The start was the establishment of MB cells in Gaza with a focus on preaching and Islamic religion

---

1 Robert Fisk, 2005.

education. The second stage was the penetration of the different professional organizations and institutions building mostly in Gaza and to a lesser degree in the West Bank. The establishment of the Islamic University and centers for social services in Gaza was the most visible achievement of this stage. The third stage was the involvement in politics and the preparation for armed struggle. When the First Intifada began, thousands of Palestinians under occupation became ardent recruits of Hamas. The final stage was renaming the organization as "Hamas" and declaring Jihad (holy war) against occupation.

Unlike the PLO and Fatah, Hamas preserved intact its political charter that calls for the establishment of an Islamic state in all of historical Palestine. It sees the Palestinian problem rooted in the ideology of Zionism. Their movement believes that "the land of Palestine [including pre-1967 Israel] has been Islamic Waqf,..., and no one can renounce it or part of it,... and no Arab king or President nor all of them in the aggregate of all organizations be they Palestinians or Arab, because Palestine is an Islamic Waqf throughout all generations and to the day of Resurrection."[1] Its leaders argue that the only solution to the Palestinian problem is a holy war (jihad) and not initiatives, proposals and international conferences that are nothing but waste of time and exercise in futility. Hamas has been labeled a terrorist organization because its members had carried out many suicide bombings against Israel in the last decades of the 20th century, killing and injuring hundreds of civilians. And its fighters have been frequently firing homemade crude rockets from Gaza into southern Israel inviting Israeli retaliation.

The Islamic movement popularity was a natural response to the defeat of the secular Arab regimes in the 1967 war and the exile of the secular PLO leadership to Tunis after the 1982 Israeli invasion of Lebanon. Hamas civilian organizations filled the vacuum in social services that were neglected by the PA which was accused by many observers of lawlessness and corruption. Even Arafat himself, when he was holed up in his Ramallah compound, relied on Hamas to provide education and medical care to the Palestinians in the West Bank and Gaza. Hamas leaders articulated a Palestinian national agenda with Islamic context and social community activism. They spread their messages from the pulpits of the mosques and through their writings. Their declared policy is a commitment to liberate historic Palestine through armed struggle and maintaining Islamic social institutions that deliver education, health and welfare services. When the PLO signed the 1993 Oslo agreement and established the Palestinian Authority, Hamas which was not a member in the PLO did not endorse the agreement, but it had to take more flexible strategy toward a possible settlement with Israel that takes into consideration the existing realities. Its short term objective is to establish a Palestinian state in the territory occupied in1967 without giving up the right to liberate the whole of historical Palestine in the long run.

Hamas won the 2006 Palestinian Legislative Council elections by a landslide against Fatah movement that had been controlling the PA institutions including the government, the security force and the presidency. The corruption of Fatah leadership and its government dismal failure to end occupation led to the massive repudiation of its policies. Hamas

---

1 Article 11, the Charter of Allah: The Platform of Hamas.

captured 74 out of 132 seats. Reaction to Hamas victory was felt in the occupied lands, in Israel and internationally, but the big impact was on the Palestinians' lives. Israel declared a government headed by Hamas unacceptable because it would undermine its security. Fatah declined the offer to be part of Hamas government. Israel and the international community decided to boycott financially and diplomatically any government led by Hamas thus punishing the Palestinians for rejecting Fatah and electing Hamas. And the governments of Egypt and Jordan that had signed peace treaties with Israel abhorred the rise of the Islamists power on their borders. Hamas has been at odds with Fatah leadership and its government since the elections. See Chapter 8 for more on Hamas and Fatah.

THE FIRST INTIFADA AND THE PLO

A 1987 fatal traffic accident in Gaza triggered a Palestinian uprising that has been called "the First Intifada." An Israeli truck hit a car carrying laborers from the Gaza Strip near the Jebalya refugee camp killing four Palestinian passengers. Rumors among the Palestinians had it that the victims of the accident had been killed in cold blood to avenge the death of an Israeli in Gaza few days earlier. Arab newspapers and leaflets denouncing the murder of the four men were circulated among the Palestinians in Gaza and the West Bank. The funeral of the victims turned into a riot and an assault with stones and bricks on the Israeli army outposts and border police in the refugee camp. Riots continued to flare up again in the refugee camp and Gaza City and spread to the southern end of the Strip, the West Bank and even East Jerusalem.

The groundwork to the *Intifada* actually started in Gaza under the inside leadership of the Islamists before the 1987 traffic accident. Waving the Palestinian flag, demonstrations, strikes and throwing stones and firebombs at IDF symbols were common place in Gaza and the West Bank months before the *Intifada*. Thousands of Palestinians protested the deportation of the Islamic "Jihad" faction leader, Abdul-Aziz Odeh, weeks before the outbreak of the *Intifada*. On the eve of the uprising, the militant "Jihad" and "Hamas" had already attracted young Palestinians dedicated to resisting occupation. In the West Bank, the unarmed youth, *Shabiba*, of Balata refugee camp had declared a revolt before December 1987. The *Intifada* caught the PLO establishment in Tunis by surprise and it had to jump on the bandwagon of the uprising once it had been in progress.

Besides refocusing the attention of the world on the plight of the Palestinians, the *Intifada* had many repercussions locally, in the relationship with Jordan and in Israel. The uprising of 1987 highlighted the suffering of the Palestinians under the occupation and their willingness even to die for their cause. It was estimated that more than 500 Palestinians died and 8,500 wounded only in the first two years of the *Intifada*.[1] An important consequence of the uprising was the emergence of indigenous leadership in the occupied territory that would overshadow the exiled PLO in leading the Palestinians against the occupation. Recognizing the failure of the Arab regimes and the PLO establishment to make any progress in liberating the occupied lands and intimidated by the Israeli brutal repri-

---

1 Ze'ev Schiff and Ehud Ya'ari, 1989, p. 31.

sals, local Palestinian leaders toyed with different ideas to change the status quo, some based on militant Islamic ideology and others on benign pragmatism. The Palestinians supported the new leaders and organizations. Unlike the PLO leaders who had been detached from the daily struggle of their constituents, the new leaders led the protest against the occupation and many were ex-prisoners in the Israeli security detention centers. Most of the Palestinians thought the PLO was indifferent to their suffering or ineffectual in dealing with the Israelis. Many perceived the PLO chief, Arafat and his associates as self-important frauds chauffeured in their limousines in Tunis or flying in private jets around the world, away from the realities of the Israeli occupation.

A group of prominent inside Palestinian intellectuals and politicians known for their affiliation with the PLO considered a novel and peaceful approach for solving the Palestinian problem in the 1980s. Hanan Ashrawi, Feisal Husseini, Sari Nuseiba and Rashid Shehadeh accepted the "Greater Israel" project over historical Palestine, thus approving annexing the West Bank and Gaza to Israel and creating a de facto bi-national state in the future.[1] Israel's right wing and religious parties rejected the proposal because they perceived it as a scheme to undermine the Jewish character of the state. The plan would indeed have changed Israel's demography in the future so that Jews would no longer be in the majority, thus bringing an end to it as a democratic Jewish state. Since the inception of Zionism, all its leaders, religious and secular, have been eager to create a "Jewish State" based on a "Jewish majority" by any and all means.

Since occupying the West Bank and Gaza, Israel's policies and actions suggest that it was not in hurry to reach a political solution. As early as 1971, Dayan stated that Israel should "plan and implement whatever can be done without worrying about the day of peace...in the meantime [the government] must create facts."[2] Yigal Allon, the minister of Labor in 1961–1968, and Deputy Prime Minister and Foreign Minister in the 1970s, provided a plan to establish settlements along the Jordan River and around the Arab population centers in the West Bank without forcibly creating a Jewish presence inside these centers.

After the 1967 war and until 1988, Jordan and Israel had a policy of cooperating openly in the administration of the West Bank, known as the "open bridges" policy. While the IDF command was in full control over security, the borders, airspace and water resources, Jordan had been paying the salaries of all the civil servants in the West Bank including public schools teachers, public health workers, the policemen, the post-office employees and civil and Islamic courts personnel. School children were taught the Jordanian curriculum, slightly modified by Israel, and the Jordanian *dinar* and the Israeli *shekel* were legally used simultaneously in business transactions.

In the spirit of the "open bridges" policy, King Hussein and Foreign Minister Shimon Peres met in 1987 in London and reached a preliminary agreement on a format to negotiate a settlement to the Palestinian issue based on Security Council Resolutions 242 and 338.[3] The settlement would be negotiated in Israeli–Jordanian bilateral committees where Pal-

---

1 Howard Sachar, 1996, p.962.
2 From Dayan's speech to the army staff college as reported by *Haaretz,* August 21, 1971.
3 Howard Sachar, 1996, p.958.

estinians from the occupied land would be included in the Jordanian delegates. The final agreement would lead to peace and security and respect for the legitimate rights of the Palestinians. Israeli Prime Minister Yitzhak Shamir over ruled his foreign minister. He rejected the plan because, according to him, it would put pressure on Israel by the Security Council to surrender the "Land of Israel" in reference to the West Bank.

In 1988 and during the First Intifada against the repressive occupation, three important events took place, Arafat denounced terrorism, King Hussein declared Jordan's disengagement from the occupied West Bank and the PLO accepted the two-state solution. The King's decision was taken when he realized Israel would not strike an acceptable peace accord with him. And in the same year the Palestine National Council declared independent Palestinian state in the West Bank and Gaza with no reference to the 1948 UN General Assembly Resolutions including Resolution 194 regarding the refugees' rights of return. This entailed terminating the legal and administrative links with the West Bank and ending the monthly pay checks for West Bank employees.

King Hussein admitted that "it was the *Intifada* that caused our decision on disengagement from the West Bank."[1] There were other reasons for Hussein's decision. In his secret talks with Shimon Peres and Yitzhak Rabin, the only substantive offer the Israelis made was "power sharing" that would have allowed Israel and Jordan to have "a joint administration of the West Bank and the Jordanian flag would be raised over the Muslim holy places in Jerusalem."[2] He rejected the offer, and he also recognized he could not compete with the new leadership in the occupied lands or the PLO for the loyalty of the Palestinians, some of whom had their own grievances against his rule. Despite the fact that Jordan is the only Arab country that provides the Palestinians access to the world and it is the only country that allows the Palestinians to live a normal life without restrictions, many Palestinians resent Jordan for its role in the 1970 civil war. They blame Jordan rather than the PLO for the 1970 Black September massacre. Others believe there is official discrimination against the Jordanian citizens of Palestinian descendents.

Another consequence of the First Intifada has been the rise of the popularity of the Islamic Resistance Movement (*Hamas*). The movement was committed to the resistance of the Israeli occupation of Palestinian lands. It joined the protesters against the occupation and played a big role in the *Intifada*. The harsh Israeli response to the uprising had its effects on the form of *Hamas* resistance. It was transformed from peaceful civil disobedience to burning tires in the streets and throwing stones to the use of fire arms then by 1994 some of its members carried out suicide-bomb missions inside Israel proper killing Israeli civilians.

The forces that participated in the First Intifada and the weapons used were mostly non-conventional. Feeling powerless against the hardships of Israeli's occupation and abandoned by their exiled political leaders and the Arab states, young Palestinians started protesting by demonstrations and engaging the IDF and the settlers with stones. The re-

---

1 Interview with King Hussein by Avi Shlaim on December 3, 1996.
2 Howard Sachar, 2007

pressive measures used by the Israelis to subdue the protestors that were captured on films inspired more youth to join the protest and led to the escalation of disobedience throughout the territories. Many unarmed Palestinian youth; some had not reached their teen-age, were killed or injured by the IDF in the confrontations.[1] Despite their rage against the occupation and the harsh reaction by the Israelis to the riots, the Palestinians did not resort to acts of terrorism inside Israel proper in the uprising. The Israelis, on the other hand, failed to justify killing and injuring unarmed civilians, mostly children, protesting occupation. The success of the *Intifada* was not measured by the number of Israeli targets that had been destroyed, but rather by the endurance of the Palestinians to bear casualties and suffering. While the evidence suggests that the uprising was a genuine popular revolt against the occupation and its effects, Israel's minister of defense, Yitzhak Rabin, accused Syria and Iran and Prime Minister Yitzhak Shamir blamed the PLO of being behind it. [2] The uprising created widespread international criticism of the harsh Israeli response and produced local political leadership in the occupied territory speaking on behalf of the Palestinians and demanding Israeli withdrawal from the West Bank and Gaza. Many in the international community recognized the human right of the Palestinians to be free from suffering under the Israeli occupation and the Israelis recognized that suppressing the uprising by force alone was unsustainable in the new international environment.

The Palestinians felt abandoned by the PLO, the Arab states and the international community. The PLO standing in the occupied land had been diminished since it had done nothing following its ejection from Lebanon. The November 1987 Arab summit that was held in Amman focused mainly on the Iraq-Iran war and ignored the Palestinian case. The Soviet Union that had been pro-Arab during the Cold War was preoccupied with re-forming itself under Mikhail Gorbachev. It reversed its previous policy of supporting the Palestinians and allowed thousands of Jews to immigrate to Israel who became potential settlers of the occupied lands and strong supporters of the right wing extremist parties. Jewish settlers in the West Bank alone increased from 64,000 in 1988 to 130,000 in the mid 1990s. Some mainstream Israeli leaders openly advocated the transfer of Palestinians to Jordan. These included Deputy Defense Minister Michael Dekel, Cabinet minister Zippori and Yosif Shapiro from the National Religious Party.[3]

THE OSLO AGREEMENTS

After the 1991 Gulf war victory and liberating Kuwait, US Secretary of State, James Baker decided to exploit the newly established good relations with the governments in the region by trying to get the Arab to negotiate their historic disputes with Israel. Jordan, Syria and Lebanon agreed to participate, but Israel's Prime Minister Yitzhak Shamir insisted that the meetings should be bilateral between Israel and each separate Arab delegation, the Palestinian representatives must not be residents of East Jerusalem and they

---

1 Mazin Qumsiyeh, 2004.
2 Ze'ev Schiff and Ehud Ya'ari, 1989, p. 25.
3 Don Peretz, 1990, p.31.

should be part of the Jordanian delegation. After bitter disputes over almost every point, the opening meeting that included delegations from Jordan, Syria, Lebanon and the West Bank was held in Madrid in the presence of US President George Bush Senior and the Soviet Union President Mikhail Gorbachev. Two parallel negotiating tracks, bilateral and multilateral tracks, were established in Madrid. There were four separate sets of bilateral negotiations between Israel and each of Syria, Lebanon, Jordan and the Palestinian delega-tion. The first bilateral meetings took place in Madrid, on November 3, 1991 right after the formal conference ended.

While Madrid Conference focused on many important regional issues, this study is concerned only with the bilateral Palestinian–Israeli talks. President Bush Senior ex-pressed hope that the end result of the negotiations would recognize the security of Israel and the right of the Palestinians to have control over their future. The venue of the real bilateral talks was shifted to Washington D.C. after the first meeting. The Washington negotiations on the Palestinian issue were held between non-PLO Palestinian delegation from the West Bank headed by Dr. Haider Abdul-Shafi and delegation from Israel headed by Eli Rubinstein. No significant progress was made in eleven meetings from Dec. 1991 through August 1993 even after the Likud coalition government lost to Labor ending its monopoly of ruling Israel since 1977.

An internal unexpected Israeli political crisis had taken place in 1992 when Prime Minister Yitzhak Shamir's government lost the support of the extreme right *Techiya* party faction in his government in protest against the negotiations on a possible limited Pal-estinian autonomy and as a result, a date for the Knesset election was set in June 1992. Labor won on a platform of negotiating an agreement with the Palestinians, and its leader Yitzhak Rabin assumed the office as prime minister. The United States welcomed the change because it had its differences with Shamir on the subject of the settlements in the West Bank. Shamir considered the settlements as a right exercised by the Jews in the land of Eretz Yisrael (all Palestine) but the US administration of President Bush Senior be-lieved the settlements were obstacles to peace. President Bush was the first to congratu-late Rabin for winning the election and announced his willingness to approve billions of dollars in loan guarantees to Israel.

The ascendance of Labor to power did not mean yielding to the demands of the Pal-estinian negotiating team in Washington to have Israel commit itself to complete with-drawal from the West Bank and East Jerusalem. Neither Likud nor Labor would com-promise on having Jerusalem united under Israeli rule, and none would dismantle all the settlements as the Palestinians demanded or react permissively to Arab violence. Rabin's government, however, was committed to have peace with the Palestinians but on its own terms that were not acceptable by Abdul-Shafi negotiators in Washington. The Pales-tinian negotiators even had to boycott the Washington talks when Rabin deported 415

Islamic activists to Lebanon in December 1992. They returned to the talks in April 1993 when the Israelis had been negotiating secretly with the PLO in Oslo.

Terje Rod Larsen, the director of the Institute for Applied Science (FAFO) in Oslo which specializes in solving international disputes told Yossi Beilin, the deputy to Foreign Minister Shimon Peres, that the PLO leadership in Tunis had asked him to explore the possibility of mediating between them and Israel.[1] The foreign ministry in Rabin's government had an agenda to get the best outcome from the peace talks by negotiating with another Palestinian team from the ranks of the PLO who might be less intransigent in opposing the Israeli demands.[2] With the talks in Washington reaching dead end, Beilin and Peres decided to accept the Norwegians, who had no strategic interests in the region, as facilitators rather than mediators for unofficial secret talks with the PLO.[3] They wanted to gauge and probe the PLO view and exploit its weakness, and the PLO leaders were eager to have more active role in the Israeli–Palestinian negotiations. The Israeli director of military intelligence suggested in 1992 that "Arafat's dire situation, and possible imminent collapse made him the most convenient interlocutor for Israel."[4] The PLO were trying to emulate their past experience in 1988 when the Swedish Foreign Minister, Anderson mediated a dialogue between Yasser Arafat and American Jewish peace activists in Stockholm where Arafat declared on behalf of the Palestine National Council his support for two-state solution.

The 1993 secret negotiations with the PLO were disguised by the Israelis as academic conference within the FAFO institute between Israeli private citizens and the PLO to circumvent the Israeli ban on contacts with the PLO.[5] Academic talks do not commit the government of Israel to comply with their recommendations, but they allowed it to explore common grounds and keep their options open to possible alternative to the ongoing Washington negotiations. The first meeting was held on January 20, 1993 between Professors Yair Hirschfeld and Ron Pundak on behalf of Israel and Abu Al'a Qurai, Maher al-Kurd and Hasan Asfoor from the PLO in Tunis. Negotiations continued with Larsen periodically acting as a mediator when there were disagreements, members of the Palestinian delegates call the PLO leadership in Tunis and the Israeli team calling Beilin and Peres in Jerusalem for consultation. The purpose of the talks in Oslo as well as in Washington had been to negotiate a declaration of principles on empowering the Palestinians in the West Bank and Gaza. In late February, 1993, Shimon Peres was able to bring Rabin on board and sanction the Oslo backchannel by convincing him that direct negotiations with the exiled PLO leadership would serve the interests of Israel.[6] He argued that Arafat would continue to hamper the progress of the peace negotiations "as long as he remained [an outsider] in Tunis." He suggested that the incentives of allowing Arafat to return to Gaza from his

1 Howard Sachar, 1996, p.991.
2 Howard Sachar, 1996, p.991.
3 David Makovsky, 1996, p. 15.
4 Avi Shlaim, 2000.
5 David Makovsky, 1996, p. 19.
6 Andrew Buchanan, 2000.

exile to speak for the Palestinians would induce him to speed up the conclusion of the negotiations (read, accept Israeli terms).[1]

Since the Palestinian's violence and the security of Israel were high on Rabin's agenda, he accepted Peres argument in the belief that only Arafat had the power to control the Palestinian uprising and the militant Islamists and implement peace agreements favored by Israel. It was the rise of the popularity of Hamas and the Islamic Jihad among the Palestinians that encouraged the Israelis to rescue Arafat from obscurity. Rabin took over the rein of government in the middle of the first Palestinian uprising. Members from Hamas were accused of inciting violence and allegedly killing Jewish settlers and policemen to discourage the Israelis from settling in their lands. In response, Rabin ordered hundreds of Hamas activists to be rounded and dumped in the buffer zone between Israel and Lebanon where they decided to remain for many months living in tents under severe weather conditions to evoke international sympathy and embarrass the Israeli government and the Arab negotiators.

Rabin allowed the talks in Washington to continue openly and under the cover of secrecy authorized the back channel talks in Oslo. Senior government Israeli officials joined the Oslo negotiators, the Americans were well informed on the progress in Oslo, but the Palestinian negotiators in Washington had no knowledge or coordination with those in Oslo. The Americans had a big role in mediating between the PLO and the Israelis in Oslo. Daniel Kurtzer from the US Department of State was conducting a form of shuttle diplomacy between Tunis and Jerusalem to narrow differences between the two parties until a final draft of the DOP was reached in Oslo. After being alerted to the Oslo channel by Peres, Egypt's President Mubarak encouraged Arafat to move forthrightly toward an accommodation with the Israelis.

Unlike members of the delegates to the Oslo talks who had not been traumatized by the Israelis, most members of the Washington team had been jailed or deported by Israel in the past. The negotiators in Washington under the leadership of Haidar Abdul-Shafi insisted on including East Jerusalem as part of the interim agreement and dismantling all settlements; they asked for a commitment by Israel to withdraw from all the territory occupied in the 1967 war, and "continued to bring the subject of human rights violation."[2] The Oslo team, on the other hand, was more receptive to the Israeli demands and conditions of postponing the talk on East Jerusalem and the settlements, prolonging the process and providing ambiguous promises. To insure that Israel would accept only the Oslo negotiations, Arafat asked the Washington team to stand firm in demanding the inclusion of Jerusalem in the interim agreement while instructing the Oslo negotiators to accept Israel's demand to exclude it. It should be noted that none of Arafat negotiators in Oslo was an international lawyer while the Israeli negotiators who framed the agreement included experts on international law.

---

1 Shimon Peres, 1995.
2 Andrew Buchanan, 2000.

Once the Oslo process began, the Washington talks faded away and Abdul-Shafi and his team were surprised by the loss of all their months of negotiations as the PLO of Tunisia signed on a different and fatally flawed Oslo agreement on behalf of the Palestinians who had been living under occupation. Abdul-Shafi was quoted saying that he had heard of the Oslo negotiations for the first time while listening to the news on a hotel radio and preparing for his next meeting with the Israelis. Israel chose to negotiate with the exiled leaders to exploit their weak position in the Arab world due to Yasser Arafat support of Saddam Hussein in the invasion of Kuwait and his weak position in Palestine after the immergence of new Palestinian leaders, living and suffering under the occupation. The new Palestinian leadership included mostly academics, civil society activists and the Islamists. What frightened Israel most was the growing strength of the religious Palestinian groups, "Hamas" and "Islamic Jihad" that had been challenging the PLO leadership living in Tunis. If it was not for the Islamic strength in Palestine, "the Israelis would have had little interest in recognizing the PLO."[1]

The recognition given by Israel to Arafat and his team, rather than the new Palestinian leadership, was used as the price to "extract concessions on key issues."[2] To get the best deal, the Israelis chose to negotiate with the PLO leaders, who were eager to return to Palestine and establish themselves in what the Israelis call the "disputed territory," rather than with the inside Palestinians who insisted on a commitment to unconditional end of occupation and "immediate and substantive withdrawal of the Israeli army from the West Bank."[3] Despite their dissatisfaction with the PLO negotiations, the inside Palestinian negotiators had to be loyal to the PLO, the only Palestinian organization that had been recognized by the sponsors of the peace talk, in order to gain legitimacy.

The DOP as well as the letters of recognition and the four annexes were clear in specifying the obligations of the Palestinians, but they were vague regarding their rights. This gave Israel, the stronger party, the power to interpret them. The PLO leaders recognized Israel without addressing Israel's status in the West Bank as an occupier, thus treating the West Bank and Gaza only as a disputed land with shared sovereignty. In return, Israel only concession was recognizing the PLO as the legitimate representative of the Palestinian people. Israel accepted the possibility of an independent Palestine state on unspecified parts and borders of the West Bank and Gaza Strip after an interim period of five years of restricted self-rule under the sovereignty of Israel and stages of negotiations and confidence building measures. By agreeing to the Oslo process under the patronage and the backing of the United States, Arafat and his advisors practically abandoned the UN resolutions that had been issued since 1948. Arafat signed five different agreements between 1993 and 1997 that constitute the legal framework of what has been called "Oslo Agreements."

The DOP or "Oslo I" document that was signed by the prime minister of Israel Yitzhak Rabin and the PLO chief Yasser Arafat in a Washington ceremony hosted by US President

---

1 Robert Fisk, 2005, p.390.
2 Mazin Qumsiyeh, 2004.
3 Nicholas Guyatt, 1998.

Bill Clinton was a promise to reach an agreement, leaving the details to be negotiated between the parties. September 13, 1993 was hailed throughout the world as a breakthrough in the quest for a durable solution to the Palestinian conflict and Arafat proudly called it 'the peace of the brave'. Many reports confirmed that Arafat signed the DOP without even reading it. An article in New York Yorker on October 14, 1996 quoted an Israeli participant in the negotiation that "Arafat had not read the agreement. He'd read the headings." Israel took the credit for agreeing to have peace and at the same time continued the occupation with the consent of the PLO on behalf of the Palestinians.[1] In his speech on the White House lawn, Rabin said in praising the Oslo Agreement: "We [Israelis and Palestinians] are destined to live together on the same soil on the same land."

The DOP agreement states that permanent status issues, such as Jerusalem, refugees, settlements, security arrangements and borders are to be excluded from the interim arrangements and that the outcome of the permanent status talks should not be prejudged or preempted by the interim arrangements. Until the permanent agreement is reached, the Israeli government retains sole responsibility for foreign affairs, defense and borders, and most important, the agreement does not restrain Israeli settlement activities. The Israeli leaders insisted in speeches, even while signing the DOP agreement, that Jerusalem remains the undivided and eternal capital of the Jewish people. Letters were exchanged and more interim agreements were concluded between Israeli leaders and Yasser Arafat after the signing of the DOP.

On September 9, 1993, Yasser Arafat signed a letter addressed to Yitzhak Rabin accepting UN Security Council resolutions 242 and 338 and recognizing the right of Israel to exist in peace and security. It promised to assume responsibility over all PLO elements and personnel in order to assure their compliance with Oslo agreements, prevent violations and discipline violators and declared inoperative all the articles in the Palestinian Covenant which denied Israel's right to exist. Rabin gave a letter in exchange to Arafat, also dated September 9, stating that Israel had decided to recognize the PLO as the representative of the Palestinian people and commence negotiations with the PLO within the Middle East peace process. Arafat letter to Rabin on behalf of the Palestinians was the recognition of Israel's legitimacy, something Israel had been seeking for half a century. Rabin recognition of the PLO was conditional upon the commitments made by Arafat letter, but Arafat's letter did not have any reference to the refugees' right of return or the Palestinians right of self determination. The agreement did not refer to Israel as an occupier nor asked for the end of occupation, removal of settlements or even freezing settlement activities, the return of East Jerusalem, and the Palestinian refugees' right of return. It only allowed the PLO under Yasser Arafat to return with their fighters to relieve the Israelis from managing and policing the Palestinians.

On May 4, 1994, the Gaza-Jericho aspect of the DOP was negotiated and concluded in an agreement signed in Cairo between Israel and the PLO as the first step in the implementation of the DOP. It included granting self-rule in Gaza Strip cities and Jericho City

---

1 Edward Said, 2000.

and the redeployment of the Israeli forces outside populated area of Gaza and Jericho. Immediately following the signing of the Gaza-Jericho agreement, the Palestinian Authority was created and Arafat returned with his lieutenants to Gaza in June. The responsibilities of education, health, social welfare, security and tourism in the West Bank were transferred to the self rule PA in 1995. An agreement regarding election of a Palestinian Council and its powers would be negotiated later on. The self rule authority would have a strong police force in order to guarantee public order, internal security and enforce compliance with Oslo.

One day before Arafat signed the letter recognizing the right of Israel to exist in peace and security, Yossi Beilin stated that "it should be clear that if the Palestinian police could not prevent terrorism against Israel and arrest those who attack the settlers in Gaza, Jericho and the territories, then the IDF will return and take over the responsibility of security."[1] Annexes were issued regarding economic cooperation between Israel and Palestinians. Negotiations between Israel and the Palestinians on the permanent status would commence as soon as possible but not later than the beginning of the third year of the interim period (May 1996). The permanent status would take effect by May 1999, five years after the implementation of the Gaza-Jericho agreement.

Another Interim Agreement on the West Bank and the Gaza Strip, called "Oslo II" or "Taba," was signed on September 24, 1995 in Taba, Egypt, and countersigned four days later in Washington. It calls for further Israeli troop redeployments beyond the Gaza and Jericho areas. Israel was first scheduled to redeploy from the major Palestinian population centers in the West Bank (the "second redeployment") and later on from all rural areas (the "third redeployment") by August 1997, with the exception of the network of Jewish-only settlements and the Israeli military installation and Israeli-designated military areas. The agreement divided the West Bank and Gaza into three areas, each with distinctive borders and rules for administration and security controls.

Under Oslo II, the West Bank was divided into three zones, A, B, C. Zone A which included the large population centers was to come under exclusive Palestinian control except for security, water, exits and entrances. Zone B was to be under Israeli military occupation and Palestinian Authority civil administration, with security, water, building permits, exits and entrances controlled by Israel. Zone C which constitutes 60% of the West Bank was to stay completely under military occupation and administration. Under the Accords only Palestinians who carry Israeli permits can reside anywhere in any of the three zones of the West Bank and Gaza. Many of the most important provisions including the withdrawal from the West Bank cities and areas A and B were delayed for security reasons. By August 1997, when Israel was supposed to have withdrawn from areas A and B except for the settlements as required in Oslo II, only 3% of area A and B was under the Palestinian control.

Hebron, a city of one hundred thousand Palestinians and a few hundred Jewish settlers was a special case. Rabin and Arafat signed a partition map for the city in September

---

1 Ha'olim Huzi, September 8, 1993.

1995, but neither Rabin nor his successors Peres or Netanyahu ordered redeployment. Netanyahu was able to renegotiate the partition plan in 1997. On January 15, 1997 the Hebron negotiations were completed and a Protocol concerning Redeployment in Hebron was signed by Israel and the Palestinians, specifying arrangements for Israeli troop withdrawals from most of Hebron and the partitioning of the city and the holy sites between Jews and Palestinians. The final agreement gave the settlers full control over one quarter of the commercial center of the city. US Secretary of State Warren Christopher witnessed the signing of the Hebron Protocol by Israeli Prime Minister Netanyahu and Yasser Arafat. Following the signing of the Hebron Protocol the two sides also signed, on January 21, 1997, an Agreement on having a Temporary International Presence in the city of Hebron (TIPH) from Norway, Italy, Denmark Sweden, Switzerland and Turkey. The task of the TIPH was to monitor and report the activities of the Israelis and the Palestinians in Hebron to prevent acts of violence similar to the 1994 Israeli terrorist attack that killed 29 Palestinian worshipers.

US President Bill Clinton held a Middle East summit conference at the Wye River Plantation, in Maryland during mid-October 1998 to clarify the responsibilities of the parties in implementing the interim Oslo II agreement. The Israeli delegation was headed by Prime Minister Benjamin Netanyahu, and Yasser Arafat headed the Palestinian group. As a result of the negotiations, the Wye River Memorandum that increased the area under the PA control to 18.2% was signed by Prime Minister Netanyahu and Yasser Arafat on October 23, 1998 in a ceremony which was also attended by the ailing King Hussein of Jordan. Under the memorandum, Security, water, exits and entrances of the areas under the PA control remained an Israeli responsibility. It required the need for Palestinian police to respect human rights norms but failed to address Israeli human rights obligations altogether. The Wye Memorandum invited the US Central Intelligence Agency to act as a monitor and arbiter on security issues between Israeli and Palestinian interpretations of compliance.

On September 4, 1999, the Sharm el-Sheikh Memorandum was signed in Egypt by Israel's Prime Minister Ehud Barak and Yasser Arafat in a ceremony attended by Egypt's President Hosni Mubarak, Jordan's King Abdullah and US Secretary of State Madeleine Albright. The memorandum restated the commitments of both sides to implement all the agreements reached since the signing of the DOP, set a new date of March 13, 2000 for a "framework" on the eventual final status agreement and the date of September 13, 2000 for the completion of the final status talks. It reiterated the obligations of both parties to put the timetable of Wye River back on track.

Seven years after the signing of the DOP and many other agreements in different locations, President Clinton called for Camp David meeting of 2000 with the purpose of ending the Palestinian–Israeli conflict once and for all. Arafat was offered an agreement to sign that would have consolidated apartheid and legitimized annexation of considerable areas of the occupied territory including Jerusalem to Israel. The agreement would have ended all future claims for Palestinian refugees' lands and property inside Israel proper and nullified fourth Geneva Convention and other UN resolutions relevant to the Palestinian refugees.

Arafat knew for sure that his acceptance signature on the offer would be his death sentence. But he also knew that Oslo agreements that he enthusiastically signed and promoted as the road to peace limited his power to extract any concessions from Israel that may satisfy the Palestinians. He and the whole Palestinian cause were captive of his own Oslo agreements. He rejected the Camp David offer and could not come up with a counter offer because the gap between the US–Israeli offer and the minimum acceptable final solution by the Palestinians was too wide to bridge.

The media claimed that Arafat turned down 95% of the West Bank and Gaza and part of Jerusalem city. But the offer made by Barak gives the Palestinians immediately Gaza and no more than 76% of the West Bank divided into three or two cantons, according to the Israeli interpretation, separated by Israeli territory. Israel does not consider the 5.4% of the West Bank that it annexed to Jerusalem municipality as part of the West Bank any more and Barak would not give up the settlements and East Jerusalem. The figure that the media referred to does not take into account the territory taken for roads joining settlements with each other and to Jerusalem and wide arterial swaths providing water, sewage services, electricity and communications. This infrastructure that supports the settlements divides the entire West Bank into multiple fragments. Israel would keep control of the Jordan River valley that constitutes roughly 10% of the West Bank for between 6 and 21 years according to different accounts of the negotiations. And there is no guaranty that Israel would ever relinquish control of the Jordan River Valley. If the Israelis were willing to surrender the Jordan Valley at some future date, then the Palestinians will have eighty-six of the West Bank.

As for Jerusalem, the Palestinians would have full sovereignty over few neighborhoods in East Jerusalem and establish their capital in the village of Abu-Dis, not in the City of Old Jerusalem. The offer would leave more than 300,000 settlers under the sovereignty of Israel, and Israel would have full control over the borders, security, the underground water resources and airspace of the promised Palestinian state. The official offer to the Palestinians "might have been the most generous offer by Israel, but it does not compare to the generosity of the Palestinians to Israel in the Oslo agreement."[1] They surrendered in the Oslo Agreements their rights in 78% of historical Palestine, where the State of Israel proper has been established in 1948. Camp David 2000 offer dictated that Palestinians accept to live with 80% of the settlements and no right of return for refugees. President Bill Clinton claimed that he was promoting peace, but there was a massive increase of settlers during his administration, mostly while Ehud Barak was prime minister. The offer was not acceptable by the Palestinians, but minor territorial adjustments to the West Bank and East Jerusalem with comparable territorial compensation could have been accepted.

The failure of Camp David meeting was not a surprise since it did not involve real negotiations. Ehud Barak supported by President Clinton tried to dictate the terms of

---

1 David Hirst, 2003, p. 25.

the final status and when they were not accepted, he simply terminated the meeting and the negotiations. Whether in the negotiations that produced 1993 Oslo Accords or the unsuccessful 2000 negotiations, the US participation in the peace process was to adopt Israel's positions. The US was teaming with Israel when it was supposed to act as a neutral mediator. President Clinton negotiating position in Camp David was to pressure the Palestinians to accept the Israeli offer. Dennis Ross, the principal US negotiator, wrote in his 2004 book, "The Missing Peace: the inside story in the Fight for Middle East," that he gave Israeli needs higher priority over the Palestinian rights in the July 2000 Camp David negotiations. He and the rest of the US team involved in the negotiations kept rejecting the Palestinians' claim for a contiguous West Bank or the sovereignty over East Jerusalem.

By signing the Oslo Accord and amending the Palestine National Charter (PNC) in 1993, Arafat's revolution was over and the 1948 refugees who looked up to him for hope would never return to their homes based on Oslo. Shimon Peres described the amendment of the PNC as the most important decision made by the Palestinians in the 20th century. Then US Secretary of State Madeleine Albright thought the PLO concessions had far reaching ramifications on the future resolution of the conflict. She stated in September 1994 that as a result of Oslo, all UN resolutions concerning the question of Palestine were contentious, irrelevant and obsolete.

After signing the 1993 DOP, Israel embarked on confiscating more land and building settlements and extensive network of roads for the settlers in these same disputed lands, doubling the settler's population and more than tripling the expropriated lands, making the complete withdrawal problematic. East Jerusalem and its surroundings are where the largest settlement blocks have been built on confiscated Arab lands. During the first quarter of 2005, building of new settlements rose by 83% than during the same period in 2004 and new settlers moving to the West Bank have risen by more than 14,000.[1] Tens of settlements were built, land was confiscated and many previously built settlements were expanded. It was estimated that by the year 2000, more than 400,000 settlers lived in the conquered territory.[2] And by 2009, the settlers' population has exceeded 480,000. Given these conditions that have been created by Israel as "facts on the ground," an independent Palestinian entity if ever materialized, will comprise only islands within an Israeli-dominated territory.

The press office of the Israeli government stated on January 21, 1997 that the policy of settlement building in the West Bank and Gaza was "consistent with the terms of the Oslo Accords." Acting Prime Minister Shimon Peres who had been described as a moderate and a man of peace said in a 1994 speech: "From our point of view... [the Palestinians] don't have land, they don't have authority, and they don't have means. In many ways, [the negotiation with the Palestinians] is a negotiation with ourselves, because what is driving

---

1 *The Guardian*, Oct. 18, 2005.
2 According to *Palestine Monitor*, there were more than 403,249 settlers in the West Bank. Of these settlers 211,788 were living in Jerusalem as of 2000.

us is the question: what sort of an Israel do we want to have in the future."[1] Peres personally helped establish Ofra settlement in the West Bank.

Oslo has become an obstacle to peace rather than a solution, and it caused the peace process to stagnate. It did not provide principles that would affect the outcome of the proposed negotiations. Israel interpreted Oslo and its subsequent phases as agreements on dividing the occupied land rather than withdrawing from it. It used the endless interim period specified in the Oslo Accords to create irreversible "facts on the ground." Arafat and his lieutenants focused only on establishing a presence in the post-1967 Palestine and ignored the issue of the refugees when dealing with Israel and Washington, even after the signing of the 1993 Accord. Oslo deprived the 1948 and 1967 Palestinian refugees of the basic right of participation in the future Palestinian elections. Unlike the Iraqis who acquired citizenship in the US, Britain and other European countries and had been given the right to vote for the Iraqi Parliament candidates, the Palestinians who are classified as refugees living in camps in Jordan and Lebanon have been denied the right to vote in the Palestinian elections. Shafiq al-Hout, a Palestinian intellectual and a PLO member said of Arafat, "He [Arafat] has given up the right of return of about three million refugees and it was all done in secret." Muhammad Heikal, the Egyptian dean of journalists, commented on Arafat after signing the Oslo agreement, "Arafat has sold the house."[2] After reviewing the outcome of Oslo agreement, the political analyst, Hasan Abu Nimah concluded that "with Oslo, PLO leaders did not liberate their people from occupation, they simply joined them."[3]

It is difficult to correct the mistakes and repair the damage inflicted on the Palestinian cause by Oslo that empowered Israel to create the facts on the ground. Oslo provided the cover for Israel to colonize what was left of Palestine and pretending that there is a peace process in place. The agreements have undermined the resiliency of the Palestinian cause; they have not ended Israel's control over what is left of Palestine; and the agreements installed a corrupt PA in power. The Palestinians under the PA had to endure not only the brutality of the Israeli occupation, but also the autocratic police rule of the PA including serious human rights violations. Five years after Oslo, the international donors were alarmed by the corruption and lack of transparency by the PA as reported by a task force.[4] They asked for a series of reform as a condition to continue providing their contributions. With no productivity or public work, the PA policies created a structural economy of dependency on exporting cheap labor to Israel. The young Palestinians had to work as day laborers in Israel just to put food on their tables, because they couldn't hope for finding jobs in the local economy.

To the Palestinians, Oslo of 1993 and the 1917 Balfour Declaration (BD) have peculiar attributes in common. First, both were based on ambiguous language authored by British politicians. Oslo was based on UN Security Council 242 resolution of November 1967

---

1 A speech by Shimon Peres to the Mayor's Conference in Jerusalem, March 15, 1994.
2 Robert Fisk, 2005.
3 Hasan Abu Nimah, *Jordan Times*, January 17, 2006.
4 "Council on Foreign Relations Report, 1999.

which was authored by Lord Caradon, the British ambassador to the UN, and the BD was in the form of a letter from Arthur Balfour, Secretary of State for Foreign Affairs, to Lord Rothschild in 1917. Lord Caradon omitted one word "the" before the word "territories" in the proposed text of the 242 UN Resolution, thus allowing the stronger party of the conflict, the Israelis, to enforce their interpretation of the Resolution.[1] Arthur Balfour omitted the word "political" before the word "rights" in the text of Balfour Declaration, "nothing shall be done which may prejudice the civil and religious rights of the existing non-Jewish communities in Palestine," thus allowing the British authorities to deprive the Arabs of their right to exercise self-determination under the Mandate by the League of Nations in 1922. The second striking similarity between Balfour Declaration and Oslo is that both were issued while the Palestinians were under occupation. Third, the Arabs were too weak to challenge Great Britain when the Balfour Declaration was issued in 1917. The British Foreign Secretary Arthur Balfour expressed his colonialist arrogance and deep contempt to the Palestinians when he said in 1917, "We do not propose even to go through the form of consulting the wishes of the present inhabitants of the country [Palestine]...[who are] totally barbarous, undeveloped and disorganized black tribes."[2] The Palestinians and their Arab allies have been too weak to challenge Israel after signing the Oslo agreements. The fourth similarity was that the Balfour Declaration gave the Zionist movement the legitimacy it needed to colonize Palestine, and the Oslo agreements gave it the legitimacy to disregard the UN resolutions pertaining to the Palestinian–Israeli conflict and international laws regarding occupied lands. Oslo has not prevented Israel from building settlements, annexing land from the West Bank with the least Palestinian population to keep its Jewish demographic character, and giving the Arab population centers to the Palestinian Authority to police. But a big difference between Oslo and the BD was that the former was negotiated by the PLO on behalf of the Palestinians, and the latter was imposed on the indigenous Palestinians by the British.

A two-state solution based on giving the Palestinians an independent state can never be implemented with hundreds of large and small settlements spread all over the West Bank and in Jerusalem. The Israeli actions became facts on the ground that could not be reversed easily. These have been symptoms of Oslo's bankruptcy that led the Palestinians living under the occupation to lose faith in the politics of negotiations and resort to violence.

THE SECOND INTIFADA (AL-AQSA INTIFADA)

The failure of the 2000 Camp David summit created a consensus among the Palestinians that the Oslo agreements had solved nothing. The Palestinians were disappointed and looking for a trigger to express anger. On September 28, 2000, Ariel Sharon and a group of his Likud deputies guarded by 2000 armed soldiers visited the "Temple Mount,"

---

1 UN 242 Resolution called for "Withdrawal of Israeli armed forces from territories occupied in the recent conflict [1967 war]."
2 Abu Sitta, Salman.

as referred to by Jews, in Jerusalem which is the site of the mosques of al-Aqsa and the Dome of the Rock. This provocative visit became the pretext for instigating large scale demonstrations and the start of the second Palestinian uprising which effectively ended the Oslo peace process. On September 29, Palestinian Arabs staged large demonstrations and threw stones at police in the "Western Wall" area in Jerusalem. Police used rubber-coated metal bullets and live ammunition to disperse the demonstrators, killing 4 persons and injuring approximately 200. Similar demonstrations took place over the following several days. Palestinians began more demonstrations against Israeli soldiers, settlers, and other Israeli civilians throughout the occupied territories. These demonstrations that lasted for more than five years, with the ensuing clashes and different forms of violence including suicide bombs in Israel, are known to the Palestinians as "the Second *Intifada*" or "al-Aqsa *Intifada*."

Sharon's visit was only the spark not the reason for al-Aqsa *Intifada*. Mitchell Report of 2001 stated that the uprising was in response to the failure of the permanent status offer at Camp David to end the Israeli occupation of the West Bank, Gaza and East Jerusalem. The offer at Camp David was unacceptable by the Palestinians. It "provided for Israel's annexation of the best Palestinian lands, the perpetuation of Israeli control over East Jerusalem, a continued military presence on Palestinian territory, Israeli control over Palestinian natural resources, airspace and borders, and the possibility of the return of less than 1% of refugees to their homes." The second *Intifada* was an uprising against Israel's continued occupation and the failure of Arafat and the Oslo agreements to end it.

As expected, "al-Aqsa *Intifada*" and the suicide bombings in Israel proper at the heels of the 2000 Camp David failure contributed to Prime Minister Ehud Barak defeat and the resurrection of the controversial hard-line Ariel Sharon as a Prime Minister in the 2001 Israeli elections. From all accounts, the Israeli public elected Sharon overwhelmingly knowing his credentials as a ruthless ex-military commander responsible for one of the most shocking war crimes against the Palestinian refugees in Lebanon.

After he was elected, Prime Minister Sharon launched "Operation Defensive Shield" to crush the Palestinian uprising. He sent the military to reoccupy the Palestinian population centers that had been under the Palestinian Authority control. Israeli tanks invaded all major towns in the West Bank except for Jericho. The military constructed physical road blocks and checkpoints to prevent Palestinian people and products from reaching the main cities. By June 2002, there were repeated military invasions, closures, homes demolition, extrajudicial assassinations of activists, kidnapping of political leaders, destruction to civil infrastructure and the Palestinians had to live under frequent 24 hours curfews imposed upon them as collective punishment. The "Palestine Monitor," a Palestine civil society that disseminates news about local developments, estimated that number of Palestinians killed by Israel between September 28, 2000 and March 1st of 2006 was 3,982 including 708 children (below 18 years) and the number of injured was more than 41,000 including 2500 Permanent Disabilities. Israeli casualties, victims of suicide bombing, exceeded 1,000. Arafat, who once was embraced as partner in peace, became demonized, isolated and, many Palestinians believe he was murdered, and the four-hundred-mile separation wall was built in and around the West Bank.

THE PALESTINIAN REFUGEES

Palestinian refugees have been described as persons normally residing in Palestine, who lost their homes or livelihood as a result of the 1948 and 1967 wars, and their descendants. The first and most significant exodus was created by the 1948 Arab–Israeli conflict when about two-thirds of the total Palestinian population of 1.2 million at the time was forced to seek refuge outside their homes. And the second wave of more than 300,000 refugees became homeless in the 1967 war. These include students, business-people, vacationing families and expatriates who had been outside the country when the war broke out. More than 100,000 of the 1967 refugees had been already refugees from the 1948 war.

The vast majority of the Palestinian Arabs did not leave their homes during the 1947-48 war willingly or in order to make way for avenging Arab armies. They were driven from their homes as part of a coordinated plan by leaders of the Zionist movement. All the Zionist leaders since 1897 wanted to rid Palestine from its indigenous Arab population to keep alive the slogan of "land without people." Chaim Weizmann, a one time President of the World Zionist Congress and later on the president of Israel said in a 1914 speech to the French Zionist Federation: "There is a country which happens to be called Palestine, a country without a people, and, on the other hand, there exists the Jewish people, and it has no country. What else is necessary, then, than to fit the gem into the ring." Many Zionist leaders perpetuated the same theme of "land without people for people without land" until they secured Britain's Balfour Declaration.

The Palestinians presence on the land became a problem that needed a solution. Yosef Weitz, the director of the Settlement Department of Jewish National Fund, wrote in his diary on December 20, 1940: "Amongst ourselves it must be clear that there is no room for both peoples in this country...The only way is to transfer the Arabs from here to neighboring countries, all of them, except perhaps Bethlehem, Nazareth, and Old Jerusalem. Not a single village or a single tribe must be left."[1] When Chaim Weizmann was asked in 1917 about the Palestinians he replied, "The British told us that there are some hundred thousand Negroes [Arabs] and for those there is no value."[2]

The idea of "transfer" was the main Zionists' solution to the demography problem. Ben-Gurion, the first prime minister of Israel submitted "line of action" recommendations for dealing with the Arab population problem in June 1937 Jewish Agency Executive (the government of the pre-Israel settlers) meeting. He stated that "The Hebrew State will discuss with the neighboring Arab states the matter of voluntarily transferring Arab tenant farmers, workers and fellahin from the Jewish state to neighboring states."[3] He suggested that the Palestinians can be transferred to Iraq and Syria and the West may pay for their

---

1 Masalha, Nur, 2001.
2 Ibid.
3 Ibid.

resettlement. And in December of 1947, Ben-Gurion asked the Haganah to "adopt the system of aggressive defense; during the assault we must respond with a decisive blow; the destruction of the [Arab] place or the expulsion of the residents along with the seizure of the place."[1] Early in 1948 before the end of the Mandate, the Haganah and other Jewish paramilitary organizations started executing *"Plan Dalet"* which called for the expulsion of the Palestinians from towns and villages in various areas of the country to ensure the establishment of Israel as a Jewish state with the smallest possible Arab minority. Plan Dale will be discussed further in Chapter 4.

Jewish fighters were determined to expel the Palestinian Arabs. They committed numerous massacres and forcibly ejected hundreds of thousands of Palestinians from their homes before, during and after the 1948 war. According to the UN, number of the Palestinian refugees of 1947-49 Arab–Israeli war was the largest exodus for any nation since Second World War. The refugees lost everything and have been denied by Israel the right of return to their homes in what became Israel; Israel destroyed their villages and took over their land and other properties. Israel seized more than 500 towns and villages and cleansed most Palestinians from the areas they controlled. Palestinians were removed to create room for millions of Jews from all over the world. The international community has been aware of the ethnic cleansing but decided to ignore it, thus encouraging Israel to adopt cleansing as a state policy.

Most Palestinian refugees have been languishing in camps in the Middle East for three generations with no equal legal rights or right to work and earn a living. With the exception of Jordan, the Palestinian refugees are officially treated with contempt and stigmatized in all Arab countries. Most registered refugees survive only on UN handouts and they have been under constant harassment by police and hundreds were massacred by militants of their host countries.

While the US military occupied Iraq from 2003–2009, it failed to protect the Palestinian refugees in Iraq from deadly attacks by some Iraqi thugs. Hundreds were killed and thousands were forced to leave their homes and run for their lives. In 2008, the UN Refugees Agency said there were about 2,500 Palestinian refugees mostly widows and orphans, victims of the violence in Iraq, languishing for years under canvas tents in the Iraqi desert at the Syrian border where temperature exceeds 122ºF in summer. Syria and Jordan had accepted more than two million refugees from Iraq but they denied entry for Palestinian refugees who have been trying to escape the attacks and persecution in Iraq.

The surviving refugees and their descendants today constitute more than 50% of the Arab Palestinians. Based on Salman Abu-Sitta research, the refugees came from 531 towns and villages.[2] According to the historian Benny Morris, 213 villages and towns were cleansed before the 1948 war while the area was still under the British Mandate and 264 localities during the war.

---

1 Ibid.
2 Abu-Sitta, Salman, 2001.

The signing of the armistice agreements with the Arab States did not end cleansing of the Palestinian Arab. A total of 54 Palestinian localities within Israel were ethnically cleansed after the signing of the armistice agreements. "Falujah" and "Iraq al-Manshiah" were two of these localities where their 3,000 remaining residents who decided to take their chances and stay in their homes were forcefully evicted by the Israelis after signing the armistice agreements. In February 1949, Israel expelled 700 internal refugees from "Kufur Yasif" and forced them to cross the armistice line with Lebanon. Israel did the same thing to the inhabitants of "Hisam," "Jauneh," "Qatia" and "Kufur Anan" villages. In August 1950, the Israeli military evicted the 14,000 Palestinian residents of Majdal, an Arab town located on the southern coast of Israel. The military trucked them all to the border with Gaza Strip and forced them to cross the border. Israel then settled the town with Jewish immigrants and changed its name to Ashkelon. These are only few examples of the forced Arab expulsion to create a Jewish state.

Prior to June 1948, Jews owned less than 10% of historic Palestine, but Israel today has established Jewish towns and cities mostly on lands owned by cleansed Arab Palestinians individually and collectively. Israel was left in control of five million acres of Palestinians' land in 1949. Don Peretz concluded that, as of 1954, the vast majority of the Israelis were living on confiscated Arab land in confiscated homes. On April 4, 1969, *Haaretz* newspaper cited Moshe Dayan proudly listing villages and towns cleansed of the Palestinian Arabs as a great accomplishment of the Zionists in Palestine. "Jewish villages were built in the place of Arab villages. You don't even know the names of these Arab villages, and I don't blame you, because these geography books no longer exist. Not only do the books not exist, the Arab villages are not there either. Nahala arose in the place of Mahalul, Gvat in the place of Jibta, Sarid in the place of Haneifa, and Kfar-Yehoshua in the place of Tel-Shaman. There is not one single place built in this country [Israel] that did not have a former Arab population."

Most Palestinian refugees live in three neighboring Arab countries and the West Bank and Gaza Strip. As of June 30, 2001, there were close to four million refugees registered with the UNRWA and more than 1.3 million unregistered refugees living in these countries. And there are between 120,000 and 150,000 refugees who remained in Israel proper but are not allowed by Israel to return to their homes. Israel calls them "Absent-Present." The UNRWA recognized a total of fifty-nine Palestinian refugee camps in neighboring Arab countries, the West Bank and Gaza, but not all registered refugees currently live in camps. As of 2001, only in Lebanon and the Gaza Strip do most refugees live in camps. In Jordan, Syria and the West Bank, most of the refugees live outside camps.

The UNRWA is a humanitarian organization and does not provide protection and other political guarantees. The reliance on UNRWA provides personal safety net for the refugees but it also gives them false feeling of having international support to their national aspiration. The camps dwellers have been viewed by the local residents as alien neighbors. This created boundaries between refugees and locals, and the refugees were treated as socially inferiors by the local host communities. The feeling of social insecurity among the refugees and discrimination reinforced their opposition to permanent settlement.

Table 1: Registered refugees living in Arab countries on June 30, 2001.

Field	Registered Population
Jordan	1,639,718
Lebanon	382,973
Syria	391,651
West Bank	607,770
Gaza	852,626
Total	3,874,738

Source: *United Nations, 2001 Report of the Commissioner-General of the UNRWA.*

The Palestinian refugees' issue is at the core of the Arab–Israeli conflict and there will be no peace unless their issue is resolved. Solving the refugees' problem is a prerequisite for the success of establishing a Palestinian state. The shared experience of the unjust enforced displacement of the Palestinians from their homeland has consolidated the refugees' sense of national identity and their opposition to resettlement schemes in Arab countries. Despite their protracted exile that has lasted for three generations, most Palestinian refugees and their descendants continue to treat their present status of being a transitional phase and they cling to the notion of one day returning to their homes or homeland. A primary reason for Palestinians' armed struggle that began in the 1950s has been the failure of the international community to enforce the UN refugees' right of return. Camps refugees in Gaza initiated the First *Intifada*, and number of refugees from Gaza and the West Bank interned in Israeli prisons was twice those of indigenous Palestinian population. The refugees publicly demand the right to return and refuse resettlement plans in Arab countries. UN General Assembly Resolution 194 was issued on December 11, 1948 concerning the Palestinians right of return. It was reaffirmed by the General Assembly during each session since 1948 with the exception of 1951, but never was implemented. The General Assembly adopted more than four dozen resolutions that have referred to Resolution 194. The key part of the Resolution 194 (III) paragraph 11 states that "the refugees wishing to return to their homes and live at peace with their neighbors should be permitted to do so at the earliest practicable date, and that compensation should be paid for the property of those choosing not to return and for loss of or damage to property which, under principles of international law or equity, should be made good by the governments or authorities responsible." Three organizations were created by the UN General Assembly to deal with the Palestinian refugees. The United Nations Commission on Palestine (UNCCP) was established by Resolution 194(III) in 1948; the United Nations High Commissioner for Refugees (UNHCR) was created by 1950 UNGA Resolution 428(V); and United Nations Relief and Works Agency (UNRWA) was established by the 1949 UNGA Resolution 302(IV) under Article 22 of the UN Charter that authorizes the General Assembly to establish subsidiary organs to perform its functions which in this providing food and humanitarian services to the Palestinian refugees.

Israel insists that Palestinian refugees who fled or were driven from their homes in 1948 and their descendents should not return to Israel as stated in many United Nations resolutions. Prime Minister Ehud Olmert and other Israeli leaders stated in many occasions that Israel would not allow the return of the refugees to their homes, proposing only to assist them find their place in the future Palestinian state. He cited President Bush's June 2004 letter to Ariel Sharon that included among other things that "the refugee issue will be resolved by settling of refugees in a future Palestine state and not in Israel."

Only Jordan makes it easy for the Palestinian refugees to become part of the local community. The Quartet envoy to the Middle East Tony Blair proposed a plan to settle the refugees' issue. It calls for the construction of a new city near Ramallah in the West Bank with the goal of repatriating hundreds of thousands of the refugees there. The plan is good for housing refugees who would choose to receive compensation rather than repatriation only if it was implemented according to the UN Resolution 194.

THE PALESTINIAN ECONOMY UNDER THE PA

Palestine's economy under the PA has been crippled as a consequence of the occupation. The shrinking of the Palestinians' economy in the West Bank as well as the poverty and starvation of the people in the Gaza enclave are an Israeli man-made affliction and sadly, this is sanctioned by the US. According to the February 2009 International Monetary Fund report, the economy of the West Bank, that was not bombed or sealed completely like Gaza, was "stalling and a failure" due to the tightened restrictions of movement and free access to the outside world. Israel's unchallenged control of the occupied lands that started with the occupation in 1967 and has been secured by the terms of Oslo agreements blocked the indigenous Palestinians from controlling their resources, the land, water, borders and commerce. Control of the Palestinians' basic economic functions was delegated to the Israelis by the economic arrangements in the Paris Protocol and Cairo agreements that followed the 1993 Oslo agreements. Israel subcontracted the PA to manage education, health, social welfare and tourism while retaining the power to control resources needed for development or for performing the functions the PA had been subcontracted to do.

The occupation military regime practices what can be described as ethnic cleansing via bureaucracy. Palestinians' houses are demolished; permits for building are not issued; the farmers are not allowed to dig wells more than one third as deep as the Israeli settlers; and Israel restricts access to the land needed to meet Palestinian population growth.

The occupation made the Palestinians captive consumers for the Israeli products and Oslo agreements gave Israel control over Palestinian's taxation. As part of Israel's security policies, it fragmented the land on which the Palestinians hope their state to rise. The Jewish only settlements and roads have divided the major population centers into communities living in multitude of disconnected enclaves and the military enforced restrictions on movement of people and products. It erected hundreds of checkpoints and constructed the separation wall that subdivided the isolated enclaves into even smaller communities thus preventing labor and products movement within the enclaves or the West Bank. Closing borders disrupted commerce and limited trade with neighboring Arab countries.

The olive and its oil have always been a major source of income for a large segment of the Palestinian farmers. The Israeli military and the settlers destroyed olive orchards in many localities and prevented the farmers from harvesting what was left of their trees. The Palestinians consider the act of olive harvesting as a form of peaceful resistance against occupation. Settlers harass and shoot at farmers trying to harvest their olive crop and quite often uproot and torch the olive-laden trees. According to Israeli human rights organizations, settlers uprooted more than 100,000 olive trees in the northern West Bank and poisoned hundreds of artesian wells in 2008 alone.

Since the Gaza Strip has been ruled exclusively by the Islamist movement in June 2006, the Strip was declared "enemy entity" by Israel with backing from the US. This entailed tightening the siege on the Strip, preventing movements of people and merchandise across its borders, shutting off fuel and power to its residents and crippling its economy in the process. Israel reduced the diesel supplies from 350,000 liters per day to only 60,000 liters which means no electricity for homes and business, no sewage treatment, no irrigation or drinking water and no fuel to power the hospitals electrical generators. The shortage of raw materials, ranging from computer spare parts to cement and steel, destroyed the industry, shut out construction and hindered any economic development. The Strip population that constitutes 40% of the Palestinians under occupation is left dependent on the meager international aid when Israel allows it to bring relief supplies shipments.

Before the siege, ocean fishing had been one of the main industries in Gaza where more than 40,000 people made their living, and fish was a major source of protein for the population. Israel has restricted Gazan fishermen from laying their nets beyond five miles from Gaza's shores. But the restriction on fishing rights enforced by Israel and the siege that prevents the fuel from reaching the Strip has decimated the fishing community and their catch. The International Solidarity Movement estimated that the average catch dropped from 3000 tons per year in the 1990s to less than 500 "due to the Israeli siege." Israeli navy vessels attack the Gazan fishing boats regularly using live ammunition and shells at boats within three miles from the coast causing significant damages to the boats and threatening the lives of the fishermen.

After the three-week Israeli attack in December 2008 on Gaza, which followed two years of economic siege, between 35% and 60% of the agriculture industry has been wrecked, according to the UN's Food and Agriculture Organization (FAO). Christine Nieuwenhuve, the World Food Programme's Director said, "We are hearing that 60% of the land in the north may not be exploitable any more."[1] The FAO estimated that the businesses of 13,000 families who depended on herding and farming suffered significant damage.

---

1 *The Observer*, February 1, 2009.

CHAPTER 4. ZIONISM

Zionism as a national movement for the salvation of the Jews may be examined from many different perspectives. It was promoted in the 19th century as a Jewish únational liberation movement intended to find a solution to what was known as "the Jewish Question" by creating a colony where Jews can constitute a majority of the population. Max Nordau, a theorist and one of the early Zionists, advocated Zionism as a means for "regenerating the degenerated Jews." Zionism began as a secular movement, embedded in socialism, by Jews who were convinced that they would remain alienated human beings until they had a country of their own. It was perceived as a reinvention of Judaism as a secular national movement rather than religious or cultural, but the boundaries between the "secular Zionist chauvinism" and the "religious Jewish ethnocentrism" ideologies were blurred. Like the religious Jews, the Zionists sought to legitimize the establishment of a Jewish state in "Zion" based on the right of return to the land that was promised by God. The Zionists did not choose Palestine because of its natural resources, but it was chosen as the territory for their nation because of its symbolism in the 19th century European version of Jewish religion. Choosing Palestine served as a good recruitment tool for Jewish immigration and a powerful tool for giving legitimacy to the Zionist project. The Zionists declared secularism, but their nationalism is culturally dependent on the Jewish religion. "Zion" is the religious name of a hill in Jerusalem and the Zionists chose their flag based on the prayer-shawl used by Orthodox Jews. The Zionists and the religious Jews claim to be reclaiming and redeeming Palestine that "had always been theirs." The secular Zionists, who are economically and numerically stronger than the religious Jews, had to surrender the definition of the Jews' identity culturally to those who practice the "*mitzvoth*." Religious Jews claimed God had given them the land of Palestine and told them to safeguard themselves against gentiles who hate them. To do otherwise, they say, they would run the risk of disobeying God.

The modern forerunner of Zionism was Jewish nationalism based on the messianic prophecy advocated by East European Orthodox rabbis. As early as 1839, a Belgrade Sephardic rabbi, Judah Alkalai, called for establishing Jewish colonies in the holy land as a phase of the spiritual redemption of the Jewish people.[1] He wrote in his booklet *Minchat Yehuda* (The Offering of Judah), "As the initial stage in the redemption of our souls, we must cause at least 22,000 to return to the Holy Land....Afterward, He will grant us, and all of Israel, additional signs of His favor." Alkalai immigrated to Palestine and attracted followers; one of them was Simon Loeb Herzl, the grandfather of Theodore Herzl.

The State of Israel today is a partial theocracy since some of its universalistic legal-judicial powers have been in the realm of the *Halachic* Religion as interpreted by the Orthodox Judaism. There are certain limits on the rights of Israeli citizens who claim they are Jews but are not classified as Jews by the *Halachic* rules. The State passed laws that discriminate against non-Jewish minorities and all Israeli governments since the 1970s have been dependent on the religious parties for their parliamentary majorities.

Because Zionism was a project to establish a state on the ruins of the indigenous Palestinian society, and due to its commonality with nineteenth-century European colonialism in Africa, and because it was conceived by European Jews, it has been recognized by many historians as a movement in the European colonial tradition. Perez Smolenskin, a 19th century Russian Jew and the founder of the *Hebrew Literary Monthly* in Vienna suggested that all methods were legitimate to sustain the Jewish national goal, including "colonizing the Land of Israel." There is similarity between the Zionists and the nineteenth-century colonizers who employed Christian ideologies to justify conquering faraway lands at the expense of their indigenous populations. Zionism has been supported by, and its project was made possible by, the European colonialists. The emergence of nationalism among the Italians, Germans, Poles, Hungarians and Slovaks in Europe and the concomitant anti-Semitism could have inspired European Jewish nationalism.

Rabbi Zvi Hirsch Kalischer, from the Polish-speaking city of Thorn in East Prussia, wrote in the 19th century, "If all other people have striven for the sake of their national honor, shouldn't we strive for our duty...for the glory of God who chose Zion?" He preached that by self-help and the colonization of Palestine by pious Jews, rather than prayers, Jews could achieve salvation.

In 1800, the number of Jews in Palestine was about five thousand out of estimated total Palestinian population of three hundred thousand. Their largest community was living in Safed town, in north Palestine. And due to immigration, mostly from East Europe, Jewish population multiplied by a factor of seventeen by the eve of World War I, with the largest concentration in Jerusalem. Zionism attracted Jews living mostly in Eastern and Central Europe, drawing on history and scripture in their claim to Palestine, a land they considered to have been abandoned by their ancestors for the last 3,000 years. The Zionists used a simplified chapter of the Jewish people's history and their vulnerability

---

1   Howard Sachar, 1996, p. 6.

in recent centuries, to promote unity of the Jews and secure the sympathy of the international community.[1]

Most of the early Zionist settlers of the 1904–1930 second and third waves of immigration in Palestine were ardent young socialists determined to create a socialist society in the "land of Israel." They evicted local Palestinian peasants from land purchased by the "Jewish Agency" mostly from absent landlords, and monopolized the local labor market and the economic concessions. They created their own autonomous national institutions in Mandatory Palestine including economic and military. They established secular collective communities (*kibbutzim*), European style trade unions and referred to their pioneering movement as the "Conquest of Labor." Their project was financed directly and indirectly by Jewish "national funds." By the end of the 1920s, members of the General Federation of Jewish Labor that was commonly called "the Histadrut" represented three-quarters of the Jewish labor force. It created hundreds of co-operatives that employed thousands in different fields which included education, health care, transportation and industries. The Hebrew language was the medium of communication in all these institutions. The Histadrut became the second largest employer in Palestine after the Mandatory government and its economic strategy was the exclusive employment of Jews. The success and dedication of the early Zionists led some observers to argue that Zionism might replace Judaism as the basic tenet of the Jewish people. For Zionists whose loyalty to the secular state overrides all else, the Jewish people were the means for one end, the creation of a Jewish state, but a struggle between moderates and extremists has its place in Zionism.

Arabs viewed Zionism as a form of Western imperialism that was conceived by Jewish and gentile elites to prevent the assimilation of the Jews in Christian societies and create a state in a strategic location that would serve the interests of the colonial powers in the Middle East. The Europeans helped implementing the Zionists program using the methods of the 19th century European colonialism. Many of the Israeli historians including Benny Morris who had been a consultant to the Israeli political and military establishment agreed with their Palestinian counterparts that Zionism was basically a settler-colonial movement, not to redeem a lost country after two millenniums of exile. Under the British occupation of Palestine, the Zionists who entered Palestine treated the Arabs in the same manner the Europeans treated the natives of their colonies. The problem with the Jewish colonialists is not their religious belief, but their political Zionism ideology based on Jabotinsky thought to possess the Palestinians' land and press an exclusive claim to the country.

Some of the 19th century Zionists, the "cultural Zionists," led by Asher Ginzberg (Achad HaAm), believed that the goal of the Zionist movement should be only to create a "national spiritual center" in the "Land of Israel" for the revival of Judaism. Ginzberg was "to many Russian-Jewish students in Europe what Gandy had been to many Indians, what Mazzini was to young Italy a century ago."[2] They believed that it was the Jewish culture

---

1 Avi Shlaim, 2001.
2 Weizmann,Chaim, 1949

that ensured the centrality of Palestine among the Russian Jews. And "political Zionism" that is based on conquest was a deviation from the Jewish traditions by creating an artificial Europeanized concoction in Palestine. "Cultural Zionists" were against conquest and uprooting the indigenous Palestinian population. Yitzhak Epstein, a cultural Zionist wrote in 1905 "The Hebrew people, first and foremost among all peoples in the teaching of justice and law, absolute quality, and human brotherhood, respect not only the individual rights of every person, but also the national rights of every people and tribe. We must enter into a covenant with the Arabs and conclude an agreement that will be of great value to both sides and to all human kind."[1]

But in 1949, Ben-Gurion, a political Zionist, told a committee that was formed to Judaize the Negev region that, "We are obliged to remove the Arabic names for reasons of state. Just as we do not recognize the Arabs' political proprietorship of the land, so also do we not recognize their spiritual proprietorship and their names!"[2] Eventually, the vision of establishing political sovereignty over the "Land of Israel" had more enthusiasts following among the European Jews, and the political Zionism prevailed.

The term "Zionism" was first used by an East European Jew, Dr. Nathan Birnbaum, in an 1893 publication describing Jewish nationalism based on the ideas of Moses Hess and Leo Pinsker.[3] In the late 1870s and before the outbreak of the pogroms hostilities toward Jews in Russia, *Chovevei Zion* ("Lovers of Zion") secret clubs were established by Russian Jews after their encounter with the wave of nationalist movements in Europe.[4] Hundreds of these organizations began to function in different cities offering courses on Hebrew language and the history of Jews. Their first conference was held in 1884 in the city of Kattowitz, Germany under the leadership of Leo Pinsker by virtue of his reputation as an influential Jewish leader. The conferees concluded that the Jewish people could be transformed into a viable nation as an alternative to their assimilation in Europe only if they settle in the "Land of Israel." Their first priority was to finance Jewish settlements in Palestine and Pinsker, as a president of the *Chovevei Zion* organizations, was charged with directing the task of immigration and settlement.

Pinsker was successful in his effort to provide an ideology and organizational structure in Europe and Russia for the purpose of colonizing Palestine. Some of the settlements that Pinkster developed with funds from wealthy Jewish philanthropists were the agricultural settlement of *Rishon LeZiyyon* near Tel Aviv, *Rosh Pina, and Zikhron Yaaqov* near Haifa and *Pitach Tikva* near Jerusalem.[5] After being permitted to function openly in Russia, *Chovevei Zion* organizations grew rapidly in Europe, Russia and the United States during the late 1890s. Their activities became known as "practical Zionism" because of their effort

1 Epstein, Yitzhak, 1905 (2004)
2 Halper, Jeff, 2008.
3 The Nathan Birnbaum pamphlet was written in German. The title translation was: "The National Rebirth of the Jewish People in Its Homeland as a Means of Solving the Jewish Problem."
4 Howard Sachar, 1996, p. 16.
5 Mazin Qumsiyeh, 2004, p. 71.

to settle immigrants in Palestine with the help of wealthy Jews. They were behind the so called *"First Aliyah"* wave of immigration between 1881 and 1884 from Russia.

Palestinian historians consider 1881 the year when Zionist organized colonization of Palestine began through the power of money. Land that many Palestinian peasants had been farming for generations was purchased mostly from absent landlords. The Jewish colonizers began evicting the native Arabs off the land they had been leasing and working. In 1891, Ze'ev Tiomkin, a member of a Russian *Chovevei Zion* organization immigrated to Palestine, established a bureau in Jaffa, and bought large tracts of land on behalf of his organization. Societies of *Chovevei Zion* were in decline in the early 1890s until the rise of Theodore Herzl when he energized the movement and encouraged many to join it. By 1897, when Herzl convened the First Zionist Congress, the movement had become international and the delegates who attended the Congress came from many countries.

Most Zionists were driven by pragmatism and politics rather than the belief in the messianic message of the Orthodox Judaism. Modern Jewish nationalism emerged among secularized Jewish intellectuals despite the skepticism and sometimes the hostility of some traditional rabbis, but the Zionists adopted symbols of Jewish traditions including the revival of Hebrew culture, observing Jewish holidays and memorializing events in Jewish history.[1] This and their yearning to immigrate to Zion, which the religious Jews consider a Jewish ancestral land, strengthened the bonds between secular Zionists and the Orthodox Jews. At the same time, some Jewish intellectuals in Germany, Britain, United States and France expressed opposition to Zionism for ideological reasons or fear of alienating the Jewish communities. Hermann Cohen and Ludwig Geiger from Germany described Zionism as dangerous as *"utramontanism"* in reference to the historical Roman Catholic Church party that advocated the doctrine of papal supremacy.[2] Lucien Wolf branded Zionism as a conspicuous treason idea that may lead to anti-Semitism.[3]

The Zionists call for the return of the Jewish People to Palestine was reinforced by the European and the Russian governments sanctioned persecution of their Jewish communities. Jewish identity according to Herzl himself was perpetuated by Europeans anti-Jewish persecution. He suggested that if there was no anti-Jewish discrimination, Jewish identity can disappear in two generations. Herzl wrote "It is only pressure that forces us back to the parent stem, only the hatred encompassing us that turns us into strangers once more."[4] The wave of the 19th century ethnic based nationalism in Europe and Russia led to the strength of Zionism as a national survival movement. After the murder of Alexander II and the ascendance of his son Alexander III to the throne in 1881, Russia entered into an oppression period directed against its ethnic minorities. Jews were stigmatized of being organized anti-government revolutionaries and harsh measures were taken against them. Anti-Jewish decrees were issued on May 3, 1882 and they were enforced until the

---

1 Shlomo Avineri, 1875, p. 103.
2 Howard Sachar, 1996, p. 52.
3 Lucien Wolf was the secretary of the Joint Foreign Committee of the Anglo-Jewish Association.
4 Theodor Herzl, 1956, p. 60

Bolshevik Revolution of 1917. The decrees included laws that prohibit Jews from establishing settlements in rural areas in Russia, thus forcing Jews to relocate in the city slums. Professional Jews lost their livelihood and their economic base was seriously undermined. Mob attacks against Jews (pogroms) that occurred more often in Russia and Poland in the late 19th century forced many Jews to seek safe residence in other countries. The Tsar decision in 1890 to encourage the departure of the Russian Jews to other countries including Palestine coincided with the launch of the Zionist movement. His government was happy to grant its Jewish constituency passports for pilgrimage to Palestine and the Russian consul in Palestine was authorized to renew the passports, thus allowing Jews to settle in Palestine legally outside the Turkish law. The Tsarist regime permitted the "Society for the support of Jewish Agriculturists and Artisans in Palestine and Syria" to raise money in support of immigration to Palestine.

Originally, German Jews who spoke the German dialect Yiddish had been referred to as "Ashkenazi" Jews, but later on the term was expanded to identify all European and Russian Jews, as opposed to the Asian and North African Jews who are called "Sephardic." According to the Biblical Book of Genesis, "Ashkenaz" was the great grandson of Noah.[1] The anti-Ashkenazi Jews sentiment in Europe and Russia formed the basis for more activism in the Zionist movement. The well-known early Zionist advocates such as Moses Hess, Zvi Hirsch Kalischer, Leo Pinsker, Moses Lilienblum, and Theodore Herzl believed that establishing a Jewish state in Palestine was the only way for self-emancipation and confronting the hatred of the Jews in Europe and Russia. Moses Hess, known for his 1862 book on Zionism, "Rome and Jerusalem," was a socialist, sometimes at odds with Karl Marx, with no interest in religion. Despite Hess assimilation in the European culture and his influence on early socialist thought, later in life he became an ardent nationalist and proposed Jewish nationalism as a solution to the anti-Semitism. He argued that if Italian nationalism is rising "on the ruins of Christian Rome" then the Jews too can achieve "national renaissance" in Palestine. He declared that he had to return to his people after 20 years of estrangement. Hess finally came to believe that a national homeland for the Jews offered the only means to transform them from vulnerable minorities "strangers among the nations" to "normal" people. He argued that the establishment of a Jewish state would fulfill not only the religious or national ambitions but would also preserve the physical existence of the Jews. Hess suggested that the European governments should support the creation of a Jewish protégé nation in the Middle East for their own self-interest and he encouraged the Jewish millionaires such as Rothschild and Montefiore to finance the colonization of Palestine. The early Jewish settlements in Palestine were actually called "colonies." In recognition of his role in promoting Zionism, Hess remains were flown from Germany to be buried in a 1962 state ceremony in Israel.

Leo Pinsker, a physician by profession and a Crimean War veteran, was a strong advocate of the assimilation in Russia and a strong believer in Jewish enlightenment and integration within a pluralist Russia during his early days. Then after the 1881 pogroms

---

1 Genesis 10:3.

he concluded that the solution to the Jewish people requires their political independence in a country where they constitute the majority. He wanted a national homeland for the Jews, but not necessarily in Palestine. In his pamphlet, *Autoemancipation*, he argued that since the Jewish people in Russia and Europe were considered foreigners they will never be accepted as equals.

The theologian Rabbi Kalischer was a strong believer in supporting immigration and settlement in Palestine. In 1870, he used his influence to convince the French "Alliance Israelite Universalle" organization that had been mainly concerned with defending the civil rights of the Jews, to finance one of the first settlements in Palestine, "Mikveh Israel," which included an agricultural school to train farmers. In the aftermath of the 1881–1882 pogroms, the Jewish humanist, Moses Lilienblum, abandoned his early views that the Jews were only a spiritual nation and called for the Jews to immigrate to Palestine. He wrote: "There is no home for us in this or any gentile land."[1]

The Zionist program was supported by Christian evangelical enthusiasts in Europe and the United States who considered the establishment of a Jewish homeland in Palestine a return to the promised land of biblical Israel that God had made to the Jews three millennia ago. Ben-Gurion perceived that "the American Christians could not imagine that the land promised to the Jewish people should be handed over to the Arabs, who for them were pagans."[2] Some Christians believed in the biblical prediction of a Jewish return before Christ second coming. The idea of a homeland for the Jews was advocated by prominent non-Jewish British thinkers and politicians such as Lord Shaftesbury, George Eliot, Holman Hunt, Colonel George Gawler, Laurence Oliphant, Edward Cazalet, Colonel Charles Henry Churchill, and Benjamin Disraeli.[3] Lord Shaftesbury, a 19th century influential political figure and a devoted evangelist encouraged the British to return the holy land to the Jewish people. Oliphant, who was a respected diplomat and a fundamentalist Christian, talked about his wish that "God's Holy People" would return to the cradle of their birth.[4] George Gawler was the cofounder of the 1852 Association for Promoting Jewish Settlement in Palestine that later became known as the Palestine Fund.[5] Many European supporters believed the claims of the early Zionists, including Herzl, the great Hebrew poet Chaim Bialik and the novelist Joseph Berditchewski, that there were no people living in Palestine.[6]

Secular Zionists claim that the Jews as a nation earned a homeland in Palestine as a solution to the anti-Semitism in Europe and as a reward for supporting the Allies in the two world wars as residents of their adopted countries.[7] The strong 19th century nationalism in Europe and the anti-Semitic pogroms that followed the assassination of the Rus-

---

1 Howard Sachar, 1996, p.13.
2 Ben-Gurion, 1973, p.249.
3 Arnold Blumberg, 1985.
4 Howard Sachar, 1996, p.21
5 Lawrence Epstein, 1984.
6 Anita Shapira, 1992, p. 40.
7 George Antonius, 1979.

sian Tsar Alexander II in 1881 drove thousands of Russian Jews to migrate and settle in Turkish ruled Palestine. The Jewish population in Palestine more than doubled between the end of the Egyptian occupation in 1840 and the beginning of the wave of Jewish immigration in 1881. The number of the *"First Aliyah"* immigrant Jews to Palestine between 1881 and 1884 exceeded 25,000. Most of them had been just seeking refuge and a small minority had been Zionists supported by *Chovevei Zion*. The immigrants established small rural settlements on land purchased by wealthy European Jews and organizations. Petach Tikva (Opening of Hope) was founded on the coast and Rosh Pina was built in the Jordan valley in 1878. Rishon LeZion (First in Zion) was established by Russian immigrants, Zichron Yaacov was built by Romanian Jews, Yesod Hamaada (Foundation) was created by Polish immigrants.

The second wave of Jewish immigrants, the *"Second Aliyah,"* fled Russia after the vicious pogroms of 1903 and 1905 and chose Ertz Yisrael over America for idealistic reasons. They were mostly militant Zionists with radical nationalist ideas of the "conquest of labor" and "conquest of land." Unlike their predecessors, the *"Second Aliyah"* immigrants were determined to create a socialist Utopia by redeeming themselves and the land. Their spiritual leader and mystical philosopher, Aharon David Gordan, set a personal example by working as a manual agricultural laborer in Petach Tikva farms. They founded more than fifteen settlements that survived World War I including Degania, the first kibbutz that was established in 1909 and the City of Tel Aviv. The *"Second Aliyah"* established the Labor movement, insisted on using the ancient Hebrew language in their daily discourse regardless of their mother language, led the *Yishuv* in the War of Independence and shaped the ideology and the institutions of Israel.[1] The leadership included the founder of the State of Israel, David Ben-Gurion, first speaker of the Knesset, Joseph Sprinzak and the president of Israel from 1957–1963, Yitzhak Ben-Zvi.

The Turks who controlled Palestine as the southern part of Syria in the 19th century opposed the idea of conceding a homeland for the Jews within its territory, but the Jewish immigration and the establishment of their colonies intensified. Jewish immigrants as subjects of great powers settled under the protection of the consuls of their countries who had become very powerful after the brief Egyptian occupation of Palestine.

THEODORE HERZL

Theodore Herzl (1860–1904), a broadly traveled well known Hungarian Jewish journalist and a writer, was obsessed with the Jewish question since his university days but he had different solutions at different times. Until the eruption of violence against the Jews in France as a result of the *Dryfus Affair*, the court martial of a Jewish officer in 1894, Herzl believed that gradual Jewish assimilation with the Christian Europeans would be the best solution to anti-Semitism. In 1895, Herzl wrote in his diary, "About two years ago I wanted to solve the Jewish question, at least in Austria, with the help of the Catholic Church. I wished to arrange for an audience with the Pope and say to him: help us against

---

1   *Yishuv* is a term that refers to the Jews in Palestine prior to 1948.

the anti-Semites and I will lead a great movement for the free and honorable conversion of Jews to Christianity."[1]

A year later after the *Dryfus Affair* he changed his belief and attempted to articulate a new ideology based on Jewish nationalism, in his formal sixty-five page essay, *Der Judenstaat*, translation, "the Jewish State," addressed to the Rothschilds banking Jewish family in 1896. He proposed a Jewish state as a modern solution to the Jewish question because Jew-hatred was inevitable fact of life. He asserted in his essay that all Jews, whether in Russia or those assimilated in Western Europe, belong to one nation and their question was a national question rather than religious or social. He stated in his essay, "The idea which I have developed in this situation is an ancient one: it is the establishment of the Jewish state." He was explicit that the Jewish state should be secular. He wrote that, "We shall not permit any theocratic tendency to emerge among our spiritual authorities. We shall keep them to their synagogues..." Despite his non-religious ideology, Herzl writings were replete with religious references. The Jews should settle in Palestine because, in his words, "the Temple will be visible from long distance, for it is only our ancient faith that has kept us together." Herzl's solution to the anti-Semitism was for the Jews to have a land of their own. He suggested Argentina or Palestine as the settlement site, but he preferred Palestine as the first choice because of its historical significance to the Jews. To establish settlements in a Jewish homeland, Herzl proposed the creation of two organizations, the "Society of the Jews" as the legal defender of the project and the "Jewish Company" as the finance company with a share capital of 50 million pounds.

Der Judenstaat was the first chapter in Herzl's diary that had become an outstanding literary work, on his views on Zionism. Addressing his essay to the wealthy Rothschilds suggests that Herzl was introducing the concept of Zionism to the European elites. He was trying to reach a wide international audience of statesmen, financiers, intellectuals, educators and newspaper editors who had the power to make the big decisions and influence public opinion. Financing was an important factor for the success of transforming Zionism from a theory into a feasible project. Despite the Tsarist censorship, copies of *Der Judenstaat* were smuggled to Russia and central Europe. In his reference to Palestine in his diary, Herzl never mentioned the Arab Palestinians, giving more impetus to the popular Zionist's slogan, "a land without people for a people without land."

Initial reaction to Herzl's solution to anti-Semitism among European prominent Jews and gentile sympathizers ranged from scorn, ridicule and exasperation to praise, admiration and even calling him a modern-day prophet. The B'nai Brith Lodge of Munich initially forced the local Jewish community to stay away from Herzl, and the "*Jewish Jules Verne*" newspaper asked "Why should we go to Palestine? Our language is German and not Hebrew, and beautiful Austria is our home land."[2] Baron Edmond de Rothschild, heir of the French banking dynasty, was reluctant to accept the political leadership of the movement although he was a strong supporter of Jewish colonies in Palestine even before the

---

1 *The Diaries of Theodor Herzl*, edited by Lowenthal, 1958, p. 7.
2 Howard Sachar, 1996, p.42.

"First Zionist Congress" when he financed the development and maintenance of *Rishon Zion* agricultural settlement. He financed more settlers and provided grants for the promotion of modern Jewish culture such as the 1904 Ben-Yehuda's Hebrew dictionary and the 1903 Jacques Faitlovitch school for reintroducing the Falashas Jews into the Jewish mainstream. Anyway, Herzl was counting on the support of other prominent individuals such as Chaim Weizmann, David Wolffson, the leading Zionist of Cologne, Dr. Moritz Güdemann, and Chief Rabbi of Vienna, Dr. Max Nordau, a distinguished literary figure, and Israel Zangwill, an eminent Anglo–Jewish novelist. There was impressive growth of Zionism popularity throughout Europe and Jewish organizations that supported him with enthusiasm included *Chovevei Zion* societies in Germany, East Europe, Russia and Palestine that asked Herzl to accept the leadership of the movement.

Riding on the publicity of his *Der Judenstaat* in the Jewish communities across Europe and the support of committed Zionists, Herzl convened the "First Zionist Congress" in Basel, Switzerland in 1897 where Jewish delegates from fifteen countries participated and an official World Zionist Movement was established with various national Zionist federations to be represented in an executive committee to be called "Greater Action Committee." The goal of the movement as presented in Basel was to establish a homeland for the Jews in Palestine by encouraging Jewish farmers, laborers and artisans to establish settlements, strengthening national consciousness of the Jews everywhere and securing the support of various governments to accomplish the goal. By declaring that its sole aim was to create a national home for the Jewish people, the Basel Congress planted the seed that gave birth to the State of Israel fifty-years later. Herzl was on target in his prophecy when he wrote in his diary evaluating the First Zionist Congress: "At Basel I founded the Jewish state...If I said this out loud today I would be answered by universal laughter. Perhaps in five years and certainly in fifty everyone will know it."[1]

In his effort for realizing his vision of establishing home for the Jews in Palestine, Herzl managed to meet Germany's foreign minister and Kaiser Wilhelm individually in 1898 and asked them to grant protection to a land company for Jewish settlements in Palestine but the German officials were noncommittal. Later on, Herzl was granted an audience with Sultan Abdul-Hamid II of Turkey in 1901 and proposed on behalf of the World Zionist Organization to establish a land colonizing company in Palestine in exchange for large amount of money. Abdul-Hamid turned down the proposal and offered protection for the refugee Jews who wish to live in different parts of the Ottoman Empire with the exception of Palestine. Pressured by the growing feeling of disappointment and restlessness within the Zionist organizations for failing to secure a charter of settlement in Palestine, Herzl decided to seek the support of the European powers especially the British politicians who had already accepted the Zionist's argument by their biblical conviction or political views.

Herzl promoted his Zionist solution when he appeared in 1902 as a Jewish expert before the Royal Commission that was formed by the British Parliament to study the threat of cheap labor posed by the East European Jewish refugees. He described the bad condi-

---

1 Entry from Herzl diary September 3, 1897, *The Complete Diary*, Volume II, p. 581.

tions of the European Jews and expressed his hope that Britain would continue to give them asylum and allow them to make living, then he added that if these refugees became unwanted then a Jewish homeland had to be found where they go legally without creating the problems that the Commission had been investigating. Lord Nathaniel Rothschild, a Zionist and a member of the Commission took Herzl proposal to the Colonial Secretary Joseph Chamberlain and suggested that a Jewish homeland could also serve the British imperial interests. Chamberlain was receptive to the idea and asked Herzl to propose any place under the British control that was not settled by white man, as a Jewish home-land. After some research, Herzl came up with two locations, the Island of Cyprus and the al-Arish area in northern Sinai of Egypt, but Chamberlain rejected Cyprus off-hand and thought al-Arish would be possible. Herzl and a team of Zionist negotiators and experts in agriculture and irrigation left for Egypt to meet Lord Cromer, the British Agent-General of Egypt. Herzl returned empty handed when the Egyptian Prime Minister, Boutros Ghali rejected the plan of having a Jewish enclave in Sinai or anywhere else in Egypt.

Soon after the rejection of al-Arish project, Chamberlain proposed East Africa Pro-tectorate (Kenya) as another location within the British possessions in Africa where Jews can settle and cultivate the land in the interior. The proposal came at a time when a savage pogrom in Russia took the life of many Jews and destroyed hundreds of their homes and businesses which required urgent Zionist solution to the plight of East European Jews. A Zionist commission of investigation was dispatched to East Africa and a law firm was commissioned to prepare a charter of Jewish autonomy. In August 1903, the sixth Zionist Congress convened and Herzl informed the delegates about London offer and asked to approve the establishment of a Jewish colony in East Africa only as an emergency measure and to strengthen the Zionist's position with the British government rather than a substi-tute to Palestine. It was treated as a temporary alternative to Palestine and an opportunity to develop relationship with the British. Supporters of the plan emphasized the impor-tance of the British government recognition of the national demands of the Jewish people. A resolution to send the investigating commission to East Africa passed with a narrow majority but most East European delegates including influential Zionists voted against it and criticized Herzl's heavy-handed leadership. Finally, the subject of East Africa was put to rest when the British colonists in the territory opposed the idea of mass influx of Jewish immigrants, and then Chamberlain declared that the area was too small to accommodate all the Jews who were expected to immigrate. The closure of the East African option by the British government was a relief for Herzl but he predicted that Britain would "do ev-erything in its power to have Palestine ceded for the Jewish state."[1]

As the aims of the Zionist movement were revealed through statements of the Jew-ish leaders in Europe, and the Jewish organizations activists in Palestine, fear among the indigenous Palestinians grew. The Zionists and their supporters ignored the presence of the half million Arabs with centuries-old roots living on the land of their devotion. Arabic

---

1 Howard Sachar 1996, p.63. Herzl prediction to Max Bodenheimer, a German lawyer accompanied Herzl in his trip to Turkey to prepare drafts of a charter of settlement in Palestine in 1901.

newspapers in Beirut, Damascus, and Cairo had been accredited for drawing the attention to the serious development in Palestine. The World Zionist Organization established in 1901 a fund, the Jewish National Fund (JNF) that would be financed by contributions from world wide Jews and their supporters. By 1907, the JNF opened offices in Jaffa; and it created the Palestine Land Development Company (PLDC) in 1908 as a step to build a Palestinian beachhead. The PLDC main function was to purchase land in Palestine, settle the land with the new immigrants, train Jewish farmers, and develop self-supporting agriculture cooperatives. The Zionist project aimed at redeeming the land and only Jews would work on the land, thus expelling the Arab farm labor who had been tilling the land for generations. PLDC purchased land from absentee landlords who gained legal title to the land from Turkey by questionable means. It is estimated that 70% of land acquired by Jews was bought by the PLDC.[1] Besides securing the land for settlers, it provided food, shelter, tools, and schools for the Jewish newcomers and their families in Palestine. The JNF became a symbol of the Jews commitment to Zionism where thousands of JNF collection boxes were located in Jewish homes, businesses and places of religious and social events in Europe and America. Prior to World War I, a wave of mostly Russian socialist committed immigrants arrived in Palestine and Tel-Aviv, a new Jewish town, was founded close to Jaffa. A total of thirty-two settlements were established by the Zionist organizations between 1897 and 1914.[2]

THE BALFOUR DECLARATION

Eighteen months after British–French Sykes–Picot Agreement of 1916 which divided the eastern Mediterranean Arab lands between the two countries, the president of the Zionist Federation, Baron Lionel Rothschild was able to extract the ground-breaking Balfour Declaration. On November 2, 1917, the British foreign secretary, Balfour, presented a letter that has been called the Balfour Declaration to Lord Rothschild, committing the British Government support for the establishment of a national home for the Jewish people in Palestine.[3] Although the declaration carried the name of Balfour, it was actually framed and authored by Jewish Zionists. It was a one sentence statement drafted by linguistic and legal experts to lay the grounds for a future Jewish statehood and limit the rights of the non-Jewish population to religious and civil rights without referring to them as Arabs. Two years after the Declaration, Weizmann said in a speech to a Jewish audience in London: "[The Balfour Declaration] is the golden key which unlocks the doors of Palestine and gives you the possibility to put all your efforts into the country...., we can pour in a considerable number of immigrants, and finally establish such a society in Palestine that Palestine shall be as Jewish as England is English, or America is American..."[4] The declaration was the outcome of several months of negotiations between the British government

---

1 Robert Smith 1995, p.89.
2 Neville Mandel 1976.
3 Pappe 1994.
4 Chaim Weizmann, 1952, p.42.

of Lloyd George and the Zionists in Britain led by Chaim Weizmann. The explanations for the reasons behind the Balfour Declaration by British policy makers at the time range from idealism to utilitarianism. The motives have been seen by some as a result of the pressure exerted by the Zionists led by Chaim Weizmann, a scientist who contributed important services to the British war effort in the World War I.

Chaim Weizmann, a Russian born, German trained chemistry professor at the University of Manchester was recognized as a Zionist leader by the Jewish community in Britain at the outbreak of the war. He was introduced to several British political leaders by the influential Zionist, Herbert Samuel who had been the home secretary in Herbert Asquith government. Weizmann established relationships with the future Prime Minister Lloyd George, the Colonial Secretary Winston Churchill and undersecretary of foreign affairs Lord Robert Cecil. He earned more recognition at the highest level of government during the war for inventing a special fermentation process to be used by the British navy guns. His devotion to Britain and his personal charm and "unrivaled gift for lucid exposition" enhanced his influence on the policies of the British leadership.[1] He was promoting the idea of creating a Jewish homeland under British protection in Palestine, thus linking the success of the Zionist program with the victory of the Allies in the war.

When Lloyd George became the prime minister in 1916, there was consensus within his cabinet regarding the benefits that can be realized by Britain in having a partnership with the Zionists where Britain can rule over a Jewish Palestine. Undersecretary Mark Sykes, a good friend of Weizmann and a strong believer in the Zionist project, suggested that a Jewish presence in Palestine might serve the British interests in defending "the Suez Canal against attack from the north and as a station in the future air routes to the east."[2] General Allenby was preparing for the invasion of Palestine in 1917 when Balfour asked Weizmann to propose a written draft of a declaration to commit Britain to a Jewish national home in Palestine that he might present to the cabinet for possible approval. Such a declaration was necessary to confirm the British intent to have control over all Palestine and prevent it from falling totally or partially under the French influence based on Sykes–Picot Agreement. Some of Weizmann associates submitted in July 1917 the following draft that consisted of two articles: "1. His Majesty's Government accepts the principle that Palestine should be reconstituted as the national home of the Jewish people. 2. His Majesty's Government will use its best endeavors to secure the achievement of this object and will discuss the necessary methods and means with the Zionist Organization."

After some deliberation by the cabinet members, the Zionist's original draft was slightly revised and written in the form of a letter to Lord Rothschild, President of the British Zionist Federation. The letter which declared the decision of the British government to facilitate the establishment of a national home for the Jewish people in Palestine has been referred to as "the Balfour Declaration." The final formal draft of the Declaration submitted by the British foreign secretary Balfour to Lord Rothschild states: "His Maj-

---

1 Sir Ronald Storrs, 1937.
2 Christopher Sykes, 1965.

esty's Government view with favour the establishment in Palestine of a national home for the Jewish people and will use their best endeavors to facilitate the achievement of this object, it being clearly understood that nothing shall be done which may prejudice the civil and religious rights of existing non-Jewish communities in Palestine or the rights and political status enjoyed by Jews in any other country." It was "the first political success of the Zionist Organization."[1] It can be argued that the Declaration by itself was not binding because it was not a treaty between two states. But it became binding when the League of Nations incorporated it almost verbatim in Article 2 of the Mandate for Palestine: "The Mandate shall be responsible for placing the country under such political administrative and economic conditions as will secure the establishment of the Jewish national home...." The Mandate was even more specific by referring to "the historical connection of the Jewish people with Palestine" to secure the implementation of the Zionist's program.

Lloyd George stated in 1936 that what induced Britain to issue the Declaration was to enlist the support of the Jewish people, including the American Jewish community, during the war when Britain lost the confidence in its allies.[2] Other motives for the Declaration had to do with the ideologies and the attitudes of the British leadership. It was suggested that Lord Balfour, the main architect of the declaration that carries his name, and Prime Minister Lloyd George were ardent supporter of the Zionist movement due to their religious belief in the Bible and the Jews right of return. They were "deeply religious men and knew the Bible" according to Chaim Weizmann.[3] Arthur Balfour closed a memorandum he wrote on August 11, 1919 by stating that whether Zionism is right or wrong, "good or bad, is rooted in age-long traditions,..., of far profounder import than the desires and prejudices of the 700,000 Arabs who now inhabit that ancient land."[4]

Some ministers and British government officials might have been influenced by their colonial thinking on the superiority of the European man and the misperception of the Arabs. They believed that the Zionists could bring a measure of civilization and improve the quality of life among the indigenous Palestinians who had been seen as backward illiterate nomads. Most British politicians believed that a Jewish state allied with Britain would serve the British interests in the Middle East and help protect the lines of communications with the Indian subcontinent, the Jewel of the British Crown. The support for Zionism and disregard for the Palestinians' grievances became the basis for the policies of the British governments that succeeded Lloyd George administration. Some analysts suggest that British policy makers might have co-operated with the Zionists in order to divert Jewish immigration to Palestine instead of Britain.[5]

---

1 Yitzhak Shamir, 1994, p. 247.
2 Furlonge 1969, p.60.
3 Chaim Weizmann, *"United Nations Special Committee on Palestine Report,"* vol III. Jerusalem, July 8, 1947.
4 Arthur Balfour, *Documents on British Foreign Policy 1919-1939, First Series, vol IV. London 1952. no. 242.*
5 John Keay, 2003.

Regardless of the motives, Balfour Declaration was "one nation solemnly promised to a second nation the country of a third."[1] The British leaders gave themselves the right to grant a national home for the Jewish people, in a territory conquered by force, without consulting with its Arab population who constituted 93% of its inhabitants. Lord Curzon wrote to Colonel French on August 4, 1919 that the terms of the Mandate for Palestine included the enforcement of the Balfour Declaration and "This should be emphasized to Arab leaders at every opportunity and should be impressed on them that the matter is a '*chose jugée*' and continued agitation would be useless and detrimental."[2]

THE ZIONISTS STRATEGIES

In the quest to establish a Jewish state over the whole of Palestine, there have been many Zionist parties and organizations, but they all strongly believed that the support of the great powers was indispensable in the struggle for creating the Jewish state. The Zionists, however, never hesitated to fight back against the great powers with acts of violence if their interests were even marginally undermined, and there are many examples that support this view. When the Zionists perceived a change in the policy of the British regarding the future of Palestine, they fought back with guns and explosives. Britain provided the Zionists with the most important tool to establish a homeland, the Balfour Declaration, but the beneficiaries of the Declaration revolted against the Mandate authority, killed and even hanged British officers when the White Paper was released. The White Paper was discussed in Chapter 3. The United States has been supporting and defending the State of Israel before and after its inception, but the Israeli air force attacked the US reconnaissance ship, Liberty, off the coast of Gaza killing 34 and injuring 171 sailors during the 1967 Arab–Israeli war. It is believed that the Israelis attacked the ship to prevent its crew from hearing incriminating radio traffic.

Mainstream Zionist leaders including Chaim Weizmann and David Ben-Gurion advocated a gradualist strategy and slow conquest through land acquisition, dunam-by-dunam, and Jewish immigration, one immigrant at a time.[3] Others such as Vladimir (Ze'ev) Jabotinsky pressed for the maximalist approach, large scale immigration and the establishment of *Yishuv* armed forces in Palestine. Jabotinsky founded the para-military Haganah organization in the *Yishuv* because he strongly believed that military power was necessary for establishing the Jewish state on both sides of the Jordan River. He argued that since the Arabs would never agree voluntarily to turn Palestine into a country with a Jewish majority, the Jews should establish settlements under the protection of their own military "behind an iron wall which they [the Arabs] will be powerless to break down."[4] Jabotinsky has been considered by some historians as the second most charismatic Zi-

---

1 Jeff Halper, 2008

2 Lord Curzon to Colonel French, Cairo, August 4, 1919, *Documents on British Foreign Policy 1919-1939*, First Series, vol.IV.. London 1952, no. 236.

3 One dunam equals a quarter of an acre.

4 Avi Shlaim, 2000, p.13.

---

onist figure after Herzl.[1] Jabotinsky, a skillful journalist, eloquent orator and an ardent Zionist, was born in Odessa, Russia in 1880, immigrated to Palestine then exiled by Jamal Pasha, the Turkish military governor in Palestine. Jamal Pasha ordered the deportation of many non-Turkish residents of Palestine, including Zionist activists, after the beginning of World War I.

To enhance the British support for the Zionist program, Jabotinsky joined Joseph Trumpeldor, another exiled Zionist leader, in establishing a Jewish volunteer military unit within the British army to fight against the Turks in the war. They created the Jewish transport Zion Mule Corps in Alexandria, Egypt, in March and April of 1915. Its five hundred volunteers from Jewish political refugees in Egypt wore the Shield of David insignia on their shoulders and both Jabotinsky and Trumpeldor were commissioned officers in the unit. The Zion Mule Corps was engaged in combat at the beaches of Gallipoli where scores of its members were killed and wounded. To protect the *Yishuv* from the Turks' retaliation for the Anglo–Zionist collaboration, groups of Jews in Palestine demonstrated against the organizers of the Zion Mule Corps. By the end of the war, Jabotinsky formed another 5,000 men military "Jewish Legion" unit to fight with the British in World War II. The decision to offer services to the war effort through several Jewish military units with their own Jewish symbols was a long term strategy by the Jewish leadership to develop and train the nucleus of the future military that would fight to establish and defend Israel.

There were two major Zionist political parties in the pre-state period, the minimalist party of Jewish workers (the Labor Party) and the maximalist Zionist "Revisionist Party." While the two factions had the same goal of creating a Jewish state and the right of every Jew to immigrate to Palestine, they differed in their tactics. Leaders of the Labor Party adopted a policy of pragmatism even supporting the 1937 British partition proposal without abandoning the long-term objectives of taking over all of Palestine. The Labor Party was advocating the interests of the Jewish workers but it opposed efforts by the Mandate government to improve the living conditions of the Arab workers in Palestine. The "Revisionist Party" platform called for revising the terms of the Mandate to include Trans-Jordan and all of Palestine as a homeland for the Jews, and the use of military force to restrain the Palestinians. The Zionist Revisionist Party that Jabotinsky founded in 1925 was the front runner of the right wing Herut Party and its successor the Likud block which rose to power in 1977 under Menachim Begin. Jabotinsky recognized the just cause of the Palestinians and their patriotism, but he argued that the "Jewish justice is greater" and the Arab patriotism "cannot be bought [but] it can only be curbed by ... *force majeure*."[2] The Revisionists were an offshoot of the European fascism that promoted the submission of the people to a single leader.[3] Jabotinsky admired the Italian fascist dictator, Benito Mussolini, formed a militant youth group "Betar" affiliated with his party with its own brown uniform and the slogan, "in fire and blood Judea will be reborn." [4] Members of

---

1   Howard Sachar, 1996, p.184.
2   Anita Shapira, 1992, p.218.
3   Simha Flapan, 1979, p. 88.
4   Benny Morris, 1999, p.108.

the Revisionist Party, Betar group and some Haganah commanders founded in 1931 the armed Jewish underground organization, Irgun Zeva'i Le'umi (Etzel). It carried out armed attacks against Arabs, and after the publication of Malcolm MacDonald White Paper in May 1939, Etzel directed its activities against the British Mandatory authorities. MacDonald White Paper was described in Chapter 3. When Jabotinsky died in 1941, Menachem Begin emerged as the successor of the right wing revisionists and became the leader of the Etzel organization. With the break of the World War II, Etzel declared a temporary truce with the British.

After the temporary halt of violence during World War II and the defeat of Fascism, Etzel and other military organizations resumed their violent campaigns demanding Jewish statehood and no restrictions on immigration. The Haganah had already instituted conscription and began its own operations. With help from the Haganah, Etzel committed many terrorist attacks against the British and the Arab civilians under Begin's leadership. Assault units from Etzel blew up the British headquarters in Jerusalem at King David Hotel on July 22, 1946, killing 88 people. Although the bulk of the Zionist movement reacted to the UN's 1947 partition proposal with pragmatism, Begin was one of the few that rejected it, demanding that Israel should be established over all Palestine. He declared that "the partition of the Homeland is illegal...Eretz Israel will be restored to the people of Israel, all of it and for ever."[1] A combined force of Etzel and Stern terrorists using weapons provided by the Haganah slaughtered two thirds of the inhabitants of the Palestinian village of Deir Yaseen on April 9, 1948.[2] Menachem Begin was elected to the Knesset in 1949 and became the co-leader of the Likud bloc. He became the prime minister of Israel from 1977 until his retirement in 1983. He received the Nobel Peace Prize with Anwar al-Sadat for concluding the Egypt–Israel peace treaty in 1978, but he also initiated massive Jewish settlement program in the occupied West Bank, annexed the Syrian Golan heights, and ordered the invasion and occupation of southern Lebanon in 1982.

THE 1948 WAR (THE WAR OF INDEPENDENCE)

Long before 1947, intercommunal fighting was taking place between the Palestinian Arabs and the Jewish communities and there was no chance for direct negotiations between the two antagonists. All Arab factions in Palestine rejected the Jewish claim to Palestine and quarrels became common between Arab village farmers and the new Jewish settlers. Each of the Arab and Jewish Yishuv communities conducted its affairs independently from the other, but there were contacts and instances of cooperation between workers and the Arab and Jewish markets remained interdependent.[3] Illegal Jewish immigration was stepped up after World War II, and in most cases when ships were intercepted, the refugees were arrested and detained by the British. As stated above, Jewish militants committed violence against the British, and the Palestine problem became the concern of the

---

1 Chomsky, Noam, 1999, p. 161.
2 David Hirst, 2003, p.249.
3 Pappe 1994; Peretz 1996.

newly formed Arab League. Britain decided to convene a conference in London in 1946 and 1947, but both of the Palestinian Arabs and the Jewish Agency refused to participate because the British did not allow some of their leadership to attend. The Zionists insisted on partition and the Arabs wanted a unitary independent Palestine. The London conference was halted on February 1947 and the British government decided to leave Palestine altogether and refer the whole problem to the United Nations General Assembly (UNGA), rather than the Security Council. The British move to abandon Palestine was partially due to the cost of maintaining security when the British economy was floundering.[1]

After months of deliberation, the UN formed special committee to investigate. An eleven-nation investigative board, United Nations Special Committee on Palestine (UNSCOP), was set up on May 13, 1947 by the United Nations to investigate the Palestinian issue and make recommendations. The scope of the Committee investigation was expanded to include the problem of the displaced Jews of World War II. The Arab Higher Committee that was controlled by Haj Amin al-Husseini, the voice of the Palestinians, decided to boycott the committee hearings and the Arab states declared that they would not be bound by the committee recommendations. But Moshe Shartok and David Horowitz, the Jewish Agency representatives, met endlessly with the Committee members.[2]

On October 21–24 the UNSCOP members presented their recommendation to the UNGA. The Committee was divided into seven (Canada, Czechoslovakia, Guatemala, the Netherlands, Peru, Sweden and Uruguay) proposing partitioning Palestine into two states, one Jewish and the second Arab, to three (India, Iran and Yugoslavia) recommending one federation state, and the Australian delegate abstained. Majority of the committee members concluded that Arabs and Jews in Palestine were unable to live together within a single state.

Based on the committee recommendations, the General Assembly passed Resolution 181 (II) on November 29, 1947 to divide Palestine into an Arab state and a Jewish state with an international regime for the City of Jerusalem area. The Resolution designated 11,800 square kilometers or 45% of Palestine excluding Jerusalem area for the Arab state and 14,500 square kilometers or 55% for the Jewish state.[3] The General Assembly members voted thirty-three to thirteen for the partitioning plan. Jerusalem was designated as an international zone to be administered by the UN. The Jews welcomed the Resolution, regarding it as the realization of the Zionist vision and they decided to establish, defend, and expand the Jewish state as stipulated by the UN resolution. They might have wished for even more than 55% of the country, which included most of the fertile regions and the coveted coastal areas overlooking the Eastern Mediterranean. But for them, the importance of the resolution was that it gave them their own state, never mind its size or borders. But the Arab Palestinians rejected the Resolution because they felt it was unfair to give more than 55% of Palestine to the Jews who constituted a small percentage of the population and owned no more than 7% of the land. The first response of the Pal-

---

1 Pappe 1994.
2 Sachar, Howard, 2007
3 Martin Gilbert, 1998, p.149; Tom Segev and Arlen Neal Weinstein 1986, p.21.

estinians to the UN resolution was three-day general strike. Their leaders rejected the Resolution without having the power and resources to challenge it on the ground. Britain as the mandatory power in Palestine refused to participate in the implementation of the Resolution and refused to transfer its authority to a proposed UN commission or allowing its members to visit Palestine in 1947. As a result, confusion, disorder and violence ensued immediately after the Resolution was announced.

Poorly armed local Palestinian Arab volunteers, inexperienced and disorganized young men, were engaging well organized Jewish military groups including the Haganah that had battle experience during the 1936–1939 Palestinian rebellion and World War II. By April 1948 and before the mandate was terminated, the Jewish fighters silenced the Palestinian resistance. The war was discussed in more details in Chapter 3.

Early in 1948, a Jewish committee appointed a thirteen-member provisional Council of State under Chairman David Ben-Gurion. The Council acted as the provisional government for the Jewish controlled area with authority to collect taxes, issue paper currency and postage stamps, acquire national loans and the military of the Haganah pledged cooperation with the Council. In comparison, the Palestinian Arab community was in total chaos, hundreds of thousands were homeless and their leaders were taking refuge in neighboring countries. They were paying dearly for their failure to plan for anything comparable to the Jewish quasi-government.

Israel was proclaimed an independent state on May 14, 1948 when the Mandate was terminated and the British High Commissioner departed Palestine, and a provisional government of the State of Israel was proclaimed. Ben-Gurion read the "Declaration of Independence" and the Soviet Union and the United States recognized it immediately. The anti-Semitic policies and the horrors of the concentration camps of Germany led to the feeling of guilt by the West for failing to prevent the Nazi genocide in the 1940s, and strengthened the morality of the Zionist's argument that the Jews should have their own state, and motivated more Jews to flee Europe to Palestine. The United States recognized Israel's statehood immediately and within a few years of its establishment, Israel was recognized by most countries of the world. Andrei Gromyko, the foreign minister of the USSR, stated in his speech before the UNGA on November 26, 1947 that one of the reasons for supporting the creation of a Jewish state was that, "— there was not a single country in Western Europe which succeeded in adequately protecting the interests of the Jewish people against the arbitrary acts and violence of the Hitlerites.."[1] The irony of this rhetoric and the bleeding hearts in sympathy with the Jews was forcing the Palestinian people to pay for the European crimes.

On September 17, 1948, four months after the birth of Israel and when it had its own provisional government, Bernadotte and his aid, Colonel André Serot were murdered in downtown Jerusalem by members of the Jewish armed ultranationalist Lehi "Stern" terrorists in a deliberate and carefully planned plot. The assassination was planned by

---

1 UN General Assembly Official Records, 2nd Session, 1947, 125th Plenary Meeting, 124, Continuation of the discussion on the Palestinian question.

Yehoshua Zetler, approved by the three-man Lehi chiefs, Yitzhak Shamir, Natan Yellin-Mor and Yisrael Eldad, and carried out by a four-man team led by Meshulam Markover one day before the release of Bernadotte recommendations. Only two of the perpetrators, Yellin-Mor and Matitiahu Schmulevitz were apprehended, tried in a military court and received a short sentence as political prisoners, then set free for promising to be good citizens. Yellin-Mor claimed that Bernadotte was an agent of the British and enemy of Israel because he had opposed Israeli take over all of Palestine and Trans-Jordan.[1] Yitzhak Shamir rose to prominence and occupied the highest office in the Israeli government later on. He was elected to the Knesset, became the Speaker from 1977–1980, foreign minister from 1980–1986, then he became the head of the Likud Party and the Prime Minister twice, in 1983–1984 and 1986–1992.

Historians claim that strategies of the Jewish maximalists and the gradualists were different, but the Labor Party leaders who have been perceived as main stream gradualist Zionists followed the same policy that Jabotinsky had advocated.[2] The main stream Labor Zionists are no different from the so-called Revisionists in dealing with the Palestinians. The policy of the Labor Party under David Ben-Gurion, a socialist and the founder of Israeli left is a case in point. At the age of twenty, Ben-Gurion emigrated from Poland to Palestine in 1906 to start working as an agricultural laborer. Through his active involvement in politics and the commitment to socialism and Zionism, he rose to prominent positions in the labor movement. He was elected in 1921 as the secretary-general of the Histadrut, the General Federation of Labor in Palestine, and in 1930 he was one of the co-founders of the Labor Party (*Mapai*).

Ben-Gurion was elected chairman of the powerful Jewish Agency Executive in 1935, assumed the *Yishuv* defense portfolio in 1946 and started planning for the confrontation with the Arabs. Although Ben-Gurion supported the British partition proposal of 1937, he stated in a speech at the time that "the boundaries of the Zionist aspirations are the concern of the Jewish people and no external factor will be able to limit them."[3] He envisioned in 1942 the whole of Palestine and Trans-Jordan as the future Jewish state, but in 1946 he reverted to his old position of establishing a "Jewish commonwealth only within Palestine." When the British government abruptly retreated from the two-state approach and endorsed the White Paper on May 17, 1939 that called for one independent state, Ben-Gurion led the revolt against the British. He issued a written statement denouncing the White Paper and closing it with strong words: "It seems only too probable that the Jews will have to fight rather than submit to the Arab rule." It was against the basic Zionist principles to accept the idea of living in a bi-national liberal democracy where the Jews would eventually become a minority and the Palestinian Arabs a majority. And it was the main reason for carrying out the mass expulsion of Arabs in the 1948 war. Ben-Gurion decided, as the chairman of the Jewish Agency and the leader of the *Yishuv*, to support

---

1 David Hirst, 2003, p.280.
2 Avi Shlaim, 2000, p.16.
3 Noam Chomsky, 1999, p. 161.

the hardliner Jabotinsky in establishing the Haganah military organization to defend the Zionists interests in Palestine and to be the nucleus for the future Israeli army.

During World War II, Ben-Gurion declared that he would fight the British in Palestine to establish a Jewish state and fight side by side with them to defeat the Nazis. He said: "We will fight with the British against Hitler as if there were no White Paper; we will fight the White Paper as if there were no war."[1] He and Weizmann attended the May 1942 American Zionists conference in the Biltmore Hotel in New York. The conference adopted a resolution to work toward establishing a Jewish commonwealth on all of mandatory Palestine. In junction with the Biltmore resolution, military Zionists conceived the "*Plan Dalet*" to insure the success of creating a state with Jewish majority in Palestine. In 1945, Ben-Gurion established in the US a business group financed by the Jewish Agency to acquire and send arms for the Haganah. "*Plan Dalet*" evolved over the years and by 1947, it included contingencies to deal with the Arabs when the British would depart Palestine. Its objective was to protect the Jewish settlements and population and to gain control of areas outside the sectors designated for the Jewish State to "make [it] as large and Jewish as possible before the Arab armies could stop them [the Jewish fighters]."[2] The plan was expanded to include methods to force expulsion of Arab civilian population from future Israel by the Jewish military using physical and psychological terror and preventing their return. It called for seizing most or all of Palestine which Ben-Gurion alluded to in an address to the Zionist Executive on the 7th of April 1948 only five days after "*Plan Dalet*" was adopted by the Haganah and other Jewish armed groups: "Let us resolve not to be content with merely defensive tactics, but at the right moment to attack all along the line and not just within the confines of the Jewish state and the borders of Palestine..."[3]

Ben-Gurion accepted the 1947 UN Resolution for the partition of Palestine because it gave the Jewish state international recognition and legitimacy, but he was not satisfied with the borders established by the Resolution or the demographic make-up of the proposed Jewish state. The designated state did not fulfill the ambitions of the Zionists who had been striving to have all of Palestine. The state was too small to accommodate all future immigrants and its population included more than 50% Arabs, but Ben-Gurion had the solution for both perceived problems. As the first prime-minister of Israel, he led the nation to victory in the "War of Independence" and he was responsible for the planning and execution of "*Plan Dalet*" to expand the state beyond the proposed borders and the forced expulsion of Arab civilian population from their towns and villages to solve the demographic problem of the new State of Israel. More than 400 Palestinian villages were taken over and their inhabitants were driven out or fled in terror and never been allowed to return. The irony is that Zionists and some of their Western supporters claim that Israel was established through anti-colonial struggle.

Ben-Gurion's first term as a prime minister ended on December 7, 1953. He submitted his resignation to the President and went to work in "Sdeh Boker kibbutz" in the Negev

---

1 Avi Shlaim, 2000, p.23.
2 David Hirst, 2003, p.264.
3 Ben-Gurion, 1954, p.239.

desert for more than two years. He served for a short time in 1954-55 as a minister of defense under Prime-Minister Moshe Sharett. Then after the 1955 elections, he was called upon to become again a prime minister from November 1955 until his retirement in 1963. For Ben-Gurion, the 1948 War of Independence was only one step toward achieving the Great Zionist enterprise. After the 1949 armistice agreements with the Arabs, Ben-Gurion treated the negotiated borders only as temporary demarcations because he planned on expanding the State of Israel to absorb the thousands of Jewish immigrants who had been arriving in Israel every year. He declared that, "We [the Jews] have to set up a dynamic state bent upon expansion."[1] Ben-Gurion talked and wrote about peace with the Arab states, but his actions suggest he was reluctant to pursue permanent peace on the basis of the UN resolutions regarding the Arab refugees' right of return. The armistice agreements provided Israel with immediate international recognition and security, and the potential to expand in the long run. With the passage of time the world has forgotten the UN resolutions regarding the partition or the right of return for the Palestinian refugees. In the meantime, Israel used its military superiority to expand its borders when there was an opportunity to conquer more land. Under binding peace agreements, on the other hand, Israel would be under pressure to give back some territory to the Arabs and may allow the return of Palestinian refugees.

THE 1956 WAR

Israel was looking for war to pre-empt the potential threat of Egypt's arms purchase and to thwart Nasser's support for the Palestinian guerrillas.[2] It found one by aligning itself with the French and the British to overthrow Nasser. The French wanted to retaliate for Nasser's support to the Algerian Liberation movement and the British wanted to prevent Nasser from nationalizing the Suez Canal.

Prime Minister Ben-Gurion, French Prime Minister Guy Mollet and the British Foreign Secretary Selwyn Lloyd held a secret meeting in Sèvres, France, on October 22–24, 1956 to discuss military action against Egypt. They planned the participation of the Israeli Defense Force (IDF) in the 1956 tripartite military plot against Egypt. From Israel's point of view, Egypt had been violating the armistice agreement and threatening its security. Ben-Gurion listed many Egyptian violations in a speech to the Knesset on January 2, 1956.[3] He complained about raids by armed regulars and irregulars across the armistice lines killing Jews and mining Israeli lines of communications that caused hundreds of Israeli casualties in the early 1950s. He described life in Israel on the borders with Gaza unbearable. He also pointed out that Egypt had "blocked the passage of the Israeli shipping in the Suez Canal and in the Straits of Tiran." Ben-Gurion asserted that the flow of military arms and the rhetoric by the Egyptian leaders represented a serious threat to Israel. He questioned Egypt's purchase of Soviet weapons and announcements by government-con-

---

1   Ben-Gurion, 1954, p.419.
2   Pappe 2004
3   Ben-Gurion, 1973, p.271.

trolled "Cairo Radio" station that the Egyptian revolution had been born in Palestine and the mission of its military was to restore Palestine and "eradicate" Zionism.

Leaders of the three countries reached a plan of attack on Egypt called the "Treaty of Sèvres" that included military and political features. Israel's large scale military attack and occupation of Sinai, including the east bank of the Suez Canal, was planned to provide the pretext for the Anglo–French military to intervene and occupy the Canal Zone. Israel would drop paratroopers in Sinai east of the Suez Canal to destroy the Palestinian guerrilla camps; then Britain and France would announce a joint ultimatum to Israel and Egypt to cease military action for fear of disrupting shipping in the Canal. Israel would accept the ceasefire, but they were counting on Egypt to reject the Allied conditions; then the Anglo–French would land their paratroopers along the Canal and seize the waterway. In the meantime the Allied airforce would attack the Egyptian airfields and destroy Nasser's airplanes.

Two members of Ben-Gurion's cabinet objected to the plan because it was in partnership with colonial powers. The staunchest political supporter of the Sinai Campaign was Menachem Begin, the leader of the maximalist *Herut* Party and the advocate of establishing the State of Israel over the whole of Palestine. Ben-Gurion territorial expansionist program was not limited to Palestine or the Balfour Declaration. His plan was to take Sinai Peninsula from Egypt, an independent neighboring country, and annex it to Israel. During the planning for the Suez War, Ben-Gurion told his French counterpart that he would like to "tear this peninsula [Sinai]" from Egypt and annex it to Israel because the British had been the ones who stole it from the Turks and gave it to Egypt, and Israel was looking forward to extracting the oil that had been discovered in the south of Sinai and transport it in pipelines to Haifa.[1]

The IDF launched the Sinai campaign on October 29, 1956, by crossing the international borders with Egypt and dropping paratroopers deep in Sinai. Prime Minister Ben-Gurion announced on October 30 that "Israeli defense forces entered and engaged *"fedayeen"* [Palestinian guerrillas] units in Ras en-Nakbeh and Quntilla and seized positions west of the Nakhl crossroads in the vicinity of the Suez Canal.

Britain and France issued their ultimatum to Israel and Egypt demanding that they withdrew their forces ten miles away from the Suez Canal, which Israel's foreign minister accepted and Egypt rejected. On October 31, Allied fighter-bombers began bombing Egyptian airfields destroying Egypt's air force on the ground. When Jordan and Syria rejected Nasser's appeal for military support, he ordered a general withdrawal from Sinai, thus opened the opportunity for the Israeli military to advance within ten miles distance from the Canal. Within a week after the invasion, the Egyptian military had to withdraw from Gaza and Sinai in front of the advanced IDF mechanized columns. By November 2, all Sinai was occupied, Gaza Strip was under full control by the Israeli "Home Guard" and "Palestinian guerrillas were rounded up from prepared lists and shot on the spot."[2] The

---

1 Ben-Gurion Diary, entry on October 25, 1956.
2 Howard Sachar, 2007, p 500

triumphant Ben-Gurion declared the death of the 1949 armistice agreement implying that Israel would annex Sinai and the straits of Tiran. When the IDF captured Sharm el-Sheikh in Sinai in 1956, Ben-Gurion's congratulation message to the unit that captured the area was: "Yotvata, or [Tiran], which until fourteen hundred years ago was part of an independent Jewish state, will revert to being part of the third kingdom of Israel."[1] Yotvata was the Hebrew name of Tiran Island at the entrance to the Gulf of Aqaba.

Within days of the invasion, "Israeli geographers, geologists, archaeologists, prehistorians, philologists and scholars of the Bible descended on the wilderness and began scouring it for traces of the Exodus route which the Tribes of Israel had followed out of Egypt."[2] The victory excitement in Israel was short lived. President Eisenhower sent a letter to Ben-Gurion demanding Israel's withdrawal from the Sinai. The Soviet Prime Minister Nikolai Bulganin threatened Soviet intervention if Israel, Britain and France did not withdraw their military forces from Egyptian lands. Britain and France decided to back down and advised Israel to withdraw in return for a peace treaty that would give Israel some economic gains, including freedom of navigation in the Gulf of Aqaba and the Suez Canal. France felt obliged to help Israel in some way as a payback for its support in the war campaign, which explains in part why they provided Israel with a nuclear reactor immediately after the war.

Ben-Gurion asserted that nuclear weapons that could be used as a deterrent to the Arab world would be the only guaranty of Israel's security, and he sought a nuclear reactor from France to produce nuclear weapons. France built the reactor in southern Israel in 1957 with the capacity to produce weapons-grade plutonium fuel, and then supplied the needed natural uranium to fuel it.[3] An Israeli whistleblower, Mordechai Vanunu, claiming to be a technician from Dimona nuclear facilities, stole classified documents from his workplace, immigrated to Australia, and published some secrets about Israel's nuclear activity in the *London Sunday Times* in October 1986. He unveiled information about a sophisticated nuclear program that had produced over 200 bombs deliverable by F-16 aircrafts and Jericho missiles. The documents revealed for the first time the capability of the plutonium separation facility to produce 40 kilograms annually, far more than previous estimates. (Mr. Vanunu spent 18 years in jail for this and is still being harassed by the Israeli government.)

THE 1967 WAR (THE SIX-DAY WAR)

In 1966, the propaganda wars among the Arabs had intensified and was fed by border skirmishes with Israel on the Syrian and the Jordanian fronts. Jordan was accused by Egypt's media for failing to repulse November 1966 massive Israeli attack on the village of Al Samu', in the Hebron area. The same media never criticized Syria, Egypt's ally, for losing six MiG 21s in one aerial battle with Israel over the Golan Heights in April 1967.

---

1 Avi Shlaim, 2000, p.179.
2 Howard Sachar, 1996, p. 506.
3 Shimon Peres, 1995, p.130.

The aerial battle was followed by heavy artillery and tank fire exchanges across the entire 76-kilometer-long Syrian-Israeli front line. Moshe Dayan admitted that Israel's deliberate border provocations were designed to engage the Syrian army in battle to justify Israel's expansion in the DMZ [Golan Heights]. The Egyptians rushed to escalate the conflict without anticipating the consequences of their action.

On May 18, 1967, Jamal Abdel-Nasser ordered the withdrawal of the United Nations observers from the demilitarized buffer zone in Sinai and moved his troops near the borders with Israel for the first time since 1957. Four days later, he made another dangerous decision. His navy blockaded the Straits of Tiran, denying Israel navigation in the Gulf of Aqaba through the Red Sea. Nasser declared that "the closing of the Strait wipes out the last smears of the 1957 War."[1] Ironically, while Nasser was delivering speeches threatening Israel if it attacked Syria, he sent his deputy Zakariyya Muhieddine to Washington to work out a diplomatic face-saving solution to the crisis which he had already created. Nasser had hoped for a victory by forcing an Israeli backdown in the war of words, not in a real war, but for Israel, what he had done was an act of war. Unfortunately for the West Bank residents, King Hussein of Jordan joined the conflict by declaring his support for Egypt and inviting Iraqi troops to take positions along the Israeli frontier. Nasser's decisions played into the hands of the Israelis, who took his actions as a declaration of war and responded with a surprise attack on June 5, destroying most of the Egyptian, Syrian and Jordanian forces.

Within six days, the Israeli army achieved an overwhelming victory. It captured the Gaza Strip and the Sinai Peninsula from Egypt, East Jerusalem and the West Bank from Jordan, the Golan Heights from Syria and Sheeba Farms from Lebanon. Israeli leaders started drawing new boundaries for their state and debating how to coexist with more than 3 million Palestinians residing in the newly occupied lands without disturbing Israel's Jewish character. Three weeks after declaring victory, Israel expanded its capital by incorporating East Jerusalem and large areas of the West Bank into its municipality. Some Israeli leaders called for annexing all the conquered territory, but the ruling Labor Party was more careful not to rush into a decision that would impact the demography of the State.

In his autobiography, Ariel Sharon referred to the capture of the West Bank and Jerusalem in 1967 as the liberation of Samaria and Judea, an area he claimed belonged to Israel but had been captured by the Arab armies in 1948. In the view he wished to promote, Israel was restoring Jewish lands that the Arabs had wrongfully taken from the Jews. And he added that he "had no interest in ruling the Arabs of Samaria, Judea, and Gaza. I [Sharon] believed they needed to run their lives with as little Israeli interference as possible."

During the Israelis' euphoria, the commander of the armored division in the war and the future prime minister, Ariel Sharon, suggested that their victory was not complete and that there was much more to do. Even when he was still with his army units in Sinai in the final days of the war, Sharon cabled instructions to move the infantry school to an already

1 Sachar, Howard, 2007

assigned location near Nablus and he advised that Israel's immediate action should be to "establish Jewish footholds [in the West Bank and Jerusalem] as fast as possible" in order to secure the area. On his return from Sinai, he "spent a great deal of time" in the West Bank and Jerusalem neighborhoods searching for strategic locations and high controlling terrains with access to road junctions to be colonized and retained. He believed that Israel should create facts on the ground because, in his words, "survival depended not on faith in someone's goodwill, but on facts, actually building on the land and actually defending it." He cited his mother warning him on another occasion while he was negotiating with the Egyptians, "Do not trust them! Do not trust them!" Sharon insisted that certain areas of the occupied lands would never be relinquished because of their strategic or historical and cultural significance to Israel and the Jewish people. These include Jerusalem, the high grounds that are "essential for defending Israel's industrial centers," and the Jordan River valley. To secure certain areas permanently in Israeli hands, Sharon suggested that Jews must establish large settlements there.

Ties to the occupied land had to be forged. The Israelis called the conquered lands by their Biblical names and drew new maps with view to settle Jews and provide their colonies with the necessary infrastructure. Sharon was only one of many Zionist individuals and organizations that were surveying the newly occupied land with one purpose, to colonize it. Immediately after the war, Israel had many plans proposed by military men, government committees and the World Zionist Organization. They all want to annex the land and its resources without giving Israeli citizenship to its Arab population. To achieve that goal, the leadership of the Labor Party decided to adopt two plans, the "Dayan Plan" and the "Allon Plan." Israeli Defense Minister Moshe Dayan's plan called for linking the West Bank and Gaza to Israel through roads, electricity, water and communications. He believed that the links would act as "open bridges" that would lead to economic assimilation of the occupied land in Israel and pave the road to coexistence and stability.

The Allon Plan had been named after Yigal Allon, a commander of the Palmach military unit in the War of Independence, the minister of Labor during the 1967 war and deputy Prime Minister after the war. Allon's objective was to absorb most occupied land into Israel, but excluding the Palestinians themselves. His plan called for dividing the West Bank into two sectors, one to be annexed to Israel and the other to be home for Palestinians under partial autonomy. The plan required the creation of two sets of borders for Israel, one for security and the other for political ends. The security borders were extended to encompass all historical Palestine. The political borders would include Israel proper and whatever settlements that can be built and as much land as possible in the West Bank and Jerusalem areas. The plan would allow the Palestinians to have their autonomy over the northern sector of the West Bank with the exception of a ten mile strip to be annexed to Israel and the rest of the West Bank to be settled by Israelis.[1]

Israeli leaders never set fixed borders for their state since its establishment. They always considered the pre-1967 borders as temporary armistice demarcation lines and that

---

1 Guyatt, Nicholas, 1998, p.149

the "Land of Israel is wherever the boots of its soldiers tread." Twenty-six years later, the expanded Allon Plan was the basis for the Oslo peace process that was concluded by the Israelis and the PLO leaders on behalf of the Palestinians.

The post-1967 era was marked by self-confidence of the IDF and the political leaders, and their disregard for the Arab aspirations of recovering their occupied lands which the Israelis called "the disputed lands." It was the territorial expansion period for Israel in the newly conquered lands. Moshe Dayan was speaking for most of the Israeli leadership when he called for building large-scale Jewish settlements and drawing a new map for Israel "from Jordan to the Suez Canal" rather than exploring the possibility of peace with the Arabs.[1] As for Palestine, Dayan claimed in 1973 that "there is no more Palestine. Finished."[2] The Labor government policy toward the occupied land for the years 1973-77 under Prime Minister Golda Meir was spelled out in a published "Galilee Document" that was proposed by Israel Galilee, a cabinet member, and approved by the ministers of the Labor Party. It called for expanding existing settlements, building new ones and constructing industrial projects in the occupied land.[3] The plan was provocative to the Arabs and inconsistent with the potential for peace. The Israeli governments have embarked on settling Jews in Jerusalem and the West Bank to create irreversible demographic and political facts on the ground. Jewish only settlements, highways and economic infrastructures to support them have left the Arab population living in disconnected enclaves.

Much was said and written about the role of the Nobel peace laureate Yitzhak Rabin in advancing the peace process, especially after his violent death on November 4, 1995 at the hands of a rightwing Jewish militant, but during his three years in office, Israel expanded the existing settlements especially in East Jerusalem, continued the policy of confiscating more Arab lands for such expansion, and constructed a network of roads that linked the settlements with Israel exclusively for the settlers use. Rabin was the commander of the Haganah military units that forced the Arab residents of Lydda and Ramle to leave their homes for good in 1948. Short time before his death, Rabin was quoted saying: "There will be no Jerusalem for the Palestinians and no return for the refugees." While he was the chief-of-staff, General Yitzhak Rabin ordered his soldiers to break the bones of the Palestinian children who protested the occupation in 1988 and the soldiers carried out his orders. More than 5% of the West Bank was confiscated and more than 40,000 homes were built in the West Bank settlements during the tenures of Rabin and his successor Peres.[4] After Prime Minister Netanyahu defeated Shimon Peres in the 1996 elections, the finance minister of the incoming government, Dan Meridor thanked Rabin and Peres governments for incorporating large areas of the West bank and increasing the settlers population, saying "[They] increased the number of Jews in Judea and Samaria [the West Bank] by 40% in the past four years."[5] The Israeli Likud, Labor and Kadima Parties have

---

1 Quoted by Abba Eban in his Autubiography, 1977.
2 *Times Magazine,* July 30, 1973.
3 Avi Shlaim, 2000, p. 317.
4 Nicholas Guyatt, 1998.
5 *Haaretz,* July 19, 1996.

been committed to the annexation of land, expansion of the settlements, and promulga-tion of many laws that contravened the Universal Declaration of Human Rights such as administration detention, assassination, torture, house demolition, schools closure and building the separation wall. Chapters 9 and 10 have more details on the Israeli policy toward the Palestinians in the occupied lands.

THE 1973 WAR (YOM KIPPUR WAR)

The Israeli arrogance and its implied contempt for the Arabs gave Sadat of Egypt and Assad of Syria the motive to go to war in 1973 and refute the Israeli's assumption that it had the capacity to perpetuate the status quo indefinitely. Unlike the previous wars with Israel, the 1973 war was limited in its scope, objectives and outcome. It was intended to re-cover parts of the Egyptian Sinai Peninsula and the Syrian Golan Heights, not Palestinian occupied land. The significance of the 1973 war was the conclusion by Anwar Sadat that there was no hope of solving the conflict with Israel through military means. The Egyptian leader decided to launch a personal diplomatic mission by traveling to Israel and address-ing the Knesset in November 1977. Israel returned all of Sinai in exchange for Egyptian recognition of its existence and demilitarizing Sinai. Israel signed a peace agreement with belligerent Egypt, the only Arab country that presented real threat to Israel. The 1973 war will be discussed in more depth in Chapter 6.

By signing the peace treaty with the most populous Arab state, Israel has become more secure and more powerful in dealing with the Palestinians, the Syrians and the Lebanese. Israel's position was further enhanced by the international and regional developments of the 1990s. Iraq's wars against its neighbors diverted the focus of politics in the region on the threat of Iraqi, an Arab state and a sworn enemy of Israel. The US led "Desert Storm," a coalition with Egyptian and Syrian participation to free Kuwait from Iraqi occupation; and Israel obtained additional weapons from the US to convince it not to retaliate against Iraq's Scud missile attacks. The collapse of the Soviet Union, the traditional supporter of Arab causes, made Israel even more secure than before. The November 11, 2001, terrorist attacks that killed close to three thousand people on US soil triggered the invasion of two countries, Afghanistan and Iraq. The wars weakened the Arab states further and allowed Israel to dismiss any Palestinian resistance to occupation as act of terrorism.

THE RUSSIAN JEWS

The last wave of immigration to Israel from Russia and East Europe in the 1990s after the collapse of the Soviet Union underscores the fact that Israel continues to be an im-migrant settler country. Jews in East Europe constituted 75% of worlds Jewry in the 19th century and the largest numbers of them were to be found in Russia. Jews in the West were integrated among their gentile fellow citizens in reformed and secular societies, but until the middle of the 19th century, Russian Jews were segregated more closely among themselves by force or choice. They maintained their religious and communal traditions including diet, dress, Hebrew prayers and daily Yiddish vernacular. Under the great reformer Alexander II who ascended the tsarist throne in 1855, Russian Jews received for the first time their civil rights as full citizens of the state. They started working in local governments, attended high education institutions and many joined the Russian middle class and excelled in their professions and intellectual activities. This was the beginning of the European Jewish enlightenment period, referred to as "*Haskalah*" in the Jewish history. This period produced the Jewish poets Mecah Joseph Lebensohn and Judah Leib Gordon and Jewish essayist Moshe Lilienblum, who told the Jews to follow Jewish traditions at home and the synagogue but to live like the mainstream Russians when leaving home. The *Haskalah* writers remained faithful for their Jewish heritage. They used Hebrew as the language of expression even in their secular literary work; they described Jewish life in Russia and contrasted it with the history of the idealized ancient Jewish life.[1] And as described above, Vladimir Jabotinsky was an accomplished Zionist Russian writer. By the end of World War I, the czarist regime was replaced by the communist Soviet government which denounced Zionism as a capitalist invention. Nationalism, including Zionism, is anathema to the communist ideology. Zionism was accused of denying the primacy of the socialist revolution and Zionist offices and periodicals were closed in early 20th century. During World War II, the Histadrut established a wartime fund in support of the Soviet Union. And in May 1947, the Soviet Union supported the establishment of Israel although it preferred the establishment of a democratic Arab–Israeli state in Palestine.

The big break for the Russian and East European Jews came when Mikhail Gorbachev assumed leadership of the Soviet Union in 1985 and introduced economic and political liberalization. Unanticipated consequence of the new policies was ethnic upheavals, nationalist unrest and the collapse of the Soviet Empire political and economic system. Under liberalization, Russian Jews were allowed to leave after decades of obstinate refusal. The floodgate of Jews immigrants opened and Soviet and El-Al planes started daily massive airlift of thousands of Jews to Israel. Russian Jews immigration in the 1990s was a historic demographic infusion of people heading for Israel, and the US was accredited for its success. To discourage the immigrants from going to the US, the United States Immigration Bureau repealed a law that granted Jews fleeing the Soviet Union automatic entrance to US. And Gorbachev government cooperated in facilitating Jewish departure to Israel.

A total of 8,144 Jewish Russians arrived in 1987, and in 1990 the number rose to 181,000. By the end of the 1990s, Israel's population increased by 20% when more than one million Russian Jews made it to Israel. Most of them were atheists and their motive for immigrating to Israel was primarily the search for a better standard of living rather than fulfilling the Zionist dream. It was a free ride; citizenship was granted on arrival, and living accommodations and financial aid were provided by the Israeli state and some US-based NGOs. Each arrival was handed 22,000 shekels to cover first year living expenses and the Jewish Agency provided health insurance and no-interest mortgage. Arriving families included three generations, the grandparents, the parents and the children.

---

1 Sachar, Howard, 2007

Russian immigrants were treated differently from the North African and Middle East or the Falashas immigrants. They were allowed to settle directly in the Israeli society at large rather than going through the absorption centers. The young arrivals mastered Hebrew easily and the middle-age immigrants learnt Hebrew but preferred the Russian language when they huddled in their social gatherings. Ten years after the first Russian immigrants arrived in Israel, Russian-language radios, newspapers, orchestras and book stores became popular in Israel.

Israel is a country of immigrants from different backgrounds, but once the immigrants settle down they make contributions to their newly adopted country and they get involved in its politics. Different reports from Israel have claimed that along with the Russian Jews, an estimated 200,000 immigrants had not met the *Halacha* (Jewish law) conditions to be considered as Jews, but they received citizenship and all other accommodations like other Jews. Russian immigrants, Jews or gentiles, augmented Israel's population, served in the military and participated in the development of science and high technology since a large percentage of them arrived with engineering training bestowed by the Soviet Union. They also started their own political parties upon arrival, but they added volatility to the already unstable political system in Israel. Most of them supported the election of Yitzhak Rabin in 1992 against Shamir, who was accused of not responding to the Russian immigrant's economic needs; then they swung to the right in 1996, helping Netanyahu win the election. In 1999 the majority voted for Ehud Barak and in 2009 election, they voted for the right-wing Yisrael Beiteinu Party that was established by the Russian born Avigdor Lieberman.

Russian Israelis, who constitute 6% of the Israeli population today, are among the most hawkish toward the Palestinians. They support settlements in the West Bank and East Jerusalem where many of them live, including Avigdor Lieberman. Lieberman suggested that the model for dealing with the Palestinians should be Valdimir Putin's 1990s bombardment of Chechnya, which caused the death of a third of the entire population. The Yisrael Beitenu Party (that has been referred to as the "Russian immigrants' party") won 15 seats in the 2009 election, making it the third largest party after Kadima and Likud. The party joined the 2009 government under Prime Minister Netanyahu, and Lieberman became the foreign minister. If the party leaders had their way, they would make Israel purely a Jewish state by forced transfer of Israeli–Arabs.

THE ISRAELI –ARABS

Jews constituted about 50,000 or 7% of the population in Palestine in 1917 when the British government officially committed itself to support the establishment of national home for the Jewish people in the "Balfour Declaration." By the end of 1948, the Jewish population had increased to 30%. And within two years after creating their new state, the Zionists succeeded in making Israel a Jewish-dominant society. The number of immigrant settlers grew and most of the Arab population was driven out or fled in fear to neighboring countries. The Jewish population doubled within the first three years and the Arab population that remained in Israel became a minority. There was mass Jewish immigration from Europe and from Arab states. The Iraqi government allowed more than 120,000 Iraqi Jews to be flown in two stages to settle in Israel, Operation Izra and Nehemia. And more than 47,000 Yemeni Jews immigrated to their new adopted state in 1949-50.

A total of 150,000 Palestinians did not flee in the 1948 war while 750,000 of their countrymen did flee for their lives when the State of Israel was established. Those who decided to stay in their homeland, under Israeli rule, constitute about 20% of the Israeli population in 2010 and they are known as the Israeli–Arabs. They have been given the Israeli citizenship but they suffer from state discrimination. The "Israeli–Arabs" have been accused by some Israeli media as a fifth column; Israel took over their lands and relegated them to second class citizens. Since 1948, Israel has formalized a dual system of governing its citizens based on their self-proclaimed ethnicity and religious affiliation to de-Arabize and Judaize the country by imposing laws that gave the Jewish communities exclusive privileges and dominate the Israeli–Arab citizens.

According to the Legal Center for Arab Minority Rights in Israel, there are many Israeli laws that explicitly discriminate against the Israeli Arabs. In its 2005 Annual Report, the US State Department said that "[There is] institutionalized legal and societal discrimination against Israel's [Arab] Christian, Muslim and Druze citizens. The government does not provide Israeli–Arab communities with the same quality of education, housing, employment and social services as Jews." When some Israeli–Arabs joined Palestinians of the West Bank and Gaza in protesting Ariel Sharon visit to al-Haram al-Sharif Mosque in October 2000, the Israeli police treated them as enemies and fired rubber bullets and live ammunition to quell the unarmed demonstrators, killing twelve Israeli–Arabs. Because no national based Arab political organization in Israel was permitted for years, the Israeli–Arabs had to join the Israeli Communist Party to protest the laws that discriminated against them and fight for their civil rights.

Israeli leaders were not satisfied with the removal of 85% of the native Palestinians within the nascent Israeli state and the plunder and destruction of their homes. The remaining Palestinians have been subjected to laws that deprived them of their land. Israel enacted more than thirty statutes for the purpose of transferring private Israeli–Arab lands to the state. Israeli–Arabs also include refugees estimated in 1948 to be around 40,000 individuals who were expelled from their homes and remained in the area occupied by Israel during the war. They were evicted by the Jewish military from their homes in Galilee, West Jerusalem, Lydda and Jaffa, but decided to move to the next safe villages hoping one day they would return to their homes. They have been living in Israel but are not allowed by the Israeli government to return to their towns and villages. After being denied citizenship for many years, they ultimately became Israeli citizens but are not allowed to reclaim their homes and lands that are within few miles from where they live. They became known as "Absent-Present," a name coined by Israel to mean they are absent from their homes and present in the state.

Within months of its birth in 1948, Israel used another form of forced eviction of Arab villagers when it decided to clear its border areas of any Arabs to a depth of four to eight miles, creating more internal refugees. Residents of many villages within this area, including Iqrit and Bir'im and Tarshiha, along the Lebanese border, and Zakariya near Jerusalem, were expelled from their homes and farms, which were suddenly declared military areas. Salman Abu Sitta lists hundreds of Palestinian localities that were ethnically cleansed between 1948 and 1950. Fifty years later, they are still not allowed to return to their homes while Jewish-only agricultural and industrial settlements and towns have been established on their land. In December 1998, the Knesset defeated a bill that would have allowed the villagers of Iqrit to return to their homes. The confiscated Arab lands have been sold or leased only to Jews. Most of the JNF landholdings, allocated to Jews only, has been expropriated by the Israeli government from Arab owners and transferred to the JNF. Arab land controlled by the JNF in 1961 exceeded 3,500,000 dounums (875,000 acres) according to a Hebrew University study.

Israeli–Arabs are the poorest, least educated citizens and unemployment among them is higher than in any other group; they have no access to welfare or subsidized housing. Israel has laws that allocate generous financial support and low interest loans for those who served in the military and other laws that provide financial compensation to the ultra-Orthodox Jews who do not serve in the military or contribute to the economy, but there are no such laws to help its Arab citizens. Israel has been continuously improving its infrastructure, building new schools and hospitals and expanding its highways and light-rail system everywhere in the country except in the Arab towns. The streets in Arab towns and Arab neighborhoods in the mixed cities are not maintained, the municipal services are poor and the classrooms in Arab schools are crowded.

Zionist leaders had one long term strategy to achieve one goal, and for more than one hundred years they have been committed to its success; and finally they succeeded. Most Israeli Jews today seem to believe that only the Jews have a just cause, not the Palestinians. They treat the Palestinian people as enemies simply because they aspire to be free from occupation and oppression. The Israeli Jewish population could better their lives and achieve a moral success if they liberated themselves from their faulty assumptions, superstitions and sense of divine entitlement, and transcended their ethnocentrism by finding ways to deal fairly with the Palestinians. The Israeli historian Yaacov Lozowick advised his fellow Israeli Jews that their role today should not be "to [seek] recompense for what they lost in the wars against the Romans; it [Israel] can enable the Jews to fulfill their prophetic visions of social justice, truth , and morality, not the geographic ones of hills and valleys."[1]

Despite their successes, the Zionists lost two symbolic arguments that have no real value for the Palestinian national cause. First, they proved the falsehood of their early claim that "Palestine was a land without people" and Golda Meir's dismissive claim that the Palestinians "did not exist." Second, contrary to the early Zionists' speculation that

---

[1] Lozowick, Yaacov, 2003

Jews would be safe only in a country of their own, the Israeli leaders' policy of conquest, domination and oppression has made Israel the only place where many Jews feel insecure and unsafe, especially since 1967, even after many war victories and political recognition.

CHAPTER 5. THE HASHEMITES AND PALESTINE

The Hashemites claim to be a noble family descended from Fatima, the Prophet Muhammed's daughter, and her husband, Ali, the fourth caliph and a scion of the house of Bani Hashim, the noblest of the ancient Arabian Peninsula tribes. "Sharif" Hussein Ibn Ali claimed to be the 37th in the line of descent from the Prophet.[1] By reason of their lineage, the Hashemite family enjoyed respect among Muslims that made them the guardians of the Holy sites in Mecca and Medina. Besides his descent, Hussein's piety and his irreproachable personal demeanor earned him even more admiration and respect of his acquaintances. He had considerable influence over the Arab tribes in Hijaz since the 19th century, but he had been perceived by Turkey's Sultan Abdul-Hamid to have symptoms of disquieting ambitions for declaring independence from the Ottoman Empire. To keep him under control, the Turkish government invited him to Istanbul in 1893 and kept him and his family, including his four children, Ali Ibn al-Hussein, Abdullah Ibn al-Hussein, Faisal Ibn al-Hussein and Zaid Ibn al-Hussein, away from his power base under the pretence of being a guest to the Ottoman Sublime Porte. He was officially referred to as a member of the Council of State. Forcing individuals to reside in Istanbul under the watch of government spies was one of Sultan Abdul-Hamid's schemes to control recalcitrant leaders who happened to be too prominent to be jailed or murdered. After nearly 16 years of this form of captivity, the Young Turks revolutionaries returned Sharif Hussein back to Hijaz in 1908 as the Grand Sharif (Emir) of Mecca where he became convinced of the need to break away completely from Turkey after failing to achieve the autonomy he aspired to have within the Ottoman Empire.

---

1 "Sharif" is the title of any one who is a descendent of the Prophet.

EMIR ABDULLAH IBN AL-HUSSEIN

Sharif Hussein never had the military and financial resources to challenge Turkey until his son Abdullah convinced him to gain the support of a great power in a rebellion against Turkey. Abdullah came up with the idea of seeking alliance with the British, but his father, the senior Hashemite and the guardian of the Islamic holy shrines of Mecca, was not fully contented with the idea of siding with a Christian power against a Muslim country. He had to seek a compromise with the Turks before making the decision. After consulting with his son Faisal and other family members, he allowed Abdullah to establish communication channels with the British. On his way back from Istanbul in 1914, Abdullah visited General Herbert Kitchener, the British High Commissioner in Cairo at the time. He described the strained relationship between his father and the Turkish government, and inquired about the possibility of receiving British support and co-operation in the event of an Arab revolt against the Ottomans. Kitchener response was discouraging, but he instructed Storrs, the British Oriental Secretary in Egypt, to meet with Abdullah and try to find more about what he had in mind. Later on, Abdullah met Ronald Storrs and requested military armament to protect his father's interests against the Turkish overlords.[1] No commitment was made by the British in this meeting, but a channel of communication was established and the two men developed a friendly relationship. The British military in Egypt decided to exploit the rift between the Arabs and the Turks by considering the offer made by Abdullah to participate in joint military effort with the Hashemite against the Turks. Negotiations were conducted in several letters exchanged between Hussein and Sir Henry McMahon, the British High Commissioner in Cairo. The direct correspondence that continued until the outbreak of the war in 1915 led to an agreement that was written in general terms. But to the Arabs in Mecca, it was treated as a firm commitment by Britain to give independence to the Arabs in exchange for Arab revolt against the Turks.

McMahon told Hussein in a crucial letter dated October 24, 1915, that Britain was prepared to "recognize and support the independence of the Arabs in all the regions within the limits demanded by the Sharif [which included Syria, Arabia and Iraq]." Some Arab land along the Eastern Mediterranean shores which the British government did not consider to be purely Arab would be excluded from future Arab independent rule. These districts included "Mersina and Alexandretta" which were later annexed by Turkey and portions of Syria lying to the west of Damascus, Homs, Hama and Aleppo districts."[2] McMahon did not specify the borders of the excluded lands especially those in the district of Damascus. The territory marked for independence by McMahon letter and the form of such independence were obscurely defined. Sharif Hussein understood that the British commitment excluded only the areas of present-day Lebanon and areas to the north along the Syrian coast, while the British insisted that the excluded area covered much of what later became Trans-Jordan and Palestine. Further more, McMahon asked the Arabs to recognize the British interests in the provinces that became present-day Iraq which re-

---

1 Avi Shlaim, 1998, p.21.
2 George Antonius

quired special administrative arrangements. The agreement fell short of the expectations of the Arab nationalists in Syria. They perceived the exchanges between Sharif Hussein and McMahon would allow only the Arab Peninsula and its Muslim holy places to remain an independent Arab state that would be committed to have special relations with Britain. The protocol that the Arab nationalists in Syria drafted demanded that Britain should grant independence to all the liberated Arab lands as a price for supporting Britain against Turkey, and perhaps awarding only Aden to the British.

The "Great Arab Revolt" under the leadership of Sharif Hussein of Mecca had been designated by pro-Hashimite Arab intellectuals as the beginning of modern Arab renaissance. But after the revolt and the war, the Arabs found themselves exchanging domination by the Turks for domination by the British, the French and the Zionists whose designs were extremely alarming. The British had been dealing exclusively with Sharif Hussein of Mecca and his children Abdullah and Faisal as the implicit speakers of the Arab nation. Recognition of Hussein and his children as spokesmen for the Arabs never meant to give them the power to rule over the British decisions. The British policy suggests that Sharif Hussein and those who represented him were to be used only as agents to further the interests of Great Britain in the Arab world rather than to satisfy the national aspirations of the Arabs. The British firmly rejected the suggestion that Sharif Hussein assumes the title of the "Caliphate of the Muslims" or the "king of the Arabs" because Britain planned on dividing the Arab lands into small colonies. They installed Hussein's son, Emir Faisal, on the throne of Iraq and appointed the younger son, Emir Abdullah, as the ruler of Trans-Jordan. The British allowed Sherif Hussein to have the title of "King of Hijaz" with a provision that gave Great Britain the exclusive responsibility of defending the Muslim holy places against external aggression. When Hussein refused to accept the commitment of the British Mandate on Palestine regarding the Balfour Declaration, the British abandoned him and supported his rival, Sultan Abdul-Aziz al-Saud of Najd, in his effort to conquer Hussein's kingdom in 1924.

By the end of World War I, Britain had entered into several conflicting commitments regarding the conquered Ottoman Empire. There was an agreement with France to share colonizing the Arab lands, a promise to support Arab independence, and the promise of a homeland for the Jewish people. In violation of the promise to support Arab independence, the April-May 1916 British–French Sykes–Picot agreement was to divide between themselves the eastern Arab territories of the Middle East, between the Mediterranean and the Persian frontier less the Arabian Peninsula. Then on November 2, 1917, and before Britain had a jurisdiction over Palestine, the foreign minister of Britain, Arthur James Balfour, declared that his government had officially committed Palestine to be a homeland for the Jewish people. The word "Arab" did not appear even once in the declaration. The only reference to the Arab Palestinians was "that nothing shall be done which may prejudice the civil and religious rights of the existing non-Jewish communities in Palestine." The declaration neither stated that the non-Jewish communities were Arabs who constituted the large majority of the population nor promised to guarantee their political rights. The declaration had violated the political rights of the indigenous Palestinians by offering their country to the Jewish people without consulting with them. Its wording implies that the Arab Palestinians were promised to have only civil and religious rights in a future Jewish state.[1] William Ormsby-Gore, the British Assistant of the War Secretary denied that Arabs lived in Palestine by stating in 1918 that "west of the Jordan [river] the people were not Arabs, but only Arab-speaking."[2]

When the contents of the Balfour Declaration became widely known by the Arab population, the Grand Sharif of Mecca, Hussein Ibn Ali, was assured on January 4, 1918, by Hograth, the British Commander of the Arab Bureau in Egypt, that Jewish settlements would be consistent with the freedom of existing population, both economic and political. Hussein was so convinced initially by the British assurances that he tried to induce the Arabs to accept the Jewish immigration to Palestine.[3] Emir Faisal co-operation was sought by the Jewish leaders because of his close relations with their main ally, the British, and the Emir official capacity as the representative of the Arabs in the planned peace conference. Chaim Weizmann never tried to meet with Palestinian notables even when he was in Palestine, but he sought to meet with Faisal in order to come to terms with him on the subject of the Jewish homeland. When the British were advancing toward Jerusalem in 1918, a Jewish commission headed by Weizmann was dispatched to Palestine to prepare for the implementation of Balfour Declaration. Weizmann visited Faisal in his army camp near Aqaba on June 4. He expressed the desire of the Zionists to co-operate with the Arabs in their effort to settle in Palestine peacefully for exchange of supporting Faisal to develop an Arab kingdom in northern Syria. A British Colonel, P.C. Joyce, a military advisor to Faisal, observed that "Faisal really welcomed Jewish cooperation [during the meeting]."[4]

For the preparation of the January 18, 1919 Peace Conference at Versailles, British officials arranged another meeting between Faisal, the representative of his father, and Weizmann, the representative of the Zionist movement, at Carlton Hotel in London. The two signed an agreement that formalized promises of mutual co-operation over Jewish immigration to Palestine on January 4, 1919.[5] The two leaders reiterated the pledges of respect for each other's communities which they had made in their previous meeting in Aqaba. They referred to the "racial kinship and ancient bonds" between Arabs and Jews. It is alleged that the agreement formalized promises of mutual co-operation over Jewish immigration to Palestine.[6] For Weizmann, the acceptance of the Balfour Declaration had been the basis of any agreement he signed and any speech he delivered. Article III of the Weizmann-Faisal agreement states: "In the establishment of the Constitution and Administration of Palestine all such measures shall be adopted as will afford the fullest guarantees for carrying into effect the British Government's Declaration of the 2nd of November,

---

1 John Keay, 2003, p.82.
2 Doreen Warriner, 1972, p.33
3 Geoffrey Furlonge 1969, p. 61
4 Ronald Sanders, 1983, p.736–37.
5 Geoffrey Furlonge, 1969, p.70.
6 Doreen Warriner, 1972, p.70.

1917 [the Balfour Declaration]. Moreover, all necessary measures shall be taken to encourage and stimulate immigration of Jews into Palestine on a large scale, and as quickly as possible to settle Jewish immigrants upon the land."[1] Below the signed agreement, Faisal added a hand written statement that he would be bound to comply with the agreement only if an Arab state were established.

In his statement to the Palestinian Royal Commission on November 25, 1936, Weizmann stated that he and Faisal had found themselves in full agreement on the subject of Palestine and "that first meeting was the beginning of a lifelong friendship." [2] He compared the significance of the Balfour Declaration to the modern Jews to the sanctity of the Jewish ancient heritage. He argued in front of the Commission in Jerusalem that the Balfour Declaration was regarded as the *Magna Carta* of the Jewish people and it "was in a sense comparable with another declaration made thousands of years before, when Cyrus allowed a remnant of the Jews to return from Babylon and rebuild the Temple."

The post-war Paris Peace Conference was convened in July 1920 to settle the dismembered Ottoman Empire and dispose of the war spoils. The Arabs were free from Turkish control but their self-appointed spokesman, Faisal, had no leverage to negotiate with the Great Powers for the independence for the Arab lands, as demanded by the Syrian nationalists who aspired to establish an Arab independent state in Greater Syria with Damascus as its capital. Faisal, a key figure in the revolt against the Turks, was treated by both Britain and France only as the envoy of his father, Sharif Hussein. He left the conference empty-handed when it came to the question of Syria's independence, although he had made significant concessions regarding Palestine in the agreement of January 4, 1919. Palestinian notables were horrified when the news leaked out about the Weizmann–Faisal agreement sacrificing their land for an ambiguous Arab independence.[3]

The nationalist Syrian Congress in Damascus challenged the Peace Conferees by declaring Syria an independent kingdom in March 1920 and offered Faisal the throne which he accepted. To gain the support of the Pan-Arab Palestinians, Faisal retracted his earlier agreement with Weizman because he could not go against the nationalist tide, but he continued to anger many Palestinian notables for courting the British to further his personal ambitions at the expense of the Palestinians. It is suggested that Faisal had second thought about his previous agreement with Weizman because of his father's opposition to the Balfour Declaration. Despite Faisal close relations with the British and his discussions with the Zionist leadership the possibility of co-operation between the Arabs and Jews, Pan-Arab Palestinians support to his ambitions in Syria was driven by pragmatism and lack of alternatives other than the endorsement of his independent kingdom. Members of the prominent Palestinian families organized a conference in 1919 and agreed to support the idea of having Palestine as a part of Syria under Faisal.[4] They hoped that Faisal would form a large Arab federation that included Palestine as one of its provinces, which

---

1 George Antonius 1979, p. 438; Ronald Sanders, 1983, p.639-40.
2 Weizmann statement to the Palestinian Royal Commission on November 25, 1936.
3 Baruch Kimmerling and Joel Migdal 1993. p.76.
4 Yehoshua Porath, 1974, p. 84.

would reduce their fear of being overwhelmed in their fight against the powerful Zionists alone. Palestine, within an independent Arab state, had a better chance of staving off the Jewish threat. To involve the Arab and Muslim worlds in their struggle against Zionism, Palestinian delegations traveled to different Arab and Muslim capitals asking for support.

In Europe, the Supreme Council of the Peace Conference decided to disregard the Syrians claim of independence and the Arab rights for self determination, placed Lebanon and Syria under the French mandatory control and Iraq and Trans-Jordan and Palestine under the British mandatory rule. The French army defeated Faisal's poorly equipped army, ejected him from Syria, and suppressed all resistance. As a consolation prize for losing the throne of Syria and within a policy of creating satellite Arab states under their influence, the British gave Faisal the throne of Iraq and appointed Abdullah as the representative of the British government in Trans-Jordan. After Faisal fall and the sorrow end of Greater Syria concept, the Pan-Arab Palestinians had to give up on the idea of a Palestine as an integral part of Syria and to think inward in dealing with their own problems on the basis of Palestinian nationalism just as other Arab peoples had to deal with their own problems.

To create a Middle East order that would serve the British colonial interests for a long time to come, in 1921 Winston Churchill offered the thrones of oil-rich Iraq to Faisal and the territory of Trans-Jordan to Abdullah as rewards for their support to Britain against Turkey. The British policy was to create small states headed by the two members of the Hashemite family, by reason of their lineage and considerable power over the tribesmen, as a means to administer the area. The mini-independence given to Iraq and Trans-Jordan was a form of indirect colonial control mechanism modeled after the qualified independence of the Gulf Sheikhdoms. It provided employment for two influential Arabs who would owe their titles as symbols of independence to the colonial power. The economically poor and perennially insecure state of Trans-Jordan that was completely dependent on annual subsidies from London gave the British control over a corridor from the Mediterranean to the Gulf.

In 1921, the Colonial Secretary of Britain, Winston Churchill and the eminent Arabists T. E. Lawrence (Lawrence of Arabia) and the High Commissioner Sir Herbert Samuel were in Cairo contemplating the best way to secure the British control over the Middle East. Churchill had already given the throne of Iraq to Faisal as a substitute for the loss of Syria to the French. While the conference was underway, Emir Abdullah arrived in al-Aqaba town at the head of Arab irregular tribesmen with a publicized plan to reinstate his brother, Faisal, in Syria. Lawrence proposed that Abdullah was the most qualified to control the anti-Zionist sentiment among the Arabs at the least cost to the British. Lawrence suggested that the ideal person who might help the British would be "a person ....who was not an inhabitant of Trans-Jordan, but who relied on his Majesty's Government for the retention of his office."[1] On May 26, 1921, Churchill summoned Abdullah to meet him in Jerusalem and offered him the Emirate of Trans-Jordan where he could reign (not rule) as Britain protégé. Abdullah would receive a monthly subsidy and Britain would provide

---

1 T.E. Lawrence, 1935.

advisers to administer the Emirate from Amman as an integral part of the Mandate under the supervision of the British high commissioner in Jerusalem with one exception. The Emirate was excluded from the Jewish homeland and at some point in the future, Trans-Jordan would be granted independence.

Thus to some ardent Zionists dismay, the arbitrary decision by Churchill to break the unity of Trans-Jordan and Palestine, limited the development of a homeland for the Jews, as stipulated by the Balfour Declaration, only to the west of the Jordan River. As early as 1917, when no central government was in control of Trans-Jordan after the defeat of Turkey, Zionist agents had been surveying Trans-Jordan lands and resources with an eye to settle future immigrants in the east of the Jordan River besides Palestine. In a report submitted to the Zionist Commission in Palestine, Baruch Basin identified 5,000 square kilometers of fertile lands in Trans-Jordan as a potential area for settlements.[1] In 1919, Moshe Shertok was authorized by Weizmann, the Chairman of the Zionist Commission, to go to Trans-Jordan and investigate the possibility of buying land from the Circassian (Caucasian) landowners in Jordan, but the Circassians refused to sell. During the 1919 Peace Conference, the Zionist representatives struggled for including Trans-Jordan in the Jewish homeland. Many Jewish leaders considered Churchill's decision to install Emir Abdullah in Trans-Jordan as the first major defeat to the Zionist project.

Abdullah accepted Churchill's offer, recognized the British Mandate of Palestine and the Balfour Declaration which his father rejected to the bitter end.[2] The reliance of Abdullah on the British for retaining his office and fulfill his personal ambitions gave Britain the leverage needed to pressure him to check the anti-Zionist agitation among his Arab constituency. In the meantime, the British were able to administer the strategic Trans-Jordan with a few British military advisors to Abdullah and a small financial subsidy. To enhance the benefits of Trans-Jordan to Britain, a British military unit invaded the districts of Ma'an and Aqaba and annexed them to Trans-Jordan in 1924. Ma'an and Aqaba were part of the Arabian Peninsula that was ruled by Abdullah's father since 1916. The expansion of this compliant entity gave Britain total control over the path to Palestine and Sinai from the Arabian Peninsula. Palestine and Sinai provided protection to the Suez Canal and secured a link between the British dominated Gulf area, including Iraq, and the Mediterranean. Iraq and Trans-Jordan under British appointed Arab royalties gave Britain control over the land and air routes to the East and the important oil resources in Iraq and the Gulf.

The strategic interest in the petroleum reserves in the Gulf and Mosul areas and the transportation of their oil through pipelines to the Mediterranean must have played an important role in the British policies. To meet the need for oil to run the newly installed combustion engines of the Royal Navy ships, the British government formed a special committee, the Petroleum Imperial Policy Committee in 1918 to draw a plan for securing control of adequate world oil resources.[3] The plan that was later on implemented, in-

---

1 Yoav Gelber, 1997.
2 Avi Shalaim, 1998, p.27
3 Marian Kent, 1976.

cluded building a modern port in Haifa with a large oil refinery to process the pumped oil from Iraq through the pipeline and facilities to export the refined oil to Britain. The politics of the big powers toward the Middle East since the 20th century have always been for oil. For almost 100 years, the British and then the US have declared wars, dispatched navy armadas, stationed troops, installed friendly regimes and toppled others to secure the region's oil.

Immediately after the 1921 Cairo conference, T.E.Lawrence was sent to Jeddah to meet Sharif Hussein and tie up the loose ends of the British objectives in the Middle East. His task was to conclude a formal treaty of alliance with the elder Arab leader, Sharif Hussein Ibn-Ali, in return for a commitment by the British to defend his Hijaz Kingdom and to continue paying him the annual subsidy that had been paid since 1917. Hussein angrily rejected the offer because of the attached conditions to accept the Mandate on Palestine and the Balfour Declaration. He refused the Declaration because it failed to safeguard the legitimate political, civil and religious rights of the Palestinians. The British stopped the support to Hussein in response, thus leaving him exposed to his ruthless arch-enemy Abdul-Aziz Al-Saud and his Wahhabi warriors of Najd. The British had already established friendly relations with Ibn Saud through their India Office. The British orientalist, Harry St. John Philby was an advisor to Ibn Saud during his military campaign against his rivals in Arabia. The British supplied Ibn Saud with money and weapons which he used first to defeat Ibn Rashid of Najd. Then in 1925, he conquered Hijaz and forced Hussein to abdicate and flee Arabia. The defeat of Sharif Hussein ended the Hashemite Sharifian rule over Hijaz, including the holy cities of Mecca and Medina, and its unbroken succession since 1201. The downfall of Hussein, the appointments of Faisal to the throne of Iraq and Abdullah to the Emirate of Trans-Jordan, and the implementation of the Balfour Declaration in Palestine suggest that the Arab countries borders and political institutions had been designed by Britain to meet its imperial needs and Zionists goals. For the British, controlling non-Palestinian Arab opposition to the Balfour Declaration and securing land access to the Gulf and to Iraqi oil were the most successful World War I missions.

Emir Abdullah, the future King of Jordan, was the brightest and most resourceful of Sharif Hussein's four sons. He must have been acquainted with the Balfour Declaration, the British Mandate which authorized Britain to facilitate the establishment of a homeland to the Zionists, and the goals of the Zionists as stated by their leaders over the years. The plans for transferring the Arab Palestinians to other countries had been common knowledge as an integral part of Zionism since its inception. Theodore Herzl wrote in his diary on June 12, 1895 among other things related to his vision of how to colonize Palestine: "We must spirit the penniless [Arab] population across the border... Both the process of expropriation and the removal of the poor must be carried out discretely and circumspectly."[1] Israel Zangwill, known for promoting Zionism under the slogan "a land without people for a people without a land" wrote in his 1920 book that for a successful colonization of Palestine, there must be an "Arab exodus." Abdullah's acquiescence with

---

1 Raphael Patai, 1960.

the British role in opening the door for massive Jewish immigration to Palestine justifies the skepticism of his Arab critics especially the Palestinians who questioned his wisdom and even his patriotism. They ask how a man of his stature cooperates with the British Mandate that had been committed explicitly to implement the Balfour Declaration without knowing that he was supporting Zionism against the Arab Palestinians. The Emirate of Trans-Jordan was created on the territory between the Jordan River, the Dead Sea and Wadi Araba in the west, the Arabian Desert in the east and south, and Syria in the north with about 250,000 mostly Bedouin inhabitants. Trans-Jordan had no sea port until 1924 when the British military invaded the districts of Ma'an and Aqaba in the Arabian Peninsula and annexed them to Trans-Jordan as stated above.

Britain gave Trans-Jordan independence, and the Mandate agreement was replaced by a Treaty of Alliance in March 1946 as a reward for Abdullah's loyalty and cooperation in implementing the British project since World War I. Abdullah was enthroned as a king on May 25, 1946, and the Emirate name was replaced with the "Hashemite Kingdom of Jordan." Even with independence, Jordan continued to depend on Britain for its survival under King Abdullah. The King was surrounded by British military officers including the commander of his Arab Legion forces, John Bagot Glubb (Glubb Pasha), and Britain continued to subsidize his budget annually.

When Abdullah accepted the British offer to administer Trans-Jordan, his subjects had been a mix of immigrants from Palestinian, Syrians who came after Faisal's defeat in Syria, Caucasians who settled in the area during the Turkish rule, North Africans and nomadic Bedouins. His control over his emirate was based on networks of personal loyalties and he was closer and more attentive to the Bedouins and the Caucasians than to the other groups. Abdullah was a pragmatic self-confident leader, skillful in dealing with his loyal Bedouin constituency who pledged their undivided allegiance to him. This freed him from any constraints in making foreign policy decisions even if they were at odds with the rest of the Arab world. The Bedouins, illiterate and ascetic, trusted that nothing could go wrong under his leadership. The loyalty and dedication of the East Jordanian Bedouins to Abdullah and his descendents had been in recognition of the Hashemite contributions to their wellbeing. The Hashemites have transformed Trans-Jordan through the years from a minor subordinate area attached to Syria, Iraq or Arabia to a self-governed country, and the East Jordanians from obscure tribes fighting each other to citizens of a modern state.

Historically and geographically, Trans-Jordan had never been a separate entity. Its western part had been a segment of Syria or Palestine and the eastern and southeast desert could have been Iraqi or Arabian territory under the Ottoman Empire from 1516 until 1918. Between 1918 and 1920, Trans-Jordan became the southern part of the Syrian State under King Faisal. Faisal managed to extend his authority over Trans-Jordan tribes by paying their chieftains monthly sums of money. Trans-Jordanian traditional tribal society had been resistant to central authority especially after the fall of King Faisal that caused its detachment from Syria. After the collapse of King Faisal regime in Syria and before Abdullah founded the Emirate of Trans-Jordan in 1921 under the British Mandate, many local governments were established by local tribe leaders. There were Ajloun government under

Ali Sharairi, the government of Deir Yousuf headed by Sheikh Klaib Shraideh, Jarash government under Muhammed al-Mughrabi and Karak government under Refaifan al-Majali. The Zionist intelligence bureau described Trans-Jordan in 1920 as a no-man land where the leaders of its tribes had been "ready to serve, ready to fight and invade wherever there is a good booty in view."[1] The Hashemites starting with Abdullah put Jordan's name on the World map as a country for the first time in recent history.

Britain provided funds needed by Abdullah to buy the loyalty of the Bedouin tribe chiefs and village notables, and the young Bedouins were recruited in the Arab Legion. Upon his installment in Trans-Jordan, Abdullah urged the population not to make any move against the Zionists because "the Englishmen are our allies, and the Jews are their friends and under their protection."[2] During the 1936–1939 Palestinian rebellion against the British, most of the Trans-Jordanians tribesmen had little sympathy for the rebels and "lacked any serious anti-Hashemite or anti-British grievance."[3] The Jordanians who sympathized with the Palestinian rebels were mostly Amman businessmen and many civil servants, including ministers and even prime ministers of Palestinian origin who had settled in Jordan since World War I. The merchants had to restrain themselves to protect their economic interests as the potential disorder and lawlessness would hurt their businesses should violence spillover into Jordan. The civil servants and the high ranking officials of Palestinian ancestry did not translate their sympathy with the rebels into action to appease Emir Abdullah who was the British protégé in the region. Abdullah was against the Palestinian rebels because counter to his personal ambitions; their goal was to have independence. His Arab Legion was guarding against infiltrating rebels across the border from Palestine. Some rebels had attacked police stations in northern Trans-Jordan and captured their weapons during 1938.[4] Abdullah visited the Bedouins in their encampments and induced them not to shelter or help Palestinian rebels who crossed the river. He helped organize opposition to the insurgency inside Palestine under the leadership of the Nashashibi faction who pledged their allegiance to him. The Husseinis and Nashashibis were discussed in Chapter 3 in more details.

During his entire political life, Arab political leaders had been suspicious of Abdullah's policies, namely his ambitions to create a kingdom over "Greater Syria" and for his close relations with the British and secret contacts with the Zionists. Presiding over a Hashemite kingdom that included Jordan, Syria, Lebanon and Palestine was the essence of his political ambitions throughout his life, but his plans were not taken seriously by his allies, the British. Creating such a large Arab state even under a loyal Hashemite was incompatible with the strategies of the British colonialists to break down the region into small entities. Most Arabs had been in favor of a union among Syria, Iraq, Jordan and Palestine but not under Abdullah for his close relations with the British. They regarded him a British

---

1 Yoav Gelber, 1997, p.9.
2 Yoav Gelber, 1997, p.15.
3 Benny Morris, 2002, P.37.
4 Yoav Gelber, 1997, p. 138.

puppet and his cooperation with the British in implementing the Balfour Declaration was perceived by the Arabs as a betrayal of the national cause.

Abdullah believed that if the Arabs and Jews acted wisely as neighbors, they could have created conditions where both can benefit. He was known for making contacts with Zionist leaders all through his life and the Zionists had been impressed by his moderation. He had made numerous friendships with Zionist leaders over the years. Abdullah had close relationship with Dr. Montague David Eder, of the Zionist Executive in 1921–22. He told Eder in the fall of 1921 that he would be disposed to the Zionist enterprise, but he wanted the Zionists to use their influence with the British to back him in his own ambitions of ruling over Syria.[1] Abdullah solicited Jewish finance and investment in Trans-Jordan to build power plant in Naharayim and to develop the potash factory on the Dead Sea beach. Weizmann, in his capacity as the president of the Jewish Organization, and F. Kisch, the head of the Jewish Agency political office in Palestine visited Abdullah in Amman in 1926 where the Emir told them that he had no problem with Jewish economic investment in Trans-Jordan, according to Yoav Gelber.

He secretly invited Jewish Agency official, Eliahu Sasson to his palace in the Jordan Valley twice in August, 1947 and presented him with a plan for partitioning Palestine and annexing the Arab part to Trans-Jordan.[2] And in January 1949, Sasson and Dayan met the king in his palace at al-Shuneh to deliver Israel's demand to take the western section of the Gulf of Aqaba. He met Mrs. Golda Meir, the acting director of the Jewish Agency Political Department and the future Prime Minister of Israel at the Jordan River power station of Naharia on the Jordan River on November 17, 1947, twelve days before the UN vote on the recommendations of the United Nations Special Committee on Palestine (UNSCOP) to divide Palestine into two separate states, one Arab and the other Jewish. She was accompanied by two of her aides, Elias Sasson and Ezra Danni. They discussed the new situation due to the pending UN resolution to partition Palestine and they reaffirmed their previous commitments. They reached a preliminary agreement to forestall Haj Amin al-Husseini's plans for a Palestinian state. Sasson reported to his superiors that the King promised not to allow his military to cooperate with any Arab armies against the Jewish fighters.[3] Abdullah stated in the meeting that he would annex the Arab sector of Palestine to his kingdom and in the process prevent the establishment of a Palestinian state under their "common enemy...the Mufti [Haj Amin]."[4] Golda Meir agreed with the King and added that Israel would not interfere with what might happen in the Arab sector of Palestine. The British helped Abdullah to take over parts of the area earmarked for the Arab state by stationing detachments from his military in main towns prior to the termination of the Mandate. The Jordanian Arab Legion had been present in Palestine since 1944 as part of the British military garrison. When the Palestinian armed groups' irregulars were

---

1 Yoav Gelber, 1997, p.16.
2 Benny Morris, 2002.
3 Sasson report to the head of the Jewish Agency Political Department, Moshe Sherett, November 20, 1947, Central Zionist Archive (Jerusalem).
4 Golda Meir, 1975.

hopelessly trying to stand their grounds in the face of the Jewish Haganah attacks in April 1948, these Jordanian army units were watching with indifference instead of helping them. The name of the Arab Legion was misleading. Until 1956 Sir John Bagot Glubb, a British, was the Legion's commander and there were at least forty British officers at every unit level of the military structure. And the Legion relied on supplies from British depots in the Suez Canal zone.[1]

In their attempt to bypass the Palestinian leadership, the Zionists always tried to establish links with leaders of Arabs outside Palestine. The negotiations with the Arabs that mattered most to Weizmann were those with Emir Faisal, not with the Arab Palestinians and once Faisal's goodwill was secured, nobody else mattered. Weizmann used his diplomatic skills to elicit the Hashemite co-operation in order to influence the attitude of the Arabs towards Zionism. The Zionists had long considered Abdullah the most accommodating Arab leader since Balfour Declaration. Abdullah and the Zionists were described by Uri Bar-Joseph as "the best of enemies" even at the height of the 1948 war.[2] Unlike other Arab leaders, Abdullah did not have deep-rooted enmity toward the Jews even while they were trying to establish a homeland in Palestine. The Iraqi historian, Muhammed Oudah, wrote that "Most of their [Jews] important writers considered his [Abdullah's] tenure on the Jordanian throne one of the greatest assurances for the preservation of Israel."

Abdullah's Emirate and the post-Balfour Zionist movement had goals in common that made their interests converge and develop into a sustained relationship before and after the establishment of Israel. They had a common protector and a common enemy, and the two parties tried to "coordinate their policies."[3] The Trans-Jordan Emirate and the Balfour Declaration project had been created and supported by the British and both the Zionists and Abdullah had been opposed to a Palestinian state under the Palestinian nationalist leadership. In 1922, Abdullah met Weizmann in London and offered to support the Balfour Declaration if the Zionists would use their influence with the British government to appoint him as the ruler of the "Semitic kingdom" which comprised Palestine and Trans-Jordan. The offer was politely rejected because it was incompatible with the Zionists' aim, especially at a time when they were confident of attaining an independent state of their own in Palestine. The Zionists found they could use Abdullah as a better partner and more flexible to deal with than the local inhabitants of Palestine. King Abdullah used his influence to thwart Haj Amin al-Husseini's efforts to establish a temporary Palestinian government once the British had left, and he ignored the AHC when important decisions regarding Palestine were made.[4]

In the 1948 war, both sides, King Abdullah and the Israelis, acted to abort the establishment of a Palestinian state. Abdullah was against allowing Palestinians to operate militarily against the Israelis. Just before the 1948 Arab–Israeli war, Abdullah's Prime Minister, Tawfiq Abul-Huda, and his military commander, Sir John Glubb, met British

1 Yoav Gelber, 2004, p. 10.
2 Uri Bar-Joseph, 1987.
3 Avi Shlaim, 2000, p.30.
4 Cohen, 1982, p. 306.

Foreign Minister Ernest Bevin in London to negotiate a new treaty and explain the Arab League's military plans in Palestine. They informed the Prime Minister that the goal of the Trans-Jordanian army in Palestine would be only to occupy the sector awarded to the Palestinians by the United Nations.[1] To accomplish the acquisition of the Arab share of Palestine, Abdullah had to co-ordinate with Israel and at the same time he had to conceal his plans from other Arabs including the Palestinians. He honored his promise to the Jewish leaders by not allowing his military to cross the borders of the Jewish state as assigned by the United Nations in the 1948 war, but the Israelis broke their promise. Their military crossed the borders into the Arab sector and captured the towns of Lydda and Ramle and their surroundings from the Arab Legion.

As discussed in Chapter 3, on December 29, 1948, the United Nation Security Council called for a permanent armistice between Israel and the belligerent Arab states. Iraq was the only Arab state that refused to negotiate armistice agreement with Israel. Its government informed the United Nations mediator, Ralph Bunche, that it had authorized Jordan to negotiate on its behalf and its military in Palestine would surrender their positions to the Trans-Jordanian army. The Egyptians officially agreed to negotiate directly face-to-face with the Israeli representatives, but through a mediator from the United Nations. The negotiations with Trans-Jordan formally started on February 24, 1949 on the Island of Rhodes.

Members of the Trans-Jordan delegation were low ranking military officers unfamiliar with the Palestinian territory and its resources and none of them was a Palestinian. They had no authority to make important decisions because the real negotiations were conducted secretly by King Abdullah himself in his palace at *Shuna* town near the Dead Sea. Meetings were held between the King and Israeli personnel in which, the armistice lines were finally decided. The first meeting was for a preliminary exchange to pave the way for the final armistice negotiations where the King wanted to convey his desire to make peace with Israel and explain the basis of his negotiations. The Israeli delegation was limited to Elias Sasson, a highly talented Jewish Arabist and Lieutenant Colonel Moshe Dayan, the future Israeli minister of defense.

The Israeli negotiators in the next meetings that started on April 1, 1949, included a foreign ministry official Walter Eytan, Moshe Dayan and the Haganah commander of operations Yigael Yadin.[2] After a week of negotiations, the two parties reached an agreement on establishing the demarcation of the armistice lines. Trans-Jordan surrendered to Israel several square miles of strategic Arab land that included the "Iron Triangle" area, the Chadera-Afula highway and Lydda-Haifa railroad. The surrendered area had been part of the territory controlled by the Iraqi military contingent before handing it to the Arab Legion and withdrawing from Palestine without signing an armistice agreement with Israel.

King Abdullah had to give it to Israel through the negotiated armistice agreement to avoid a clash with a superior IDF force that was poised to take the whole area by force.

---

1 Sir John Bagot Glubb, 1957.
2 Howard Sachar, 1996, p.349.

After concluding the armistice agreement with Egypt and removing a formidable opponent from the circle of belligerency in Palestine, the entire Israeli military was ready to be deployed for the first time along the Jordanian front. The King, who knew the limitations of his own army, realized that Israel would use its military advantage over the Arab Legion to achieve its vital territorial objectives. Short on ammunition and stretched too thin, the Arab Legion was incapable of defending the area with only 2,000 men against overwhelming Israeli forces. After extensive negotiations between the King and Israel and with the involvement of Britain and the US, Israel accepted a belt only 5 kilometers wide instead of 15, stretching from Lydda to the north of Jenin and including fifteen villages with 12,000 inhabitants. The Arab Legion took over the Iraqi front and surrendered to Israel the required territory. This agreement prevented an Israeli conquest of the whole area.

Most likely all of the Iraqi-controlled sector could have been saved if the Iraqis had joined the armistice negotiations, but the Iraqi leaders in Baghdad were adamant in their refusal to negotiate with Israel — despite efforts by the Jordanians and the British to persuade them.[1] The Iraqi decision to withdraw without negotiations defies comprehension; it was a blatant act of betrayal to the thousands of Palestinians who had been living under their protection. The Palestinians, especially the villagers who lost land beyond the armistice line, and their supporters, blamed King Abdullah for the surrender of the "Iron Triangle." But the facts suggest that Abdullah should be commended for using his diplomatic skills to minimize the damage done by the Iraqi decision to withdraw unilaterally without negotiating an armistice agreement. He was able to save the cities of Jenin, Nablus, Qalqeelia and Tulkarm from Israeli takeover, although large areas of their agricultural lands did end up on the Israeli side. The problem is that King Abdullah failed to tell the Palestinians the reasons behind his decision to surrender the land.

After the ceasefire agreement with Israel, some 3,000 Palestinian notables who included mayors of the large cities and mostly educated elites convened in Jericho on December 1, 1948. They passed resolutions in favor of a united Palestine under Abdullah as king. They asked Abdullah to be the "King of United Palestine" and authorized him to resolve the Palestinian problem by war or peace.[2] King Abdullah deferred the proclamation on the union until the conditions with Israel permitted such action.

The King established a temporary military administration to handle the civil affairs of the area under his control with the intention of annexing it, but he failed to obtain tacit support from members of the Arab League for his plans to annex the West Bank.[3] The resistance of many Arab governments to the partition was driven by their leaders' personal aversion of Abdullah. They were suspicious that Abdullah would use his influence with the British to take over other Arab land beyond Palestine. Syria and Lebanon opposed the merger of Palestine with Trans-Jordan because they perceived such a merger as a step toward the creation of "Greater Syria" that would include Syria, Lebanon, Trans-Jordan and Iraq under the Hashemite dynasty. Saudi Arabia was against the merger because it

---

1 Yaov Gelber, 2004, p. 81.
2 Yoav Gelber, 2004, p. 42.
3 Mary C.Wilson, 1987, p.174-75.

would strengthen the Hashemite who had ambitions to recover their ancestral province in Arabia. The Egyptian government under King Farouq was trying to preserve its leadership role in the Arab League by going along with the majority that opposed Abdullah's aspirations to swallow the Arab parts of Palestine. Egypt gave Haj Amin al-Husseini a refuge in Cairo and supported him to establish a Palestinian government not as a foil against Israel but rather to reduce the Jordanian monarch influence among the Palestinians.

Most Palestinians, even some supporters of al-Husseini, eventually accepted the annexation because they were frightened by Israel and there were no other alternatives after the departure of the Egyptians and the Iraqis from the area. In December 1949, the part of Palestine under the Jordanian control, which came to be known as the West Bank (including Jerusalem), was annexed and the Emirate of Trans-Jordan became the Hashemite Kingdom of Jordan. The incorporation of the West Bank fulfilled King Abdullah's territorial ambitions and brought a large number of professional and educated Palestinians into his kingdom. On the negative side, he had to deal with the needs of more than 400,000 native West Bankers and some 500,000 refugees from the Israeli-controlled areas of Palestine. The Palestinians including the refugees on both sides of the river were offered the Jordanian citizenship and the right to vote, but many refugees refused to accept the franchise for fear of losing their right of return to their homes and property that they left behind in Israel. The Arab League accepted the West Bank to be held in trust by King Abdullah until a final settlement could be realized.[1]

In defense of King Abdullah, this study believes that the King was a pragmatic ambitious politician and a realist. He had no resources other than his claim of being a member of the Hashemite family. Abdullah was determined to establish a state under his rule but he realized two facts regarding the international relations. First, Zionism was too powerful and the Arabs lack the power, the discipline and resources to defeat it or even to slow down its project. Second, he was convinced that he would never achieve his goal without the material and political support of a super-power. By his alliance with Great Britain, Abdullah was able to keep the West Bank and Jerusalem in Arab Hands in the 1948 war even when his military was no match to the IDF. And most important, he was behind the British decision to abort the Zionists' plan to establish their state on both banks of the Jordan River.

Abdullah managed to maintain nonbelligerent relations with Israel and at the same time claiming to be the defender of the Palestinians. In 1952, King Abdullah was assassinated in Jerusalem at the entrance of the al-Aqsa Mosque by a 19-year-old Palestinian, and a member of al-Husseini clan was convicted for ordering the killing. The involvement of al-Husseini clan in this crime suggests that it was a violent act to settle scores with the King for his opposition to Haj Amin al-Husseini leadership. There was a culture of violence against the Arab political leaders in the aftermath of the 1948 Palestinian war. Egyptian Prime Minister Nukrashi was assassinated by a member of the Muslim Brothers (MB) organization and later on the director of the MB, Hasan El-Banna was gunned down.

---

1 Gelber, Y., 1997, p. 283.

Prime Minister Riad al-Sulh of Lebanon was assassinated in 1951 by members of the Syrian Social National Party to revenge the execution of the party's leaders after the failure of a military coup. Abdul-Karim Kassim carried out the 1958 military coup in Iraq and murdered several members of the Iraqi royal family and all cabinet members of the government.

The sudden departure of King Abdullah, the founder of the State of Jordan, changed the political landscape of the region. He was the most controversial heavy weight Arab leader with independent political agenda. He never followed the crowd; he believed in the power of diplomacy and compromises; he would not go to war unless he was certain he could win; and he had close allies in the West and even in Israel. His death created uncertainty for a while in the future of the Hashemite Kingdom. His elder son Emir Talal Ibn Abdullah had been sick under psychiatrist treatment in a Switzerland clinic. And Abdullah younger son, Emir Nayif Ibn Abdullah was unacceptable by the palace old guards and the British allies. At the advice of the British Ambassador Alec Kirkbride who was recalled from leave in Britain, Talal was brought back from Europe, declared fit to rule just to thwart the ambitions of Nayif. He was sworn a King but for a very short time. In August 1952, the parliament declared Talal deposed for health reasons, sent into exile in Turkey, and a regency council was formed until Prince Hussein, the son of Talal came of age in 1953. As for Jerusalem and the West Bank, there was no change in the status quo; East Jerusalem remained Jordanian and the west sector of the city stayed under Israeli control. The transition was smooth; Prime Minister Tawfiq Abul-Huda used the Arab Legion that was under the command of British officers, to insure security and deal with any opposition.

KING HUSSEIN OF JORDAN

The young king was enthroned in November 1953 only one year after the military coup that brought Nasser to power in Egypt, and the surge of Arab nationalism in most Arab countries. New parliament elections in Jordan produced a lower house that had many pro-Baath and pro-Pan-Arab members who were less supportive of the monarchy. That parliament was too liberal in a country that had been ruled by an autocratic regime since its inception. The palace old guards counseled the young inexperienced monarch to dissolve the parliament and replace Prime Minister Fawzi al-Mulqi with Abul-Huda, one of the old Hashemite loyalists. Abul-Huda government managed to have a new docile Parliament elected.

The 1954–56 period was critical for Hussein because he had to manage his good relations with Britain and the wave of anti-British sentiment among the Jordanians of Palestinian origin especially at a time when Nasser was the most popular Arab leader among the masses. Nasser revolutionary movement sought independence of Arab countries and his propaganda machines that dominated the airwaves were delivering unfriendly commentaries against the Hashemite Monarchy. The struggle between Nasser and Britain over the future of the Suez Canal and the aftermath of the 1956 British–French–Israeli attack on Egypt forced Hussein to make major decisions to appease Arab public which had been hostile to Britain and the West.

By 1956, the King's actions suggest he had already acquired the political skills needed for survival. Despite his anti-Communist stance and desire to win the US support, he refused to join the Baghdad Pact that was proposed by Britain; he negotiated the British forces withdrawal from Aqaba; and most important, he dismissed Glubb, the British commander of the Arab Legion; and later in 1956, the rest of the British officers left their posts. Hussein improved his standing among his people and in the Arab world without abandoning his opposition to communism. He retained the British defense obligations agreement and when President Eisenhower declared his 1957 doctrine for protecting the Middle East against Communism, the king asked if the US would be willing to support Jordan financially. The US pledged a $30 million annual subsidy and some military equipment for the kingdom. Hussein had to withstand another crisis in 1958.

The 1958 merger of Egypt and Syria into the United Arab Republic (UAR), the first step toward the anticipated Pan-Arab state, posed a serious threat to the monarchy in Jordan due to the popular pressure for more Arab unity under the leadership of Nasser. Jordan and Iraq formed the United Arab Kingdom under the Hashemite dynasty to counter such a threat, but it was a very short-lived union. Abdul-Karim Kassim carried out a military coup d'état, and his men killed King Faisal II Ibn Ghazi and most of the royal family in Iraq. Kassim claimed that Iraq was liberated and the monarchy would be replaced with a republican government. The cruelty of the coup leaders toward the Iraqi royal family suggests deep aversion to the pro-Britain policies of the royal family.

Hussein lost his supporters in Baghdad and recognized that his Kingdom was surrounded by hostile republics and there was a strong anti-Western sentiment in the region even among his own people. He appealed to the United Nations, the US and Britain for help. The United Nations passed a resolution calling for Middle East states to abstain from hostile actions to change established governments and Britain activated its defense treaty with Jordan by dispatching few thousand paratroopers to defend it against possible invasion by neighboring countries. American tanker planes flew over Israel to supply Amman with its gasoline needs. Hussein survived the 1958 crisis, but his country emerged more dependent on the US for financial support and defense. The US replaced Britain as the main protector of Jordan. The young king was destined to face one crisis after another when he had to deal in the 1960s with the PLO challenge. The PLO and its military wing, the PLA that were created by the Arab League had support of many Palestinian-Jordanians, then King Hussein made a fatal mistake by allowing his kingdom to be drawn into the 1967 war when it was not prepared to fight. The problems with the PLO in Jordan were discussed in Chapter 3.

King Hussein had stubbornly rejected the idea of a Palestinian entity as proposed by Nasser in 1960 in any form because it meant the disintegration of his kingdom. Jordan claimed that Egyptian and Syrian government intelligence with the cooperation of the Jordanian exiles tried to create internal instability through subversive activities with the aim of overthrowing King Hussein regime.[1] Terrorists, weapons and ammunition smuggled

---

1 *Middle East Record*, 1960, p. 326.

from Syria and Egypt were intercepted by the Jordanian security forces. Many attempted military coup d'état against the monarch were forestalled, and in 1960, Prime Minister Hazza' Majali was killed by a time-bomb in his office. It was widely assumed that Majali was killed by agents of the United Arab Republic for his strong Jordanian nationalism. After the assassination of his Prime Minister, King Hussein ordered his military to prepare for an attack on Syria in September of 1960, but he was pressured by the British to abandon the plan.[1] The Moroccan security uncovered an attempt by Egyptians to assassin King Hussein during his visit to Morocco in 1962.[2] The Palestinians of the West Bank, who believed that Nasser can lead the Arabs to liberate Palestine, were the target of Nasser's propaganda machine against King Hussein. They were receptive to Egypt's campaign against Jordan. This led King Hussein to rely on the support of his military and security forces that had demonstrated loyalty and dedication to him. King Hussein had been always known for his independence and rational politics, but in June of 1967 he must had been under too much pressure from Nasser and the Arab nationalists. His decision to go to war in 1967 must have been very painful to the young monarch because it was against his nature and policies to follow popular sentiments on issues that affect the integrity of his kingdom.

Jordan lost the 8,086 sq. miles of the West Bank and Jerusalem land and 2.5 million populations in the 1967 war. It lost the walled City of Jerusalem and its surroundings, the city that contains Jewish, Christian and Islamic holy sites. On the thirtieth anniversary of the 1967 war, King Hussein delivered a speech to his people acknowledging that his participation in that war was a regrettable mistake. King Hussein disclaimed his sovereignty over the occupied West Bank and Jerusalem in 1988, revoked the Jordanian citizenship of the residents of the occupied lands, and recognized the PLO as the sole representative of the Palestinians.

The Palestinians have the right to have their own state and representatives, but when they are under occupation there is no rational explanation for them to break their ties with Jordan and choose to be citizens of a truncated mini-state dependent on the goodwill of Israel, which they have been fighting for a century. Palestinians have been the losers in severing the traditional union with Jordan and leaving their fate in the hands of the PLO and Israel instead.

First, and most important, as a result of the disengagement Jordan had an excuse to negotiate a separate peace treaty with Israel. Separate talks and treaties with the Arab states has been an Israeli demand, as it weakens the solidarity of Arab states and neutralizes their potential role in support of the Palestinians. Jordan could have given the Palestinians the option to have their own state after liberating the occupied lands through negotiations.

Second, the Jordanian decision to disengage was an emotional one influenced by bad memories of "Black September" of 1970 rather than by rational choice. In August of 1967, a long time before Black September, 82 prominent West Bank civic leaders signed an open

---

1 *Al-Ahram*, September 18, 1960.
2 Moshe Shemesh, 1988, p. 21.

manifesto rejecting any attempt to create a Palestinian entity separate from Jordan but unfortunately, their request was ignored.[1] Many of the East-Jordanian public lost interest in the Palestinian problem and the Palestinians were oversold by the PLO promises of ending the occupation and providing freedom, security and prosperity within a state of their own.

Third, the PLO leaders were too weak politically and they were only interested in their return to the West Bank and Gaza after their long exile. The repression and humiliation that the Palestinians endured at the hands of the Israeli settlers and the PLO security forces after the 1993 Oslo Accord with Israel suggest that the PA was called upon to protect the Israelis from the growing anger of the Palestinian people.

Fourth, the West Bank is landlocked and had been dependent on the East Bank of Jordan as an outlet to the world. Severing the historical and traditional links with Jordan forced the Palestinians of the West Bank to be dependent on Israel for their economic survival and succumb to the status of inferior partners with the Israelis. A Palestinian entity if ever materialized will be an Israeli protectorate that does not satisfy the interests and ambitions of the Palestinians.

Fifth, Palestinians in the West Bank under the PLO are left completely dependent on the international aid to pay the salaries of the bureaucracy. The threat of cutting off aid has become a weapon to manipulate the politics of the Palestinians.

The Israeli leaders shunned King Hussein's effort to negotiate with them a peaceful solution to the West Bank and Jerusalem for the same reasons they refused to negotiate seriously with the Haider Abdul-Shafi delegation in 1993. Israel chose to negotiate with the exiled PLO leaders, not with King Hussein or Abdul-Shafi, to exploit their weak position financially and politically. Details regarding Abdul-Shafi were discussed in Chapter 3, "Oslo Agreement" section.

---

1 Howard Sachar, 1996, p.680.

CHAPTER 6. EGYPT AND PALESTINE SINCE 1914

Egypt's governments up until the early 1930s did not seem to realize what was coming in Palestine, across its eastern borders, as a result of Britain's promise of a homeland for the Jewish people. There was an attitude of animosity by the government officials toward the Palestinian Arabs and more sympathy for the Palestinian Jews during the 1920s.[1] When the Jewish community celebrated the opening of the Hebrew University in Palestine in 1925, the British foreign secretary, Arthur Balfour, who committed Britain to the establishment of a Jewish national home in Palestine and Ahmed Lutfi Al-Sayyed, the official representative of Egypt were among the attendants.[2] And in 1929, the Egyptian Prime Minister Muhammad Mahmoud, showed impartiality regarding the Palestinian conflict by condemning the Palestinian Arab riots against the Jewish neighborhoods in which the small Jewish community in Hebron was attacked and driven from the city.

The Egyptian government-controlled newspaper, *al-Siyasah*, threatened the Palestinian nationalists for their inflammatory attacks on the Egyptian leadership. A year later, the office of the Arab Palestinians newspaper, *al-Shoora*, was closed for instigating public opinion against Egypt's foreign policies, and the mosque's speakers were not allowed by the government to mention Palestine in their payers. At the same time, the government allowed an Egyptian Zionist newspaper to continue its publication. The unfriendly attitude toward the Arab Palestinians is attributed to many factors. The Egyptian elites were more concerned about their national independence and ending the British occupation than in Arab nationalism. Another reason was the desire of the Egyptian politicians to appease the British authorities in order to remain in power, and some Egyptians were influenced by their European education which called for religious tolerance and the Palestinian-Jewish dispute was perceived as a religious issue.

---

1 Khalil 2003, p.127.
2 Abdel-Aati 1995.

It was in 1936 when the Prime Minister Mustafa al-Nahhas from al-Wafd Party for the first time declared Egypt's support to the Arab Palestinians in a speech to the parliament. His foreign minister declared in the League of Nations that Egypt would refuse the partition plan for Palestine. He expressed concern about the establishment of a Jewish state and demanded a just resolution to the conflict, but Egypt's influence on the course of events was limited because it was still under British control. The policy of the Egyptian governments since 1936 has been to back up the Arab Palestinians position of refusing to recognize the right of the Jews to establish a home land in Palestine. This policy was reinforced by the desire of the King to achieve leadership in the Arab world and improve his image as a statesman at home. Egypt led the Arab delegation to the 1939 Round Table conference that was held in London to discuss the Palestinian issue. The establishment of the Arab League in 1947 with its headquarters in Cairo gave Egypt officially a major role in Arab politics. It inaugurated Egypt as the leader of the Arabs and the defender of their causes including the Palestinian issue. The support was transformed from the speeches and symbols to the material, then to participation in the 1948 war.

All Egyptian political parties were supportive of the Palestinians but the degree and the reason for the support depended on the ideology of the party. The Muslim Brothers treated the conflict in terms of religious clash between the Muslims and the Jews. They defended the right of the Palestinians to protect their Islamic sanctuaries and denounced Muslim countries for their failure to stand by them. The secular al-Ahrar al-Dustooryin Party argued that the solution to the Palestinian issue must be through peaceful coexistence. The Egyptian Left defended the right of the Arabs to prevent the division of their country, while the fascist Misr al-Fatah policy was based on its hatred to the Jews.

Egyptian journalists with their different political orientations followed the development of the Palestinian issue from all its dimensions since the 1920s. They were mostly supportive of the Arab Palestinians from the beginning and more farsighted regarding the future of the conflict than the government. Even after the defeat of the 1948 War, the Muslim Brothers and Misr al-Fatah opposition newspapers defended the Egyptian participation in the war, but they blamed the setbacks on the policies of the ruling class "the Pasha."[1] The anti-Pasha attacks by the opposition press could have been the pretext that led to the 1952 military coup which put an end to the monarchy, the political power of the dominant Pasha class, and regrettably Egypt's experiment in democracy.

Unlike the government's policy that was faltering in the 1920s then changed to the support of the Arabs in the 1930s, the public opinion had been firm in its backing of Arab Palestinians. The Egyptians demonstrated against Arthur Balfour in 1925 when he stopped in Cairo on his way to attend the opening of the Hebrew University in Palestine. There was outrage in Cairo streets when the Egyptians heard the news about the 1929 al-Burak (the Wailing Wall) incident in which quarrels between Muslims and Jews over access to the Wall led to altercations. The Egyptian people, motivated mostly by religious zealous, were ahead of the government in their material support to the Palestinian rebel-

---

1 "Pasha" is a title of nobility originally used in the Ottoman Empire.

lion against the British Mandate in 1936. Islamic organizations collected contributions to be donated to the victims of the uprising while the government could not participate due to the British political pressure. The Egyptian radio did not engage in the politics of Palestine because until independence, the air-waves were under direct control of the British colonial authority.

At the end of World War II, people became even more concerned about the future of Palestine and its effect on their country.[1] They reacted with outrage, strikes, and street demonstrations against the 1947 UN resolution to partition Palestine. The widespread sympathy with the Palestinians and the support for their rights forced the government to pay more attention to what was happening in Palestine. Despite the protest and call for arms struggle against the partition plan, the military intervention was not supported by all political parties. Such differences on policies were common in Egypt under its fledgling democracy in the pre-1952 era.

Palestine became even more of a national cause after the 1948 War defeat. Rather than reconsidering the policy toward Palestine, the Egyptian public was discussing the reasons and who was responsible for the humiliating outcome. Nasser had firsthand experience with the 1948 war when he and his infantry battalion were besieged and he was wounded in a Palestinian place called Faluja. The 1948 war defeat was a major justification for Nasser's revolution. The collapse of the Arab armies, according to Nasser, was caused by the corruption of the existing Arab order, the monarchies, the regimes of the *beys* and *pashas*, the large landlords and the feudalists.[2]

After the establishment of Israel and the defeat of the Arab armies in 1948, Egypt signed the 1949 armistice agreement in Rhodes, and later on failed to reach an agreement with Israel on the Palestinian refugee's issue. The victorious Israelis allowed Egypt to retain only the overpopulated poverty stricken Gaza Strip, with mostly Palestinian refugees, because it was not in the interest of the Israeli State to have the refugee camps within its borders. The 1952 military coup that ended the monarchy and transformed Egypt into a military dictatorship under Nasser was the most important outcome of the 1948 War. The underground Egyptian "Free Officers" opposition organization that staged the coup was born in 1941 to fight the British and free Egypt from their rule. Under the leadership of Nasser, the group spread far and wide and became more powerful in Palestine during the 1948 War. Nasser wrote that while he and his comrades were fighting in Palestine "all their thoughts were concentrated on Egypt." The 1948 war was followed by the UN supervised armistice which unfortunately did not prevent more wars in 1956, 1967 and 1973.

After the Egyptian–Israeli armistice agreement was signed and Gaza Strip with mostly refugee residents was under the Egyptian control as stated in Chapter 3, there was tension along the armistice line. Between 1949 and 1956, some Palestinian refugees tried to return to their properties in Israel and others were armed guerrillas on military missions against Israel. Israel responded with a devastating retaliatory raid on Gaza in February

---

1 Abdel-Aati 1995
2 Nasser, 1959

1955 where paratroopers led by Ariel Sharon attacked and destroyed the Egyptian military headquarters in Gaza killing 37 Egyptian soldiers and wounding another 31. The Egyptian army was unprepared, ill-equipped, and too weak to cope with the Israelis during the raids.[1] This happened at a time when Nasser had rejected the West conditions to assist in building the High Dam on the Nile River, and his need to demonstrate Egypt's strength to ward off the dangers of the American sponsored Baghdad Pact. It forced Nasser to give the needs for defense high priority that culminated in the signing of the Czechoslovakian arms deal in September of that year. The purchase of the Soviet weapons made the Soviet Union a major political player in Middle East affairs. After the 1955 Israeli raid, Nasser terminated secret negotiations with the Israeli government and supported more Palestinian guerrilla infiltration into Israel. At the same time, he started talking about nationalizing the Suez Canal that was a major strategic asset for Britain.

The 1956 war was discussed in detail in Chapter 4. The war was waged by Israel, the French and the British. As stated before, Israel wanted to pre-empt the potential threat of the arms purchase, the French wanted to retaliate for Nasser's support to the Algerian Liberation movement and the British wanted to prevent Nasser from nationalizing the Suez Canal.

After the withdrawal of the invading armies, Sinai Peninsula was demilitarized and the international waterway of the Straits of Tiran was opened up to the Israeli shipping. Despite Israeli gains, Nasser emerged as a champion in Egypt and the Arab world for winning the political war. He nationalized the Suez Canal, confiscated British and French holdings in Egypt, and took over the properties of native Egyptian Jews. Approximately 90% of the Egyptian Jewish community had to leave Egypt and Nasser terminated all contacts with Israel after the invasion. He promoted Arab nationalism and claimed himself the defender of the Palestinian cause. Recovering Sinai was a triumph for Nasser, but his anti-Israel warlike rhetoric that was broadcast in public speeches and publicized in local press did not help the Palestinians. On the contrary, it convinced large sections of the Israeli population to oppose reconciliation with the Palestinians.

Nasser is credited for laying down standards of Pan-Arab political agenda that forced even the moderate Western-supported regimes in the region to adopt. Following the 1956 War, Egypt became the model for the revolutionary forces in the Arab world. Nasser legitimized authoritarian rule and called for Arab unity as the means to face the Israeli threat, but he also created enemies from the ruling Arab elites. His call for overthrowing the Arab conservative regimes as a step toward unity deepened the feeling of animosity toward him among many Arab rulers. It can be argued that despite their token support to the Palestinians, some Arab conservative regimes saw Israel as their indirect ally because both were threatened by Nasser, and both were supported by the United States. Besides being a charismatic revolutionary with domestic and foreign policy achievements, Nasser's influence was derived from Egypt's stature as the most populous, with the most developed bureaucracy, the largest GNP, and the largest military in the Arab region. Another reason be-

---

1 Perez 1996, p.57

hind his influence was his total control over the Egyptian media that was transformed into an effective propaganda machine. His regime nationalized all private-owned newspapers and installed radio and television sets in coffee shops in the cities and villages all over the country. Free battery-operated radios were distributed in villages that had no electricity.

Nasser was involved in the 1962 civil war in Yemen and could not extricate Egypt from that war to meet his obligations to come to the defense of Syria in 1967. Periodic incursions into Israel by the Palestinian guerrillas and the dispute over Jordan River water led to clashes between Israel and Syria. The clashes eventually led to the 1967 war which gave Israel the golden opportunity to end Nasser's threat once and for all. (The 1967 war was discussed in Chapter 4.) In just six days Israel destroyed the military of three neighboring Arab countries and conquered their lands. The image of Nasser as the defender of the Arabs was severely tarnished. Conservative Arab rulers should have felt more secure because Nasser would not have time to de-stabilize their regimes after the war.

The Egyptians and the rest of the Arab world population were in a shock and disbelief after the humiliating defeat. They had been misled by their leaders and the controlled media before and during the war. Their radio, newspapers and televisions reported the leadership rhetoric that exaggerated the strength of the Egyptian military and its readiness to destroy the Jewish state. Israel succeeded in using such threat as announced in the Arab news media, word by word, as a proof of the Arab aggression and painted itself as a vulnerable victim who had to defend its people with all means. Egypt and its Arab allies lost on the battlefield and in the world public opinion, but the big losers were the Palestinians. Israel conquered what had remained of Palestine, the West Bank, East Jerusalem and Gaza, and immediately started colonizing the occupied land. A new wave of Palestinian refugees crossed the river into Jordan and those who had been outside the occupied land including workers in the Gulf States, traveling businessmen and students in foreign countries were denied the return to their homes and families in the newly occupied lands.

The 1967 war caused a radical change in the Arab world toward Israel. Arab writers and intellectuals began considering Israel a part of the global order with which they had to deal, even while they feel hostility toward it. Others dared to criticize the undemocratic Arab political systems. Many Arab thinkers argued that Israel's triumph over the Arabs is a triumph of democracy over authoritarianism rather than a superiority of the Jewish people. The aftermath of the 1967 defeat brought out sharp criticism of Nasser's qualities that were anathema to the Egyptians temperament. He was described as an adventurous ruthless leader determined to suppress his political adversaries. The defeat and the occupation of Sinai including the eastern bank of the Suez Canal was a self-fulfilled prophecy of the Israeli threat that had been the basis for justifying Nasser's fifteen years of authoritarian rule. Instead of the call for regime change after its failure to defend the country, the Egyptians renewed their allegiance to Nasser because he was the only leader they had known and there were no alternatives under his authoritarian regime. The opposition had been either behind bars, in exile, or disfranchised, and the military would not take orders from other than Nasser. Nasser, in effect, had institutionalized the personalized authoritarian regime in Egypt and the region.

The Egyptians never intended to go to war in 1967, according to many observers in-cluding Muhammad, a close advisor of President Nasser.[1] Heikal claims that the Egyptian intention for removing the UN forces from the Egyptian–Israeli border, which triggered the war, was only to warn Israel not to attack Syria. The fact that Egypt kept some of its best military units in Yemen to prop its government against the royalist insurgents sup-ports the argument that Egypt was not ready to fight Israel in 1967. Egypt's involvement in the Yemeni civil war was a drain on the military and economic resources in the 1960s even before 1967.

Nasser never intended to go to war in 1967, and he had missed a golden opportunity back in 1955 to solve the Arab–Israeli conflict peacefully under the auspices of the US.[2] He turned down an American offer to solve the Arab–Israeli conflict peacefully. The United States offered to finance the High Dam on the Nile River if Egypt would play a leading role in reaching a peaceful solution to the Arab–Israeli conflict. Muhammad Heikal, a confi-dant of Nasser wrote that Herbert Hoover, Assistant Secretary of State in the Eisenhower administration, met Ahmad Hussein, Egypt's ambassador to the US in June 1956 and of-ficially offered on behalf of the US to finance the High Dam project in exchange for Egypt's help to settle the Arab–Israeli conflict peacefully, but Nasser rejected the offer.[3] Chester Cooper confirms that John Foster Dulles, the US Secretary of State, was eager to link the High Dam financing to the Arab–Israeli conflict in order to stop the Soviet Union influ-ence in the Middle East. Financing the High dam was decided in a NATO meeting on December 15, 1955, by the foreign ministers of the US, Britain, and France in order to limit the Soviet involvement in the Middle East.[4] But Nasser rejected the offer because it would mean siding with the West in the Cold War.

Solving the Palestinian problem peacefully and building the High Dam would have been a win-win proposition for Egypt if Nasser was serious about supporting the Pales-tinian cause. After the 1967 war, Sadat changed Egypt's alliance from the Soviet Union to the US in exchange for the peaceful return of Sinai to Egypt. Was the quasi-alliance with the Soviets more important than solving the Palestinian issue peacefully? Geopolitical questions are decided by national interests as a rational choice. In hindsight it seems that if Nasser considered the solution of the Arab–Israeli conflict as important as the return of Sinai was for Sadat, he should have considered the offer to ally Egypt with the US as a reasonable price, but he did not. Since the alternative to a negotiated settlement was war with unpredictable consequences, Nasser's refusal to accept the negotiation offer was irrational.

Sadat succeeded Nasser in 1970 and promised his countrymen that he would recover Sinai, but he also knew that he would not keep his promise without help from the US. In

---

1 Heikal 1973
2 Heikal 1973, p.62; Cooper 1978, pp. 94-95; Hofstadter, 1973, p.121
3 Heikal 1973, p.62
4 Hofstadter, 1973, p.121

the first two years of his rule, Sadat tried to resolve the Arab–Israeli conflict peacefully, but he was rebuffed by Israel and the US. Israel was confident that Egypt and Syria could not recover their occupied lands militarily and the status quo was acceptable to the US since the death of Nasser and the defeat of the PLO by King Hussein of Jordan had diminished the Soviet Union influence in the region. Sadat agreed without any reservation to the 1971 Yaring proposal to enter into peace negotiations with Israel, and he offered to open the Suez Canal for the international navigation, including Israel, in return for partial Israeli withdrawal from the northern edge of the Canal. He was not taken seriously by the Americans even when he dismissed the Soviet military advisors as demanded by the US. The Egyptian leadership discovered that their peaceful gestures were ignored by the American policy makers for some reasons, which Kissinger described later on as "shortsighted." After failing to resolve the conflict through diplomacy, Sadat decided to prepare for war without the usual announcements and media fanfare. He formed alliances with the moderate Arab states and he provided his military with Soviet-made arms.

The Egyptian armed forces surprised the Israelis on October 6, 1973 by storming their "Berleev Line" defenses across the Canal and establishing foothold in Sinai. Syria's simultaneous military attack on Israel north border forced Israel to fight on two fronts. The Egyptian military won a battle against the Israelis for the first time. It destroyed the bulk of the Israeli war machine in the first two days, and forced the US to intervene by airlifting military equipment to the Israelis. When the Israeli military encountered difficulties and began running short of military supplies, Nixon ordered a full scale airlift of military equipment paid for with a grant of supplemental military aid.

The 1973 war possibly marked the end of the inferiority complex and the myth of the Israeli invincibility for a while. It was focused on recovering Egyptian land, not on issues that concern the Arab Palestinians in the occupied land, and therefore it differed from the previous wars in objectives, preparation, execution, and outcome. It was the bloodiest of all the Arab–Israeli wars, and it was the only war that weakened the hegemony of the Israeli elite and might have ended with an even more devastating Israeli defeat had it not been for the US intervention. Israeli losses were so high that US Galaxy planes had to rush replacements of war equipment directly to the front lines. The number of casualties and the level of the defense expenditures prior to the war are the best indicators for the intensity of the war. The number of dead Israeli soldiers was 2,527 in the 1973 War, compared to 777 in the 1967 War, 190 in the 1956 War, and 222 in the "War of Independence."[1] The number of Israelis wounded was 8,800, while 840 tanks were lost, and the cost of the war equaled approximately one year's gross national product for each of the combatants.[2] Egypt's defense expenditure as a percentage of its GNP was 19.9 % in 1972 and 31.0% in 1973, as compared to only 11.7% in 1966 and 11.5% in 1967.[3] Seven months before the 1973 war, Sadat appointed himself as a prime minister. This made him "the president, the prime minister, the supreme commander of the armed forces, president of the Arab Social-

---

1 Evron 1978, P. 100
2 Perez 1996, p.74
3 Evron 1978, p. 115

ist Union (ASU) central committee, and the military commander," with the undeclared purpose of preparing for the war. Sadat was committed to win because with such authority, it was his war, and if he failed he would have no one to blame but himself. In short, unlike the previous wars, Egypt took the war to recover Sinai seriously.

The Egptians' relative success in the 1973 War supports the argument that Egypt was not serious about recovering land for the Palestinians when they intervened on behalf of the Palestinian Arabs. They could not or they were not willing to fight the Israelis in 1948 and 1967 when Israel was militarily most vulnerable, but they were able to stand up to Israel in 1973 when it was the strongest military power in the Middle East, Egypt's economy was in the worst shape ever, and the Soviet Union was slow in sending arms. They were serious only when the objective was to recover Egyptian lands.

The success of the Israeli counter-offensive that trapped the Third Egyptian army and brought the Israeli forces to within 101 kilometers of Cairo in the 1973 war had no negative effect on the morale of the Egyptian people, because it was attributed to America's intervention rather than Israel's military superiority. Sadat wrote: "Suddenly I found myself confronting the United States, and this was what made me announce to the whole world on October 19, 1973, that I wasn't prepared to fight the USA."[1] Despite its military recovery on the Egyptian and the Syrian fronts, Israel's casualties reached disastrous level and its military intelligence was discredited for its failure to predict the attack. The Egyptian news media focused on the theme that the US would never allow an Israeli defeat. Sadat rightfully claimed credit for the 1973 Egypt's success in the war and used the news media to portray himself as "the hero of the crossing," and for two years he was virtually free from political challenge.

Six days after the start of the military action in 1973, Sadat accepted the UN Security Council resolution 338 and ordered his armed forces to ceasefire. Egypt and Israel signed a disengagement agreement mediated by then US Secretary of State, Henry Kissinger on January 17, 1974. The agreement called for Israel to withdraw 15 miles east of the Canal but the pull back promised of no more to come. On September 1, 1975, Kissinger was able to get the two sides to sign the "Sinai Two" agreement which included a further Israeli withdrawal and the stationing of Americans in the buffer zone. Sadat gave Israel a non-belligerency pact and gave Kissinger a secret promise to keep Egypt out if Syria attacked Israel.[2] "Sinai Two" marked the end of the step-by-step diplomacy but Israel continued to retain 90% of Sinai. The Arab world condemned the Egyptian–Israeli settlement as a defection from the alliance and a repetition of the discredited armistice agreement after the 1948 war. (King Farouk had been the first to sign an armistice agreement after the defeat of 1948 war.)

Sadat declared on October 16, 1973, that the purpose of the war was only to recover occupied lands and restore the rights of the Palestinians, and that Egypt was ready for a ceasefire. Even when Sadat had created an obvious split in the Arab ranks and his press

---

1 Sadat 1978, p.290
2 Hirst and Beeson 1981, p.193

was mocking and insulting his Arab and Palestinian critics, he claimed he was fighting for the Palestinian cause. In his March 1975 speech to the UNGA, Sadat stated that "Jerusalem, Nablus, and Gaza [Palestinian cities] are no less dear to [him] than Egypt and Kantara."

His rhetorical promises to restore the Palestinian rights were forgotten in his 1979 peace treaty with Israel, which had nothing tangible for the Palestinians. Sadat's go-it-alone diplomacy was successful in achieving the Egyptian goals of recovering Sinai and securing generous US economic aid but made it harder for the Palestinians to recover their territory. The Egyptian–Israeli peace treaty freed the Israeli governments and settlers to consolidate their hold on the Palestinian, Syrian and Lebanese occupied land. The treaty even weakened the position of the Israeli peace advocates who had argued that significant territorial concessions to the Palestinians were necessary to obtain peace with the Arabs. The 1973 War was a turning point in Egypt's political strategies toward the conflict with Israel. Egypt opted for peace with Israel regardless of its Arab allies' reaction. There were two important reasons behind this decision. The outcome of the 1973 War was the best Egypt could achieve for itself in war with Israel, and Egypt did not have the economic resources or the desire to fight any more wars. Egypt was tired of the Palestinian issue.

In his annual opening of parliament on November 9, 1977, Sadat surprised his audience and even his closest advisors by announcing that he was "ready to go to the Knesset, to talk to them [the Israelis]" peace.[1] Yasser Arafat was among the audience as an invited guest of the President. The Israeli Prime Minister, Menachim Begin, extended an invitation through the US embassy and the visit was materialized on November 20, 1977. In his address to the Knesset, Sadat declared that Egypt "would accept to live with [Israel] in permanent peace based on justice." Sadat's foreign minister, Ismael Fahmi resigned and most of the Arab world including Egypt's close ally, Syria, and Sadat's principle paymaster, Saudi Arabia, were outraged. Sadat was depicted by his Arab constituency as a traitor but in the US and Europe, where he had been described previously as a warmonger, he was immediately hailed as a hero and the most admired Arab leader.

Sadat's historic visit to Jerusalem on November 20, 1977, reflected his determination to make peace. He treated peace as a sacred matter, part of Egypt's tradition, and beyond criticism. He enacted laws that would allow dissolving parties that object to the peace treaty openly, and would deprive citizens who oppose his peace policy from exercising their political rights and prevent them to run for offices in labor unions or clubs or to work in the media. When the Egyptian Bar Association officials criticized the peace accord, Sadat threatened to cancel its license and downgrade its status to a social club, and later on he dissolved it when its leaders ignored the threat. The Parliament approved the peace agreement by an overwhelming majority, but even with this approval, Sadat was angry because eleven members dared to disagree. Like any authoritarian ruler, he did not treat the opponents of his policy with the respect they deserve.

---

1 *Al-Ahram,* November 10, 1977.

Sadat's peace initiative was a calculated rational choice move motivated by Egypt's state of the economy and the impossible task of recovering Sinai by military means. The January 1977 riots that rampaged through the streets of Egypt's cities triggered Sadat's decision to make the trip to Israel in search of peace. Sadat sought peace out of necessity rather than altruism. The riots were in response to an austerity program that was intended to convince the international financial community that Egypt was determined to have fiscal responsibility. The program reduced the subsidies of basic commodities by 50% and raised the custom duties levied on certain unsubsidized imported commodities. The riots were a reminder that with a drastic reduction in subsidies, millions of Egyptians feared they would cross the line between subsistence and starvation.

The rioters in Cairo unleashed their anger on targets that symbolized the differences between the rich and the poor as well as the symbols of the regime. They destroyed imports boutiques, exclusive hotels, nightclubs, fancy cars, police stations, and in Alexandria demonstrators ransacked the offices of the ASU and pillaged the home of then Vice-President Mubarak.[1] Heikal wrote that things were so bad that a presidential plane was ready to take Sadat and his family to exile in Tehran, Iran.[2] Sadat realized how bad the economic conditions were and that there was a direct link between the state of the economy and the cost of the Arab–Israeli wars. He rescinded the subsidy reduction measure that caused the riots and he planned on doing something dramatic in his quest to end the state of war with Israel. Sadat's decision to make the journey to Jerusalem was inspired by the food riots ten months earlier. The elections of President Carter in the US and the hard-liner Prime Minister Menachem Begin in Israel and the departure of Henry Kissinger from government did not deter Sadat from pursuing his peace mission even with no idea of the concessions that the Israelis were willing to make. The Shah of Iran was the only one who knew about Sadat's plan to go to Jerusalem before his announcement in the parliament.[3]

Sadat should not be faulted for his peace initiative because it was the only approach to guarantee the recovery of Sinai. His trip to Jerusalem succeeded in dramatizing his quest for peace internationally and forcing Israel and its allies in the West to respond favorably to his peace gesture. He had good reasons to exclude the war option with Israel, but he may be faulted for not explaining these reasons for the initiative to his Arab allies especially the Palestinians. He could have used his persuasion skills by presenting his case to the Arab people and appealing to their common sense. The Arab people including the Palestinians were fed-up with the Arab leadership who had been misleading them for so long by using the Israeli threat only to justify their authoritarian rule.

Sadat wanted the formal peace process with Israel to go at high speed without taking into consideration the long and bitter historical experience of the Egyptians in their struggle with the Israelis. The peace and normalization sought by Egypt and Israel were viewed differently by the two parties, but both sides were motivated by political pragmatism. The Egyptians wanted peace for internal reasons, and the Israelis for external and

---

1 Lippman 1989, p.116
2 Heikal 1983, p.92
3 Heikal 1983, p.97

long term goals. What inspired the Egyptians to seek peace was their desire to recover Sinai and devote their resources for solving their internal economic problems. The Israelis, on the other hand, view peace with Egypt as a big step toward acceptance in the Arab world. They sought to establish relationships in the spheres of trade, tourism, sports, culture, agriculture, and education.

Egypt understood normalization within the following terms:

- All of Sinai was to be returned and it would be excluded from any future Israeli interests.
- A normal relationship would be established with Israel without giving it any special treatment.
- Normalization would lead to peace and stability which were necessary for devoting attention to reforming Egypt's economic structure and improving the standards of living.
- Peace with Israel meant increased economic and military aid from the US and investments by American corporations.
- Areas of normalization with Israel would start with economics, education, transportation, and air traffic.

For Israel, normalization with Egypt was a strategic breakthrough based on the following principles:

- Normalization and the free passage of Israeli shipping in the Suez Canal were the price that Egypt had to pay for the Israeli withdrawal from Sinai.
- Peace with Egypt would ameliorate tension with the most powerful Arab state and neutralize its role in the Arab–Israeli conflict.
- Singing a separate peace with Egypt weakened Arab solidarity and consequently improved Israel's sense of security.
- Peace with Egypt would be the first step in ending Israel's political, economic, and cultural isolation in the Middle East and encourage other Arab countries to make peace with Israel.
- Peace would open new markets for Israeli products. The long term objective was to play a major roll in the economic development in the region.

THE ECONOMY AS A FACTOR IN SADAT'S PEACE INITIATIVE

When Sadat took office in 1970, "the treasury was empty and Egypt was bankrupt."[1] His minister of finance told him that the country might not be able to pay the salaries of its soldiers and civil servants. Egypt's external debt exceeded the value of the GNP during the early years of Sadat's government. There were 700,000 refugees who were forced to leave the Canal towns of Port Said, Suez, and Ismaelia as a result of the 1967 War. Egypt was deprived of the oil revenues in Sinai, the Suez Canal was closed, and tourism was at standstill. Only six days before the 1973 War, Sadat warned his National Security Council that the economy had "reached zero." Under these economic conditions, the aim of the

---

1 Sadat 1978, p.214

1973 War must have been limited in scope and objective because Egypt did not have the resources to wage a sustained all out war to recapture Sinai. The purpose of the war must have been mostly non-military. It was part of a strategy to force the US to take Sadat seriously, break the deadlock and bring Israel to the negotiating table to discuss peace.

Sadat had external and internal motives to take a new course of economic policy. Egypt reintegration in the world economy would improve the chances of more sympathy from the United States, and liberalizing the economy would strengthen his support among the Egyptian bourgeoisie who were his main constituency. Sadat enacted the 1974 economic openness law, known as "Infitah," which liberalized the economy and allowed the creation of private companies that would be exempted from the labor laws imposed on publicly owned companies. The new policy was intended to integrate Egypt's economy into the world capitalist system by opening it to unrestricted foreign imports and investments. Sadat, however, continued to keep major industrial enterprises under state control and maintained the commitment to solve the economic problems with socialist practices. The government continued to provide guaranteed unconditional employment for the college graduates, universal free health care and education, protection from increase of the cost of living, low cost utilities, and subsidized food and other necessities.

Initially, the Infitah policy gave the Egyptians a sense of optimism, but by 1976, the policy began to expose the country to many explosive problems. The flood of imports created a trade deficit that exceeded $3.0 billion in 1976 and the cost of government subsidies climbed to more than $1.7 billion.[1] Many of the rich Egyptians acquired wealth through import schemes, representing foreign companies, and black market exchanging money. The surge of foreign aid and business provided opportunities for people with political clout and connections to engage in tax-free commissions and unproductive consulting work. The Infitah policy adopted the consumption concept from capitalism and dropped from capitalism the stringency of market competition and the responsibility for quality control. For example, Halwan steel mill had never shown a profit, even though the iron ore was locally mined and the state provided subsidized energy, subsidized transportation and guaranteed market for its product.[2] The government chose to absorb the losses rather than close the mill because it employed 20,000 workers.

Egyptian Planners in 1974 concluded that Egypt could earn enough to pay for its food requirement if it had increased its industrial exports thirty-folds by the year 2000, a goal beyond its capabilities.[3] Many small and medium businesses lost their markets in the Eastern block and could not establish markets in the West due to generally inferior quality of their goods. The new policy created a new economic class of employees working for the private sector or catering to the needs of foreigners receiving wages several times higher than those in the public sector. Due to the income disparities, the private sector was able to raid public sector talents at all levels of skills hierarchy. Those who had acquired business experience in public sector joined higher-paying private companies or started busi-

1   Beattie 2000
2   Lippman 1989, p.92
3   Waterbury 1978, p.290

nesses of their own. Another serious problem was caused by the new rich capitalists who kept their cash reserves, estimated at $40 billion in foreign banks abroad in the 1970s.[1]

These factors and the continued expansion of subsidy programs worsened the problems of deficit financing and created runaway inflation which was felt by the Egyptians on fixed income. As a result, violent protests became commonplace. The 33,000 employees of Mahalla-al-Kubra textile demonstrated in 1975 and 1976 demanding higher wages and improving working conditions. On the New Year's Day in 1975, thousands of Egyptian workers, who earned the minimum wage of £E12 a month, demonstrated against Sadat's economic policy in front of a Nile-side luxury hotel where rich Egyptians, who benefited from Sadat's Infitah policy, were celebrating the New Year.[2] The demonstrators were chanting "Where is our breakfast?" Despite these signs of discontent, Sadat decided in 1977 to take some measures to comply with the IMF requirement to reduce the deficit by lifting subsidies on some goods. As a result, riots in Egypt from Alexandria in the north to Aswan in the south broke out on January 18 and 19. Police stations were besieged, homes were ransacked, and shops were looted and burned. The army was called in to restore order and more than 20 people were killed. The riots were viewed by observers as a despairing protest against the new liberal economic policy. Sadat publicly denied that the uprising was a grass-root reaction to his infitah policies, called it the "thieves uprising," and accused the opposition left of instigating it. But *al-Ahram* newspaper argued that the economic policies were behind the riots: "The majority of Egyptians have come to feel that they are unwelcomed in the new consumer society. [The economy] deprives the majority of the essentials of life while bestowing benefits upon a tiny segment of society."[3]

Ten months after the riots, Sadat made his historical trip to Jerusalem for the quest of peace against the wishes of Egypt's ally in the 1973 War, Syria. The West hailed the move as an act of courage and most Arab nations and their governments viewed it as abandonment of Arab unity. But within the context of Egypt's poor economic conditions, Sadat's peace initiative must have been mainly economically motivated. Faced with the US ready to help Israel with everything it possesses, unreliable Soviet ally, and a bankrupt Egyptian economy, Sadat must have recognized that he had no choice other than peace with Israel.

EGYPTIAN PUBLIC OPINION REGARDING NORMALIZATION

An intensive media campaign was launched by the Egyptian government to sell the peace initiative to the public and even to call into question Egypt's Arab identity which had been the cornerstone of Nasser's policy. Some of the intellectual elites suggested that it was time to reconsider Egypt's role as the defender of the Arab causes and focus on its own problems. The Egyptian writer, Tawfiq al-Hakim published his book, *Awdat al-Wa'i*, in which he launched an attack on Nasser's Arab nationalism legacy, and tried to assert that Egypt's culture belongs more to the Greeks and the Romans rather than to the Arab

---

1 Beattie 2000, p.150
2 Hirst and Beeson 1981
3 *Al-Ahram*, February 1, 1977.

and Muslim civilizations. The anti-Arab campaign was even more effective because of the imposed restrictions against the political opposition that had been denied the right to voice their opinion. As a result, most Egyptians felt satisfied with Sadat's policy before and immediately after the signing of the peace treaty, but later on this feeling switched to opposition. The change was due to the difference in circumstances rather than contradiction in the direction of the public thinking.

Sadat and the media sold peace as the means to resolve the Palestinian problem, end wars, and guarantee improvement in the economic development without spilling Egyptian blood. Government officials continued to declare that Egypt did not abandon the Palestinian cause and did not make any concessions harmful to Egypt's interests. The Egyptians liked what they heard about the benefits of peace, and Sadat believed that he had a Mandate to go ahead with his policies. It did not take too long for the public to discover that the promised prosperity and abundance did not materialize, and the economic liberalization policy led to inflation and more poverty. Certain events such as Israel's attack on Beirut in 1981 only two weeks after Sadat and Begin met led the Egyptians to question Israel commitment to peace. Further more, Egypt was not successful in establishing independent relationship with the United States. Egypt was judged by the US on the basis of its conduct toward Israel which gave Israel control over the Egyptian–US relations.[1] Sadat was surprised when large segments of society had complained for not benefiting from the promised peace dividends. He responded with laws to silence his critics through coercion. Enacting such laws was an admission that he was losing the public support to his policy.

Most opponents of normalization do not propose alternatives in dealing with Israel; the opposition political parties and major trade unions refused dealing with Israel, and some Egyptians, mostly radical Islamists, opted for violence against Israeli interests to interrupt normalization. Opposition parties had declared their disapproval through their spokesmen and publications whenever they were not censored. The exception was *al-Ahrar* Party which was represented in the parliament delegation that visited Israel in 1981.

Members of Muslim Brothers (MB) have been the most vocal critics of normalization. They continued their relentless criticism of the peace agreement in a publication titled "*al-Basheer*" when the government closed their *al-Da'wa* magazine for its anti-peace stand in 1981. Normalization, according to the MB, is a form of cultural invasion that will contaminate the minds of the youth and make it easy for Israel to spy on Egypt. Although the cycle of wars and a Pan-Arab military option against Israel is over, Israel's relations with Egypt have not been truly normalized even under Sadat. Business communities on both sides try to normalize, but the Egyptian bureaucracy and civil societies, secularists and Islamists, have turned the peace into a cold relationship where the ghost of the past hatred remained intact.

Relations with Israel in the 1980s

The Egyptian–Israeli peace treaty has continued to be the basic framework for the relationship between the two countries since 1979 despite controversial accusations lev-

---

1 Eliots 1988

eled by some Israelis that Egypt has not lived up to the spirit of the treaty. The conditions that made the treaty necessary for Egypt at the time of its signing have remained in place, even worsened, in the 1980s and beyond. Estimates of families below poverty line in the urban areas increased from 44.4% in 1981-82 to 51.1% in 1984, then dropped to 49.0 in 1991, and in the rural areas it increased from 43.0% in 1981-82 to 47.2% in 1984 and 64.5% in 1991.[1] There is no question that Egypt "needs the peace process to solve its internal problems."[2] Besides avoiding the possibility of war with Israel, staying with the treaty has given Egypt economic resources badly needed to sustain its population above the destitution level. There is no pressure from within the state for repealing the treaty because the alternatives cannot be rationalized. Some Israeli actions in the occupied West Bank and in the region such as the invasion of Lebanon in 1982 and the massacres at Sabra and Shatila refugee camps have dismayed and angered the Egyptian public. The only reaction by the government was to condemn the Israeli actions. No Arab nation lifted a finger on behalf of the Palestinians.

After the complete return of Sinai in 1982, Mubarak returned the focus of his government to the Palestinian issue that had been neglected when the regime was dealing with the more pressing fate of the Egyptian lands. The rhetoric support to the Palestinians and obstructions to normalization have become the weapons of choice used by Mubarak to shore up the legitimacy of his government. Angry Egyptians called on Mubarak to freeze the normalization process, and some even demanded abrogating the peace treaty when Israel invaded Lebanon in 1982. Egypt called its ambassador to Israel and decided to freeze official contacts with Israel. The government spokesman stated that normal relations with Israel cannot be sustained while Israel pursued unreasonable regional policies. Egyptian Minister of Defense Marshal Abu Ghazala testified in a closed parliamentary committee meeting in 1987 that Israel was Egypt's chief enemy. Egypt was reluctant to cooperate with Israel in some economic projects including a USAID's financed for trilateral projects involving US, Israeli, and Egyptian personnel and technology as part of the normalization process prescribed in Camp David accord.[3]

The Egyptians demonstrated in protest against Israel's 1985 bombing of the PLO headquarters in Tunis, and the protest developed into incidents of violent actions against the Israeli interests in Egypt. An off-duty Egyptian soldier killed seven Israeli tourists in 1985 and an Israeli diplomat was assassinated in the same year only one week after *al-Ahali* newspaper reported the discovery of an Israeli–American spy ring in Cairo. One Israeli was killed and three more were wounded in Cairo's International Industrial and Agricultural Exposition in 1986. A group of armed men in the Egyptian side of the international border with Israel fired at an Israeli army patrol in 1987. The Israelis complained about the attitude of the Egyptian press and the Egyptian Bar Association for slandering the victims

---

1 Zaki, 1994

2 *International Herald Tribune*, February 24, 1984.

3 Dina Gallal, "America and Egypt: The Aid and the Relation," *al-Ahram al-Iqtisadi*, July 20, 1987.

and providing support to the criminals and depicting them as innocent civilians in the wake of each attack.

The Israeli practices for controlling the 1988 Palestinian uprising were condemned by most Egyptians. Many demonstrated in protest and demanded to break diplomatic relations with Israel, and all professional associations and trade unions took actions to undermine the normalization process.[1] The Engineers Association rejected the justification for normalization, and declared its official boycott of Israel in the areas of commerce and professional conferences. The Artists Union decided to boycott all forms of cultural and artistic contacts with Israel, and the Egyptian Bar Association petitioned the courts to force the government to expel the Israeli ambassador from the country. The Journalists Association asked its members not to travel to Israel or interview any Israeli official, and the Medical Doctors Association withdrew from an international conference for inviting Israel to attend. Egyptian educators announced their solidarity with the Palestinians and asked the minister of education to withdraw a school text book for showing a map of Israel and ignoring Palestine. Egyptian intellectuals opposed Israel's participation in the annual Cairo's International Book Fair, and the Conference of College Teachers Clubs called for boycotting the Israeli universities until the Palestinian issue is resolved.

RELATIONS SINCE THE 1990S

The 1990s witnessed some international and regional development related to the Arab–Israeli conflict, and as a consequence, it had its effects on the Egyptian–Israeli relations. Iraqi troops invaded Kuwait setting off the Persian Gulf War in 1990 and the US organized a multinational coalition military force to seek Kuwait's freedom and the restoration of its sovereign government. The "coalition force" defeated the Iraqi troops and liberated Kuwait in four days of combat. The Soviet Union was dissolved in 1991 and the cold war ended with the emergence of the US as the only international superpower. Israel and its Arab neighbors, including the Palestinians held the 1991 "Madrid Peace Conference" under the auspices of European countries for the purpose of resolving the Arab–Israeli conflict peacefully. The Conference was followed by the 1993 Israeli–Palestinian Oslo Agreement, and later on the 1994 Israeli–Jordanian Peace Treaty. These positive developments improved the prospects of peace in the region, some Arab intellectuals and professionals including Egyptians visited Israel at the invitation of its government, but most Arab civil societies and Arab elites were suspicious of Israel's intentions. In its criticism of the Arab–Israeli rapprochement, the 18th Conference of Arab Writers and Thinkers which was held in Amman Jordan in 1992 stated that the Arab–Israeli struggle was regarding existence rather than borders. The Arab Artists Union refused in 1994 all attempts of normalization and refused Israel participation in the 1994 Cairo Cinema Festival. The final proclamation of the 1994 National Islamic Conference in Beirut had very strong words

---

1 Eliots 1988

against any attempt of normalization with Israel and denounced the visits of Arab artists and journalists to Israel.[1]

Despite the public opinion opposition and the lack of progress in the peace talks between Israel and the Palestinians, the Egyptian government has been determined not to retreat from its commitment to peace. Mubarak who had participated in the previous war campaigns was aware that war with Israel had contributed to the collapse of the monarchy and discrediting of Nasser's presidency. He followed the same line that President Sadat had devised during his tenure regarding peace and normalization. Even the opposition, who were against normalization, did not for the most part advocate the return to the state of war. The government has been meeting its obligations as stated in the Peace Treaty. Some Egyptian products, including the crude oil, have been exported to Israel, some Israeli products are sold in the Egyptian markets, Hebrew language programs are shown daily on the Egyptian TV and Israeli visitors are occasionally seen around the Pyramids and in the bazaars, but very few ordinary Egyptians, if any, travel to Israel. The attitude of the Egyptians toward normalization today is not encouraging. Most people surveyed do not support it now and in the future. In 1998, 350 professionals from diverse socio-economic backgrounds were asked about their impression about Israel. Of them, 96% had very negative or negative impression. In a 2003 survey of 354 teachers, conducted by Center for Political Research & Studies, only 5.9% would accept to teach in Israel at attractive salaries. The loss of confidence in the peace process and the Israeli hostile actions in the occupied lands has contributed to the Egyptian people animosity toward the Israelis. And after the 2008–2009 Israeli attacks on Gaza, some Egyptian politicians in the opposition camp called for abrogating the peace treaty, but not to return to the state of war. They criticize their government cooperation with the Israeli siege against the people of Gaza by restricting the movement of people and merchandise across the borders with the Strip since Gaza has been controlled by the Islamist Hamas and declared an enemy by Israel. Hamas draws its ideology from the Egyptian-based Muslim Brothers movement which is prohibited from engaging in politics as a party in Egypt. The government spokesmen argue that Egypt will play more constructive roles in the peace process as a mediator and enabler by keeping the channels of communications and strengthening its diplomatic relations with Israel as stipulated by the peace treaty.

---

1 "Arab Strategic Report," Center for Political and Strategic Studies, Al-Ahram, Cairo 1994: pp. 221-222.

CHAPTER 7. THE ROADMAP AND ROADBLOCKS

Representatives of the "Quartet," an ad hoc American-dominated committee made up of the US, the European Union, Russia, and the UN indorsed a US proposed schedule of conditions and events referred to it as the "Roadmap" for breaking the Palestinian–Israeli impasse and lead to a peace settlement based on a two-state solution. The US State Department released on April 30, 2003, the text of the "Roadmap" for a permanent solution to the Israeli–Palestinian conflict. The "Roadmap" is a "performance-based and goal-driven" plan rather than a treaty. It is vaguely linked to the Oslo Accords agreement and to other different plans that had been formulated since the Palestinian *Intifada* of 2000. They include the Tenet security cooperation plan of June 2001, the Mitchell report and the initiative of Crown Prince Abdullah of Saudi Arabia at the Beirut Arab League Summit Meeting of 2002. The Crown Prince initiative called for Israel to withdraw to its 1967 borders in exchange for normalization of relations with all the Arab states. The Saudi initiative came in the post September 11 frenzy following the wave of anti-Arab and anti-Muslim provocations in the United States. Feeling insecure, Arab regimes put forth the initiative to prove that they wanted peace rather than confrontation with the strategic ally of the US in the region.[1] The Tenet security cooperation plan was proposed by US CIA director George Tenet in 2001 to forge security agreements between Israel and the PA. The Mitchell report was released in 2001 by an American fact-finding committee headed by ex-Senator George Mitchell. The purpose of the committee was to investigate the state of the Palestinian–Israeli conflict and get the peace process back on track, shortly after the start of the 2000 *al-Aqsa Intifada*.

The "Roadmap" required action by the Palestinians to disarm the Palestinian resistance and by Israel to ease the wide range of security-related, humanitarian, and policy

---

1 Bishara, Azmi, *Al-Ahram Weekly*, September 28-October 4, 2006.

matters. International donors, Quartet members, and neighboring states also have obligations to fund the Palestinian Authority, to provide international political support, and to end any public or private financing of armed Palestinian groups that resist the Israeli occupation. The "Roadmap" specifies three steps for the two parties to take to reach the settlement that would lead to a permanent agreement for ending the Palestinian–Israeli conflict through negotiations based on the UN Security Council resolutions 242, 338 and 1397 but ignored the UNGA Resolution 194 that called for the refugees right of return to their homes in what is now Israel. The "Roadmap" included a timeline for carrying out each step and a deadline for completion by 2005. Phase 1 required the Palestinians to end terror and violence, normalize Palestinian life, and build Palestinian institutions to be completed by May 2003. It calls on Israel to withdraw from Palestinian areas occupied since September 28, 2000. The two sides need to restore the status quo that existed at that time, as security performance and cooperation progress. Israel also needs to freeze all settlement activity, consistent with the Mitchell report.

The second phase would start after Palestinian elections and it should focus on creating a Palestinian state democratic institutions and provisional borders by the end of 2003, as a step to a permanent status settlement. The office of a Palestinian prime minister should be formally established, consistent with the constitution. There should be effective security cooperation on the bases laid out in Phase I. Provisional borders should be created through a process of Israeli–Palestinian engagement, launched by the international conference. "Prior agreements should be implemented to enhance maximum territorial contiguity, including further action on settlements in conjunction with establishment of a Palestinian state with provisional borders." The international community should be encouraged to have an active role in monitoring the transition and providing support to the Quartet. The final phase of negotiations between the two parties aimed at achieving a permanent solution by the end of 2005 would result in the emergence of an independent, democratic, and viable Palestinian state living side by side in peace and security with Israel and its other neighbors.

The Palestinian Authority accepted the "Roadmap" as it is, but Israel had fourteen reservations against it, thus stripping it of its meaning and content. Israel has practically rejected the "Roadmap" basic premises with its unacceptable caveats and prerequisites. Given the experience with the Oslo Accords and the lack of mechanism to force compliance and prevent delinquencies, there is no guaranty that Israel, the stronger party, can be forced to comply with its provisions. Prime Minister Sharon said "yes" to the initiative so that he would be perceived by the US as a peacemaker while placing conditions that had the effect of subverting it. Sharon stated on many occasions that there would be no negotiations on Jerusalem, no return to the 1967 borders and no to the Palestinian refugees' right of return. Sharon did not even recognize the principles of "exchange land for peace" because it is "philosophically wrong and politically naïve." [1] The "Roadmap" according to Sharon is based only on "exchange security for a Palestinian state."

---

1   Statement by Eyal Arad, the spokesman for Sharon, November 23, 2005.

The Palestinian state that Sharon would accept had been defined by Israeli security concerns, settler land grabs and facts on the ground. The "facts on the ground" have become a reference to the irreversible alterations accomplished by Israel in the occupied territory. They have been established every day especially since the signing of the Oslo Accord to the point where they constitute big percentage of the West Bank area. They include establishing and expanding settlements, the separation wall that continues to cut off the Palestinian villages from each other and the villagers from their land, security fences around settlements, security roads, and bypass roads. They will determine the area and the shape of the promised "Palestinian state." After discounting the "facts on the ground," land left for the future state will be only for a Bantustan entity rather than a viable state. It will consist of three suffocating enclaves cut off from one another inside the West Bank in addition to the impoverished and overcrowded Gaza Strip which is separated from the West Bank by Israeli proper land.[1] President Bush pledged on April 14, 2004 to support Prime Minister Sharon promise that in any final peace agreement with the Palestinians the refugees would be denied the right of return to their homes in Israel and the large settlement blocks would be annexed to Israel because they were facts on the ground. He declared that "in the light of new realities on the ground [in the occupied West Bank], including already existing major Israeli population centers, it is unrealistic to expect that the outcome of final status [Palestinian–Israeli] negotiations will be a full and complete return to the armistice lines of 1949." Thus the US President put a major roadblock against implementing his own government proposed "Roadmap." Giving Palestinians' land to Israel without their approval amounts to US version of the Balfour Declaration. There is not even a guarantee that Israel would abandon any settlements inside the Palestinian autonomy enclaves in the final agreement.

The Nablus and Jenin northern enclave is separated from the center by the large settlement bloc of Ariel-Eli-Shiloh. The central enclave of the Ramallah area is separated from the southern Hebron and Bethlehem enclave by clusters of Israeli settlements, highways and tunnel roads. The area of East Jerusalem has been isolated by Jewish settlements from Ramallah in the north by Givat Ze'ev, from Bethlehem in the south by Gush Etzion with its 15,000 settlers and from the east to the Dead Sea by Ma'ale Adumim which has 28,000 settlers. Jewish enclaves have been established in the Old City of Jerusalem and in the surrounding Arab neighborhoods of Silwan, Ras el-Amoud, Wadi el-Joz and Sheikh Jarrah. The three Palestinian enclaves are divided so that people traveling from one to the other have to go through areas controlled by Israel. Under the security cover, Israel has appropriated large areas of agricultural land around Jerusalem for building the separation wall.

An unpublished report prepared by top European diplomats in the 25 EU countries criticizing Israel's colonizing policy suggested that Israel has completed the annexation of East Jerusalem with its 230,000 Arab residents by building settlements in and around it,

---

1 One million Palestinians live on 360 square kilometers of land in the Gaza Strip, making it the most densely populated area in the world.

and "the prospects for a two state solution with East Jerusalem as the capital of Palestine are receding."[1]

With half a million settlers living in more than 200 settlements strategically placed throughout the occupied lands, miles of roads and the separation wall, nothing is left of the "Roadmap," which was supposed to create a Palestinian state by the end of 2005.[2] Even its author, President Bush, gave up on the "Roadmap." He noted that a Palestinian state might not come to life during his presidency (which ended in 2008). Israel has been building its West Bank separation barrier and expanding Jewish settlement blocks that it wants to hold onto under a final deal. Some Israeli observers speculate that Sharon or his successors would impose a unilateral final solution where the separation wall would become the de facto border. Israel would keep Greater Jerusalem area, large Jewish West Bank settlements, and enough territory around the settlements to keep them safely connected to Israel and the West Bank's Jordan Valley on the border with Jordan. The wall that has been built on Palestinian lands extends Israel's range beyond the pre-1967 borders by 20 kilometers inside the West Bank in the Ariel settlement area and ten kilometers around the Ma'ale Adomim settlement. The military controlled Jewish-only roads and the by-pass network prevent the expansion and development of Palestinian towns and villages. The Israelis claim that their imposed unilateral solution is in accord with the "Roadmap."

Prime Minister Sharon decided in September 2005 to end Israel's military presence in Gaza and destroy its settlements inside the Strip. This was Israel's response to the collapse of the 2000 Camp David II, but the decision to disengage from Gaza had more to do with Israel's strategic and demographic needs and security than the quest for peace. Sharon realized that the "Greater Israel" that he had been advocating, which included Gaza, meant the end of Israel as a Jewish state. Besides the demographic concern, Gaza is home to more than a million hostile Palestinian refugees who threatened Israel's security and made it too costly to protect the settlers. It became increasingly difficult to protect the more than 7,000 settlers living among 1,400,000 Palestinians in the over-crowded Strip. After pulling out of the Gaza Strip, Israel has reinforced its presence in the West Bank and East Jerusalem, hoping to retain areas heavily settled by Israelis in the future. Most of the Jewish settlers were relocated from occupied Gaza to the occupied West Bank and the number of settlers in the West Bank has since increased by more than 4% within a year. Two months before the withdrawal from 19 square miles of settlement area in Gaza, Israel seized more than 23 square miles of the West Bank around the Ma'ale Adumim settlement in the West Bank.

Israel had offered to withdraw from Gaza in the 1978 Israeli–Egyptian Camp David Accords, in the final peace treaty with Egypt in 1979 and in the second Oslo agreements. Because it had been so costly to control a rebellious Gaza, Prime Minister Yitzhak Rabin

---

1 The report was leaked to the news media on November 25, 2005.
2 *Le Monde*, November 23, 2005.

once said: "I wish that Gaza would sink in the Sea." And in 2005, Sharon's government found that besieging Gaza was less costly than occupying it.

Demographic forecasts predict that Israel will lose its character as a Jewish and democratic state if it retains the population centers in the occupied lands, since the Arab population is increasing. This explains in part why Sharon might have decided to withdraw from Gaza and remove its 7,000 Jewish settlers unilaterally. After the withdrawal of the Israeli soldiers and settlers from the Gaza Strip, Arabs living under direct Israeli control including those in Israel proper dropped from 51% to 40% of the total population. Most Palestinians by far believe that it was the armed resistance, waged mostly by militant Islamists, that forced Israel to withdraw from Gaza. And many attribute the victory of Hamas in the January 2006 parliamentary elections to this belief.

Although Gaza's borders, shores and airspace continued to be under complete Israeli control, the Palestinians were happy that the IDF and the settlers left Gaza. But the unilateral disengagement without coordination with the Palestinians suggests that Israel is trying to bypass the "Roadmap" and enforce its own solution to the conflict. Israel has transformed Gaza into a large concentration camp and invades its towns regularly, including a three-week massive offense in 2008–09 in retaliation for crude rockets fired by Hamas and other Palestinian groups.

An electronic fence surrounds Gaza on three sides with few crossing points, and those are controlled by the Israeli army; and the Israeli navy enforces a siege on the fourth. When Israel withdrew its settlers and soldiers from Gaza in August 2005, it retained absolute control over who and what was allowed in and out of the Strip. There are no longer any settlements in Gaza, but the Gazan population remains impoverished and isolated inside a "big prison." Palestinian farm produce rots at checkpoints because Israel has refused to allow it to be exported, and small Palestinian industrial businesses that had once subcontracted with large Israeli companies were forced to close. And to make things worse, Egypt kept Rafah Crossing, the only lifeline to the outside world for the 1.4 million Gazans, closed since Hamas took control of the Strip. The Palestinians were forced by their instinct of survival to dig underground tunnels to counter the ongoing siege and import their basic needs from Egypt. The tunnels have become targets for daily Israeli air-strikes and Egypt demolition operations. It has been reported by the Israeli *Haaretz* that the US Army Corps of Engineers have been helping Egypt since July 2008 to build a US-financed steel wall along its 10-km-long border with Gaza to further isolate the Strip. The wall extends not only above ground but sixteen meters deep in the ground to prevent the Palestinians from digging the tunnels.

A six-ship flotilla carrying thousands of tons of humanitarian aid sailing to thwart the Gaza blockade and bring in food, medicine and building material was intercepted in international waters by Israeli commandos on May 31, 2010. The Israeli armed military descended from helicopters on the deck of the Turkish-flagged *Mavi Marmara*, attacked the unarmed pro-Palestinian activists and journalists aboard the ship, and killed at least nine passengers and injuring dozens. During the brutal attack, "the Israeli troops fired live ammunition and rubber coated bullets, electroshock weapons and tear gas at the civilian passengers." Hundreds of activists and journalists from different nationalities were towed from international waters to Israeli detention centers. The high-seas attack led Israel's only regional ally, Turkey, to withdraw its ambassador to Israel. The bloody attack came at the time when the PA had resumed the "peace negotiations" with Israel which broke down after Israel invaded Gaza and destroyed it in 2008.

Israel's reliance on violence to solve political issues and its disregard for international law foreclose the possibility of negotiating peace through a political agreement. The platform of Kadima, the new political party that has been established by Prime Minister Ariel Sharon after the Gaza disengagement, states that the Jewish nation has a national and historic right to the whole of Greater Israel (historical Palestine). But in order to maintain a Jewish majority, part of the "Land of Israel" (i.e., the West Bank) must be given back to the Palestinians so that Israel remains a democratic Jewish state; Jerusalem and large settlement blocks would be kept under Israeli control.[1] The hawkish Prime Minister Benyamin Netanyahu, the leader of the right-wing Likud Party, has repeatedly expressed his firm opposition to ending the Israeli occupation. And his coalition partner Avigdor Lieberman calls for more settlements, tighter military control and no two-state solution.

Israel continues to control the population registry of the Palestinians in all the occupied land and who is permitted to live there. Israel will recognize only residents of the Palestinian cantons who carry Israeli issued cards and Palestinian Authority passports are issued only with Israeli permission. At the same time, the Palestinian Authority would act as proxy organization to police the Palestinians on behalf of the Israeli occupiers.

Following Arafat's death on November 11, 2004, at the age of 74, Mahmoud Abbas, a senior in the PLO hierarchy, won the January 2005 presidential elections and replaced Arafat as the leader of the PA, Fatah and the PLO. The elections were described as peaceful and democratic. Abbas was the architect of the Oslo agreements; he renounced terrorism and he has declared in every occasion that he was for negotiated settlements with Israel. The departure of Arafat and the election of Abbas was an ideal opportunity for the US to push the peace process forward especially since President Bush was in a strong position after he had just won re-election for the second term. But instead of helping the pro-US Palestinian leader by making it easy for him to negotiate an agreement with the Israelis, Bush decided to commit the US to support Sharon's plan to disengage unilaterally from the Palestinians. The plan doomed the President's own "Roadmap," thus undermining the leadership of Abbas. When Ariel Sharon suffered a stroke and was unable to carry out his duties in 2006, Ehud Olmert was elected Prime Minister and the leader of Kadima Party.

Prime Minister Olmert claimed in Washington that abiding with the "Roadmap" process was the way to achieve peace with the Palestinians. At the same time Israel had begun building a new Jewish settlement, Maskiot, in the Jordan Valley violating the letter and spirit of the "Roadmap." Families from the former Gaza Israeli settlements would be the first to move in Maskiot. The "Peace Now" group said that the Maskiot construction is an attempt to grab more land from the West Bank and annex it to Israel. Prime Minister

---

1 Justice Minister Tzipi Livni statement on November 28, 2005.

Ehud Olmert claimed that there was no Palestinian partner ready to negotiate peace with Israel. Therefore, he had a unilateral plan for ending the conflict without an agreement with the Palestinians by imposing Israeli permanent borders with the West Bank by 2010 to secure a long-term Jewish majority for Israel.

Referring to the plan to annex parts of the West Bank to Israel as "realignment," Olmert told reporters after his meeting with French President Jacques Chirac on June 13, 2006: "The realignment plan is unstoppable. It is unpreventable. It will be carried out with or without talks with the Palestinians." The realignment plan would give the Palestinians less than the offer made by Prime Minister Ehud Barak in September 2000 Camp David conference, and rejected by Arafat because it fell short of the Palestinian minimum demands. Olmert told Nobel peace laureate Elie Wiesel in Petra-Jordan: "There will be blocks of settlements that can't be evacuated, they will not be evacuated."[1] Olmert and other Israeli leaders may go ahead with unilateral plans because it is hard to find a Palestinian leader who might be willing to accede to Israel's annexing of large segments of the West Bank, including East Jerusalem, and give up the Palestinian refugees right of return. A plan for dividing the West Bank unilaterally is certain to exacerbate the already tense situation. If the failure of the 2000 Camp David talks to produce an acceptable final status agreement was responsible for the Second Intifada, imposing an Israeli version final status will be a recipe for more turmoil and violence.

When Prime Minister Ehud Olmert visited the White House in 2006, President Bush hailed the unilateral disengagement plan that Olmert had adopted, but Middle East politics are extremely volatile and unpredictable. The plan was abandoned immediately after the abduction of Israeli soldier Gilad Shalit by the Palestinian militants in Gaza.

---

1 *Jordan Times*, June 23-24, 2006 on Nobel Prize laureates conference in Petra-Jordan.

CHAPTER 8. THE PALESTINIAN DEMOCRACY EXPERIMENT

This study strongly supports the right of people to choose their own government in free democratic pluralism and transparent elections and their right to practice any religion they choose — or no religion. But it uttely rejects mixing religion and politics by governing on the basis of a certain religious belief, regardless whether it is Islamic, Jewish, Christianity or any religion.

On January, 25, 2006, the Palestinian legislative elections took place in the occupied lands after a series of postponements and delays by the Fatah leadership. The elections were monitored by many foreign observers who testified to their fairness, transparency and democratic nature. Ironically, even under occupation, it was the second parliamentary elections in the Arab world that was not rigged and manipulated by the elites in power, and the opposition won by landslide. Only in the 1991 first round multi-party Algerian elections, the Islamic Salvation Front won, then the military intervened, cancelled the second round and more than 160,000 Algerian people were killed in a decade long civil war as a result. The Palestinian experiment in democracy sadly had the same fate of the Algerian failed democracy.

Fatah corruption and Sharon refusal to negotiate with Abbas contributed to Hamas electoral victory. Hamas won 75 seats and Fatah took 47 of the 132 seats make up of the Palestinian Legislative Council. The remainder went to a few independents and a number of small leftist, liberal and secular parties. The outcome of the elections represented a challenge to Hamas which opposed Fatah policies in dealing with Israel, and it was a humiliating defeat for Fatah that viewed itself since its inception as embodying the hopes and aspirations of the Palestinian people. Hamas, as described in Chapter 3, is a branch of the Muslim Brothers movement in Palestine which draws its political charter, beliefs and way of life from the teachings of Islam. Its members claim, "Allah is its goal, the Prophet Muhammed its model, the Quran its Constitution, Jihad [holy war] its path and death for the cause of Allah its most sublime belief."[1] They regard nationalism as part of the Islamic faith.

To form a government, Hamas tried to engage in talks with Fatah, but it was clear from the beginning that Fatah had made a decision not to be a junior partner in any government dominated by Hamas. Eventually Hamas was forced to form a government from its own party, headed by Ismael Haniyah. Israel found a new excuse not to negotiate with the Palestinians and the Bush administration was less likely to push Israel to talk peace when Hamas was in power. As soon as the government was formed and before it started functioning, the Israeli army declared war on its members, including rounding-up newly-elected Islamist lawmakers, raiding Hamas offices in the West Bank and detaining central political figures in the new government. Most of these officials remained hostages in Israel without charge or trial. Hamas decided that the main base of its government would have to be in the Gaza Strip, not Ramallah as was traditionally the case, because the Israeli occupation army could easily arrest the prime minister if his office was in the West Bank.

Hamas stamped out the rampant corruption at the highest levels of government but unless it changes its charter, it will never bring Israel to the negotiating table. Hamas had difficulty controlling the bureaucracy because its members including the security forces are loyal only to Fatah and Mahmoud Abbas. The bureaucrats refuse to take orders from Hamas ministers, threatened them and denied them entry into their own ministerial offices. At the same time, Israel branded Hamas government a "terrorist authority." It decided to halt the transfer to Hamas government tens of millions of dollars of the Palestinian tax money that it levies on Palestinian imports which pass through its seaports. The Oslo Accords gave Israel the power of taxation and the transfer of such taxes to the PA through vouchers, thus depriving Hamas of a basic function of governing, to collect taxes as part of its budget. By withholding the taxes that constitute nearly 40% of the Palestinian government financial revenues, Israel decided to punish the Palestinian people for exercising their right to elect their own representatives. Before the Palestinian elections and when the PA was headed by the secular Fatah, Israeli Defense Minister Shaul Mofaz declared that Israel could not reach a peace agreement with the present Palestinian generation. He asked the Israelis to "wait for the next [Palestinian] generation" to negotiate a peace agreement with Israel. The Israeli government has claimed the absence of a Palestinian partner for peace since Arafat rejected Prime Minister Ehud Barak offer in September 2000 as a base for final peace, when Fatah was in power under the Oslo signatories. Now, with the more militant Hamas-led government in charge, it will be easier for Israel to justify ignoring the Palestinians all together and undertaking unilateral actions. Hamas refusal to recognize the legitimacy of the "Zionist State" frees the Israeli leaders from having to deal with the democratically elected government without being criticized by the West.

In an op-ed published by *The Guardian* of London on April 2, 2006, Ismael Haniyah spelled out Hamas views on peace with Israel: "No [peace] plan will ever work without a guarantee, in exchange for an end to the hostilities by both sides, of a total Israeli with-

---

1 Article 8, the Charter of Allah: The Platform of Hamas.

drawal from all the land occupied in 1967, including East Jerusalem; the release of all the Palestinian prisoners, the removal of all settlers from all settlements; and recognition of the right of all refugees to return." Hamas position is not much different from previous UN resolutions including 242 and 338 as interpreted by the Palestinians, but it has been ignored by Israel and the West because the UN resolutions have been superseded by "Oslo" and the "Roadmap" as points of reference. Israel decided cutting all ties with the Hamas-led Palestinian government and ruled out peace talks with the Palestinian president, Mahmoud Abbas, as long as the Islamic group refuses to recognize Israel. Israel's tough stance against Hamas received widespread international backing, especially by the United States.

The "Quartet for Peace" mediators called on Hamas to renounce violence and recognize Israel and the interim peace deals it signed with the Palestinians since Oslo even those Israel no longer recognizes. The US and the EU governments boycotted Hamas-led government and suspended the foreign aid that had kept the Palestinian Authority afloat since it was created in 1994. They labeled Hamas a terrorist group because its members had carried out many suicide bombings against Israel over the past decade, killing and injuring hundreds of civilians. Finally, the United Nations joined the US and the EU by advising its aid agencies on April 11, 2006, to avoid having political contacts with the cabinet ministers and other high-level appointees in the Hamas led Palestinian government. The punitive actions suggest collective effort by Israel and the West to force the government to fail and resign if it does not comply with their demands.

The US has spearheaded the movement to delegitimize the only democratically elected government in the Arab world while at the same time declaring that the lack of democracy is the core problem in the Middle East. Despite intense international pressure and a growing financial crisis, Hamas rejected the ultimatum, but it abided by its year-old ceasefire. With no control over borders and no territorial contiguity or economic development and the loss of the foreign financial aid, Hamas government could not raise revenue outside international aid to provide for public education, healthcare, security, maintaining the infrastructure and social services. The Khartoum Arab League summit which was held in late March 2006 pledged to fund Hamas government, but the money has not been forthcoming. The Arab states have yielded to the Israeli–US-led campaign for denying aid to the Hamas-led PA. The World Bank forecast that poverty in the Palestinian areas would rise to 67% by the end of 2006, up from 44% in 2005 if the economic siege continued.

The Palestinians who had been denied the opportunity to develop their national economy cannot be expected to dig themselves out of the hole with no aid. The inability of the government to pay salaries for the 160,000 civil service workers threatened the main source of Palestinian employment. Hamas leaders managed to collect tens of millions of dollars from some Arab and Muslim private groups to counter the Western sanctions. The money, however, couldn't be transferred to Palestine because banks were afraid of running afoul with Washington's anti-terrorism regulations. Failure of the Arab states to break the Israeli–US siege and help the starving impoverished Palestinians tells much about the Arab states irrelevance in the international arena individually and collectively. Leaders of the so called moderate Arab regimes agreed to comply (directly or indirectly) with the Israeli–US imposed boycott of Hamas-led government and even refused to meet members of its cabinet. Mohammed Ameer, an editor at Saudi Arabia's Riyadh newspaper suggested that part of the problem was that Hamas did not share the vision of these Arab countries on peacemaking with Israel. He said: "The Arab governments were embarrassed in the first place when Hamas came to power."

President Abbas and his Fatah Organization have been at odds with Hamas and its government since the elections. Abbas stripped Hamas-led government from its inherited powers of controlling the security forces and the entry points at the border with Egypt. After losing a power struggle for control over the Palestinian security forces, Hamas formed its own 5,000-man security force, known as the "Executive Force," in April of 2006. Abbas outlawed the unit early in January 2007, prompting defiant declarations by Hamas that it would more than double the unit in size. To make things worse, Hamas and Fatah military forces were involved in a series of deadly open clashes that left at least 22 people dead by the middle of June 2006. Abbas announced on May 25 that he would call a national referendum in 10 days on a proposal drawn up by imprisoned political leaders in Israeli jails unless Hamas and his Fatah party settled their differences through dialogue. The prisoner's proposal called for a national unity government to negotiate with Israel for establishing a Palestinian state in the Gaza Strip and West Bank, including East Jerusalem. The document demanded that the issue of the refugees to be settled in accordance with UN Resolution 194, which calls for their repatriation or indemnification. The proposal asked Hamas and the Islamic Jihad to join the Palestine Liberation Organization, the only recognized representative of the Palestinians.

Hamas leaders claimed that Palestinian law did not give the president the right to hold a referendum. It branded the referendum an attempt to overthrow its three-month-old government. Abbas saw the document as a way to restart negotiations with Israel and circumvent Western sanctions against the Palestinian Authority. Hamas political chief Khaled Mishaal, who resided outside the Palestinian territories, stated on June 1st, 2006 in Qatar, that Abbas' plebiscite would annul the results of the January elections. But Abbas responded on the same day during a visit to the Tunisian capital that it was his constitutional right to convene a plebiscite without the need to have the endorsement of the Hamas-dominated legislature. Clashes erupted across the West Bank and Gaza between Hamas and Fatah loyalists after Abbas announced the ultimatum.

The real problem, according to Hamas leaders, is Israel's refusal to withdraw from the West Bank, not its non-recognition of Israel. They point to the fact that no matter how many times Palestinians recognized Israel, Israel had not agreed to withdraw from the occupied lands. Settlements and a gigantic concrete separation wall have reduced most Palestinian population centers to open air prisons. Israeli government spokesmen had already dismissed the prisoners' proposal as "an internal Palestinian affair," and rejected any suggestion that Israel would return to its 1967 borders, let alone allow the repatriation of refugees. Abbas believed that the acceptance of "the Prisoners' Document" was a way to end Western-led economic sanctions that had crippled the Palestinian economy and it would be a basis to restart peace negotiations with Israel. But the UN special envoy to the peace process, Alvaro De Soto, said even if the referendum was passed it would not be enough to see sanctions lifted. This reduced the significance of the proposed referendum to nothing but public relations.

Arab states never came to the defense of Hamas government. Only the State of Qatar invited Prime Minister Haniyah to visit it. Hamas leadership had been advised by Husni Mubarak of Egypt and King Abdullah of Saudi Arabia on June 1st, 2006 to accept the Arab peace initiative that was adopted by the 2002 Arab League summit meeting in Beirut, Lebanon. The US openly sided with Fatah faction against Hamas by providing weapons and military training to bolster Abbas forces. According to the Israeli press, the Israeli government approved the transfer of weapons provided by the US through Jordan to Abbas' Praetorian guards that had been known as Force 17. The head of the Foreign Relations in the Knesset said that weapons had been delivered on June 14, 2006. Providing such weapons at a time when there is a potential confrontation between the two factions was an inducement to escalate the tension between them to a civil war. For Israel, internal Palestinian strife is an excuse to refuse carrying on serious negotiations with the Palestinians and expand the settlements. And the Palestinians may blame their own leadership for the Israeli attempts to throttle their national cause.

The tension between Abbas and Hamas and the failure of the Arab states to compensate for the loss of the Western aid may hasten the collapse of Hamas government but that may also radicalize its movement. The budget situation will make the Palestinian government gravely lacking in legitimacy and the Palestinians will become disillusioned with democracy and resort to violence. If the failure of Hamas government leads to total collapse of the PA, Israel would be forced to reinstate direct administration of the West Bank and Gaza Strip, a prospect Israel tried to avoid when it installed the PA in 1993.

Hardships due to the siege began to take their toll on impoverished Palestinians. Hundreds of civil servants who had not been paid for months burst into the parliament building in Ramallah twice in the week of June 11, 2006, when the parliament was in session, demanding their overdue salaries. They climbed over the lawmaker's offices throwing water bottles and small objects at the deputies screaming "We are hungry." Against a backdrop of the economic and political problem, Fatah and Hamas have been negotiating an agreement on the so-called Prisoners' Document that implicitly called for the recognition of Israel. The two factions have disagreement on three areas of the Document. Hamas refused to recognize the PLO as the "sole" representative of the Palestinian people as stipulated in the Oslo Agreement, arguing that the PLO could be accepted as the "sole and legitimate representative of the Palestinian people" only if it is reformed democratically. Once it is reformed, Hamas could join the organization. Hamas also opposed the view that the PLO should have the monopoly of endorsing any final status agreement with Israel to legitimize it. Its leaders argued that such an agreement would have to be approved by a majority of Palestinians, both in Palestine and in the Diaspora, to acquire legitimacy. Hamas also opposed the Prisoners' Document call to confine the armed struggle against Israel to the occupied territories of the West Bank while Israel attacks the Palestinian civilians.

After weeks of negotiations, an agreement was reached on the Prisoners' Document with some modification among all factions except for the Islamic Jihad, which had some reservations about certain items. The agreement was supposed to be the basis for a unified political strategy to deal with Israel. Immediately after the agreement was concluded, two Israeli soldiers and two Palestinian guerillas were killed and a third Israeli soldier was captured in a daring operation by Palestinians against an Israeli army outpost inside Israel close to the border with Gaza on June 25, 2006. The factions that captured the soldier demanded the release of Palestinian prisoners for the release of the 19-year-old captured soldier. From the onset, the capture of the soldier was intended to pressure Israel into releasing Palestinian children and women in Israeli jails. According to Israel, there were more than seven thousand Palestinian men, 95 women and over 313 children in Israeli jails and detention camps. Leaflets issued by Hamas's military wing, the Izz al-Din al-Qassam Brigades, which was one of the factions that held the abducted soldier stated it would not give any information about the abducted soldier unless Israel released all female prisoners and the children under the age of 18 in Israeli jails. Musheer al-Masri, a Hamas MP stated on June 28, 2006: "Hamas wants a deal similar to what the Lebanese Hizbullah achieved in January 2004 when Israel freed 400 Palestinian prisoners in return for one soldier and the remains of three dead soldiers." While the Palestinians considered the captured Israeli soldier in a military confrontation as a prisoner, Western and moderate Arab leaders and Arab media embraced the Israeli claim that the abducted soldier was a kidnapped victim, and issued appeals for his release. The Palestinians wondered why none of these Arab leaders had issued a serious appeal to Israel for releasing hundreds of Palestinian women, children and political leaders in Israeli jails. Release of the prisoners in Israeli jails ranks high on the Palestinians' political agenda.

Israeli leaders ruled out any negotiations with the captors because it would compromise Israeli deterrence strategy and encourage Palestinian fighters to kidnap more Israelis in order to swap them for Palestinian political prisoners in Israeli jails. Israeli tanks and armored personnel carriers rolled into the south of Gaza Strip on June 28, 2006 in what looked like a full scale invasion. The invasion was preceded by the Israeli air-bombing of three bridges in central Gaza, main water pipelines and the main power plant that provided electricity to most of Gaza Strip residents. Israel also detained ten members of the Hamas Cabinet and nearly two dozen lawmakers and other Hamas officials in the occupied West Bank. Within a week, Israel stepped up its ground offensive and moved troops into the northern Gaza Strip killing and injuring hundreds of Palestinian civilians. The Palestinian fighters remained defiant, firing Qassam rockets into the southern Israeli city of Ashkelon for the first time. Hamas leader Mishaal, who resided in Syria and was considered more hardliner than local Hamas leaders, held "Olmert and his hostile policies" responsible for what happened to the Israeli captured soldier. Olmert ruled out negotiations with either Mishaal or the Hamas-led government.

The abduction of the Israeli soldier is the first operation involving the military wing of Hamas since halting its attacks on Israel in a unilateral self-imposed truce since March 2005. Hamas had honored a ceasefire reached with President Abbas in Cairo while Israel had been carrying on unhindered bloody campaign of targeted assassinations and unwarranted home demolitions. The abduction was also the first test to Prime Minister Olmert and his Defense Minister Amir Peretz leadership in dealing with the Palestinian militants. Unlike most previous Israeli premiers and defense ministers, Olmert and Peretz had not come from the ranks of the military generals, but their response to the soldier abduction suggested that they were no different from their predecessors, resorting to wage their own war against the Palestinians. This war might not have freed the kidnapped soldier, but at least it would have protected Olmert and Peretz from the accusation of being "weak," an accusation that can end the political career of any Israeli politician.

Israel's armed forces are superior to those of all its neighbors combined. With such an advantage, its leaders have a long term strategy of using overwhelming force when confronted with a perceived challenge. Their defense posture views any threat as an existential threat to the country's very survival. Nobody can stop them so long as the real superpower supports them. The invasion of Gaza was similar in many ways to the 1982 campaign against Lebanon under then defense minister Ariel Sharon. As stated in Chapter 3, the justification used by Israel to invade Lebanon was Palestinian's attempt to assassin the Israeli ambassador in London, and the pretext to invade Gaza was the Palestinian's abduction of an Israeli soldier. Israel was using the soldier's capture as an excuse to try to topple the government led by Hamas, and the 1982 invasion of Lebanon was to bring about the destruction of the PLO. The PLO and the Palestinian refugees in Lebanon were left on their own to face the Israelis and their Lebanese allies in 1982, so as Hamas government and the Palestinians in Gaza had to defend themselves with no help expected from the Arab states in 2006.

Israel can count on its major ally, the US, for support economically, militarily and politically. Since the 1967 war, the US has been providing Israel with material and political support regardless of whatever it does to the Palestinians. By 2007, Washington vetoed forty-two UN Security Council resolutions critical of Israel and many resolutions focusing on Israel that never reached a vote due to threat of US veto. The US routinely backed Israel when the UNGA passed non-binding resolutions calling for actions on behalf of the Palestinians. But the support the Palestinians receive from their Arab allies is only occasional rhetoric and advice to accept Israeli–American dictates. The Arab states assumed the role of mediators rather than defenders of the Palestinians. Despite their close relations with Washington, the moderate Arab regimes have no influence on the US policy toward the Palestinians if they wish to intervene on their behalf. The failure of the Palestinian leadership to speak with one voice and President Abbas refusal to allow his Fatah organization to join Hamas in a national dialogue created divisions among the Palestinians and paralyzed their government.

Reasons for aborting the Palestinian democracy that rejects occupation are rooted in Oslo Agreements that rendered any challenge to Israel's supremacy unacceptable and should be prevented by Israel and the international community.

CHAPTER 9. THE 2006 LEBANESE-ISRAELI WAR

While the region was embroiled in the crisis of the abducted Israeli soldier by the militant Palestinians and the Israeli military campaign in Gaza to retrieve him and destroy Hamas-led government, another serious one suddenly erupted that eventually over-shadowed the conflict in Gaza. The Lebanese Shiite military group, Hizbullah ambushed an Israeli military patrol in a cross-border raid on July 12, 2006, killing eight Israeli soldiers and capturing two. Like Hamas in Gaza, Hizbullah demanded the release of Lebanese detained in Israeli prisons in exchange for releasing the two captured soldiers. Israel responded by bombarding Lebanese roads, bridges, ports and airports, as well as Hizbullah targets. Within two weeks after the raid, the ports were placed under siege, cellular communication towers were destroyed and roads and bridges to Syria were bombed. It was the most destruction inflicted on Lebanon by Israel since the 1982 invasion to expel Palestinian militias. The air, land and naval strikes that killed hundreds of civilians besides destroying the country's infrastructure were intended to punish Lebanon for allowing Hizbullah guerrillas menace Israel's northern border. Hizbullah's response was firing hundreds of rockets on Israeli targets across the border and even hitting the industrial city of Haifa, 20 miles away from the border, killing Israeli civilians including Israeli Arabs. An Israeli navy ship was hit by rockets causing extensive damage to the ship and killing four of its crew.

Hizbullah is more influential in Lebanon than the country's fragile democratic government and Hizbullah military wing is more powerful than the Lebanese army. The Lebanese government has been too weak to control Hizbullah, but Israel held the government in Beirut responsible for its action. The Lebanese prime minister, the UN Secretary General Kofi Annan, France and the Russians pleaded for an immediate ceasefire but there was no sign Israel was ready to heed the pleas especially since the US was openly supporting its action. UN relief coordinator Jan Egeland expressed alarm on July 22, 2006, over the humanitarian crisis in Lebanon and in Gaza and the inability of his organization to provide badly needed relief supplies amid the Israeli offensives there. The US vetoed a Security Council ceasefire resolution and obstructed peace efforts during the July 26 conference in Rome in order to give Israel enough time to achieve its political objectives regardless of the destruction and human suffering. US Secretary of State Condoleezza Rice was openly rude and cruel when suggested that the destruction of Lebanon and the killing of civilians including children and their parents was nothing but the "birth pangs" of a new Middle East. The US refusal to call for a ceasefire or a truce "until the time was ripe for a sustainable ceasefire in Lebanon" confirms the perception that Israel is fighting an American war in Lebanon and will continue to fight until Washington's political aims are accomplished or defeated.

The Lebanese war has been described by many observers as a proxy war between the US through Israel and Hizbullah that had been supported and armed by Iran. In the aftermath of the Israeli air strike on July 30, 2006, that killed more than 60 Lebanese in Qana, most of them children and women, Condoleezza Rice expressed "sorrow" but refused to join the international community in condemning Israel. Muhammed Mahdi Akef, the supreme guide of the Muslim Brothers in Egypt described the new Middle East that Rice was talking about as alliances between the corrupt and autocratic regimes in the region and the US to terminate all forms of resistance to the US–Israeli grand design and undermine Islamist movements in the region. Rice's "new Middle East" had been mid-wifed by Israel's ruthless war machine in order to neutralize any resistance to the Israeli occupation in Palestine or Lebanon.[1] The US was giving Israel the diplomatic cover, time and space in which to pursue its military assault on Lebanon. Instead of encouraging the secular reformers and the so called moderates in the Arab world, the US policies had created an environment where only the radical Islamists would have more support by the Arab population.

Hasan Nasrallah vowed never to release the two captured Israeli soldiers even "if the whole universe comes [against us]," unless it was a part of a prisoner exchange brokered through indirect negotiations. But Israel was too busy destroying Lebanon and the release of the two Israeli soldiers had been all but forgotten. The purpose of this assault had not been to free the captured soldiers. Israel was waiting for an internationally accepted excuse to use their military superiority against the militants in Lebanon. Hizbullah, like its counterpart in Palestine, Hamas, took the bait and gave Israel what it wanted. The Israelis quickly shifted their aims from retrieving the soldiers to destroying, or at least crippling Hizbullah. They decided to widen the war by launching a ground offensive deep into Lebanon and Hizbullah kept firing its missiles into northern Israel. The human cost was mounting in Lebanon and to less extent in Israel. Four weeks after the start of the conflict in Lebanon, more than 1,000 Lebanese, mostly civilians, were killed, about one-third of the dead were children under the age of 13. Three-thousand Lebanese were injured and another one million displaced, but "Hizbullah seemed to be holding strong and its

---

1 *Al-Ahram Weekly*, July 27, 2006.

morale intact," because it enjoyed the support of the Shiite Lebanese according to Shaul Mishal, an Israeli professor and political analyst. Rather than strengthen the pro-Western Lebanese central government, Israel was weakening it because Israel was not just attacking Hizbullah, it was attacking the country as a whole destroying civilian and military infrastructures that took decades to build. The Israeli air strikes and the ground assaults failed to subdue Hizbullah or stop its rocket attacks on Israel that fell on Northern Israel at more than one hundred per day. The 10,000 Israeli troops fighting inside Lebanon and supported by artillery, the air force and navy guns had been meeting fierce resistance from Hizbullah fighters. More than 70 Israeli soldiers had been killed in combat in the first four weeks of the war and an estimated 500,000 Israelis were displaced. Hizbullah's relative success in resisting the Israeli invasion of South Lebanon coupled with the uproar over the Israeli massacre in Qana, earned Hizbullah the popular support in the Arab and Muslim people worldwide.

Israel massive blitz against Lebanon triggered a major humanitarian crisis and the US continued to oppose an immediate ceasefire even when Israel committed many massacres of innocent civilians including children and women. The systematic bombardment of Lebanon reduced residential neighborhoods, factories, bridges, roads, tunnels, electricity generators and government buildings to rubble and burned out ruins. Israel even dropped anti-personnel cluster and phosphorous bombs against the Lebanese, according to the Israeli Cabinet Minister Yaakov Edri. Arab governments especially those friendly with the US lost legitimacy among most of the Arab public for their failure to use their influence with Washington to stop the deliberate destruction of an Arab state. They were unable or unwilling to pressure the US into calling off the Israeli assaults and they never established a consensus on how to deal with Hamas and Hizbullah. Despite the Arab public overwhelming anti-Israeli opinion, Arab governments allied with the United States had shown willingness to accept Israel's justification for its extreme action and blame Hizbullah and Hamas military for the flare-up of the violence in the region. Pro-US Arab governments fear that Hizbullah and Hamas challenge to Israel might bolster the image of the Islamic opposition groups in their own countries. Egyptian and Jordanian governments had been fearful of the rise of Islamist movements to power after Hamas' election victory in Palestine and the Muslim Brothers' electoral gains in Egypt. Arabs demonstrated in many Arab capitals to protest the Israeli incursion and in support of Hizbullah and Hamas which were perceived as the only organizations that challenge Israel and its illegal and brutal occupation of Arab land. Nasrallah was riding a wave of popularity in the Arab world especially among the Palestinians who have been searching for a hero to confront Israel. The Palestinians may be divided between Hamas and Fatah in politics, but they were united in their support for Hizbullah.

Pro-US Arab governments capitalized on Nasrallah's close relations with Iran to discredit him, but that did not stand in the way of his popularity in the Arab world. For the Arab people in the region, Hizbullah's performance in showering northern Israel with rockets and creating havoc in Haifa for weeks cut down to size the Israeli military power, something no Arab army had been able to do since the founding of Israel in 1948. The war that was intended to weaken the Islamists had at the end exactly the opposite results in the region; it strengthened the popular base of the Islamist movements and weakened the Arab autocratic regimes. Even if Israel and the US managed to dislodge Hizbullah's fighters from southern Lebanon, Hizbullah had been significantly strengthened by the conflict and Nasrallah will likely remain the most powerful politician in Lebanon and the most popular in the Arab world.

Arab rulers allied with the US have taken the diplomatic stance that armed resistance against Israel is either "adventurous" or irresponsible. Saudi Foreign Minister described Hizbullah attack on Israel as "unexpected, inappropriate and irresponsible act." The political futility of the Arab League was exposed at the emergency foreign ministers' meeting in Cairo. The irreconcilable differences among its members on how to confront the situation in the region rendered them irrelevant in dealing with the crisis. Secretary General of the League, Amr Musa, declared: "The Middle East peace process is dead," after the foreign ministers convened on July 15, 2006 to discuss the Israeli offensives in Lebanon and Gaza. He added that "The only way to revive the peace process is to take it back to the Security Council." Arab League members abandoned their responsibility to protect the national security of their people or to have a say in the destiny of one of its state-members by failing even to produce a communiqué with Pan-Arab recommendations at the conclusion of their foreign ministers meeting. The chairman of the Egyptian and Arab bar associations, Sameh Ashour, declared that "In their emergency meeting, Arab foreign ministers didn't live up to their people expectations."[1] Arab governments' irrelevance gave credence to the perception that since the liberation of Kuwait in 1991 by the US, Pan-Arab system had collapsed and most Arab regimes have become docile American protégés. Political observers have reported a strong public backlash against the governing elites in the Arab world who had acquiesced in the face of the Israeli actions in Lebanon and Palestine with explicit American support. Tens of thousands demonstrated in solidarity with the Lebanese and the Palestinian resistance in Cairo, Amman, Bahrain and Baghdad to name few.

The military confrontation with Hamas and Hizbullah made it difficult for Prime Minister Ehud Olmert or any future Israeli prime governments to implement unilateral disengagement plan in the West Bank which includes withdrawal from some Jewish settlements. Immediately after the war in Lebanon ended, the Israeli Prime Minister declared that his plan for unilateral disengagement was not on his agenda anymore. The Israelis would not leave the Palestinians territory and risk rocket attacks on Tel Aviv and Jerusalem by militants in the West Bank. Hard-line Israelis blame the unilateral withdrawals from Southern Lebanon in 2000 and from Gaza in 2005 as the root causes for the latest confrontation with the Islamic organizations. Yuval Steinitz, a member of the right-wing Likud Party stated that "The territorial concessions by Israel [withdrawal from Gaza] have been perceived in the Arab world as evidence to Israel's weakness."

Hamas and Hizbullah are viewed by Israel and the West as terrorist organizations allied with Iran and acting as its pawns in the Middle East. Arab political analysts argue

---

1   *Al-Ahram Weekly*, July 20-26, 2006.

that these organizations are "far less attached to Iran than Israel and its military establish-ment to the US."[1] Linking Hamas to Hizbullah will render the two-state solution to the Palestinian issue in doubt under the present conditions. Eliminating the Islamists militar-ily and politically may become the condition for Israel and the US to participate in serious peace talks. But because they are indigenous movements with solid constituencies, Israel may kill enough of their members and deplete their weapons but it is unlikely to kill more fighters than it creates. Even if Israel succeeds in destroying Hizbullah and Hamas move-ments through its military superiority and the support or neutrality of the international community, it will not end the conflict. The West is concerned only about the security of Israel while ignoring the core of the conflict, the Israeli occupation of Arab lands. By leaving the Arabs humiliated and living under occupation with no hope of real statehood, the militants or their children will regroup and come back to fight again. By making war, Israel cannot achieve peace without addressing the underlying political issues that caused it to attack Lebanon repeatedly since the eighties of the last century.

Four weeks after the start of the Israeli–Hizbullah conflict, the US and France drafted a resolution that called for a "full cessation of hostilities," but without a time frame. It called on Hizbullah to immediately stop its attacks on Israel and return the two abducted Israeli soldiers, and asked Israel to immediately stop its "military operations offensive." Soon after the resolution draft was revealed, the Arab League convened an urgent meeting for its foreign ministers in Beirut to press ahead with Arab amendments to the draft reso-lution before it is put to a vote in the UN Security Council. Arab governments were forced to change tactics and speak up against the US–French draft resolution because they could not overlook the growing public anger among their population against their stance that had been perceived as "a cover" for the expanding Israeli hostilities against Lebanon. The Arab governments that were initially critical of Hizbullah daring actions had in the end to come around and to save face before their people. They realized that Hizbullah was there to stay as a political force inside Lebanon, and they had to adjust to that fact. Ironically, the Arab foreign ministers had to take permission to travel to Beirut from Israel which controlled the skies over Lebanon. After listening to the prime minister of Lebanon deliv-ering his opening speech sobbing and wiping his tears, the foreign ministers only decision was to adopt the Lebanese cabinet seven-point plan. They avoided taking any measure against Israel or even condemning its atrocities, and there was no mention of the US sup-port to its aggression.

The Lebanese prime minister plan called for: 1) an immediate and comprehensive ceasefire to be exercised by both sides on an equal basis, 2) the withdrawal of all Israeli forces from Lebanese areas that it has recently occupied, 3) implementing the Taif accord which calls for extending Lebanese control over the entire country and exercising sole sovereignty over its territory and on confining the carrying of arms only to the Lebanese army, 4) the exchange of prisoners between Lebanon and Israel, 5) placing the Sheeba Farms area, which Israel still occupies, under UN control until there is a settlement of

---

1 Azmi Bishara, *Al-Ahram Weekly,* July 20-26, 2006.

the issue on a permanent basis, 6) the delivery of a map designating the location of Israeli mines still buried in Lebanese soil, 7) the return of the displaced Lebanese to their homes, towns and cities as soon as possible. Arab foreign ministers delegated Arab League Secretary-General Amr Moussa, Qatari foreign minister and the foreign minister of the United Arab Emirates, who had chaired the Arab ministerial council, to fly to New York for talks with UN Secretary-General Kofi Annan and members of the Security Council to amend the proposed US–French draft resolution that had been rejected by the Lebanese government and Hizbullah.

After 34 days of fighting, the draft was amended and UN-brokered Resolution 1701 calling for an end to hostilities took effect on August 14. The plan called for a full cessation of hostilities and a joint Lebanese-international force to act as a buffer in South Lebanon. Both Hizbullah and the Israeli leaders accepted it and both claimed victory, but the clear losers were the civilians on both sides. The war that left in its wake death and destruction was unnecessary. It increased hatred for Israel among the Lebanese and worsened the US' image throughout the Muslim world. The Lebanese war intensified hatred of the US and discredited its Arab allies in the region. The cost of the conflict in life and property was high. More than 1,181 Lebanese were killed and 4,000 injured most of them civilians. Israel, battered by 4,000 inaccurate Hizbullah rockets fired from Lebanon, lost 41 civilians as a result and 117 soldiers were killed in combat. Besides the destruction of their country's infrastructure, more than 15,000 Lebanese families lost their homes in the ruined villages of South Lebanon and the southern suburbs of Beirut. The repair of the damaged country infrastructure may take as long to recover from this incursion as it did to recover from its civil war.

Among the different types of explosive ordnance that Israel dropped were cluster bombs, leaving millions of unexploded deadly bomblets, effectively small land mines, scattered in fields or buried in rubble in the densely populated villages of Southern Lebanon. Israeli commanders admitted dropping 1.2 million such bomblets while the United Nations observers put the figure at closer to 3 million on southern Lebanon. The cluster bombs have blocked a return to normality in a region heavily dependent on agriculture. According to UN officials, more than 13 civilians, mostly children, were killed and another 49 injured by such bombs in the first two weeks after the end of hostilities.[1] Lebanese authorities claim that four months after the cease-fire, 35 people have been killed, thirty of them civilians and the others army bomb defusal experts, and some 190 wounded by the cluster munitions. Israel has violated agreements with the United States when it fired the US-supplied cluster bombs in Lebanon. The agreements prohibit the use of cluster bombs against populated areas, but the US officials defended Israel for using them by claiming that Israel's use of the weapons was for self-defense. Israel's use of cluster bombs has been described as a war crime by human rights organizations.

Israeli commentators and some high level officials suggested that Hizbullah was weakened but had not been defeated. Others across the political spectrum in Israel accuse

---

1 *The Independent*, August 30, 2006.

their civilian and military leaders with incompetence in planning and preparing for the war. Israel's failure to accomplish any of its declared objectives de-legitimized its government in the eyes of its critics. The two Israeli soldiers captured by Hizbullah were not freed, Hizbullah military infrastructure was not destroyed, its stockpile of rockets was not decimated and its forces were not driven north of the Litani River. And the war did not ward off the rockets that continued to strike deep into Israel until the last day of the war. Further more, the ill thought fiasco of the war worsened Israel's global standing due to the damage on the Lebanese civilian population. Eight months after the end of the war, an Israeli government war probe released on the end of April 2007 blamed Prime Minister Olmert for the failure of Israel to achieve the objectives of the war. It was an admission that Israel was defeated and humiliated by a lightly armed paramilitary Arab force.

From the Arab people point of view, the Lebanese resistance was a winner only because it was not defeated, and the UN was a big loser. The UN failed to intervene immediately to stop the bloodshed and carry out its duties as stated in its charter that calls for protecting world peace and security. The wording of the Resolution 1701 allowed Israel to justify further offensive military actions as being within the terms of the resolution. It called for "the immediate cessation by Hizbullah of all attacks and the immediate cessation by Israel of [only] its offensive military operations." It further called for the withdrawal of Israeli troops from Lebanon to be replaced by fifteen thousand multinational forces with the aim of preventing future attacks against Israel. But the resolution had not included any measures to prevent future Israeli attacks against Lebanon, and any country that contributes troops to the multinational force must be approved only by Israel.

One week after the UN resolution passed, Israeli commandoes staged an attack in the central Bekaa Valley under the pretext that its action was "defensive" to prevent the delivery of weapons to Hizbullah from Syria. Even when the ceasefire resolution was adopted after a month of violence, Kofi Annan gave Israel additional 48 hours to continue its deadly assault on the Lebanese putting more civilians at risk. That allowed Israel to continue its offensive occupying more Lebanese land, killing more civilians and dropping thousands of cluster bombs in residential and farming areas before the ceasefire took effect. The international community under the leadership of the US lost credibility among the Arab population by establishing that violence against Lebanese civilians is a viable solution to political issues.

THE PALESTINIANS AFTER THE 2006 LEBANESE WAR

While the political and media attention was almost exclusively focused on Lebanon and distracted attention from Gaza, Israel continued to punish Palestinians without any Arab governments or international protest. Israel used the Lebanese invasion as a smoke screen to liquidate the Palestinian resistance, among other things. The war against the Palestinians in Gaza and the West Bank became "the forgotten war." The Israeli military activity in the Gaza Strip had been escalated and the already impoverished and beleaguered Strip had been sealed off from the rest of the world. Palestinians in Gaza and the

West Bank continued to be killed on a daily basis, prompting the UN on August 3, 2006 to caution that, "With the international attention focusing on Lebanon, the tragedy in Gaza is being forgotten." Figures compiled by the Israeli human rights watchdog B'tselem showed the army killed more than 163 Palestinians in Gaza in July 2006, seventy-eight of them were not involved in hostilities including 40 children and 12 women. Besides the dead, 620 people had been injured according to the UN. Twenty-three Palestinians including children and mothers were killed by Israel on July 26, 2006 alone.

According to the Palestinian Authority (PA) Health Ministry, from mid-July to September 11, 2006, a total of 272 Palestinians have died and 1,463 have been injured as a result of Israel's incursion, with only one soldier killed on the Israeli side. The international humanitarian organizations operating in the Strip warned of a full-scale humanitarian crisis, where poverty affects nearly three-quarters of the population and the residents are living in darkness. There is shortage of fuel, food and medicine, and the electricity supply is scarce after Israel bombed the Strip's only power distribution plant. Israel continued its policy of targeting elected Hamas officials. Hamas PA's officials, whether elected or appointed were being arrested by the Israeli military or prevented from movement within the territory. On August 4, Israeli forces arrested the speaker of the Palestinian parliament, Aziz Dweek, from his home in Ramallah, branding him a terrorist. Half the cabinet and more than 65 members of the Palestinian parliament including the speaker were held in Israeli jails. President Abbas was touring the Arab capitals and the Palestinian Authority had no presence in Gaza or the West Bank. All this and the scourge of starvation on the impoverished Palestinians who were tormented by unrelenting Israeli campaigns of violence forced Prime Minister Ismael Haniyah to acknowledge the obvious, an overwhelming crisis of governance. He questioned the benefits of having a Palestinian Authority.

Haniyah warned on August 9 that Israel's offensive against his government raised questions over the future of the Palestinian Authority. He said in a teleconference address to remaining members of the Palestinian assembly from Gaza who managed to attend: "Following the kidnapping of its second highest ranking official and the attempt to assassinate its prime minister, we need to ask if the Palestinian Authority can continue to operate and function in these circumstances." Haniyah suggested that the Palestinians should consider the dissolution of the Palestinian Authority, but the most members of the Palestinian leadership, including Abbas, opposes giving up the PA that has become the national identity even if it was powerless and under siege. In spite of all its failures, the survival of the PA is perceived by many Palestinians as a form of resistance against the Israeli occupation. For the time being, the supporters of the PA dissolution are a minority but this can change any time if there is no improvement in the daily life of the Palestinians. The crippling financial and economic blockade on the West Bank and Gaza that had been imposed by Israel and the international community since Hamas won the parliamentary elections pushed most of the Palestinians into abject poverty. Thousands of demonstrating Palestinian civil servants, demanding payment of overdue wages clashing with riot police outside parliament and other government ministries, became daily scenes in Gaza and the West Bank since Hamas took office. On the first day of school in

September, teachers across the territory went on open-ended strike shutting down all public schools. They were openly supported by Fatah, the party of President Abbas to pressure Hamas into accepting its conditions for joining the unity government. Palestinian security officers joined the strike and demonstrated in Gaza City on the third day of the teacher's strike, firing rifles in the air, assaulting the parliament building and demanding their own overdue salaries. Middle-class Palestinians and Fatah loyalists joined ranks and organized demonstrations in Ramallah against Hamas. Housewives demonstrators brought out their pots and pans.

With the end of the fighting between Israel and Hizbullah, Palestinians expected the international community to refocus attention on their plight, but the major international players and Israel had refused to deal with the Hamas-controlled government. The United States and Israel were more concerned about implementing the terms of the Lebanese ceasefire outlined in UN Resolution 1701 that would disarm the Iranian-backed Hizbullah. Israeli foreign ministry spokesman Mark Regev said on August 18: "We think that anything that would take attention away from 1701 would play into the hands of Iran and Syria." The US was concerned that Iranian money for rebuilding south Lebanon which had already started to flow would increase the influence of Iran in Lebanon on the expense of the US and its Lebanese allies. The preoccupation of the US in Iran's threat to its interests in Lebanon and Iraq suggests that the Palestinian issue had to wait a long time before it might be addressed seriously.

Another major obstacle to the peace process has been the lack of common agreement among the Palestinian factions on the policy toward Israel. The divided Palestinian Authority had been effectively paralyzed since Hamas formed the government. Abbas and Ismael Haniyah needed to develop meaningful internal and external strategies and unify their ranks. The two leaders attempted with no success to form a unity government on the basis of the so-called National Reconciliation document issued by Palestinians held in Israeli jails. Friction was deepening between the two factions with accusations flying in both directions regarding who is responsible for the failure to reach an agreement. Abbas was exerting pressure through his supporters to foster the collapse of the Hamas-controlled government and replace it with a cabinet that meets Israel-US demands.

The US State Department had set a budget of 42 million dollars to support the opposition to Hamas. It declared that this funding was intended to support Palestinian groups it deemed capable of "democracy building as an alternatives to authoritarian or radical Islamist political options."[1] Another $20 million was proposed to train President Mahmoud Abbas' Praetorian guards. President George Bush asked Congress to provide $84 million to train and equip Abbas' security forces. By financing the opposition to Hamas, the US is openly embracing Abbas and his Fatah party. Washington meddling in Palestinian affairs by supporting Fatah and preventing Hamas from receiving money will backfire by creating a perception that Fatah and Abbas are acting as Washington's stooges. The US is widely viewed by the Palestinians with deep suspicion and distrust for its unwavering

---

1   Micaela Schweitzer-Bluhm, spokesperson for the US consul in Jerusalem.

support of Israel. The Palestinians have been aware that the US had vetoed 32 United Nations Security Council resolutions that were critical of Israel since 1982. Palestinian NGOs' Network (PNGO) and the "Arab Thought Forum" had to turn down the US funding that was conditioned on a written pledge not to have contacts with Hamas.

Demonstrations by security forces loyal to Abbas in Gaza demanding back pay owed to them often erupted into violence. Hamas has stubbornly refused pressure from Abbas for an eventual unity government that accepts the political program which included recognition of Israel and past Israeli–Palestinian agreements. Qatar's foreign minister tried to mediate between Abbas and Haniyah for ending the standoff but his attempts ended in failure after Hamas rejected the key demands that it recognize Israel and renounce armed resistance to occupation. Hamas is not willing to bow to the international demands. Its leaders continue to argue that, as an occupied people, the Palestinians have the right to resist the occupier, violently or otherwise especially since Israel refuses to recognize their rights.

Daily incidents were part of the ongoing violence between the Palestinian rival factions. Eighteen Palestinians have been killed and more than 120 wounded in clashes between the Fatah faction and Hamas in the first two weeks of October, 2006, sparking fears of a civil war. Al Aqsa Martyrs' Brigades, an armed wing of Fatah, threatened to kill leaders of the governing Hamas group. In Gaza Strip, masked gunmen killed a senior activist from Palestinian Mahmoud Abbas' Fatah group on October 21. The struggle between the two factions weakened them both and boldened Israel to continue its military and political offensive against the Palestinians. While the Palestinians were fighting each other, Israel was expanding its settlements, carrying out ethnic cleansing of Jerusalem and transforming the Palestinian population centers into concentration camps. A national unity government is necessary for the Palestinians to speak in one voice in confronting the political and economic crisis facing their society. But it is doubtful that any Palestinian government which includes Hamas will prompt Israel to end its siege on the Palestinians or release the withheld PA tax revenues estimated at $ 55 million/month. The siege on the three million Palestinians is the weapon to bring their Hamas-led government down and soften the Palestinians' stance on the conflict with the occupation. Choking off the people access to food may reduce their resistance to unjust settlement. Israeli Deputy Premier Shimon Peres told Israel's TV on October 6, 2006: "in the end [Palestinian] people will be disappointed" with Hamas' inability to govern and turn it out of office.

The United States adopted the Israeli line and made it clear that it would not accept the terms set for a Hamas-led unity government unless they meet the three conditions the "Quartet" of peace mediators had set for lifting the sanctions. US approval is essential if international sanctions are to be lifted. Besides a national unity government, alternatives had been considered by the Palestinian elites since Hamas government was installed in power. One was to have new parliamentary elections, which might be perceived as a coup to remove Hamas from power and could lead to more internal violence. Another alternative to a national unity government or new parliament elections was to give up the notion of an independent state all together and surrender the administration of the West Bank and Gaza to Israel or Jordan or the United Nations.

Abbas was coming under pressure by the US and some Arab governments to get tough with Hamas. US Secretary of State Condoleezza Rice arrived in the Middle East on October 3, 2006 where she met with eight Arab foreign ministers, Prime Minister Olmert and Abbas. She urged the "moderate" Arabs, namely the six Gulf Cooperation Council countries plus Egypt, Jordan and the Palestinian president, to work together against the "extremists." The so called "extremists" according to the US are those countries and organizations that resist American and Israeli policies. They include the states of Iran and Syria, Hizbullah, Hamas and other Islamist and nationalist organizations. Rice had declared that the US was going to help shore up the leadership of the beleaguered Palestinian president, Mahmoud Abbas, suggesting that something was in the offing regarding the Palestinians.

The US involvement that was necessary for reviving a Mideast peace process focused only on bolstering the firepower of President Abbas security force as a counterweight to Hamas. The US Consul in Jerusalem stated that US military personnel would train the Palestinian presidential guards in the Palestinian town of Jericho. General Keith Dayton, the American security coordinator in the occupied territories, would oversee the training of some 400 Force-17 men, using American, British, Egyptian, and Jordanian military instructors. Israel allowed Egypt to deliver large arms shipment to forces loyal to Mahmoud Abbas to help him in a possible bloody confrontation with Hamas.

Arab news media reported on October 28 2006 that Abbas asked Israel to allow troops from the Jordan-based PLO Badr Brigade to enter Palestinian areas, and Israeli officials had agreed to grant the request. The troops would bolster Abbas in his showdown with the Hamas group, which does not belong to the PLO. Hamas announced plans to re-enforce its military by recruiting 1,500 forces in the West Bank, Fatah's stronghold. The confrontation between Hamas and Fatah had the potential of triggering a bloody interior warfare as the two sides fail to reach agreement on forming a coalition government that would satisfy the US conditions to lift the embargo. Lifting the imposed open-ended financial blockade on Hamas-led government reduced the Palestinians' national struggle to a question of salaries for the over-staffed bureaucracy and transformed the national project to a humanitarian cause. Abbas stated on October 17 that putting food on the table for the Palestinians was more important than democracy. He later hinted that he would sack the government for its refusal to accept the conditions set by the United States and the European Union to lift the sanctions imposed on the government. The Palestinian laws as interpreted by Hamas do not give the president the power to dissolve the parliament at his pleasure as in Jordan or Kuwait.

CHAPTER 10. THE "PEACE PROCESS"

The Palestinian Authority President Mahmoud Abbas was clinging to the now-moribund US "Roadmap" plan for peace, but his government's institutions were not functioning due to the political deadlock over policies toward Israel between him and his prime minister. Abbas believed the "Roadmap" can lead to the establishment of a viable Palestinian state within reasonable time. His prime minister argued that the "Roadmap" as well as Oslo had failed to produce any tangible results for the Palestinians. He offered a 10-year ceasefire, during which Israel and the Palestinians could seek a more permanent settlement. Israel rejected Hamas ceasefire proposal, and the US brokered "Roadmap" plan could not be revived because Israel rendered the very concept of a "two-state solution" unachievable by adding 14 reservations to the plan, building and expanding the settlements and constructing more Jewish only highways and the separation wall. And the Arab states that had been too weak to influence the US or Israel policy makers were trying to resurrect their own peace plan that was rejected in 2002. But Israel had no plan for building a long-term peace as an alternative to violence, land grabbing and building walls on Palestinian lands. Even the Ariel Sharon plan for unilateral Israeli withdrawal from parts of the West Bank was abandoned immediately after the war in Lebanon. Prime Minister Olmert declared that the unilateral West Bank pullback plan, that swept him to power in March 2006, had been shelved.

Instead of withdrawal, his government issued bids in early September to build 700 homes in major settlements in the West Bank. He struck an alliance on October 23, 2006 with the hawkish Yisrael Beiteinu Party, the most extreme party when it comes to dealing with the Palestinians. Its leader, Avigdor Lieberman who became a deputy prime minister, had called for stripping Arab Israelis of their citizenship to make Israel more Jewish, executing lawmakers for talking to Hamas and blanket-bombing of Palestinian population centers, gas stations and banks. Arab Israelis constitute 20 % of the Israel's population.

By bringing Yisrael Beiteinu Party into his coalition government, Olmert abandoned his pledge to pull out of much of the West Bank, and created conditions where peace with the Palestinians will be even more difficult to achieve. A proponent of ethnic cleansing takes his seat in the Israeli government without a condemnation by the international community that sanctioned the Palestinian people under military occupation for electing a party which does not recognize their occupier. The West decided to boycott an elected government and starve its people, while continuing to do business as usual with an Israeli government that included a fascist deputy prime minister. This is another example of the US and the Europeans' hypocrisy and double standards in dealing with the Middle East peoples. Even the so called moderate Arab governments that criticized Hamas for vowing to resist the occupation chose not to criticize the new Israeli government coalition. King Abdullah of Jordan urged the Palestinians to "meet the conditions of the Quartet." He did not ask Israel to reciprocate by recognizing a Palestinian state or withdrawing from the occupied territory.

Israel's policy toward the Palestinians is reduced to military attacks, bombing, demolition, killing and arresting Palestinians with impunity under the pretext of securing the release of the captured soldier or crushing the Palestinian resistance. Israeli troops continue incursions into Gaza and the West Bank, killing activists and arresting more ministers and elected members of the Palestinian Authority but the savagery of the assaults failed to free the captured soldier. They arrested Nasser Shaèr, the deputy prime minister and Mahmoud al-Ramahi, secretary-general of the Palestinian Legislative Council on August 20. And on November 2nd, they arrested the minister of public work and housing, Abdul-Rahman Zaidan. None of the detained Palestinian legislators and ministers has been charged with a crime. Israel has been carrying out ground and air attacks in the besieged Gaza Strip in order to stop cross-border rocket attacks. The rockets are notoriously inaccurate and have rarely caused casualties among Israelis. These ineffective "rockets" are the desperate Palestinians' response to Israel's unceasing and unrelenting campaign of attacks against the encircled and starved Gaza Strip. Firing rockets into Israel and injuring or threatening any civilian is morally wrong and counter productive. This work condemns it in the strongest terms, but in the three years since the Palestinians started firing these projectiles against Israel, three Israelis civilians have been killed while the Palestinians' death in Gaza exceeded 400 in three months. The Palestinians and the Israelis are locked in a perpetual vicious cycle of violence that does not seem to end.

Abbas appealed to the groups that had been holding the Israeli soldier to release him and for Israel to release Palestinian prisoners. Number of Palestinian political prisoners and internees in Israeli jails at anytime exceed 10,000, including hundreds of women and children. Many of the prisoners have been languishing in Israeli jails for over 20 years, some with virtually no chance of being freed while alive. Within nine years since the occupation of the West Bank and Gaza in 1967, number of Palestinians arrested by Israel had exceeded 750,000 or 25% of the permanent Arab residents of the occupied territory. Once it disengaged from Lebanon, the Israeli government moved even more forcefully against the Palestinians in the occupied territories for many reasons that were mostly related to the Lebanese war.

First and most important reason was the desire to silence the government's political critics who had accused the Prime Minister and the Defense Minister of mismanaging the opportunity to destroy Hizbullah and failing to accomplish the war aims. Sending their soldiers to fight the war without a clear mission and insufficient supplies, as the political critics claim, have horrified the Israeli public. Polls taken immediately after the war showed nearly 70% of the Israelis disapproved of Olmert's job as a prime minister. After his popularity plunged over the perceived failure in Lebanon, his government was under attack by the right wing Israeli leaders. To make things worse for the Israeli governing elites, Olmert was investigated for shady real estate deals and unlawful political appointments; and sex charges were leveled against President Moshe Katsav and former Justice Minister Haim Ramon. The opposition capitalized on the leadership weakness and increased the pressure on the government not to compromise with the Palestinians. Former prime-minister and the leader of the Likud Party, Benyamin Netanyahu, who led the opposition against Olmert's government, called for escalating the war against Hamas-led government even more to discredit it in the eyes of the Palestinians and bring it down. The persistent criticism dragged Olmert's ratings in 2007 to unprecedented lows. According to some poles, only 2% of Israelis trusted him and Benjamin Netanyahu would win the premiership if elections were held then. A government war probe released by the end of April 2007 tarred the Prime Minister as acting rashly "and without adequate preparations" in the war against Hizbullah fighters and some Kadima lawmakers demanded that Olmert step down. Members from his own cabinet including his own foreign minister Tzipi Livni were calling for him to resign. The desire to rehabilitate his image among the Israelis may explain in part his heavy-handed policy toward the Palestinians. The 34-day war that was celebrated by Hizbullah as a victory was a massive setback for Israel's regional designs and for those who wanted Hizbullah removed from the country's political equation. The war backfired, achieving the exact opposite; Hizbullah emerged stronger and more popular. A year later, Israel's own investigation into the war admitted, if somewhat circuitously, Israel's defeat. The Winograd Commission's report released in January 2008 indicted the army and described the failure of the war as a "serious missed opportunity." But to the surprise of many observers, it largely absolved Prime Minister Ehud Olmert, and the report didn't chastise the war, but criticized its lack of effectiveness and poor execution.

Second, Israel embarked on more aggressive campaign against the Palestinians in order to boost the morale of the Israeli public and the IDF that had suffered from the ill-fated war in Lebanon. It wanted to apply the lessons from the Lebanese war in Gaza by making sure that Palestinians would not acquire significant military weapons that could harm the Israeli army during incursions into their territory. Israel has vowed not to turn Gaza into a "second Lebanon."[1] Defeating the Palestinians, who have been under siege since 1967 militarily, is easy to achieve compared to the Lebanese resistance. The Israeli

---

1 Senior defense ministry official Amos Gilad told army radio on October 12, 2006.

intelligence succeeded in penetrating the Palestinian militant groups through thousands of paid collaborator informants recruited from the ranks of poor unemployed Palestinians. Besides, Hamas had no way to bring in the occupied lands the type of arms that the Lebanese acquired and used against the Israelis. Third, Israel tried to punish the Palestinians for expressing their solidarity with Hizbullah fighters during the Lebanese war. The Palestinian public had demonstrated in support of Hizbullah and cheered for Hasan Nasrallah and his fighters. Fourth, the Israeli leadership maintained that moderate leaders of the Arab governments had been secretly encouraging Israel to deal a fatal blow to the Islamist militants in Lebanon and the occupied lands despite their occasional anti-Israel rhetoric intended for Arab public consumption. While Israel continues expanding its territorial boundaries, arresting Palestinian elected officials, starving and ravaging the besieged West Bank and Gaza Strip, the Arab governments have been silent if not complacent. Olmert stated in many occasions that the Lebanese war created new momentum in relations between Israel and moderate Arab countries and expressed appreciation for their restraint in criticizing Israel's war in Lebanon. The so called moderate Arabs are apprehensive that Iran would emerge stronger and more popular even among their own populations in the wake of the Lebanese war after Hizbullah, the ally of Iran, stood firm and steadfast against Israel. US Secretary of State Condoleezza Rice said on September 24, 2006 that "moderate Arab states do not wish Iran to gain too much power in the region."

Fifth, with the US approval, Israel has portrayed the fight against the Palestinians as part of the war on terrorism. Hamas is on the short US list of the terrorist organizations. The brutal assault against the West Bank and Gaza was hailed by Israeli supporters as part of the global war on terrorism. The US military response to terrorism strengthened Israel's belief in the legitimacy and effectiveness of military brutality to defeat Hamas and end its political role despite the failure to defeat Hizbullah in Lebanon. The announced reason for increasing the intensity of the Israeli assault on the Palestinians is to secure the return of the Israeli soldier captured by Palestinian fighters and to halt the firing of homemade projectiles from Gaza into Israel. But the real reason was to overthrow Hamas government. Until 2008, Israel had refused to accept a prisoner swap deal with the Palestinians hoping that the military would succeed in locating and freeing the captured soldier, thus giving the government of Ehud Olmert a military victory over the Palestinian militants.

Israel escalated its attack against the Palestinians in November when the first week of the month was one of Gaza's deadliest until then. Sixty-two people were killed and more than two-hundred wounded as Israel launched an operation on Beit Hanoun town in north Gaza Strip. Two women were among the dead and more than ten wounded when hundreds of unarmed women tried to rescue Palestinian gunmen trapped in a local mosque surrounded by Israeli troops. Later on, the Israeli military bombed homes including the residence of a woman who led the demonstration, Jamila Shanti, killing two members of her family. This was followed on November 8, 2006 by another massacre of civilians where 18 members of a family, including eight children, were killed and 34 adults and 26 children were wounded in an Israeli artillery barrage on the densely populated town. Israel blamed the attack on faulty targeting radar. South Africa's Archbishop Desmond

Tutu, who served as an independent UN human rights envoy, said in a report to the UN that Israel's deadly shelling of Beit Hanoun may constitute a war crime. As the Palestinians were trying to bury the dead civilians, the Israeli prime minister declared that Israel would keep targeting Palestinians suspected of firing rockets at Israeli border towns from Gaza despite the risk of inadvertently hitting civilians. An Arab-sponsored draft resolution in the UN Security Council that would have condemned the Israeli attack on Beit Hanoun was vetoed by the United States on November 11, 2006. The US Ambassador, John Bolton, called the text of the resolution "unbalanced" and "biased" against Israel. From the Palestinian perspective, the US veto was a license for Israel to kill more civilians in the name of self-defense regardless even if it was in occupied lands. It encouraged Israel's aggression and increased the distrust in the American role in the Arab–Israeli conflict. The veto reinforced the Palestinians perception that the US is an enemy rather than an unbiased mediator. The US previous use of the veto was in July to block a draft resolution that would have condemned Israel's military onslaught in Gaza as "disproportionate force" and demanded a halt to Israeli military operations in the territories.

Following the November US veto, the Arab League convened a meeting in Cairo attended by foreign ministers to discuss the brutal Israeli massacres against innocent Palestinian civilians and the Security Council's failure to approve their draft resolution. The Palestinian Hamas foreign minister was in attendance but Saudi Arabia, Kuwait, Iraqi and Lebanon were represented by low level delegates. This was the first time Arab foreign ministers talked to a cabinet member of the Palestinian Hamas government. The conferees did not criticize the US for the use of the veto, but they unexpectedly declared that they would break the economic siege imposed on the Palestinians by Israel and the West since Hamas was elected to office. The announcement was nothing but an empty rhetoric because none of the Arab states authorized the banks to transfer funds to the PA government.

All Arab states had observed the US–Israeli economic embargo without admitting they were implementing it, even when it was obvious that the Palestinians were starved and suffocated under the Israeli occupation. The League ministers also called for an international peace conference to deal with the Palestinian issue under the auspices of the permanent members of the Security Council that had just failed to stop or condemn the Israeli massacres in Gaza. Israel rejected the proposal and no country took that call seriously. A week later, an Islamic States ministerial conference was convened in Jeddah, Saudi Arabia. It also announced, on behalf of their governments, breaking the economic embargo on the Palestinians. It turned out that the announcements of the Arab and Islamic states regarding the Palestinians were only talk and no action. The Palestinians and Arab public learnt through past experience not to pay attention to the Arab League or the Islamic states posturing on the Palestinian issue. Arab League summit held in Khartum on March 2, 2006 pledged to fund the PA, but the money has not been forthcoming. After sixty years since its establishment, the Arab League proved incapable of dealing with the Palestinian issue.

Besides being under occupation, the Palestinians were not willing to close ranks and formulate one strategy toward Israel. While Israel continued its military offensive in the

West Bank and Gaza, rival Hamas and Fatah had been engaged in talks to form a unity government acceptable by the West but deep differences raised questions about the ability of the two sides to reach a speedy conclusion of an agreement. The two parties were so far apart that Prime Minister Haniyah, who had been elected in March, met Palestinian President Mahmoud Abbas only once as of the end of November 2006 since the two men took office. Fatah proposed a "government of experts," with absolutely no political affiliation with Hamas or Fatah. Hamas wanted a "national unity" government that represented all political factions. It insisted on controlling the portfolios of interior, health, finance, and education in return for Fatah taking the foreign affairs ministry. Fatah demanded that the government accept all previous agreements with Israel including Oslo. Its leaders claim Oslo as one of their triumphs despite the obvious that it was used by Israel to empower a Palestinian partner to accept the partition of the West Bank and deny the refugees the right of return. Another issue was the 6000-strong "Executive Force" that Abbas called illegal. Fatah had been demanding that the force be dissolved or incorporated into the Palestinian security groups that were dominated by Fatah.

Fatah sought to appease the international community in the hope of resuming the financial aid, but Hamas is set against forming a government that would be vulnerable to international pressure or abandon the resistance to occupation and yield to American-Israeli dictates. The discussions among the Palestinians to form a government took too much time considering that such a government had no real power in a territory under occupation. While Fatah and Hamas were bickering on the cabinet portfolios, many Palestinian ministers and parliament members were behind bars in Israeli jails. President Abbas or Prime Minister Haniyah had to obtain a permit from the Israeli military authority to travel between Gaza and the West Bank. The Palestinian people must feel let down by their leaders' infighting on imaginary political power. How long is it going to take them to negotiate a settlement with the Israelis if they could not sort their own differences and agree on forming a unity government in a year? At the same time, Israel continues to expand its settlements and build the separation wall on the occupied land. The daily life of half million Palestinians is adversely affected by the wall. Israel had been carrying out ethnic cleansing of Jerusalem, and escalating its violence against any and all who try to resist, peacefully or otherwise.

During a joint press conference with visiting US Secretary of State Condoleezza Rice in Jericho on November 30, 2006, Abbas stated that he would explore alternatives to end the suffering of the Palestinians due to the Israeli siege. The Palestinian President decided that early elections were the only way to lift the debilitating direct aid freeze imposed on the Palestinian government after Hamas took power. To break the political deadlock with the Hamas government, Abbas called on December 16 for early elections, although Fatah's chances of winning the election are not guaranteed and Hamas could emerge from the polls stronger than now. Hamas leaders rejected the move and described it as a "coup" against their democratically elected government. Haniyah accused Abbas of conspiring with the US to bring down his government. The rival factions, engaged in a war of words, tension simmered and disagreement developed into violence where gun battles raged in the Gaza Strip. Several Fighters from the two groups were killed and scores wounded after days of factional bloodshed in Gaza during December 2006. Haniyah's convoy came under fire at Rafah when he returned from a suspended trip to Arab countries and Iran. One of his bodyguards was killed and his son as well as his political advisor was injured in the attack.

Resurgence in factional violence in January 2007 killed 80 Palestinians, including women, and children caught in the crossfire and more than 200 wounded. Following the killing of a high-ranking Fatah officer in full view of his family allegedly by members of the government's "Executive Forces" brought the conflict between the two factions to a new depth. Thousands of Fatah supporters held a rally in downtown Gaza where the keynote speaker was a Fatah leader, Muhammed Dahlan. He referred to Hamas as a "gang of murderous agents of Iran" and threatened to make the movement "pay twofold for every provocation." Sporadic gun battles between the two factions continued across Gaza despite a Saudi offer to mediate an end to the violence. Hamas-Fatah fighting spilled over into the West Bank, with assailants abducting Deputy Health Minister Bashar Karmi of Hamas from his home in the town of Al Bireh. Suspected Fatah militiamen went on a rampage of arson, shooting and abduction, targeting individuals and businesses affiliated with Hamas. In Ramallah, masked men armed with AK-47s torched malls, department stores and money-changing offices, reportedly in full view of PA police and security forces. The prevalence of the culture of violence in the Palestinian society can be attributed to the frustration and hopelessness of a generation that has known nothing but a brutal occupation, restriction of movements, human rights violations and the failure of the "peace talk."

It took the mediation of Saudi Arabia to get the leaders of the two factions to meet in the Holy City of Mecca and try to resolve their differences. The reconciliation meeting in Mecca was the second attempt to avoid civil war after the failure of Egypt, Syria and Qatar to end the struggle between the two factions. Finally, the rival factions agreed on February 2, 2007 to end the fighting and form a national unity government headed by Haniyah. They signed an accord that was called "the Mecca Declaration." The two factions would form a unity government where Hamas would hold nine cabinet posts, six go to Fatah and an independent would become interior minister. Hamas as a partner in the unity government would "respect" previous Palestinian agreements with Israel, a wording that implies acceptance of Israel but falls short of an explicit recognition of the Jewish state. The agreement authorized Fatah and the PLO to resume negotiating peace with Israel even according to President Bush "Roadmap."

Palestinians hoped that the agreement that facilitated the formation of the government would end the showdown between Hamas and Fatah and lift the economic sanctions that have rendered most Palestinians unemployed and living well below the poverty line. Abbas asked Haniyah to form a coalition government despite a warning by the US that Washington might not deal with its members. The government in which all Palestinian political factions were represented was approved by an overwhelming majority among the free Palestinian Legislative Council members and welcomed by the Palestinian public. Some European governments indicated a certain willingness to deal with non-

Hamas ministers. The EU decided to take a wait-and-see stance on the new government and urged it to accept the three conditions for direct aid to resume. As expected, Israel ruled out holding talks even with Abbas once he formed a coalition with Hamas. Olmert stated that he would not deal with the new government until it agreed to meet the Quartet conditions. Washington, too, remained adamant in its refusal to deal with any Palestinian government that does not abide by the Quartet conditions. Finally when Israel and the US refused dealing with the Hamas-Fatah coalition government, the Europeans decided to maintain the embargo. Condoleezza Rice stated that the Mecca Declaration had complicated the situation, and the US decided to reconsider its previous commitment to contribute 84 million dollars for President Abbas security forces. The US would not deal with a Palestinian government that includes Hamas even if it ends the infighting and chaos among the Palestinians.

The US is the only broker that has influence on Israel in any dialogue that could eventually lead to a solution. But the US never exercised its leverage to make any substantive progress toward achieving peace during George W. Bush presidency. It sided publicly with the Israelis on the main contested issues. Visits by the Secretary of State provided only stopgap measures for opening a crossing gate for a short period of time or a fragile cease-fire in Gaza or talk about maintaining contact between Olmert and Mahmoud Abbas to discuss nothing of substance. The most the US was willing to do was getting the two parties talking to each other while enforcing the economic blockade against the Palestinians. The meetings were perceived as merely a formality taking place at the US request mainly to give a false impression of a continuing peace process that is either dead or dying.

On November 25, 2006 and four days before President Bush was scheduled to arrive in Jordan for talks with the Iraqi prime minister, the Palestinian Authority and Israel agreed to a ceasefire after a phone conversation between Olmert and Abbas. Abbas initiated the call telling the Israeli premier that the Palestinian factions were willing to stop firing rockets if Israel stopped its attacks on Gaza and withdrew its forces which were mostly deployed in northern Gaza. If the truce holds, it would end a five-month offensive in Gaza to counter Palestinian rocket attacks and rescue the captured Israeli soldier. In Gaza Strip alone, more than 467 Palestinians, among them 96 children and 59 women were killed and over 1,000 injured in the five months. Three Israeli soldiers and four civilians have been killed since the military launched the massive offensive. Death tolls on both sides show the disparity of power. Arab proposal to stop firing rockets into southern Israel suggests that the Palestinians realized that violence cannot end the occupation. And by accepting the ceasefire, Israel in effect conceded that its military action cannot squash the Palestinian resistance in Gaza. The agreement, however, did not declare the end of land and sea siege of Gaza or the withdrawal from the West Bank and the removal of the more than 500 checkpoints and roadblocks Israel operates in the West Bank, which restricted the movement of people and goods. The timing of the agreement suggests that the US might have advised Israel to create an environment that would dampen a possible hostile reception for the American President in the streets of Amman, Jordan.

Despite hope that the truce might ease their suffering in Gaza, the Palestinians were not too optimistic that it would move the peace process forward. Palestinians have been desperate to see serious progress towards having a state of their own in the territories occupied in 1967, but they have seen many agreements declared and in short time collapse. The fate of this ceasefire would be the same as of the past agreements unless it was followed by serious political negotiations toward ending the occupation.

Prime Minister Olmert was too weak to make the necessary concessions to the beleaguered Palestinians whose land is being rapidly swallowed up by the settlements and the separation wall. Some Palestinians read the Israeli decision to accept the Gaza truce as a victory for the resistance. In a two-hour meeting with Abbas on December 16, 2006, Olmert promised to release $100 million in frozen funds to the Palestinian President and ease West Bank travel restrictions by removing several roadblocks. But Israel attached conditions for releasing the Palestinian tax money to President Abbas. The conditions were not easy to meet; funds were not released; the roadblocks were not removed; settlements were expanded; and military raids and attacks against the Palestinians resumed.

In the first week of January 2007, the Israeli undercover military forces burst into a West Bank vegetable market killing 5 Palestinian civilians and wounding 25. The significance of the raid, that turned downtown Ramallah into a battle field, was its timing. It came on the same day of a scheduled meeting between Olmert and Husni Mubarak of Egypt in Sharm el-Sheikh to revive the long-stalled peace process. And on January 14 when the US Secretary of State was calling for reviving the "Roadmap" during a visit to the Middle East, the Israeli housing ministry announced tenders for 44 new housing units in the largest West Bank settlement, Maaleh Adumim, in violation of the "Roadmap." In April, Israel started building a new Jewish settlement, Nev Tzion, in the middle of the Arab East Jerusalem that was conquered from Jordan in the 1967 war.

The "Roadmap" specifically called on Israel to end settlement expansions and not to start new ones. Israel never accepted the "Roadmap" and continues to violate it. Olmert spokeswoman Miri Eisin told the Associated Press that the Israeli government was committed to the continuing natural growth of the settlements. Olmert makes a mockery of the "Roadmap" by telling lawmakers from his own Kadima Party that the "Roadmap will continue to form the basis" of the "peace process" while Israel never accepted it and continues to violate it. The military raids into Ramallah and other Palestinian towns, the disregard to the international laws that consider the settlements in occupied territory illegal and the daily assassination of Palestinian civilians suggests that the Israeli leaders were not ready for peace.

REVIVING THE SAUDI PEACE INITIATIVE

Twenty-one Arab League states held the 19th summit meeting in March 2007 in Saudi Arabia. They unanimously decided to re-launch the land-for-peace proposal that had been offered by Saudi Arabia in 2002 to solve the Arab–Israeli conflict and rejected by then Israeli PM Ariel Sharon and ignored by the US. When it was initially offered, Israel response was to launch a military invasion of the West Bank and Gaza Strip. The Arab leaders who had been helpless spectators in the face of the Israeli atrocities against the Palestinians activated the old initiative only to save face before their angry and frustrated public. It calls on Israel to give back all territory captured in the 1967 war and accept an agreed just solution to the issue of the Palestinian refugees, in accordance with UNGA Resolution 194. In return, Arab nations would offer Israel full recognition and permanent peace. The resolution included direct call "to the government of Israel and all Israelis to accept the Arab Peace Initiative and seize the opportunity to resume the process of direct and serious negotiations on all tracks." Arab League foreign ministers and their Palestinian counterpart selected Egypt and Jordan to pursue contact with Israel and push for the plan. They also set up working groups to drum up support for the initiative in the United States, United Nations and the European Union. The Israeli Foreign Minister rejected it immediately. Tzipi Livni was quoted saying that her government would not accept the Arab peace plan without significant changes.

Livni asked that the Arabs should drop any reference to the UN Resolution 194 that gave the Palestinian refugees, who fled or were driven from their homes when Israel was founded in 1948, the right of return to their homes in Israel. The Israelis believe that the influx of any number of Arabs into Israel would threaten its Jewish demographic and political supremacy. If the land-for-peace proposal is accepted and the refugees are granted the right to return, it will be up to them to choose to exercise it. But Olmert told the Israeli press that Israel would not allow a single Palestinian to return to his or her homeland in Israel; and Tzipi Livni insisted that Israel would not withdraw to the pre-1967 war borders. Olmert has hailed the idea of normalization in the Arab League initiative as a "revolutionary change" but he also expressed reservations. He rejected the main points of the initiative and called on Saudi Arabia to hold a regional conference that included Israel. Shimon Peres told Arab officials at a 2007 World Economic Forum panel in Jordan that Israel would make a counter offer to the peace blueprint but he declined to be more specific about its contents and gave no time frame for its release. Because the Israelis have the backing of the US, they felt confident that they could easily shift the focus of the discussion regardless of what the Arabs may offer.

The Israeli leadership wants the normalization part of the initiative with the Arab states, but without paying a price. Arab governments are eager for a political solution and the Palestinians have already declared their support for the plan, but the Arabs offered no alternatives if Israel rejected it. If there is an obstacle to peace now, it would be the combination of Israel's intransigence, the Palestinians in-fighting and the Arab states weakness. The Arabs lack the political power to promote the initiative among Israel's supporters in the US and Europe and Israel does not plan to make peace by giving up land occupied in the 1967 War. The Israelis view the Palestinians themselves as the problem in the "Land of Israel" rather than a people with legitimate rights and partners in the quest for peace. While the leaders of the Arab states were reaching out for peace, Israel decided to step up its daily incursions into the West Bank towns and villages to arrest activists. Its military killed eleven Palestinians including a 17 years old boy in two day shortly after the Riyadh

Arab League summit had re-launched the Peace Initiative. Izz al-Din al-Qassam Brigades, Hamas' armed wing, declared it would not abide by the shaky Gaza truce Palestinian President Mahmoud Abbas and Israeli Prime Minister Ehud Olmert reached in November. Hamas fired a barrage of rockets across the Gaza border at Israeli targets causing no injuries, and Israel responded by sending helicopter gun ships over Gaza airspace.

For moral reasons, the world community should not allow this historic feud to continue for generations to come until the weak side is exterminated. There is no way out of this deadlock without the US involvement. One cannot imagine peace happening in Palestine without American active engagement. But Washington and the Europeans have not taken a clear public stand on the Saudi Peace Initiative. US Secretary of State Condoleezza Rice visited the region many times but she never made any substantive progress toward achieving peace. Few days before the March 2007 Arab summit meeting, she used her shuttle diplomacy between Jerusalem and Arab capitals to make the pending Arab peace proposal acceptable by Israel. Olmert considered the Arab peace plan a positive development because it leads to normalization but he and all Israeli leaders asked Rice to demand that the Arabs drop clauses in the initiative pertaining to the right of return and withdrawal to 1967 borders. The US Secretary of State asked the Arab governments to "moderate" the initiative to make it more "palatable" to Israel before any progress is achieved on the Palestinian–Israeli issue. She wanted the Arab governments, including Hamas-led Palestinian government, to recognize Israel before it can even be engaged as legitimate partners in the peace negotiations. Israeli rejection of the main points from the Arab perspective in the peace plan in exchange for ending the century old conflict once and for all suggests its unwillingness to integrate in the region. The normal political and economic relations with all Arab countries that had been the goal of the early Zionists are being rejected by the Israeli leaders today. The Arabs failed to seize opportunities of peace in the 20th century then regretted their inaction when it was too late. They never had plans or political, military and media powers to back up their positions. The Israelis refuse to embrace peace that is offered by the Arabs in the 21st century, but unlike the Arabs, they knew when and how to reject without paying any price. The Israelis do not feel they need to make concessions to the Palestinians in exchange for recognition. The Arabs had recognized Israel when they accepted the UN Security Council Resolution 242 that called for "acknowledgement of the sovereignty, territorial integrity and political independence of every state in the area and their right to live in peace within secure and recognized boundaries free from threats or acts of force." Israel feels secure militarily and economically since signing the peace treaties with Egypt and Jordan.

Arab states demonstrated their ineffectiveness to influence the peace process when Egyptian and Jordanian foreign ministers failed in their diplomatic mission to sell the Arab League initiative to the Israeli leadership. They visited Israel, met its top policy makers and explained how the Arab Peace initiative was a good basis for Israel to achieve a lasting comprehensive peace with all the Arab states. Israel rolled out the red carpet for the visiting VIPs and scheduled meetings with Israeli political and legislative personnel and nothing little beyond that. Instead of the focus on the issues at hand, the visit was transformed into a silly debate whether the visitors were a delegation of the Arab League as Israel referred to them or only representatives of their respective countries as the visitors claim. Unfortunately, Israel had no urgency to start discussions on the final status solution with Arab states that can play a constructive role in the peace process.

THE RIFT BETWEEN FATAH AND HAMAS

A Missouri Democrat who was fed up with people fighting over the "Alcohol Prohibition" in the US during the Great Depression told one of President Franklin Roosevelt's top lieutenants that it was "ridiculous for a jobless wet Democrat [pro-legalizing alcohol] to wrangle with a jobless dry Democrat [against legalizing alcohol] over liquor when neither could afford the price of a drink."[1] So it is with Fatah and Hamas, who are ridiculous to keep fighting over an authority that neither faction has under the Israeli occupation.

In early May 2007, the US proposed a plan that calls for both sides of the Palestinian–Israeli conflict to take "confidence-building" steps. This included actions by President Abbas Fatah dominated police forces to crack down on the Palestinian militants involved in rocket attacks and for Israel to ease restrictions on the movement of Palestinians in the West Bank. Like previous US stop-gap plans, this one did not address the root cause of the conflict, ending the occupation or even lifting the economic siege. The plan fell short of achieving peace with Israel and created a new conflict between Fatah which accepted the plan and Hamas which rejected it. To the dismay of the Palestinians and delight of their enemies, forces from the two factions clashed in Gaza leaving scores of people dead and many more wounded in May 2007. Each side accused its rival in starting the fighting. Fatah accused Hamas' armed men of attacking a Presidential Guard base that had been set up by a US team to train security forces loyal to Abbas. The two factions battled in the Gaza Strip raising death toll to more than 40 in two weeks and injuring more than 50. The senseless eruption of the factional violence ended the two-month-old power-sharing alliance between the two factions that had been ushered by the Saudis.

Political leaders of both sides condemned the confrontation and the infighting, but their armed fighters on the ground ignored their pleas. Israeli physical and economic siege of Gaza and the Palestinian authority failure to provide the basic needs of the population weakened the government partners control over their respective armed wings. Gaza, one of the world's poorest and most populated places, with no prospects for better future, breeds nothing but anarchy. In the words of Azmi Bishara, "the violence that has erupted inside [Gaza] is not dissimilar to a prison riot." Gaza became a lawless territory where hundreds of rival gang members took up positions on street corners and buildings rooftops. It is the disintegration and fragmentation of a hopeless besieged starved population. Long life under siege dehumanizes the victims and leads to more defiance. The economic embargo imposed on the Palestinians after Hamas came to power, and US military assistance for Abbas, exacerbated tension between the two factions and fuelled Islamists anger. The US efforts to marginalize Hamas and strengthen Fatah backfired when Hamas

---

1 The historian William E. Leuchtenberg.

preempted such efforts by seizing power in Gaza. Hamas fighters stormed and overran the headquarters of Fatah's National Security Forces in the Strip and took total control of Gaza Strip on June 15, 2007. The last three days of fighting left 110 people dead and hundreds wounded after bitter internecine fighting. But the big casualty in the naked power struggle was the Palestinian cause. It was shameful act and criminal, Palestinians killing each other, dragging the sick from hospitals and throwing each other from high rising rooftops. The unity government collapsed and the Palestinians territory disintegrated into two separated by 30 miles of Israeli territory, one controlled by Hamas and the other by Fatah.

On June 17, Palestinian President Mahmoud Abbas used his constitutional power to sack the coalition government and strip Hamas of its representation on the Palestinian national Security Council. Then he swore in a new emergency government headed by Prime Minister Salam Fayyad excluding the Islamic group. Abbas violated the Basic Law which gave Abbas "power to dismiss Haniyah but did not allow him to appoint a new government without parliamentary approval." It was expected that the term of the Fayyad government would be extended indefinitely despite its illegality. The new government immediately gained regional and international support and recognition. The US, the EU, Egypt and Jordan recognized it as the legitimate government. Israel promised to release millions of dollars of the Palestinian tax money to Fayyad government and the US pledged to end the 15-month-old economic embargo against the West Bank. The US Secretary of State promised on June 18, 2007 to resume direct full economic assistance to the emergency government. She also stated that America was committed to moving towards a two-state solution between the Israelis and the Palestinians, a statement that had lost its meaning among the Palestinians especially after the collapse of the unity government.

Hani al-Hasan, a Fatah leader gave his account of what took place in Gaza. He stated on Al Jazeera Arabic language television that what happened was a failed American-planned putsch against Hamas by a Fatah faction headed by Muhammed Dahlan, the security aide of Abbas. He added that the US coordinator with the PLO, General Keith Dayton, planned the unsuccessful uprising with Dahlan. Al-Hasan referred to Dahlan supporters as "Dayton Group." Even without Hani al-Hasan allegations, the Palestinian public had already viewed the Gaza events as an Israeli–American plan implemented in coordination with Abbas and Dahlan to overthrow Hamas government that won a large majority in the legislative elections.

With the blessing of the US, Israel and some neighboring Arab governments, Abbas issued a decree declaring the "Executive Force" and Hamas outside the law for cracking down on Fatah fighters in Gaza. He suspended articles in the Palestinian basic law that requires parliamentary approval of decisions he makes. And he ordered the dissolution of all NGOs that must now reapply for licenses which will not be granted to Hamas-affiliated organizations, thus making them illegal. The deposed Prime Minister, Ismael Haniyah, dismissed the new PA government as "illegitimate" and insisted he remained the legitimate prime minister. But the continued Israeli blockade and the US embargo against Gaza would lead to further economic deterioration in the besieged Strip. The West Bank and Gaza Strip effectively have two bitterly divided governments, both claiming sole legitimacy to rule the embattled Palestinian people. Abbas embarked on a campaign delivering speeches attacking Hamas and ruling out any dialogue with the "traitors." Haniyah as a leader of Hamas offered to have to talk with Fatah to bridge their differences, but Fatah officials rejected the offer as long as the Islamists control Gaza. Haniyah repeatedly announced that Hamas neither wanted to keep Gaza separate, nor to establish an Islamic "emirate" there. After his meeting with French President Nicolas Sarkozy on June 29, Abbas called for an international force to be deployed in Gaza Strip, an idea that had been also proposed by Avigdor Lieberman, the deputy prime minister and the head of the extremist Yisrael Beiteinu Party. Hamas spokesman rejected the idea and warned that it would not accept any foreign troops in Gaza and would treat them as an occupying power.

In order to bolster the Palestinian US and Israel-backed government, Egypt called for a four-way Middle East summit to arrange for "peace talks" to be held in the Red Sea resort of Sharm el-Sheikh on June 25, 07. The meeting was attended by Mahmoud Abbas, King Abdullah II of Jordan, Ehud Olmert of Israel and Husni Mubarak of Egypt. The announced purpose of the summit was to reactivate the "peace process," but holding the conference with the participation of Israel only one week after the fall of Gaza into Hamas hands suggests it would focus on how to contain Hamas and strengthen Abbas. The summit did not strengthen the leader, who just lost control of half his constituency. It was convened at the time when Abbas was most vulnerable. The summit would be mainly to review how Israel would reward Abbas for overthrowing Hamas government rather than to discuss resumption of peace talk. Olmert was not expected to promise stopping building the separation wall or the expansion of settlements and he did not agree to start political negotiations on the final settlement of the conflict. Olmert can only return to Abbas some of the Palestinian money that Israel controls. One day before the conference, Israel agreed to transfer hundreds of millions of dollars to Palestinian President Mahmoud Abbas' new government. The money, part of the Palestinian tax revenues, is intended to bolster Abbas standing among the Palestinians. Hamas spokesman dismissed it as "bribery" to fuel tensions with the Islamists in Gaza. Olmert referred to the Palestinians as either terrorists or moderates. He announced his intention to release as many as 250 Fatah prisoners who did not have blood on their hands out of more than 11,000 Palestinians Israel currently holds including more than four thousands who are affiliated with Fatah. He told a joint news conference with the three Arab leaders that he would work with "moderates" like Abbas against "terrorists" to secure peace in the Middle East.

Only one week after the conclusion of the Sharm el-Sheikh summit, Israel unleashed air attacks on Gaza and rounded Hamas supporters in the West Bank. Series of deadly air strikes against Hamas targets in the Gaza Strip killed scores of people, among them many civilians. And in the West Bank, Israel resumed assassination and arrests of Hamas activists. At the same time, security forces loyal to Abbas in the West Bank took hundreds of Hamas supporters and leaders into custody. Fayyad government security agencies were collaborating with Israeli military to pursue Palestinian active resistance cells in the West Bank. The PA arrest of Hamas activists was coordinated with the Israeli occupation forces which tightly controls every square inch of the territories. News media reported that sometimes the Israeli military targeted the same individuals arrested by the PA security forces. Olmert decided to release $120 million of frozen Palestinian tax revenue to Ramallah government on condition that Abbas must not renew contacts with Hamas. Abbas and his prime minister did not pay the salaries of 19,000 civil servants in the West Bank because they were hired by the previous government of Hamas. Discriminating against Palestinians who were affiliated with Hamas did not make Abbas the president of all Palestinians. The economic boycott of the Palestinians in Gaza is intended to persuade the people to mobilize against Hamas leadership. But the collusion between the PA and the Israeli military against Hamas is bound to backfire and harm the image of Abbas and his Fatah faction among the Palestinians especially if there is no progress in the peace talks on the major issues or no improvement on the daily life in the West Bank.

The emerging factional violence under the Israeli occupation is reminiscent of the inter-Palestinian fighting in the 1936 uprising when Palestine was under the British Mandate. Hamas-Fatah fighting will kill the last hope of ending the occupation and establishing their independent state.

ANNAPOLIS PEACE MEETING

After neglecting the Palestinian issue for seven years, President Bush called for a Middle East peace conference to be held in Annapolis, Maryland, on November 27, 2007, only one year before the end of his presidency. The conference turned out to be just a meeting where representatives of the Middle East governments and other international organizations were invited to witness another start of peace negotiations. Olmert and Abbas had met more than six times to formulate an agreed on perception of the final settlement of the issues. Palestinian and Israeli negotiating teams held series of meetings in an effort to draft a joint document to be presented to the Annapolis peace meetings but they failed to agree on anything substantive. Their opening statements in the meeting reflected deep differences on how to revive the peace talks. The Palestinians wanted the pre-conference joint document to address future borders, Jerusalem and the fate of the refugees. But the Israelis wanted the joint statement to address these issues in general terms without mentioning any principles regarding the final status issues. Israel wanted the memorandum to include two points: a commitment by the PA to fulfill its obligations under the first phase of the "Roadmap" and, secondly, a reference to US President George Bush's letter of guarantees to former Prime Minister Ariel Sharon of June 2004. While the two negotiating teams were trying to find common grounds, Abbas declared in a televised speech that he was open to the idea of Palestinian land swap with equivalent Israeli land. He stated that he was willing to make some border adjustment to the 6205 square kilometers in the West Bank and Gaza that the Palestinians claim as long as they end with the same number of square kilometers. In exchange for the West Bank land that Israel intends to keep in any final settlement, Israel is reportedly considering transferring to the Palestinians part of the area separating the Gaza Strip and the West Bank in a final peace agreement. The two areas are separated by about 40 kilometers of Israeli territory. When the swap idea was floated by the Palestinian leaders, the Israeli military confiscated 279 acres of Palestinian land in the West Bank to continue the expansion of Jewish only settlements and divide the Palestinians into disconnected areas. The expropriated land belongs to residents of four Palestinian villages between Jerusalem and Jericho.

Despite the failure to reach a joint document for the Annapolis conference, Arab states including Saudi Arabia and Syria decided to attend it, each for their own reasons, but the announced reason for their attendance was the hope that it would jump-start the stagnant Palestinian–Israeli negotiations. The Egyptian President, Hussni Mubarak and the Arab League Secretary-General Amr Moussa talked about "sincere hopes," rather than optimism that the meeting would lead to success. From Olmert's point of view "the mere convocation of the Annapolis meeting was considered a success" simply by showing up and sitting down with representatives of sixteen Arab states, some of them for the first time. Representatives from the Arab League, the Organization of Islamic Conference and the UN and the European Union attended the meeting. Olmert would not commit Israel to any outcome or a deadline for the final talks. Arab states that attended the meeting in effect surrendered the Palestinian issue to the US government and the meeting became another milestone on the road to the illusive peace.

The pledges for peace negotiations are meaningless if Abbas does not speak for the Palestinians in both the West Bank and Gaza. The plight of the 1.4 million Palestinians in Gaza was not on the agenda. Hamas, the Islamist movement that won 2006 elections seized full control of Gaza in 2007 after a near civil war with its rival, Fatah. Crossing to Egypt or entry to Israel has been completely closed since then. The closures and reduction of fuel and electricity supplies by Israel since September when Israel declared Gaza a "hostile entity" was intended to pressure Hamas to relinquish control of the Strip. The closures prevented the Gazans from traveling in and out of Gaza and stopped the export of the agricultural products and the import of supplies including food, medicine and medical equipment and spare parts. The effect of these measures resulted in economic collapse and the reliance of the population on the UN food hand out and the smuggled basic needs from Egypt through underground tunnels to counter the ongoing siege.

THE 2008 ISRAELI WAR ON GAZA

Despite the siege and starvation of the world's most densely populated strip, Israel failed to dislodge Hamas from Gaza; and Gaza under Hamas became more defiant, a symbol of resistance against the occupation. With no outside help, Gaza became a base for home made primitive projectiles fired against Israel, causing little damage and widespread fear in the towns of southern Israel. Hamas and Israel agreed on a six-month truce to start on June 19, 2008, but none of the two parties complied with the truce completely and Israel continued the siege of the Strip that was imposed in June 2007. On November 4, 2008, Israeli military violated the truce by carrying out a raid into the Strip, killing six Palestinians, and then Hamas and other militant groups retaliated with sporadic rocket fire. Israel launched more across-border attacks killing several more Palestinians and Hamas fired more rockets into Israeli towns that did not kill or injure any Israelis.

Although Israel's military took many steps to undermine the six month ceasefire with Hamas and escalated the crisis, Israel claimed it had no choice but to launch a massive offensive on Gaza to stop rocket attacks on its southern area. Israel unleashed and sustained heavy bombing assault from air, sea and ground on Gaza on December 27, 2008. Israel turned the Strip into a target practice area using all sorts of munitions including banned weapons against the Palestinians while the world including the Arab and Muslim states stood by and watched. Its first targets were government and civilian institutions and humanitarian infrastructures, police stations, schools, social centers, universities, mosques, clinics, farms, small factories and water and sewage systems. The Israeli Air Force dropped more than 500 bombs in the first few minutes of the assault on Gaza killing more than 400 Palestinians according to the UN Office of the Coordination of Humanitarian Affairs (OCHA). After three weeks of continuous assault on the crowded neighborhoods, ambulances transporting the injured, relief trucks carrying food supplies, UN schools while housing families running for their lives from the Israeli indiscriminate bombing, and the UNRWA compound injuring some of its employees and setting fire to food and fuel while the UN Secretary-General, Ban Ki-Moon was holding talks in Jerusalem. Israel attack killed more than 1,400, most of them children and women, and injured more than 5,300.

It was very troubling and sad that more than 80% of the Israeli public supported, with no reservation, their government's aggression against the Palestinians that murdered more than 440 children and 300 mothers and left about 600 children wounded, with thousands needing urgent psychotherapy. These "military" actions, which have been described by the Red Cross, the UN human rights organizations and Amnesty International as war crimes and breaches of the Geneva Convention, include "bulldozing houses with civilian families inside, killing civilians who were raising white flags attempting to escape the bombed war zone, opening fire on ambulances trying to reach the injured and firing white phosphorus shells and dime bombs on crowded civilian residential areas." The findings published in the UK medical and research journal *Lancet* in February 2009 revealed the atrocities were greater than any picture or television image could convey.

The popularity of this massacre's architects, Prime Minister Ehud Olmert, Foreign Minister Tzipi Livni and Defense Minister Ehud Barak, rose significantly among the Israelis, and some demanded that the military should hit the Palestinians even harder. It was suggested by the Israeli media that the attack on Gaza had been planned by the Israeli leadership to rehabilitate the Israeli military for its failure in its July–August 2006 war against the Lebanese Hizbullah. The attack was carried out during the holiday season and the political transition in the White House when the US was less likely to disapprove or restrain Israel.

The *Independent* newspaper reported that more than 8,000 homes had been destroyed completely, some of them on top of their occupants and 21,000 homes seriously damaged. The indiscriminate killing of the Palestinians in Gaza, where people have no where to go and no means to defend themselves, is a mindless tragedy that will make peace less likely to reign in Palestine. The Israeli atrocities created an environment among the Palestinians that guarantees the resurgence of armed response by surviving victims. The *Observer* suggested that the "status of Hamas as a preferred vehicle for resistance is enhanced" among the Palestinians because of this aggression. The bloody attack on Gaza provoked countless calls from all over the world and even from the Israeli peace advocates for bringing Israel's political and military leaders to the international courts to answer for their criminal actions. Amid worldwide condemnation of the death and destruction caused by the Israeli war, the UN Human Rights Council (HRC) adopted a resolution setting up a committee headed by a South African Judge Richard Goldstone to investigate the likelihood that war crimes and crimes against humanity were committed by Israel and Hamas during the onslaught on Gaza. Hamas cooperated fully but Israel refused to cooperate with the investigating team then the fact-finding committee was forced to collect data and probe into the Israeli practices from the physical evidence and the eyewitnesses in Gaza and the Arab countries bordering Israel. The committee report said Israel used disproportionate force and failed to protect civilians during its December 27–January 18 offensive against the Palestinians in Gaza. Goldstone recommended referring the report conclusions to the International Criminal Court prosecutor in The Hague if Israel fails to conduct credible investigations within six months.

Mahmoud Abbas complied with American and Israeli demands by instructing his representative in Geneva to ask for delaying the vote on the report for six months. That would have buried the report, but the uproar among the Palestinian public at what was perceived as a betrayal by Abbas to his people forced him to change course. He could not ignore the popular rebellion against him by his own people demanding his resignation. He ordered his representative in Geneva to reinstate the report resolution for voting by the Human Rights Council (HRC). The report was endorsed by the HR 25 votes to 6, with 11 abstentions. The report asked Israel to investigate its own actions against the Palestinians, but the US under Obama took sides with Israel against the report, suggesting the massacres of a defenseless and long-persecuted civilian population were justified as self-defense.

After the Fatah and Hamas factions failed to bury their hatchets and rejected efforts to present a united front, Mahmoud Abbas issued a decree to hold presidential and legislative elections on January 24, 2010, across the occupied territory including Hamas-controlled Gaza Strip. Hamas leaders branded the decree unconstitutional and questioned its political motives. They decided not to allow the presidential or parliamentary elections to take place in Gaza as called for by Ramallah based President Abbas. They accused Abbas of exceeding his legal authority because his term had been over since January 2009, and his action was a "deliberate attempt to make Palestinians division permanent." Abbas could have waited until there was conciliation with Hamas, because elections without Gaza participation would not give him the legitimacy needed to negotiate on behalf of the Palestinian.

With the deep intra-Palestinian rift, it is difficult for the Palestinians to be optimistic. As long as the Palestinians are divided, their power to explain their case to the international community will be limited. Unless they reconcile their differences and unite, they will have nobody to blame but themselves for being locked into truncated Bantustans on no more than 15% of historical Palestine and nothing to show for the sacrifices that they offered over the years.

CHAPTER 11. THE NEED FOR LIBERATION WITHOUT VIOLENCE

This study concludes that an independent Palestinian state is impossible to achieve as long as the endless cycle of violence is not broken; the Palestinians are bitterly divided politically with Hamas governing the Palestinians in Gaza and Fatah only nominally governs the Palestinians in the West Bank; the Israeli people elect right-wing governments bent on aggression and expansion; and the US follows a policy of blind support for Israel even when the latter breaches the peremptory norms.

If there is any hope for establishing the sovereign Palestinian state, there have to be basic course correction in the positions of the key players in the conflict. Palestinians should end factionalism and develop a common political agenda and methods of non-violent struggle; the Israeli electorate political orientation should move away from the ideology of conquest and the persecution of the Palestinians; and the US traditional Middle East foreign policy of blind support to Israel should be transformed into a real even-handed approach. But none of the players is ready to correct course.

Extremism by one side of the conflict breeds extremism on the other side. The 1936 Palestinian revolt was a response to the second wave of Jewish immigrants from Russia after 1903, the "Second Aliyah," They were militant Zionists with radical nationalist ideas of the "conquest of labor" and "conquest of land."

The Israeli society militarism and the culture of violence against the Palestinians in the lands occupied since 1967 led the Palestinians to carry out violent acts against the settlers and civilian targets in Israel in the Second Intifada. Ariel Sharon was elected in 2001 on a platform to break the Palestinian resistance using disproportionate force to end the Intifada threat. He promised the Israelis to keep beating the Palestinians "until they get the message." When Israel followed policy of incursions, abductions, killing of civilians, and targeted assassinations against the Palestinians, then the militant Hamas won the 2006 Legislative Council elections. The Palestinians elected Hamas because of the despair brought on by the occupation and the systematic Israeli terror against them, not because they wanted an Islamic state. The Israeli peace camp has been weakened, as a result, and the Israeli-Jews became even more radicalized, electing right-wing governments.

Israel holds all the cards to the solution and the absolute power to prolong the conflict; and it has the means to convince the international community that the Palestinian resistance in any form is an act of terror for the sake of terror and that the Palestinians are not willing to live in peace.

The Palestinians lost each time they or their "Arab allies" resorted to violence for reasons that have been covered in the previous chapters. They lost in their 1936-1939 uprising and the Yishuv community won; they lost when the Arab states declared war to liberate Palestine in 1948, and Israel was established over 78% of historical Palestine; they lost again in the 1967 war when the Arab states surrendered the rest of Palestine. They lost in the 1973 war that was followed by the Egyptian-Israeli peace treaty which freed Israel to consolidate its hold on the Palestinian occupied land. The Palestinians lost when the PLO established military bases in Jordan and challenged the state institutions of the host country. They lost the good will of the Lebanese people when the PLO participated in the Lebanese bloody civil war making it easy for Israel to send them to exile in 1982. And the Palestinians lost the international public support when they carried out suicide bombings in the Second *Intifada* and Israel responded with mass killings, executions, imprisonment, land seizure, human right violations, and convinced the world it was acting in self-defense and portrayed the Palestinians as savages and terrorists.

The Palestinians won in the First *Intifada* by resorting to civil disobedience campaign and stone-throwing as the expression of discontent against the repressive occupation. They demonstrated that the Palestinians can resist peacefully and win without conceding their rights. As explained in Chapter 3, the Israeli army lost the battle for world public opinion and the Palestinians won even among many Israeli Jews in the First *Intifada*. The Palestinians' right to be free was recognized — until the PLO leaders stepped in and squandered the gains of the *Intifada* by signing the Oslo Agreements that disregarded international law as applied to occupied land.

Chances for a just solution today are diminished due to structural constraints created by the militants in both sides of the conflict. The Palestinian factions in Gaza and the hard-line Jewish settlers in the occupied lands have developed institutional infrastructures that circumscribe the authorities of their respective central administrations. Hamas which governs Gaza and commands sizable support in the West Bank and East Jerusalem does not recognize Israel as long as there are settlers in the occupied lands and the refugees are denied the right of return; and the right wing Israeli settlers warned their government, which emphatically rejects Palestinians' rights, against compromising on the occupied lands. Settler Council leaders oppose any curb on Jewish settlement expansion in the occupied land. When Netanyahu announced in 2009 his government would stop issuing building permits for 10 months, they decided to bar the Israeli government construction inspectors from going into their communities. Netanyahu's moratorium excluded East

Jerusalem as well as construction of public buildings and allows for the completion of hundreds of units already under construction.

Israeli Jewish population elect right-wing governments following a policy of territorial expansion, denying the Palestinians their fundamental right of statehood and rejecting the UN resolutions, knowing well they enjoy immunity for their actions through the US backing. Israel's ideology of conquest has prolonged the conflict and subverted the peace initiatives and it has not been held accountable for its illegal acts. The Israelis deny they are occupiers; they offer the Palestinians a truncated, non-viable semi-sovereign state on part of the "disputed lands" (occupied lands) and maintain a tight grip on the areas where the Palestinians live.

The century old Palestinian–Israeli conflict has been a global issue and its eventual resolution cannot be achieved in isolation as a local conflict between Israel, the Middle East super-power, and the PA leaders of the occupied defenseless, impoverished besieged Palestinians. The international community must get involved to enforce solutions according to the international laws and protect the interests of the weak party. The Oslo Accords agreements that were negotiated by Israel and the PLO are a prime example. The Accords side-stepped the international laws and the UN resolutions only to realize the long standing Allon Plan which would give Israel more than 35% of the West Bank and all of East Jerusalem, and allow the Palestinians to have a limited autonomy in fragmented cantons. Chapter 4 described Allon Plan in more detail.

The Palestinian–Israeli negotiations failed to conclude an agreement after seventeen years since the signing of the 1993 Declaration of Principles (DOP), but it took only five years between the 1977 Anwar Sadat historic visit to Israel and the withdrawal from all Sinai in 1982. Even under a right-wing Likud government, Israel had to withdraw from Sinai because the US crafted a strategy of solving the Egyptian–Israeli conflict as a top priority that persisted from one administration to the next. But the US administrations have paid only lip service to the Palestinian–Israeli conflict, and their involvement can best be described as episodic. They called conferences or assigned special envoys, and when the presidents participated, they did that during the waning months of their administrations and sided with Israel. When President Clinton was briefly involved in the failed 2000 Camp David summit that was predicated on a sense of Israel's absolute security needs, he acted as "Israel's lawyer," rather than a mediator, by pressuring Arafat to accept Israel's offer of a Palestinian Bantustan entity. Despite the skewed imbalance of power in favor of the Israelis, the US chose to side with the dominant party that had exercised its occupation power to unilaterally impose and sustain facts on the ground. To exercise its moral authority, the US should have balanced the scale of power between the two parties to protect the interests of the weak negotiators, the Palestinians. Peace in Palestine based on international law and justice serves the interests of the US and Israel, but Washington leaders have been unwilling to act as honest brokers. There is no contradiction between having special relations with Israel and to be tough as an impartial mediator, but the blind bipartisan support for Israeli hardliners has limited the US capacity to act as an effective mediator. Such support to Israel is so deeply entrenched that it has become institutionalized.

Without reconciliation and end to the strife between the Palestinian factions, no effort from within or outside would help them achieve independence. Israel, the US and the Pro-West Arab governments took sides in the Palestinian faction rivalry. They supported Fatah by recognizing Abbas and his faction as the legitimate Palestinian leadership. When Hamas came to power, and especially since it routed Fatah forces and established its own administration in Gaza, the leadership of the Egyptian regime treated Hamas at its border as a national security threat. Hamas has roots in Egypt's illegal Muslim Brothers Party (MB). The Egyptian regime fears the military wing of Hamas links with disgruntled members from the MB which maintains popular support among the Egyptian people. Leaders of Egypt, the PA and Israel have common interest in overthrowing Hamas regime in Gaza. Israel that supports only "moderate" leadership and holds the people of Gaza hostages has the power to make their lives under Hamas intolerable especially after securing the collaboration of Egypt and the PA. Israel opposes any dealing with Hamas, calls it a terrorist organization and accuses it of being a proxy for Iran, the country that is perceived as the greatest threat to Israel. Egypt tries to end or at least contain the Islamic movement militarism within the Palestinian territory and not to spill over to Egypt. Both of Israel and Egypt sealed their borders with the Gaza Strip, effectively cutting off the Strip from the rest of the world. The life of the 1.4 million Gazans became a daily reminder that Hamas brings nothing but suffering and sense of insecurity. This raises doubts about Egypt's ability to mediate an accord between Hamas and Fatah. The PA self-rule security agencies have been carrying out a campaign against Hamas supporters in the West Bank. They closed down charitable organizations, clinics, schools and sports clubs that had been linked to Hamas.

Palestinian militants' attacks on civilian targets in Israel proper played a major role in alienating the Israeli public against a just peace by encouraging them to vote for the militant right-wing parties and ultra-Orthodox factions. The attacks on civilians made it difficult for the Israeli peace advocates to compete against the militant extremists and attract supporters to influence their government policy. Israelis and Palestinians, like people all over the world, are potentially fair-minded and compassionate. Many Jewish people and organizations in Israel, the US and Europe are against the policies of Israel's human rights abuses of the Palestinians and the illegal annexation of the occupied territory. This constituency must be addressed by the Palestinians instead of the exclusive focus on the official Israeli policy makers. Hard-line Israelis dominate the Israeli political establishment today, but many Israelis and Diaspora-Jews and Jewish intellectuals and civil rights organizations have opposed the ideology of conquest and the colonization of the occupied lands.

The late Martin Buber, a renowned Israeli Jewish philosopher and educator, was an advocate of the establishment of a bi-national liberal democratic state in all Palestine even before Israel occupied the West Bank and Gaza. Professor Israel Shahak, an outspoken critic of Israel's policies towards the Palestinians and a former president of the Israeli

League for Human Rights, was a strong supporter of an independent Palestinian state. Professor Uri Avnery, a one time member of the terrorist organization Irgun, then he denounced violence and Zionism and became a peace and civil rights activist. He was a victim of assassination attempt for his stand against the West Bank settlers. The historian Ilan Pappe wrote extensively on the deliberate Israeli military campaigns to cleanse Israel from the Palestinians in the 1948 war. Professor Zeev Sternhell, a 73-year-old Holocaust survivor and a peace activist, is against the occupation and settlements. He referred to the settlements as Israel's imperial expansion. Sternhell was wounded by a pipe bomb detonated at his front door in September 2008. Israeli settlers are suspected of planting the bomb because of his stand against settlements. Simha Flapan, an Israeli writer and a peace activist, argued that it was the Israelis who had forced the Palestinian refugees to flee their homes in 1948 war. Professor Neve Gordon of Ben-Gurion University of the Negev and a human rights advocate published an article in the *Los Angeles Times* on August 20, 2009 explaining why Israel needs external pressure including sanctions, divestment and economic, cultural and academic boycott to force it end the occupation and the suffering they inflict on the Palestinians. Jeff Halper, an Israeli peace activist and co-founder of the "Committee against Home Demolition" led protests against the Israeli government policy of arbitrary decisions to demolish Palestinian homes in East Jerusalem. He argues that Cultural Zionism in a Jewish and Arab bi-national state "would preserve a vibrant Israeli culture, a powerful economy and a possibility of reconciliation [with the Palestinians]." The organization of "Machsom Watch" is an Israeli women's group that watches the behavior of Israeli soldiers at check-points in the West Bank and opposes the occupation. Its members document and write about the suffering of the Palestinians who wait for hours to be searched by the Israeli soldiers; sometimes the sick die in ambulances because they are not allowed by the soldiers to get to the hospitals. Gideon Spiro, an Israeli peace activist, arrived on a boat with more than 20 pro-Palestinian European activists from Cyprus to Gaza on October 29, 2008, breaking the Israeli embargo against the Palestinians in Gaza Strip. The group included the Irish co-recipient of the Nobel Peace Prize, Misread Corrigan. Several times a week during 2008 and 2009, some Israelis and international supporters join the Palestinian villagers of Nihlin in the village olive fields protesting the bulldozers that had been tearing up the land to make way for the separation wall that cuts off 40% of the village farmland, effectively annexing it to the settlements that surround the village. Their non-violent protest included praying in the path of the heavy machinery, and banging pots and pans.

Some officials in the UK are against the Israeli occupation and the policy of settlement. The British Foreign Office warned Britons in December 2008 against buying property in all areas occupied by Israel during the 1967 war. The Norwegian government pulled all its investment in the Israeli company Elbit for its participation in building the separation wall in the West Bank. The December 2008 Israeli attacks on Gaza provoked anger by people and organizations from all over the world including Israel itself. World-wide peace activists and human rights groups ran relentless campaigns to hold Israel to account for the alleged war crimes against the Palestinians in Gaza. Due to their tireless efforts, the

UN Human Rights Council decided to reactivate Goldstone's report to the UN Security Council despite the US pressure and boycott by the Europeans. At the same time, lawyers in Britain, The Netherlands, Spain, Belgium and Norway were drawing up criminal indictments against Israeli military officers who participated in the Gaza operation based on "universal jurisdiction." J-Street, a US political action committee was established in 2008 by US Jews who believe Israel will better its-self and improve its image internationally by withdrawing from the occupied lands including the Syrian Golan area. The J-Street members vow to support American diplomatic engagement to achieve peace in the Middle East based on the two-state solution. On December 7, 2009, a resolution passed by the EU foreign ministers to recognize Jerusalem the capital of both Israel and a future Palestinian state. The original draft did not recognize Israel's claims to East Jerusalem, but pressure from pro-Israel groups and the US to make the necessary changes to the original text, prevailed. The pressure groups persuaded the foreign ministers to include the "Jewish character" issue in the statement calling for the EU to "promote direct negotiations between the parties, while considering Israel's security needs and understanding that Israel's Jewish character must be preserved in any future agreements." Even after complying with the demands of the pressure groups, Israeli Jerusalem Mayor Nir Barkat rejected the EU recommendation to give the Palestinians any rights in East Jerusalem claiming it would "never work."[1]

If left alone, Israel will continue its program of land grab and naked abuse. It can unilaterally use its military and economic powers to impose facts on the ground. The right-wing Israeli leaders believe in the Law of "might is right." But Israeli wars on Gaza and Lebanon have demonstrated that sheer military force cannot accomplish everything in international disputes. Israel succeeded in creating one of the most powerful military systems in the world but it certainly could not guaranty its own security or resolve the ongoing conflict that spans more than a century of open hostilities. It has tried in its wars to achieve security at any cost including strangulation and death, starving non-combatant civilians and the destruction of homes and infrastructures. The campaigns against the Palestinians and the Lebanese provided for an impressive display of the Israeli military power, but the strategy was counter-productive. It demonstrated the futility of Israel's conviction that the use of its military advantage is the answer to all its problems with its neighbors. Instead of destroying Hizbullah, the 2006 war transformed it from a Lebanese organization to a popular militant group in the Arab and Islamic world. The war and the financial blockade on Hamas controlled Gaza led the Palestinian resistance to establish closer ties with Hizbullah and Iran. Another casualty of Israel's wars was the influence, legitimacy and credibility of the moderate Arab regimes that had made peace with Israel. The wars might have even spurred the proliferation of radical groups bent on undermining the security of Israel. The underlying cause of the conflict is Israel's decades-old occupation of the West Bank and Gaza, East Jerusalem and other Arab lands, and denying the refugees right of repatriation and compensation for their losses.

---

1 *Jerusalem Post*, December 8, 2009.

The 2006 US bipartisan advisory "Iraq Study Group" headed by James Baker and Lee Hamilton concluded that solving the Israeli–Palestinian conflict is a key element in achieving stability and rein in extremism in the Middle East. The report stated among other things that, "The United States cannot attain its goals in the Middle East unless it deals directly with the Arab–Israeli conflict." The US can solve the century old conflict if it acts as an impartial persistent mediator. It has the power, the means and the moral authority and the motives to influence the policies of Israel and induce it to end the occupation for the sake of peace with justice. The last time the US used its power to settle a major Middle East conflict and enforce peace was under President Eisenhower, when it forced Israel to withdraw from Sinai and the Gaza Strip after the 1956 war with Egypt. But under President Clinton, the US conception of peace was to grant the Palestinians limited rights and no sovereignty. President George W. Bush administration even became part of the problem rather than the solution. He provided unlimited support and blind endorsement of Israel's policy to ensure hegemony over all of historical Palestine. The US made Israel less amenable to make decisions required for implementing the United Nations resolutions.

President Obama's tone in speeches and interviews differs substantially from that of his predecessor, but there is nothing in practical terms that suggests his administration policy will be different on the Palestinian issue. Obama has never condemned the Israeli attacks on civilian targets in Gaza and his special envoy to the Middle East, George Mitchell, visited the region many times in 2009 — but he never included Gaza in his itinerary. Gaza was the site of Israeli attacks that resulted in thousands of Palestinians dead and injured and reduced homes, schools, mosques, government civil administration and civil infrastructures to rubble. The UN fact-finding mission report on the possibility of war crimes in the December–January Israeli war on Gaza Strip was described by Obama's administration as "flawed" instead of insisting that Israel comply with international law. The report concluded that both Israel and Hamas committed war crimes and possible crimes against humanity during the conflict. Regarding the Israeli settlements, Obama's position against their expansion, early on, promised to be a positive step toward peace. He was very clear when he announced that there should be no construction in any of the settlements or outposts, not even to meet natural growth. Then his position on the settlement freeze softened and Israel's drive to expand the settlements prevailed. In a significant departure from her previous statements demanding a total settlement freeze without exception, Secretary of State Hillary Clinton praised Israel on October 31, 2009 in Jerusalem for making "unprecedented concessions" on West Bank settlement construction by deciding to build "only" 3,000 housing units in the West Bank and continue construction in East Jerusalem. If Obama's administration does not have the will to make Israel freeze settlements expansion, then there will be little hope it will use its influence to make it vacate settlements and end the occupation. Obama's policy in the Middle East will be an extension of Bush foreign policy. There is little hope for a just solution under the US sponsorship because it supports the Israeli hegemony and its policy of controlling the entire "Land of Israel." Merely for the sake of closing the issue and proving its policy is not a complete failure, the US is willing to encourage Israel to make slight modifications to its plans for a truncated Palestinian mini-state that could be sold as an Israeli "painful concession" for the two-state solution.

When the Palestinians are denied their human rights and social justice and forced to succumb to eternal occupation or apartheid, every group or person throughout the world aspiring to be free of oppression and all free and decent people will lose as well. The US and the European countries have proved singularly and collectively unwilling to impose international law on Israel. If the US fails to correct course and act as impartial mediator, the Palestinians should find other means to plead their case. After sacrificing so much over the years and, under the aegis of the PLO, the willingness to settle for only 22% of their historic homeland, the Palestinians must continue to adhere to nonviolent options; but they must not accept the status quo which constitutes nothing but a form of apartheid.

This is a review of some nonviolent options that the Palestinians may be contemplating:

The first option is the focus on establishing a bi-national state or a "one-liberal-democratic-state" in all historical Palestine that grants equal rights to all its citizens including the Palestinians. This concept was promoted by the early Cultural Zionists, who opposed the establishment of a Jewish state and called for a bi-national-Jewish-Arab state or one-liberal-democratic state, like Asher Ginzberg (Achad HaAm), Yitzhak Epstein, Martin Buber, Albert Antebe, Henrietta Szold, David Yellin and Rabbi Judah Leib Magnes, and it was the main demand by the Palestinians prior to 1988. The one-liberal-democratic state solution where both peoples live together in a secular country realizes the dream of these visionaries who believed Zionism should create a "national spiritual center" for the revival of Judaism and that the policy of conquest was a deviation from the Jewish traditions and teaching of justice and human brotherhood. The "Cultural Zionists" lost to the "political Zionists" from the beginning and Israel was established and sustained by Jabotinsky and Ben Gurion militarism on the basis of ethnocracy and transforming Palestine into the "Land of Israel." The prevailing ideology among Israeli Jews and the policies of their governments today leave no room for any Palestinian claims in the "Land of Israel." Israeli leaders today are committed to keeping Israel an ethnocratic state, demanding that the Arabs should recognize the Jewish character of Israel — which makes the Israeli–Arabs vulnerable to expulsion because they are perceived as "demographic time bomb." The bi-national state based on religion has been tried in countries like Lebanon, Sri Lanka and recently in Iraq; the model established limited stability but has not created happy societies. Israelis across the political spectrum fear a one-state solution would lead to a Palestinian majority. Housing and Construction Minister Ariel Attias suggested Jews and Israeli–Arabs should not live together in the same neighborhood. He was quoted by the *Jerusalem Post* telling the Israeli Bar Associations in July 2009, "We can all be bleeding hearts, but I think it is unsuitable to live together.... Arabs don't have anyplace to live, so they buy apartments in places with a Jewish nature, which causes unwanted friction." The one-liberal-democratic state option is a genuine solution to the conflict, but it is a non-starter for most Israeli Jews, and the international community cannot be persuaded to impose it on Israel. The Israeli President Shimon Peres was combative in his response to a question about the call for one-state solution option. He said on November 7, 2009: "Those who reject the two-state solution must not bring a one-state solution. They will instead bring one war, not one state."

The second option is accepting a state with provisional or temporary borders. A state with temporary borders recognized by Israel and the US is not the solution to the Palestinian issue but it is better as a starting point than the self-rule authority based on Oslo agreements if it includes major changes to the status quo. The Palestinians who have been living under occupation may have good reasons to consider this option if it is tied to halting colonization, ending the Israeli siege, withdrawing the military and ending the military incursions. The offer should not end the Palestinians' claim to sovereignty over all the occupied land and the refugees' right of return. If these conditions are not met, then the proposed state with temporary borders will be nothing but the status quo under a new name and dignified with the label of a "state." Palestinians living in non-viable prison-Bantustan will not feel the difference if their homeland is called "self-rule" or "state." The problem with this option is that Israel may transform the temporary situation into a permanent political fact accepted by the international community. Offering temporary borders at this moment when Obama and the Palestinians ask for freezing the settlements expansion suggest Israel will certainly use a transitional state to prolong the negotiations so as to maintain the status quo and strengthen its hold over the occupied lands.

The third option is declaring unilaterally a Palestinian state on all the occupied lands and asking for recognition from the international community. Frustrated at the lack of progress in peace negotiations with Israel and disappointment by the US failure to halt Israeli settlements expansion, leaders of the PA announced in November 2009 a plan to unilaterally declare a Palestinian state in the occupied lands and ask for recognition by the UNGA and the Security Council. Should the Palestinians decide to declare their state and the UN Security Council approves it, any Israeli presence across the 1967 borders, including the settlements and the military bases, will be a breach of the UN resolution. The Palestinians had declared such a state in 1988 but it was ignored by the international community and the subject has been forgotten after the Oslo agreements. The PA that was created by the Oslo agreements is wholly dependent on the flow of aid from the US and the economic ties with Israel. It is in no position to make decisions without the approval of its two benefactors, the US and Israel. Should the Palestinians declare their own state, most nations represented in the UNGA would recognize it, but the countries that count most are Israel and the Untied States. The unilateral proposition by the Palestinians was immediately rejected by the Israelis, who claim a monopoly on illegal unilateral practices in the occupied lands — because they have the power. The Israeli leaders have threatened to annex more Palestinian lands if the Palestinians declare their state. And the US will certainly use its veto power to kill the proposal altogether, if it reaches the Security Council, as it always has done. Delaware Senator Ted Kaufman said of this proposal on November 18, 2009, "It is a waste of time." Even if the Security Council approved the unilaterally-declared Palestinian state, it would not address the refugees' right of return and the US will not allow Israel to be forced to comply. The UNGA issued many resolutions regarding the Palestinian conflict in the past, and they have been ignored by Israel.

A fourth option is for the Palestinians to disband the PA negotiating team and surrender the negotiations to the pro-West Arab states. This entails abandoning the outdated 1993–1995 Oslo Accords that Israel has been using as a cover to further colonization and to bypass the UN resolutions and the international laws. Disbanding the PA negotiating team casts doubts on the legitimacy of the PA leadership among their people since the only reason for the PA existence has been to negotiate. If the PA cannot negotiate and cannot live without negotiations, then it must disband itself, but the PA leaders will not give up the privileges they enjoy under the status quo even if there is no progress in the negotiations. Saudi Arabia, Egypt and Jordan may like to play a role in the process to provide a face-saving option for the PA leadership and because they do not want the Palestinians to abort the stagnant "peace process." They are strong backers of the PA leadership; they have good relations with the US; and King Abdullah of Saudi Arabia was the author of the 2002 Arab peace initiative when he was the Crown Prince. Jordan and Egypt have peace agreements and full diplomatic relations with Israel, but Jordan will most likely excuse itself from accepting a major role in negotiating on behalf of the Palestinians lest the Israeli Foreign Minister Avigdor Lieberman raises the subject of Jordan as a substitute homeland for the Palestinians. Lieberman advocated expelling the Arab–Israelis to the PA controlled area or to Jordan. He never concealed his desire to see no Palestinian left living in historical Palestine. Even most Jewish Israelis share his views today. In a survey of 6,400 Israelis as to the best solution to the Palestinian–Israeli conflict, 53.2% of the respondents chose transferring the Palestinians from the PA to Jordan.[1] Egypt's government leaders are the only Arabs who have been actively mediating between Israel and Hamas to secure the release of Gilad Shalit, the Israeli soldier captured by Palestinian fighters in Gaza. They also mediated between Fatah and Hamas. Saudi Arabia has no diplomatic relations with Israel, but it would use its close relations with the US to pressure Israel to respond positively to the comprehensive Arab peace initiative. The international community, especially the US, will be most supportive to a comprehensive regional approach for peace. But the success of such a strategy depends on Israel's willingness to make the necessary concessions. Arab peace initiative that had been announced in 2002 was rejected by Israel at the time, but in the 2008 two-day UN Interfaith Conference, the Israeli President Shimon Peres praised King Abdullah of Saudi Arabia call for all peoples and nations to promote peace, harmony and tolerance. When Shimon Peres took the floor in the conference, he told the delegates that building a new future in the Middle East "seems more feasible today in light of the Saudi proposal which evolved into an Arab Peace Initiative." Peres looked directly at the King and said, "I was listening to your message. I wish that your voice will become the prevailing voice of the whole region." But President Peres had no executive power in Israel and the Arab states are too weak, disunited and lack common purpose or power to back any decision they make individually or collectively. The Arab states became passive spec-

---

1 American Friends of Magen David Adom, November 19, 2009.

tators when Arafat was holed up in his Ramallah compound and perhaps killed because he had outlived his usefulness to Israel, or when the Israeli military attacked Lebanon in 1978, 1982 and 2006, or when Israel destroyed Gaza in 2008–09. The problem with the Arab states is they cannot be trusted. They have been accomplices in the Palestinians infighting and partners with Israel in Gaza siege even after they pledged to break the siege and fund Hamas-led PA government in March 2006 summit meeting. The Arab states that surrendered Palestinians' lands in 1948 and 1967 through their incompetence and corruption, instigating mutual antagonism and promoting their own agendas in secret cannot be trusted to help the Palestinians achieve their national goals.

A fifth option is a nonviolent campaign demanding the enforcement of the Fourth Geneva Convention and the previous UN resolutions in the occupied lands. The Palestinians have the right to use all means to resist occupation, but by adopting a strategy of peaceful protest, civil disobedience and boycotting the Israeli products, the Palestinians can produce needed international support for their struggle and strengthen Israel's peace camp. Civil disobedience makes occupation too costly to maintain and unacceptable by the international community. Palestinians can use non-traditional methods to challenge the international community to exercise its moral responsibility, enforce the provisions of the Fourth Geneva Convention and pressure Israel to end the occupation. Palestinians and their Arab and Jewish supporters should appeal for freedom and justice to human rights advocates, churches, synagogues, temples and other faith-based organizations, trade unions, political groups and intellectuals everywhere. The new forms of communications, the internet, twitter, blogs, real-time chat rooms and discussion forums can be employed to breakdown borders, transmit text and video, reach and inform potential supporters all over the world. The strategy is to provide people of good will sufficient facts about life under occupation where millions of the indigenous Palestinians are confined to tiny enclaves surrounded by massive Jews-only settlements, Jews-only highways, roadblocks and the separation wall. The Palestinians should invite liberal journalists and human rights activists and organizations from Israel, the US and Europe to monitor the behavior of the Israeli government and the settlers in the occupied lands and hold the Israelis accountable for their failure to accede to the international laws.

When people who value justice and the right of a people to self determination are given sufficient information and rudimentary tools of understanding, they will demand justice for the Palestinians in this century-old conflict. Supporting Israel's right to exist does not mean supporting Israel in subordinating the Palestinians' claims to their historical rights and controlling their destiny. For legal justice, they should turn to the international courts, The Hague International Court of Justice (ICJ), the International Criminal Court and the High Commissioner for Human Rights who holds the rank of Under Secretary-General of the UN.

The case of the Palestinians for justice is easy to explain. The Fourth Geneva Convention prohibits the occupying power from making the control of occupied lands permanent. The right for self-determination and rejection to live under occupation or apartheid conditions in a non-sovereign Bantustan state is an inherited right for the Palestinians.

And Israel's need for "security" or the historical claim to the land based on the Old Testament prophecy cannot justify violating the international laws. But the Palestinians learnt from previous experiences that there is no guaranty that Israel will abide by international courts ruling without international pressure to enforce it. The ICJ ruled in July 2004 the Israeli built separation wall was illegal, because it was built in the occupied lands, and the UNGA ratified the verdict with only five dissenting votes including Israel and the US. Israel ignored the verdict and continued the construction of the wall incorporating more than 7% of the West Bank.

Options of the endgame for the Palestinians must be the establishment of a truly sovereign state over the land occupied in the 1967 war or joining a multi-ethnic liberal democratic state over all historical Palestine. Even if an independent state or a multi-ethnic state is created, there will be no closure to the Palestinian conflict without a just resolution to the refugees' issue. Eighty percent of Palestinians are refugees and any sustainable peace must include Israel's acceptance of its responsibility for the refugees' problem. Israel's acknowledgement of the refugees' right of return on the basis of the UN Resolution 194 should lead to mutually agreed upon repatriation and fair compensation. Arab states too should consider inviting their former Jewish citizens, who immigrated to Israel by choice or force, to return back to their Arab countries of origin, resettle there or compensate them for their abandoned property.

This work condemns all forms of violence and urges the international community (US and Europe) to avoid a replay of the 2000 Camp David summit collapse that led to the second Palestinian uprising which claimed the lives of thousands of Palestinians and Israelis. The status quo has the potential of growing extremism that may lead to even more destruction and bloodshed. The US and Europe must exercise their moral authority by supporting a viable non-violent option to solve the Palestinian issue according to international laws and UN resolutions after wasting decades of empty promises. It is a challenge to their moral conscience, and if they fail to act, they will betray the principles of justice that they claim their civilized societies hold dear.

BIBLIOGRAPHY

Abdel-Aati, Badr Ahmed, *The Egyptian policies toward the Palestinian case: A Study of the Egyptian conception of the Palestinian Autonomy, 1979–1982*, Cairo University, College of Economics and Political Science, 1995.

Antonius, George, *The Arab awakening; the story of the Arab national movement*, Paragon Books, 1979.

Abu-Sitta, Salman, "The Right of Return: Sacred, Legal and Possible." In Aruri, Naseer, ed. *The Palestinian Refugees*, Pluto Press, London. Sterling, VA, 2001.

Avineri, Shlomo, "Political and Social Aspects of Israeli and Arab Nationalism," In Michael Curtis, Joseph Neyer, Chaim Waxman and Allen Pollack, eds.

The Palestinians, Transaction Books, New Brunswick, New Jersey, 1975.

Bar-Joseph, Uri, *The Best of Enemies: Israel and Trans-Jordan in the War of 1948*, London: Frank Cass, 1987.

Bar-On, Mordechai, *In Pursuit of Peace: A History of the Israeli Peace Movement*, Washington D.C.: United States Institute of Peace, 1996.

Bar-Zohar, Michael, *Ben-Gurion: A Biography*, New York: Delacorte Press, 1977

Beattie, Kirk, *Egypt during the Sadat Years*, Palgrave publishing, 2000.

Ben-Gurion, David, *Rebirth and destiny of Israel*, Philosophical Library, New York, 1954.

Ben-Gurion, David, *My Talks with Arab Leaders*, Translated by Aryeh Rubinstein and Misha Louvish, Joseph Okapaku Publishing Company, N.Y, 1973

Ben-Gurion, David, *The War of Independence: Ben-Gurion's Diary*, Gershon Rivlin and Elhannan Orren, editors, Tel Aviv: Israel Defense Ministry Press, 1982.

Blumberg, Arnold, *Zion Before Zionism 1838–1880*, Syracuse University Press 1985.

Brown, Nathan , *Palestinian Politics after the Oslo Accords*, UC Press, 2003.

Buchanan, Andrew, *Peace with Justice*, St.Martin's Press, LLC, N.Y, 2000.

Chomsky, Noam, *The fateful triangle : the United States, Israel and the Palestinians*, South End Press, Boston, 1999.

Cohen, Michael, *The Origin and the Evolution of the Arab-Zionist Conflict*, Berkeley: The University of California Press, 1989.

Cohen, Michael, *Palestine and the Great Powers, 1945-48*, Princeton: Princeton University Press, 1982.

Cooper, Chester, *The Lion's Last Roar: Suez 1956*, New York: Harper and Row, 1978.

Dawn, Ernest, *From Ottomanism to Arabism: Essays on the Origin of Arab Nationalism*, Urbana, Ill., 1973.

Divine, Donna Robinson, *Politics and Society in Ottoman Palestine*, Lynne Rienner Publishers, Boulder, Co 1994.

Eliots, Herman Fredrick, "The United States and Egypt," in Quandt (ed.) *The Middle East: Ten Years After Camp David*, Brookings Institution, 1988.

Epstein, Lawrence, *Zion's Call: Christian Contributions to the Origins and Development of Israel*, New York: University Press of America, 1984.

Epstein, Yitzhak, "the Hidden Question." In Adam Shatz (ed.), *Prophets Outcast: A Century of Dissident Jewish Writing about Zionism and Israel*, Nation Books, New York, 2004.

Evron, Yair, "Two Periods in the Arab–Israeli Strategic Relations." In Itmar Rabinovich and Haim Shaked (eds.), *From June to October: The Middle East between 1978 and 1973*, New Brunswick, N.J.: Transaction Books, 1978.

Fisk, Robert, *The Great War for Civilization: The Conquest of the Middle East*, Alfred Knopf, 2005.

Flapan, Simha, *Zionism and the Palestinians*, Croom Helm ;Barnes & Noble Books, London, New York, 1979.

Furlonge, Geoffrey, *Palestine is my country: the story of Musa Alami*, Murray, London, 1969.

Garner, Deborah, *One Land, Two Peoples: The Conflict Over Palestine*, 2nd edition, Boulder, Colo.: Westview Press, 1994.

Gilber, Yoav, *Jewish-Transjordanian Relations, 1921–1948*, Frank Cass, London, 1997.

Gilber, Yoav, *Israeli–Jordanian Dialogue: 1948–1953*, Sussex Academic Press, Brighton. Portland, 2004.

Gilbert, Martin, *Israel: A History*, New York: William Morrow, 1998.

Glubb, Sir John Bagot, *A Soldier with the Arabs*, London: Hodder and Stoughton, 1957.

Grossman, David, *The Yellow Wind*, translated from the Hebrew by Haim Watzman, New York: Farrar, Straus, and Giroux, 1988.

Guyatt, Nicholas, *The Absence of Peace*, Zed Books, London, 1998.

Halper, Jeff, *An Israeli in Palestine*, Pluto Press, 2008

Heikal, Muhammad Hasanayn, *The Cairo Documents: The Inside Story of Nasser and his Relationship with World Leaders, Rebels and Statesmen*, Garden City, N.Y.: Double-day, 1973.

Hirst, David, *The Gun and the Olive Branch: The Roots of Violence in the Middle East*, London: Faber & Faber, 1977.

Hirst, David and Irene Beeson, *Sadat*, Faber and Faber publishing, 1981.

Hirst, David, *The Gun and the Olive Branch: The Roots of Violence in the Middle East*, N.Y. Thunder's Mouth Press, 2003.

Keay, John, *Sowing the Wind, The Seeds of Conflict in the Middle East*, W.W. Norton, New York, 2003.

Kent, Marian, *Oil and Empire: Brtish Policy and Mesopotamian Oil, 1900–1920*, Barnes and Noble, New York, 1976.

Khalaf, Issa, *Politics in Palestine: Arab Factionalism and Social Disintegration, 1939–1948*, Albany New York, 1991.

Khalidi, Rashid, *Palestine Identity: The Construction of Modern National Consciousness*, New York: Colombia University Press, 1997.

Khalidi, Walid, *From haven to conquest; readings in Zionism and the Palestine problem until 1948*, Institute for Palestine Studies, Beirut, 1971.

Khalil, Aadel Abdel-Ghaffar, *The Media and the Public Opinion*, Center for Arab Unity Studies, Beirut, Lebanon, 2003.

Kimmerling, Baruch and Joel Migdal, *Palestinians and the Making of a People*, The Free Press, A Division of Macmillan, N.Y. 1993.

Karpat, Kemal, "The Land Regime, social structure and modernization in the Ottoman Empire." In W.Polk and R. Chambers, eds, *Beginning of modernization in the East*, Chicago: University of Chicago Press, 1968, pp. 58-89.

Lawrence, T.E, *Seven Pillars of Wisdom*, Doubleday Doran & Company, Garden City, N.Y., 1935.

Lesch, Ann Mosely, "The Palestine Arab Nationalist Movement Under the Mandate," in William Quandt, Fuad Jabber, and Ann Mosely Lesch, eds. *The Politics of Palestinian Nationalism*, University of California Press, Berkeley and Los Angeles, California, 1973.

Lippman,Thomas, *Egypt After Nasser*, Paragon House, New York 1989.

Lozowick, Yaacov, *Right to Exist*, Doubleday, Random House, Inc, N.Y. 2003.

Makovsky, David, *Making Peace with the PLO: The Rabi Government's Road to the Oslo Accord*, Boulder CO: Westview Press, 1996.

Mandel, Neville, *The Arabs and Zionism before World War I*, Berkley: University of California Press, 1976.

Masalha, Nur, "The Historical Roots of the Palestinian Refugee Question." In

Aruri, Naseer, ed. *The Palestinian Refugees*, Pluto Press, London. Sterling, VA, 2001.

Meir, Golda, *My Life*, Putnam: New York, 1975.

Morris, Benny, *The Birth of the Palestinian Problem 1947-49*, New York: Cambridge University Press, 1987.

Morris, Benny, *Israel's Border War, 1949–1956: Arab Infiltration, Israeli Retaliation, and the Countdown to the Suez War*, Oxford University Press, Oxford, 1997.

Morris, Benny, *The Road to Jerusalem*, I.B. Tauris Publishers: New York, 2002.

Nasser, Jamal Abdel, *The Philosophy of Revolution*, Smith Keynes & Marshall, Buffalo,N.Y. 1959.

Oliphant, Laurence, *The Land of Gilead*, New York, 1981.

Pappe, Ilan, *A History of Modern Palestine*, Cambridge University Press, 2004.

Peres, Shimon, *Battling for Peace*, London: Random House, 1995.

Peretz, Don, *Intifada: The Palestinian Uprising*, Boulder, Colorado: Westview Press, 1990.

Peretz, Don, *The Arab–Israel Dispute*, Facts on File, Inc. 1996.

Porath, Yehoshua, *The Emergence of the Palestinian-Arab National Movement 1918–1929*, London 1974.

Qumsiyeh, Mazin, *Sharing the Land of Canaan*, Pluto Press, London 2004.

Sachar, Howard, *A History of Israel*, Alfred A. Knopf, New York, 1996.

Sadat, Anwar, *In Search of Identity*, Harper & Row Publishers, New York, 1978.

Sai'd, Edward, *The End of the Peace Process: Oslo and after*, Pentheon Books, New York, 2000.

Sanders, Ronald, *The High Walls of Jerusalem: A History of the Balfour Declaration and the Birth of the British Mandate of Palestine*, New York: Holt, Rinehart & Winston , 1983.

Sayigh, Rosemary, *Palestinians: from peasants to revolutionaries: a people's history*, Zed Press: London, 1979.

Schiff, Ze'ev and Ehud Ya'ari, *Intifada: The Palestinian Uprising*, Simon and Schuster Publishing, New York, 1989.

Schleifer, S. Abdullah, "Izz al-Din al-Qassam: Preacher and Mujahid," in E. Burke III, ed, *Struggle and Survival in the Modern Middle East*, Berkeley: University of California Press, 1993.

Segev, Tom, and Arlen Neal Weinstein, *1949, the First Israelis*, Free Press ;

Collier Macmillan, New York, 1986.

Shamir, Yitzhak, *Summing Up: An Autobiography*, Little, Brown and Company, 1994.

Shapira, Anita, *Land and Power: The Zionist Recourse to Force, 1881–1948*, New York: Oxford University Press, 1992.

Sharabi, Hisham, *Arab Intellectuals and the West: The Formative Years 1875–1914*, Baltimore, 1972.

Shlaim, Avi, *Collusion Across the Jordan: King Abdullah, The Zionist Movement, and the Partition of Palestine*, Oxford: Columbia University Press, 1988.

Shlaim, Avi, *The Politics of Partition*, Oxford University Press, 1998.

Shlaim, Avi, *The Iron Wall : Israel and the Arab World*, New York : W.W. Norton, 2000

Shlaim, Avi, "Israel and the Arab Coalition in 1948." in Eugene Rogan and Avi Shlaim, editors, *The War for Palestine*, Cambridge University Press, 2001.

Shemesh, Moshe, *The Palestinian Entity 1959–1974*, Frank Cass and Company Limited, 1988.

Smith, Barbara, *The Roots of Separation in Palestine: British Economic Policy, 1920–1929*, Syracuse: Syracuse University Press, 1995.

Storrs, Sir Ronald, *Orientations*, London: I. Nicholson and Watson, 1937.

Sykes, Christopher, *Crossroads to Israel, 1917-68*, World Publication Company: Cleveland, 1965.

Tamari, Salim, "Factionalism and Class Formation in Recent Palestinian History," in Roger Owen, ed., *Studies in the Economic and Social History of Palestine in the Nineteenth and Twentieth Centuries*, Carbondale, Ill. 1982.

Tibi, Bassam, "Modern Arab Culture at a Cross-Road." In *Arab Affairs, no.15*, May 1982: pp 61-47.

Tibawi, A.L., *Modern History of Syria including Lebanon and Palestine*, London 1969.

Stein, Kenneth, *The Land Question in Palestine, 1917–1939*, Chapel Hill: University of North Carolina Press 1984.

Warriner, Doreen, *Palestine Papers, 1917–1922: Seeds of Conflict*, London: John Murray, 1972.

Wasserstein, Bernard, *The British in Palestine: The Mandatory Government and the Arab–Jewish Conflict, 1917–1929*, Oxford: Basil Blackwell, 1991.

Waterbury, John, *Egypt, Burdens of the Past, Options for the Future*, Indiana University Press, Washington and London 1978.

Weizmann, Chaim, *Trial and Error*, New York, 1949.

Weizmann, Chaim, *Chaim Weizmann. Excerpts from his historic statements, writings, and addresses; a biography*, Jewish Agency for Palestine, Publishers: New York, 1952.

Wilson, Mary C., *King Abdullah, Britain and the Making of Jordan*, Cambridge University Press, Cambridge 1987.

Zaki, Moheb, *Civil Society & Democratization in Egypt, 1981–1994*, The Ibn Khaldoun Center, 1994.

INDEX